Driven into Paradise

Driven into Paradise

The Musical Migration
from Nazi Germany to the United States

EDITED BY

Reinhold Brinkmann
and
Christoph Wolff

UNIVERSITY OF CALIFORNIA PRESS
Berkeley   Los Angeles   London

Funding for the "Musical Migration" symposium and this publication was granted in part by the Kurt Weill Foundation for Music, Inc., New York, New York, and in part by the Lucius N. Littauer Foundation, New York, New York.

Editorial assistance: Mary Davis, Alexander Fisher, John Johnson

University of California Press
Berkeley and Los Angeles, California

University of California Press, Ltd.
London, England

Library of Congress Cataloging-in-Publication Data

Driven into paradise : the musical migration from Nazi Germany
    to the United States / edited by Reinhold Brinkmann and
    Christoph Wolff.
        p.   cm.
    Includes bibliographical references and index.
    ISBN 0-520-21413-7 (alk. paper)
        1. Music—United States—20th century—History and criticism.
    2. National socialism and music.   3. Germany—Exiles—History—
    20th century.   4. Austria—Exiles—History—20th century.
    5. Musicians—Europe—Biography.   I. Brinkmann, Reinhold,
    1934– . II. Wolff, Christoph.
    ML198.5.D75   1999
    780'.943'0973—dc21   98-28956
                                                                    CIP
                                                                    MN

Printed in the United States of America
9 8 7 6 5 4 3 2 1

CONTENTS

NOTES ON CONTRIBUTORS

MILTON BABBITT is William Shubael Conant Professor Emeritus of Music at Princeton University. A member of the National Institute of Arts and Letters and a fellow of the American Academy of Arts and Sciences, he is one of the most prominent composers of the twentieth century.

REINHOLD BRINKMANN is James Edward Ditson Professor of Music at Harvard University. Having written extensively on the history and aesthetics of music from the eighteenth to the twentieth centuries, he is the author of *Late Idyll: The Second Symphony of Johannes Brahms* and *Schumann und Eichendorff: Studien zum "Liederkreis," Opus 39.*

HERMANN DANUSER is Professor of Musicology at Humboldt University, Berlin. He has written extensively on the history and aesthetics of nineteenth- and twentieth-century music; his publications include *Die Musik des 20. Jahrhunderts* and *Musikalische Interpretation.*

PETER GAY is Sterling Professor Emeritus of History at Yale University. A specialist in the history and culture of Europe from the eighteenth century to the twentieth, he is the author of *Reading Freud: Explorations and Entertainments, Weimar Culture: The Outsider as Insider,* and the multivolume series *The Bourgeois Experience: Victoria to Freud.*

BRYAN GILLIAM is Professor of Music at Duke University. A specialist in the music of Richard Strauss and in film music, he is the author of *Richard Strauss's Elektra* and coeditor of *Music and Performance during the Weimar Republic.*

LYDIA GOEHR is Professor of Philosophy at Columbia University. She is the author of *The Imaginary Museum of Musical Works: An Essay in the Philosophy of Music* and *The Quest for Voice: Music, Politics, and the Limits of Philosophy*.

STEPHEN HINTON is Associate Professor of Music at Stanford University. A specialist in the music of Kurt Weill and in the music of the Weimar Republic, he is the author of *The Idea of Gebrauchsmusik: A Study of Musical Aesthetics in the Weimar Republic* and coeditor of *Musik und Theater*, a selection of Weill's writings.

DAVID JOSEPHSON is Associate Professor of Music History at Brown University. He specializes in the music of Tudor England and in the twentieth-century musical emigration to the United States, and his writings include *John Taverner, Tudor Composer*.

KIM H. KOWALKE is Professor of Musicology at the University of Rochester / Eastman School of Music. President of the Kurt Weill Foundation for Music, he is the author of *Kurt Weill in Europe* and coeditor of *A New Orpheus: Essays on Kurt Weill*.

WALTER LEVIN is Professor Emeritus of Music at the University of Cincinnati, and is the former first violinist of the LaSalle String Quartet. He is a sought-after teacher and coach of chamber music on both sides of the Atlantic.

BRUNO NETTL is Professor Emeritus of Ethnomusicology and Anthropology at the University of Illinois at Urbana-Champaign. Among his writings are *The Study of Ethnomusicology* and *Blackfoot Musical Thought: Comparative Perspectives*.

PAMELA M. POTTER is Assistant Professor of Music and German at the University of Wisconsin–Madison. She is a specialist in German musical scholarship in the twentieth century and in the music of Nazi Germany.

ALEXANDER L. RINGER is Professor Emeritus of Music at the University of Illinois at Urbana-Champaign. Having written on music from the Middle Ages through the twentieth century, he is the author of *Arnold Schoenberg: The Composer as Jew* and editor of the volume *The Early Romantic Era* in the series "Music and Society."

ANNE C. SHREFFLER is Professor of Music at the University of Basel, Switzerland. A specialist in American and European music of the twentieth century, she is the author of *Webern and the Lyric Impulse: Songs and Fragments on Poems of Georg Trakl.*

CHRISTOPH WOLFF is William Powell Mason Professor of Music and Dean of the Graduate School of Arts and Sciences at Harvard University. A music historian with special interests in seventeenth- and eighteenth-century music, he includes among his publications *Bach: Essays on His Life and Music, The New Bach Reader,* and *Mozart's Requiem: Historical and Analytical Studies, Documents, Score.*

CLAUDIA MAURER ZENCK is Professor of Musicology at the Hochschule für Musik in Graz, Austria. A specialist in the works of Ernst Krenek and in exile studies, she is the author of *Ernst Krenek: Ein Komponist im Exil* and co-editor of *Musik im Exil: Folgen des Nazismus für die internationale Musikkultur.*

PREFACE

If the title of this book has a somewhat euphemistic ring because its key-
words, *migration* and *paradise*, have connotations that can be perceived as
either neutral or prevailingly positive, this is in no way meant to distract
from the gruesome reality of the Nazi period. We know only too well that
emigration—or more accurately, desperate escape—was possible for only
very small numbers of Jews, as opposed to the millions who perished in the
Holocaust. Many of those who had wanted to be no more than normal
Germans became the innocent victims of a criminal ideology that swayed,
blinded, compromised, and corrupted the broader mass of their fellow citizens. Then too, although the actual situation in which a displaced minority
of fortunate refugees finally ended up provided first and foremost freedom,
safety, and new opportunities, it hardly ever resembled an actual paradise.
Nevertheless, both terms are appropriate in specific ways. *Migration,* on the
one hand, indicates that the events of the 1930s and 1940s led to a permanent shift: Europe's loss and largely America's gain. Examples of forced emigration followed by voluntary remigration remained extremely rare. *Paradise,* on the other hand, far removed from any religious or romantic ideals,
signifies a set of circumstances that provided the émigrés with uninhibited
freedom and opportunities for contributing to and influencing the cultural
life of an unfamiliar New World.

The story of this unprecedented migration resulting from the Nazi ter-
ror is immense, with global implications and covering individual as well as
collective fates from all walks of life. We are now more than a half century
removed from the events in question, and those who were directly involved
are for the most part gone, yet today we are no less affected by what happened. On the contrary, as we approach the end of the twentieth century
we are intensely aware of major shortcomings in our historical memory. As

xi

Saul Friedländer put it, "For the next generation of historians—and by now also for the one after that—as for most of humanity, Hitler's Reich, World War II, and the fate of the Jews of Europe do not represent any shared memory. And yet, paradoxically, the centrality of these events in present-day historical consciousness seems much greater than it was some decades ago."[1] From a somewhat different vantage point, Martin Jay underscores this very point when he writes that "the experiences and ideas of those who sought refuge from Hitler in America strike a deep chord in our contemporary culture as well, even if the actual refugees have virtually passed from the scene."[2]

Realizing the enormous size and weight of the subject as a whole, this book approaches it highly selectively. First of all, it focuses on the musical migration, a small but significant segment of what is often referred to as the intellectual migration, and aims at uncovering, describing, analyzing, and understanding the conditions, ramifications, and impact of the scenario in which individuals involved in the world of music—performers, composers, and scholars alike—found themselves.[3] But even within this limited scope, the approach is necessarily selective. At the center of virtually all these essays are individuals or small groups of musicians, some more prominent than others. In other words, we are not dealing here with an anonymous phenomenon. Instead we gain the perspective available only through personal experience, recollection, and reflection; explore aspects of acculturation and identity; and use case studies to discuss the role musicians have played at different times in various places or institutions; and the appendix—even though it consists only of a long list of names—complements the material presented in the preceding sections and, at the same time, broadens the outlook of the whole.

The majority of the essays collected here were presented, in preliminary versions, at an international conference entitled "The Musical Migration: Austria and Germany to the United States, ca. 1930–1950" that took place 5–8 May 1994 at the Harvard University Music Department. This conference complemented one held two years earlier at the Folkwang Hochschule in Essen, Germany.[4] Whereas the Essen symposium concentrated on the the situation in Germany specifically (with some emphasis on Jewish musicians prior to and immediately following the decisive year 1933), the Harvard conference deliberately put the American scene at center stage. This focus also played a role in the shaping of the present volume, which grew out of the Harvard conference but does not not represent its proceedings. For not only were the conference papers included here substantially rewritten, but several essays were also commissioned only after the conference.

The editors—also the conveners of the Harvard conference—take this opportunity to express their gratitude to all contributors for their willingness to participate in this project and for their understanding, prompt, and expert response to often rather specific requests. The editors also wish to thank the Lucius N. Littauer Froundation and the Kurt Weill Foundation for Music, both of New York City, for their most generous support of the 1994 conference and the editoral preparation of this volume. Mary Davis, John Andrew Johnson, and Alexander Fisher, former and present graduate students at Harvard, deserve our special thanks for their expert editorial assistance, as does Ruth Libbey of the Graduate School's Dean's Office for providing both English translations of German quotations and additional editorial help. Finally, we express our gratitude to Lynne Withey and Juliane Brand of the University of California Press for their good advice and welcome support.

Christoph Wolff
Cambridge, Massachusetts

NOTES

1. Saul Friedländer, introduction to *Nazi Germany and the Jews,* vol. 1 (New York: HarperCollins, 1997), 1.

2. Martin Jay, "The German Migration: Is There a Figure in the Carpet?" in *Exiles and Emigrés: The Flight of European Artists from Hitler* (exhibition catalog), ed. Stephanie Barron (Los Angeles: Los Angeles County Museum of Art, 1996), 335.

3. Donald Fleming and Bernard Bailyn, *The Intellectual Migration: Europe and America, 1930–1960* (Cambridge, Mass.: Harvard University Press, 1969). According to official records, 104,098 German and Austrian refugees arrived in the United States between 1933 and 1941, and 7,622 of them were academics; see Donald P. Kent, *The Refugee Intellectual: The Americanization of the Immigrants of 1933–1941* (New York: Columbia University Press, 1953), 15. According to Martin Jay, "another fifteen hundred or so were artists, cultural journalists, or free-floating intellectuals" ("German Migration," 326). No estimates are available for the number of musicians among them.

4. Horst Weber, ed., *Musik in der Emigration, 1933–45: Verfolgung, Vertreibung, Rückwirkung* (Stuttgart: J. B. Metzler, 1994).

PART ONE

Introductory Thoughts

Reading a Letter

Reinhold Brinkmann

Dear friend: I am happy that you could escape hell. To be sure, after that anything is a kingdom of heaven—however little it looks like that. How much I would like to tell you that I could do something for you, in the sense in which you request. But unfortunately, to my knowledge there is, for the time being, no such opportunity. At least I do not know of any. It has become rather difficult to procure positions. There are so many gifted people here, though few of your reputation and ability.

Let me tell you of my experiences and give you some advice: (1) be patient; (2) take anything that, in whatever way, will earn you a living; (3) and above all, never lose heart, because (4) you will find something, even if it takes one or two years or longer. It was no different for me, and I myself—who am accustomed to changing life circumstances—have acted according to these principles. I find that for us, who have achieved the highest in the highest positions, no labor would be degrading. I myself, who would rather teach "finishers," now have to teach beginners. But I passionately love teaching, and so I can by now feel quite satisfied with my situation.

If you can survive for a year without income, I am certain you would be able to enter the movie studios also. But whether one should wish that for oneself is questionable. Be assured that I will think of you if I hear of something. For this reason, it would be good to hear from you more often—let alone that I shall of course enjoy it. But then, everything has become so dismal!

At any rate, I am happy to have heard from you now and to know that you are taken care of, at least for the moment. From my heart I wish that it will soon be something permanent, something that matches your ability and reputation.[1]

Arnold Schoenberg wrote this remarkable letter on 26 February 1940 to Adolf Rebner, the renowned Austrian violinist, former Frankfurt concertmaster, and first violin of the Rebner Quartet. Rebner was in fact facing his second life-threatening expulsion from home and work. Already in 1934 he had been forced to leave Frankfurt; now the Nazis, after the 1938 An-schluß, also controlled his native Austria, and he had departed Vienna for Cincinnati in 1939. In a letter written on 25 February 1940, Rebner asked Schoenberg for advice and help in his new country.[2] Schoenberg's answer aims to be encouraging, but it remains ambivalent. By citing the basic con-frontation of heaven and hell, Schoenberg alludes to the mixed experience met by those emigrants who escaped Nazi Germany and safely reached the United States.[3] His confession of a difficult, problematic state of mind like-wise casts a shadow over the tone of optimism he wants to convey.

Not only is this a moving text, in tone as well as content, but it is also an important historical document. The letter sheds light on central aspects of the forced migration of artists and scholars from Nazi Germany, address-ing both the often traumatic experience of being exiled and the difficult task of finding one's feet as an immigrant in a foreign country. And in this sense the letter indirectly circumscribes the field of memories and scholar-ship explored by this collection of essays. The title of our volume, *Driven into Paradise*, taken from Schoenberg's 1934 speech on the Jewish situation,[4] certainly mirrors the dichotomy of heaven and hell that his letter uses to characterize both the act of expulsion and the subsequent status of the immigrant.

Schoenberg's advice is directed at a professional musician shortly after his arrival in a foreign country. More specific artistic problems remain un-touched, for the moment at least. Thus the letter does not reveal Schoen-berg's own creative dilemmas, nor does it reflect specifically on the situation of a European classical composer facing a new social and cultural environ-ment. As a result, the possible aesthetic as well as compositional conse-quences of this cultural reconfiguration are not mentioned.[5] Nor is the in-tricate issue of a mutual artistic exchange between a genuinely American musical culture and the traditional European heritage, as embodied in the figure of the composing immigrant, touched on, not even in passing.[6] What matters at this point are questions of the first hour: survival and the secur-ing of a life.

PERSPECTIVES: EXILES AND IMMIGRANTS

I am very happy that you could escape hell. The first sentence of the letter brings to mind the fact that at the center of the historical event which we so neu-trally designate the "musical migration" is the Holocaust—its prehistory (the persecution before the exile commenced),[7] its actual beginning in 1933 (the year of the *Machtübernahme*, the rise to power of the National So-cialists), and its enduring presence throughout the early 1940s, including the time of the Rebner-Schoenberg correspondence. Indeed, as both his-torical reality and personal memory, the Holocaust is the measure for any historical judgment about German fascism and its consequences. In it lies the background for racial, political, and artistic persecution, and thus for the exile.[8]

The conviction that any scholarly activity in this area must first argue politically justifies a critique of the early phase of *Exilforschung*.[9] Despite some claims to the contrary, such critical assessment should not be directed at the area of source studies. Finding the sources (endangered personal estates, institutional documents, "oral history" interviews),[10] securing them, and making them available was an immediate duty and needs to continue even today. Instead it was the interpretive perspective of the early research that was problematic. Particularly noteworthy is the fact that the historical events were completely subsumed under the almost neutral concept of "emigration." The scholarly debate of the 1960s and 1970s concerning the terms "emigration" and "exile" was not just a methodological or academic quarrel; rather, the arguments were informed by clearly divergent political positions. In 1973 Peter Laemmle defined emigration as "the event of involuntary expatriation" and exile as "the state of banishment."[11] In later scholarship, however, the term "emigration" does not suggest expulsion so much as "voluntary migration" (though it remains questionable whether in regard to Nazi Germany any migration could be considered strictly "voluntary"), whereas the entire process of the forced expatriation is designated by the term "exile." "Exile," then, is multivalent, covering the act of expulsion, the process both of leave-taking and of arrival in the new land, and the status of the immigrant. As early as 1980 Claudia Maurer Zenck convincingly argued for this distinction with regard to exiled musicians; more recently it has been emphasized by the editors of the volume *Musik im Exil*.[12]

This new concept of "exile," however, has its problematic aspects too. The understanding of the immigrant as being in exile was propagated primarily by prominent immigrants from the political left. Bertolt Brecht's "On the Name Emigrants," a set of powerfully articulated verses from 1937 that are clearly informed by personal concerns, expresses this concept in an exemplary manner:

> I always found the name false they gave us: Emigrants.
> That means those who leave their country. But we
> Did not leave, of our own free will
> Choosing another land. Nor did we enter
> Into a land, to stay there, if possible forever.
> Merely, we fled. We were driven out, banned.
> Not a home, but an exile, shall the land be that took us in.[13]

The imperative of this last line is based on hope, indicating both the strong feeling of a national identity that remains unchanged and the politically motivated will to resist displacement and return home. Moreover, both seem paired with a secret contempt for "the land that took us in," resulting in the feeling of permanent "exile": the immigrant is a foreigner in a country that is strange to him; or, to use a terminological pun: the immigrant willfully remains an emigrant. This disturbing message is voiced even more strongly in Brecht's poem "On Thinking about Hell":

> On thinking about Hell, I gather
> My brother Shelley found it was a place
> Much like the city of London. I
> Who live in Los Angeles and not in London
> Find, on thinking about Hell, that it must be
> Still more like Los Angeles.[14]

Obviously, this is not Schoenberg's view of Los Angeles, and many others of his fellow refugees would not agree with Brecht's statement. Such subjective differences in artists' own evaluations of their immigrant status in fact reflect fundamental differences among the various arts, differences inherent both in the nature of the artistic "material" being tapped and in the social structures that sustain the individual arts. For poets and authors, for actors, for journalists, the medium of professional expression, language, is nationally defined. Such artists are therefore not easily uprooted and moved to a new country with a different language. In addition, the social network of institutions that support the literary culture in the homeland—newspapers, journals, publishers, distributors, critics, book clubs, libraries, theaters, academies, prizes—cannot be transposed to, or rebuilt in, the new country. Absent, too, is the corresponding readership or audience. Thus, with the exception of a few international authors, writers who were successful even in translation (Thomas Mann, Lion Feuchtwanger, and Franz Werfel, for example), almost inevitably a strong feeling arose of being artistically without resonance and professionally isolated. This experience contributed fundamentally to the negative definition of immigration as exile. For musicians, however, and for performing artists in particular, the task of relocation, and of professional reestablishment in a new country, was much easier.[15] Many of them had already performed in the United States; they were well known and were themselves familiar with the country, its social and professional conditions, and its cultural institutions; the more prominent among them already had American agents, even audiences. For these privileged immigrants, the transition was less problematic and the chances were good to get a permanent job, often at the level of their European positions.

For specific groups, of course—and the ordinary musician belongs here: the violinist in the back row of the orchestra, for example, or the second horn player from the town band—the situation was more uncertain, especially given institutional and organizational differences between Germany and the United States. Nevertheless, music itself, as a seemingly "universal language"—or better: Western music as a common language for members of the Western musical culture—does not require "translation"; thus, the active integration of the immigrant musician, of whatever caliber, into the professional life of classical music in the United States was—in general—easier than for writers, actors, and others dependent on the written or spoken word. And that shaped the immigrants' view of their new country decisively. Scholars of the musical exile must therefore be very careful not to succumb to the influence of studies of the literary exile, where the problems and conclusions are in many ways different.

The second phase of exile studies, beginning in the mid-1970s, suffered from the uncritical readiness of scholars to study and generalize from personal experiences of the exile, such as Brecht's.[16] The positive aspects that many emigrants assigned, or tried to assign, to their new status were ridiculed, as was the fact that many of them never intended to remigrate, but instead learned to accept their new country as the second, the "other," if not the only, homeland. For quite a number of refugees, the old homeland, Germany, had compromised itself forever.[17] In Schoenberg's letter, for example, the new citizen's overall-positive view of his new homeland is manifest.[18] The judgments of Brecht and Schoenberg, indeed, seem almost opposed. While Brecht calls Los Angeles his "hell," for Schoenberg that characterization goes to Nazi Germany, and the new country is not just "heaven" but—emphatically poetic—*ein Himmelreich* (kingdom of heaven) or—plainly religious—"Paradise" (as in the speech mentioned above).

DAMAGED PSYCHE: "ES IST JA ALLES SO TRAURIG WORDEN!"

The overall positive attitude toward the country of immigration is based on a strong feeling of gratitude. And Schoenberg's willful insistence on the positive—it is a *Himmelreich* even if it does not look like one!—can be understood as an effort to resist self-doubt and force the process of integration. In general, such an attitude has implications for the cultural activities of the immigrant, and for political engagement in particular: there is an unquestioned desire to support the new country and fight the old one and its fascist regime. In Schoenberg's case this includes loyalty to the United States as a prospective and then actual citizen as well as support for the cause of Jewry and, in a broader pro-Jewish, antifascist sense, for the foundation of the state of Israel; but it also concerns his work, specifically the late political compositions: the *Ode to Napoleon Buonaparte* (1942) and, most important, *A Survivor from Warsaw* with its antifascist eschatology (1947).

Calling on his own experience, Theodor W. Adorno noted an enormous psychic strain resulting from exile: "Every intellectual in emigration is, without exception, mutilated, and does well to acknowledge it to himself, if he wishes to avoid being cruelly apprised of it behind the tightly-closed doors of his self-esteem."[19] This is apparent with Schoenberg as well. The encouraging, constructive words "never lose heart . . . you will find something" are immediately taken back: *But then, everything has become so dismal!* The overall assessment of the situation remains ambivalent. Certainly, the factor of time may bring some comfort—*I can by now feel quite satisfied with my situation*—but that is by no means an enthusiastic reassurance.

Thus, with the end of the letter, we again face the psychic repercussions of exile and the immigrant's ability to endure them—the term "immigrant" now being used to denote the refugee who has accepted his new citizenship. Yes, the letter assures: *you will find something;* yes, the letter confirms: *I feel satisfied with my situation.* But just as it began by noting the persistence of "hell," the letter ends on a melancholy note: *Es ist ja alles so traurig worden!*—sounding much like a line from Heine. In its second paragraph, too, we find a reflection on the many changing life circumstances experienced even before the Nazis seized power.[20] And indeed, particularly for Jewish citizens, the dis-integration of life began in many cases very early, with the "exile before the exiling," and continued through the various stages of flight from the Nazis.

The complicated mixture of the refugee's negative and positive self-diagnosis is encountered almost paradigmatically in Ernst Krenek's American diaries.[21] In powerful words, these diaries describe how the experience of the violent expulsion resulted in a life of "constant *angst* for catastrophes."[22] They also register the repression of this angst, this existential fear, and show how the image of the enemy Hitler becomes demonized; in this sense they display, writes the diaries' editor, the "tying of the individual situation with the political events, in order to understand the former through the latter and thus find a kind of solution for them."[23] As Krenek puts it, "My basic attitude is fear, deadly fear, with brief intermittent spells of fearful hope." Under such psychic conditions, the quasi-normal professional uncertainty about the renewal of his appointment at Vassar College develops into a crisis of fundamental self-doubt:

> Terribly, almost unbearably depressed. I am so completely terrorized by the insecurity of my future that I am in a state of real despair. I think this has little to do with the objective status of my affairs, which, by the way, may be pretty bad. I feel with growing apprehension how much of a stranger I am in this world, somehow on probation, just tolerated at times on some artificial assumptions of usefulness just the same. But in point of fact, I have the terrible feeling that all the "right" people agree definitely that I am not good at anything they care for.[24]

The arrogance that members of the old middle European nations displayed toward the much younger culture of the United States, a nation they perceived as lacking in tradition, often lead to an exaggerated sense of artistic self-esteem.[25] At the same time, because the anxiety of losing their identity was stronger for artists for whom an intact self represented a secured tradition, these immigrants experienced a distinct feeling of self-isolation.[26] The central problem was to keep a balance between the preservation of an artistic identity based on the European tradition and the necessary adaptation to the new cultural and professional situation in America. It is interesting to observe that Krenek sought already early on to find, "instinctively and purposefully, a modus vivendi with America."[27] He deliberately chose not to join one of the circles of immigrants, wanting instead to become an accepted member of the American scene. As far as Krenek's composing is concerned, both the turn to tradition, that is, the reflection on history as a basis for his work, and the adoption of the twelve-tone method as a means to guarantee aesthetic unity can be understood as responses to this status of the immigrant. History and order are relied on to banish the catastrophic anxieties and artistic self-doubts that the diaries reveal with such intensity.

ACCULTURATION

Besides the traumatic experience of the expulsion itself, the problems connected with social and professional integration led to reactions of ambivalence as well. Schoenberg's letter names these problems in a simple manner: *It has become rather difficult to procure positions. There are so many gifted people here.* The statement alludes to professional conditions in the United States and the economic difficulties of the 1930s depression: the unstable level of unemployment, among musicians in particular; protectionist measures instituted by the unions, resulting in quotas; and the restrictive policy of issuing visas—an additional hurdle faced by immigrants.

A fair approach to these problems of integration needs to start with a quantitative analysis of the immigration, in our case with the number of immigrant musicians (in the most general sense) who entered the labor market and their professional specializations. Unfortunately, no statistically secure numbers exist for the migration to the United States during the period in question; a general discussion must therefore suffice.[28] Despite preexisting sympathy for the refugees, their reception into American society, and American cultural life in particular, was problematic. Nevertheless, as a response to the intensification of persecutions in Nazi Germany, culminating in the infamous *Reichskristallnacht* of 1938, one discerns a growing philanthropic readiness on the part of the American people to support the immigrants. Indeed, it seems that the private willingness of Americans generally to welcome and integrate the refugees was greater than the official governmental policy.[29] Private agencies were immensely supportive, of scholars in particular.[30] In spite of prevailing economic problems, then, there was in the United States a basic "readiness of the preexisting situation," as Herbert Strauss put it, to provide opportunities, especially for musicians, whether artists, scholars, or educators. And this situation was in many cases met by a readiness, on the part of the immigrants, to accept and adjust to conditions in the new country.

But there was another side to this as well. Differentiation in degree of acculturation was inevitable, deriving primarily from such subjective factors as age, family status, political orientation, cultural expectations, ideological prejudices regarding the country of origin, life experiences and self-reflections, and psychological flexibility. Schoenberg's letter prepares for exactly this and advises his newly arrived colleague to: *(1) be patient; (2) take anything that, in whatever way, will earn you a living.* This includes not only the acceptance of lesser work in one's field but also a possible change in occupation—a necessary step for many immigrants.

The admonition to exercise restraint and modesty needs no clarification. Although Rebner is a man of unqualified professional excellence—*There are so many gifted people here, though few of your reputation and ability*—there is, Schoenberg warns him, no place for European arrogance. On the contrary, the European elite are expected not to be afraid of work—any kind of work: *I find that for us, who have achieved the highest excellence in the highest positions, no labor would be degrading. I myself, who would rather teach "finishers," now have to teach beginners. But I passionately love teaching, and so I can by now feel quite satisfied.*

Obviously, this reminder to accept the situation as given reflects Schoenberg's own experience with immigrant colleagues arriving from Europe. The feeling of superiority of the "cultivated" Old World relative to the only just "civilized" New World was, as Krenek remarked, widespread among immigrants, especially in the realm of culture. Werner Vordtriede tells the rather primitive anecdote of a refugee who, after many years in the United States, returned to Europe; asked by a friend about renting a piano in New York, the man answered: "You want to rent a piano there? In New York you will not be able to rent pianos. One does not have pianos there."[31] Though more refined, Theodor W. Adorno's first reaction to his new country, as reported in "Scientific Experiences of a European Scholar in America," is similar. When he learned that the building that housed the Princeton Radio Project in Newark, New Jersey, was a former factory hall, he said, "I was very much taken by the lack of embarrassment about the choice of a site that would scarcely have been conceivable by the lights of the European academic community." Adorno begins his essay with another report on a confrontation with cultural superficiality: "I still remember the shock that a housemaid, an emigrant like ourselves, gave me during our first days in New York when she, the daughter of a so-called good home, explained: 'People in my town used to go to the symphony, now they go to Radio City.'

In no way did I want to be like her." Indeed, for Adorno the essential distinction between the American and the European intellectual lay in the difference between the "expert technician" and the *gebildeter Mensch*—the person of learning and culture.[32] It is well known that Schoenberg, too, cultivated such cultural biases. His letter of 13 May 1935 to an old friend in Vienna, David Joseph Bach (who later escaped the Nazis and settled in London), is a telling example: "One must never tell the truth, not even if I wanted to warn someone of a danger. Here in the partly (the greater part) still Wild West, one sees warnings like one I saw written on a house: 'If you want to shoot, do it now, otherwise you won't ever shoot again!' . . . Here everything wants to be praised . . . here, where everything is all wrong, there is uncertainty and fear of exposure which can endure only praise." Characteristically, however, the letter continues with an immediate rationalization of this deeply felt Old World conviction: "But I won't fall into European mistakes and merely grouse. . . . I have really found very many people whom I like."[33]

EXTREMES: "AMERICANIZATION" AND
"AGGRESSIVE DEFENSE"

The scope of reactions to the immigrant status is broad. On the one side is the consciously complete integration into the new environment, or, expressed with a somewhat negative European accent, "Americanization." The paradigm of an artist who embraced immigration without reservation as absolutely positive and who integrated himself, both artistically and personally, thoroughly into his new homeland and its culture (so much so that even the term "immigrant" seems no longer applicable) is Kurt Weill—not just by chance, a musician. Probably this easy integration explains why the so-called American Weill is greeted by postwar German musicologists and writers on music with almost hostile skepticism.[34] The old European cultural arrogance and a general anti-Americanism go hand in hand.

At the other end of the spectrum stands, as a similarly paradigmatic case, Paul Hindemith.[35] Although Hindemith was an enormously successful and influential composer and teacher of composition in the United States, his missionary convictions as an artist as well as his personal temperament led him to engage in rather aggressive verbal attacks and actions. His reaction to the spectacular artistic and political success of Shostakovich's *Leningrad* Symphony, no. 7, in 1942 is highly characteristic. Hindemith attacked, with rather vulgar aesthetic verdicts, that work, which has the German siege of Leningrad as its symphonic plot. As is well known, a microfilm of the score was smuggled out of the beleaguered city and reached the United States, where the declared antifascist Arturo Toscanini premiered and broadcast the symphony nationwide. The German immigrant Hindemith felt it

necessary to compose *against* this antifascist symphonic manifestation in order to demonstrate "what music and what composition in fact are [i.e.,
should be]." For Hindemith, in short, the concrete political dimension of
Shostakovich's symphony did not matter; rather, his own abstract didactic
cycle of fugues and interludes à la J. S. Bach, *Ludus Tonalis*, was conceived
as a "moral conquest" over an artistic outcry about the possible military
conquest of Leningrad by the German army.[36] Even if, as a work of art, the
Leningrad Symphony might legitimately be considered an "embasement of
musical values," as Richard Taruskin asserts, Hindemith's lack of political
sensibility is surprising.[37] His reaction can only be explained (though not
justified) in historical terms. In other words, as an artistic demonstration of
his fundamental belief in the superiority of German musical culture, *Ludus
Tonalis* came at a crucial point in his life: with the United States having entered the war with Nazi Germany, the cultural climate was about to change
decisively, understandably turning against anything German.[38] Professional-
political anxiety mixed with basic aesthetic and ethical convictions about
the true art of music thus apparently caused the German immigrant to lose
his orientation and lash out in an aggressive act of self-defense.[39]

CURRENT TRENDS

Martin Jay has commented on the various stages of *Exilforschung* in general, taking into account the differently motivated approaches both in the
two German states, together with their political implications, and on both
sides of the Atlantic Ocean.[40] Following Ernst Loewy, Jay sees a change in
attitude and direction since the merger of the two Germanys, leading to a
reconsideration of the dominant political interpretation of the "émigré
legacy."[41] For the editors of *Musik im Exil,* the trend Jay observes may be
an example of depoliticized *Exilforschung* and thus suspect.[42] But the new
stage of scholarship does not necessarily neglect a political orientation. Although the political aspect may not always be accented in recent studies,
one can perceive it as *aufgehoben* in the Hegelian sense, as an integral part
of the subject matter itself.

Most important, there exists a new international collaboration in the exploration of the musical emigration. This can be observed in the cooperation between American and German/Austrian as well as French scholars on
issues of exile studies—in joint publications, in efforts to secure sources, in
the organization of symposia.[43] This combining of interests and approaches
by scholars from various countries and of different political persuasions
should introduce a broader, more open, dialogical atmosphere and better
understanding of the perspectives and problems on both sides of the Atlantic. Undoubtedly, the continuing importance of exile studies is also sup-

ported by recent scholarly interest in the Holocaust and by a new emphasis in research on the history of Nazi Germany—on fascism and anti-Semitism in general, and on the role of the arts in particular. What was exceptional a decade ago, when the commendable reconstruction of the infamous "Degenerate Art" exhibit was undertaken in Europe and the United States, seems to be a sign of normalcy today: the 1997 Los Angeles art exhibit "Exiles and Émigrés: The Flight of European Artists from Hitler" subsequently traveled to the Neue Nationalgalerie in Berlin. Indeed, not only was the forced migration of artists and intellectuals from Nazi Germany to various places all over the world a phenomenon with international ramifications but its historical importance and lasting impact as well as its moral dimensions can only be fully understood from an international perspective.

"RETURNING HOME?"

The suspicion of depoliticization was in a sense confirmed a few years ago with the appearance of a German guidebook on the Los Angeles émigré colony, one in a series of illustrated tours of such places as Goethe's Weimar, the Pierre Lachaise Cemetery in Paris, and the literary haunts of the Côte d'Azur.[44] This commercialization of the exile—with maps, walking tours, bus excursions, and so forth—can certainly be perceived in terms of depoliticization, but it also testifies to the fact that the German *Bildungsbürger* has finally accepted emigration, as well as the decision not to remigrate, as an honorable action. The émigrés are no longer perceived—as was the case in the bitter debates directly following World War II, at least in West Germany—as "deserters" and thus questionable as to moral virtue. Works born of and reflecting the exile (in particular, the American immigration) are now considered part of the canonic German repertory, in all the arts equally. For that reason, I prefer to call the current reassessment not depoliticization, but historical normalization.

Still, we need to be careful. "Normalization" should by no means imply losing a sense for the historically and morally extraordinary dimension of the expulsion from Nazi Germany: as stated above, this forced migration was part of, or for non-Jewish exiles, parallel to, that subhumanly unique event, the Holocaust—Schoenberg's "hell." And the presence of the Arnold Schoenberg Institute housing the composer's archive on the campus of the University of Southern California, Los Angeles, for several decades made the expatriation and immigration visible, serving as a memorial to that historical event. In 1998, however, the ASI, as it was internationally known, ceased to exit, and the archives were moved to Vienna. Indeed, a Viennese journal announced the move with the headline "Schönberg kehrt heim!"—"Schoenberg returns home!" For the émigré, though, home once become "hell" could therefore never be "heaven" again—if, for a Viennese Jew, it ever had been. With the passage of time, then, and with witnesses no longer alive, there is the danger of forgetting. And in the case of the Viennese headline, the suspicion may be allowed that the unreflected intention was to make us forget, to erase the exile from the map of the émigré's life, to bring about a late, posthumous reconciliation between him and his native country through a connection with the great tradition of Viennese music from Haydn and Mozart through Beethoven, Schubert, and Brahms to Mahler. It is our, the historians', duty to insist that it was in fact the perversion of this tradition and its sublime ethics that shaped the émigré's life and art. For the forced migration in the shadow of the Holocaust, the line to be remembered and to be engraved in people's memory forever is *Es ist ja alles so traurig worden!*

NOTES

Translations from German texts into English are by the author if not otherwise acknowledged. Special thanks to Anne Canright and Karen Painter for their critical reading and editing of this essay.

1. The letter is in the Schoenberg Collection of the Library of Congress, Washington, D.C. Thanks to Lawrence Schoenberg for his permission to publish it.

Lieber Freund, ich freue mich, daß Sie aus der Hölle entkommen konnten. Demgegenüber ist ja doch alles ein Himmelreich, wie wenig es auch danach aussehen mag. Wie gerne würde ich Ihnen sagen, daß ich etwas tun kann in dem Sinn in dem sie es verlangen. Aber leider: meines Wissens ist fürs erste kaum eine solche Möglichkeit vorhanden. Wenigstens ist mir keine bekannt. Es ist bereits sehr schwer geworden, Stellungen zu verschaffen. Es sind so viele fähige Menschen hier. Allerdings wenige von Ihrem Ruf und Können.

Wenn ich Ihnen etwas von meiner Erfahrung sagen und raten darf, so ist es: 1. Geduld haben; 2. alles annehmen, was irgendwie ein Erwerb ist; 3. und vor allem den Mut nicht verlieren, denn 4. Sie werden etwas finden, wenn es auch ein bis zwei Jahre oder noch länger dauert. Es war nicht anders bei mir und ich, der ich wechselnde Lebensverhältnisse gewöhnt bin, habe nach den vorgenannten Prinzipien gelebt. Ich finde es gibt für uns, die wir Höchstes an höchster Stelle geleistet haben, keine Arbeit, die uns entehren könnte. Ich, der eher "Aufhörer" unterrichtet habe, muß nun Anfänger unterrichten. Aber, da ich leidenschaftlich gerne unterrichte, fühle mich nunmehr ganz wohl.

Ich bin sicher, wenn Sie hier ein Jahr ohne Einkommen leben könnten, würde sich auch für Sie der Eintritt zu den Movie-Studios öffnen. Aber: ob man sich das wünschen soll, ist zweifelhaft. Seien Sie versichert, daß ich, wenn ich etwas höre, an Sie denken werde. Es wird deshalb gut sein, daß ich öfters von Ihnen höre—abgesehen davon, daß es mich selbstverständlich freuen wird. Es ist ja alles so traurig worden!

Jedenfalls freue ich mich, jetzt von Ihnen gehört zu haben und zu wissen, daß Sie, für den Augenblick wenigstens, versorgt sind. Herzlich wünsche ich, daß es bald etwas dauerndes, das Ihrem Können und Ihrem Ruf entspricht, wird.

Herzliche Grüße, Ihr Arnold Schönberg

2. Rebner arrived in Cincinnati in July 1939, acting on the advice of friends who said that this was a city with rich musical activities and thus a good place to start an American career. About his arrival, see Frederick Yeiser, "A Famous Musician Comes to Town," *Cincinnati Enquirer,* 22 October 1939. Thanks to Marilyn McCoy from the Arnold Schoenberg Institute in Los Angeles for this information.

3. Schoenberg took the hell metaphor from Rebner's initiating letter ("It has been about a year now since I escaped hell . . . ") and expanded on it.

4. Arnold Schoenberg, "Two Speeches on the Jewish Situation" (first speech), in *Style and Idea: Selected Writings of Arnold Schoenberg,* ed. Leonard Stein (London: Faber & Faber, 1975), 502.

5. For some summary remarks on the issue of artistic "deradicalization," discussed in particular in American exile studies, see Martin Jay, "The German Migration: Is There a Figure in the Carpet?" in *Exiles and Emigrés: The Flight of European Artists from Hitler* (exhibition catalog), ed. Stephanie Barron (Los Angeles: Los Angeles County Museum of Art, 1997), 331–32.

6. The letter does not contribute to the current debate about the role of the musical immigration for a genuinely American classical musical culture. This discussion concerns what has been called a "re-Germanization" (following the "liberation" of an independent American compositional voice after the nineteenth century, with its predominantly Germanic orientation) of American compositional practice by the immigrant composers, primarily through their teaching, though regarding the latter—thinking only of Schoenberg and Hindemith versus Milhaud and Nadia Boulanger—German and French influences seem to balance each other since the 1930s. (As I write this footnote I think of today's newspaper, the *New York Times* of 4 August 1997, with an essay by K. Robert Schwarz, "In Contemporary Music: A House Still Divided," debating the controversial role of serialism in American classical avant-garde music—a vivid testimony that the issue of émigrés influencing the American composition scene is still a burning question.) Another item is the important impact German immigrants on the development of musicology in the United States.

7. For Michael Winkler (*Deutsche Literatur im Exil, 1933–1945: Texte und Dokumente* [Stuttgart: Philipp Reclam, 1977], 16), too, "exile as ostracism" existed long before the "legalized beginning of the dictatorship"; for that matter, we can say equally that "exile" persisted as a psychic state long after the actual reign of the Nazis.

8. See Klaus Emmerich's analogous statement: "I advocate that the link with fascism should be considered very seriously as the decisive new historical quality [of literature produced in exile]." Quoted in Wulf Koepke and Michael Winkler, eds., *Exilliteratur, 1933–1945* (Darmstadt: Wissenschaftliche Buchgesellschaft, 1989), 119.

9. Another deficit of the early German scholarly literature on the exile is its focus on German perspectives without fully recognizing the pertinent American studies, some of which appeared even earlier. Besides the books by Duggan and Drury, Fermi, Heilbut, and Fleming and Bailyn cited elsewhere in this essay, major American studies are Rex W. Crawford, *The European Scholar in America* (Philadelphia: University of Pennsylvania Press, 1953); Robert Boyers, ed., *The Legacy of the German Refugee Intellectuals,* 2d ed. (New York: Schocken, 1972); R. Stewart Hughes, *The Sea Change: The Migration of Social Thought, 1930–1945* (New York: Harper & Row, 1975);

and Jarrell C. Jackman and Carla M. Borden, eds., *The Muses Flee Hitler: Cultural Transfer and Adaption, 1930–1945* (Washington, D.C.: Smithsonian Institution Press, 1983); see also Martin Jay, *Permanent Exiles: Essays on the Intellectual Migration from Germany to America* (New York: Columbia University Press, 1985). For biographies, memoirs, and studies related to specific fields, see Martin Jay, *German Migration*, 330–31. Among publications in the German language, the following also discuss immigrants in the United States: Habakuk Traber and Elmar Weingarten, eds., *Verdrängte Musik: Berliner Komponisten im Exil* (Berlin: Argon, 1987); Juan Allende-Blin, *Musiktradition im Exil: Zurück aus dem Vergessen* (Cologne: Bund, 1993); Walter Pass, Gerhard Scheit, and Wilhelm Svoboda, *Orpheus im Exil: Die Vertreibung der österreichischen Musik von 1993 bis 1945* (Vienna: Verlag für Gesellschaftskritik, 1995).

10. The indispensable foundation for any investigation of the German immigration in the United States was established by John M. Spalek; see his *Guide to the Archival Material of the German–Speaking Emigration to the United States after 1933*, vols. 1 (Charlottesville: University Press of Virginia, 1978) and 2 (Bern: Francke, 1992). For the importance of oral history, see Hans Sahl's reminder in his poem "Die Letzten" (The last ones): "We are the last ones./Interrogate us./We are responsible./ We carry the file boxes/with our friends' warrants of arrest/before us like a vendor's tray" (excerpted in Winkler, *Deutsche Literatur im Exil*, 15).

11. Peter Laemmle, "Vorschläge für eine Revision der Exilforschung," *Akzente* 20 (1973): 510. See also Matthias Wegner, *Exil und Literatur* (Frankfurt am Main: Athenäum, 1967); and Benita Luckmann, "New School: Varianten der Rückkehr aus Exil und Emigration," in *Exil, Wissenschaft, Identität: Die Emigration deutscher Sozialwissenschaftler, 1933–1945*, ed. Ilja Struber (Frankfurt am Main: Suhrkamp, 1988). Laura Fermi, in *Illustrious Immigrants: The Intellectual Migration from Europe, 1930–1941*, 2d ed. (Chicago: University of Chicago Press, 1971), 15, took a rather practical approach: "The word 'refugee' is out; 'exile' and 'expatriate' do not apply to those who intended to become American citizens; and 'émigré' is awkward, though 'émigré scholar' is used in scholarly books. The intellectual wave has been called 'the cultural migration,' and I have done so, but 'migrant' is not used in this context. There is, in conclusion, not a single word descriptive of a group whose motivations and intentions were as varied as those of the European-born intellectuals, who came here. Accordingly, I shall avail myself of the existing terms, selecting in each instance the most appropriate to the person under consideration." For another American perspective on this issue, see Lewis A. Coser, *Refugee Scholars in America: Their Impact and Their Experience* (New Haven: Yale University Press, 1984). In *Musik im Exil: Folgen des Nazismus für die internationale Musikkultur* (Frankfurt am Main: Fischer Taschenbuch Verlag, 1993), 16, editors Hanns-Werner Heister, Claudia Maurer Zenck, and Peter Petersen stress that "the real and not just the mere ideological transformation of exile into immigration" was valid for "the vast majority of Jewish musicians (as for artists and scholars in general), who did not want to return to Europe, much less to one of the Germanys or Austria." Despite prominent advocates (see the round-table discussion "Probleme der Erforschung und Vermittlung von Exilliteratur" in Koepke and Winkler, eds., *Exilliteratur*, 102ff.), the ideologically charged term "antifascist exile" has not been widely accepted.

12. Claudia Maurer Zenck, *Ernst Krenek—Ein Komponist im Exil* (Vienna: Elisabeth Lafite, 1980), 11. In the introduction to her study (11–42), Maurer Zenck com-

petently discusses the methodological problems, including a brief characterization of main trends in the early history of *Exilforschung*. In *Musik im Exil*, 15, Heister, Maurer Zenck, and Petersen observe "a tendency . . . during the last years . . . to substitute the concept of 'exile' with the more harmless one of 'emigration.'" Probably rightly, they understand this political "diffusion" as "a subversion of the relevant history and of the identity of those people who were forced to flee the Nazis."

13. *Bertold Brecht Poems*, ed. John Willett and Ralph Manheim with the cooperation of Erich Fried (London: Eyre Methuen, 1979), 301. The original German title is "Über die Bezeichnung Emigranten."

14. *Bertold Brecht Poems*, 367. The German title is "Nachdenkend über die Hölle." See also Brecht's poem "Die Auswanderung der Dichter" (The poet's emigration). Using the term "existentially banished poeple," Werner Vordtriede, a refugee himself, broadened the view of the exile to suggest a permanent "state of mind" and arrived at a "typology of literature written in exile" for both the nineteenth and twentieth centuries. With terms such as "homesickness," "loneliness," "cottage life," "falling silent," "hatred," and "suffering from the fatherland," he characterized the experience of alienation as typical for the modern poet in general. See Vordtriede's essay "Vorläufige Gedanken zu einer Typologie der Exilliteratur," in Koepke and Winkler, eds., *Exilliteratur*, 24–43. For a brief critique of Vordtriede's attempt, see Jost Hermand, "Schreiben in der Fremde: Gedanken zur deutschen Exilliteratur seit 1798," ibid., 65. Because Vordtriede does not reflect on the specifics of various political situations, the concept of exile remains abstract; the extraordinary and thus singular dimension of the Holocaust is neglected in particular.

15. Concerning this issue, see also Herbert A. Strauss, *Essays on the History, Persecution, and Emigration of German Jews* (New York: K. G. Saur, 1987), 353; and Winkler, *Deutsche Literatur im Exil*, 27–30.

16. Typical seems Hermand's polemical characterization of those emigrants who did not repatriate to Germany. Hermand calls them "the already assimilated and bourgeois-unpolitical representatives of the theory of collective guilt" and describes the status of immigration as a "no man's land of being without citizenship" ("Schreiben in der Fremde," 90).

17. Herein lies the controversy between Bertold Brecht and Thomas Mann. See the discussion (though a partisan one) by Hermand, "Schreiben in der Fremde," 85–90.

18. Stephen Hinton, for example, has criticized the understanding of "immigration" as a "permanent exile" (see his contribution to this volume). However, it should not be overlooked that, for psychological or tactical reasons, many immigrants forced a positive attitude.Consider, to cite just one example, the anecdote that Anthony Heilbut relates about Schoenberg: "Schoenberg advised his son-in-law to avoid debates and keep 'smiling, always smiling'—talking in German but switching to English for 'smiling' as if it were an American aberration" (Heilbut, *Exiles in Paradise: German Refugee Artists and Intellectuals in America, from the 1930s to the Present* [New York: Viking Press, 1983], 59).

19. Theodor W. Adorno, *Minima Moralia: Reflections from Damaged Life*, trans. E. F. N. Jephcott, 3d ed. (London: Verso, 1985), 33. See the specifications in E. Stern, *Die Emigration als psychologisches Problem* (Boulonge-sur-Seine: E. Stern, 1937); and Maurer Zenck, *Ernst Krenek*, 11, 23–27. In particular, see the poignant memories

recorded by Henry Meyer, "Mußte da auch Musik sein? Der Weg eines Geigers von Dresden über Auschwitz nach Amerika," in Heister, Maurer Zenck, and Petersen, eds., *Musik im Exil*, 29–40.

20. For the biographical background of Schoenberg's remark, especially his confrontations with aggressive anti-Semitism, see Reinhold Brinkmann, "Schoenberg the Contemporary: A View from Behind," in *Constructive Dissonance: Arnold Schoenberg and the Transformation of Twentieth-Century Culture*, ed. Juliane Brand and Christopher Hailey (Berkeley: University of California Press, 1997), 196–219.

21. Ernst Krenek, *Die amerikanischen Tagebücher, 1937–1942: Dokumente aus dem Exil*, ed. Claudia Maurer Zenck (Vienna: Böhlau, 1992). In her commentary the editor discusses the "psychopathology" of the exiled (10).

22. Ibid., 145.

23. Ibid., 10.

24. Ibid., 198, 186.

25. Regarding this lack of tradition and attitudes toward the United States in general, see Strauss, *Essays*, 385–400.

26. See Maurer Zenck, *Ernst Krenek*, 180–184. See also Erna M. Moore, "Exile in Hollywood," in *Die deutsche Exilliteratur, 1933–45*, ed. M. Durzak (Stuttgart: Philipp Reclam, 1973). Certainly, behind the reference to history (that is, European history) lies the political conviction to represent the "other Germany," the better one. See also Winkler, *Deutsche Literatur im Exil*, 25.

27. Krenek, *Amerikanische Tagebücher*, 136.

28. Regarding statistical information, see Strauss, *Essays*, 340–45. For an earlier study, see Fermi, *Illustrious Immigrants*, 11–17; Donald Peterson Kent, *The Refugee Intellectual: The Americanization of the Immigrants of 1933–1941* (New York: Columbia University Press, 1953), 15; and Helge Pross, *Die deutsche akademische Emigration nach den Vereinigten Staaten, 1933–1941* (Berlin: Duncker & Humblot, 1955), 45. Maurer Zenck calls the expulsion from Nazi Germany a "mass phenomenon" (in Krenek, *Amerikanische Tagebücher*, 11). Donald Fleming and Bernard Bailyn, conversely, state: "This migration was not a mass movement. Of the millions of Europeans uprooted by the fascist regimes, only a small portion was able to reach safe refuges abroad and of those only a trickle managed to settle in the United States" (Fleming and Bailyn, eds., *The Intellectual Migration: Europe and America, 1930–1960* [Cambridge Mass.: Harvard University Press, Belknap Press, 1969], 3). Given such uncertainties, these are approximate numbers of immigrants admitted from Germany and Austria to various countries in the period 1933–41: United States, 132,000; Latin America, 80,000; Great Britain, 72,000; Palestine/Israel, 56,000; France (prewar), 30,000 (plus many more in transit going overseas); Shanghai, 17,000 (from all countries of origin); Czechoslovakia (until 1938), 6,500; Holland, 30,000 (in transit); Switzerland, 30,000 (in transit). Immigrant professionals from Germany/Austria in the United States are as follows: 1,000 educators (including academics); 2,350 medical personnel; 810 lawyers, 470 musicians; 300 visual artists. Again, these numbers are merely approximations.

29. See Strauss, *Essays*, 340–42; also Jay, *German Migration*, 329, with older studies mentioned 336n.11.

30. Most prominent was the Emergency Committee in Aid of Displaced Foreign Scholars (see the report by Stephen Duggan and Betty Drury, *The Rescue of*

Science and Learning: The Story of the Emergency Committee in Aid of Displaced Foreign Scholars [New York: Macmillan, 1949]), but also the Institute for Advanced Study in Princeton and the University in Exile, part of the New School for Social Research in New York, to name only a few. For an account of difficulties with social integration, see Fermi, *Illustrious Immigrants,* 28–31. Other earlier American studies are Maurice R. Davie et al., *Refugees in America: Report of the Committee for the Study of Recent Immigration from Europe* (New York: Harper, 1947); Franz Neumann et al., *The Cultural Migration: The European Scholar in America* (Philadelphia: University of Pennsylvania Press, 1953).

31. Vordtriede, "Vorläufige Gedanken," 25.

32. Theodor W. Adorno, "Scientific Experiences of a European Scholar in America," in Fleming and Bailyn, eds., *Intellectual Migration,* 342, 338, 350. See also the presentation of a "cultural shock" mentioned by Winkler, *Deutsche Literatur im Exil,* 21ff.

33. Quoted in Hans Heinz Stuckenschmidt, *Schoenberg: His Life, Worlds, and Work,* trans. Humphrey Searle (New York: Schirmer, 1978), 405–6.

34. Even Hanns-Werner Heister's attempt to reevaluate the "American Weill" from a leftist perspective is not free of such a prejudice. Heister sees "Weill's production in the U.S. perhaps not always at the level of quality of his pre-exile works"; typically his argument points to a missing "congenial 'American Brecht'" as the reason for Weill's perceived failure. This judgment implies that the outstanding quality of Weill's "European" works rests primarily on Brecht's merits. See Heister, "'Amerikanische Oper' und antinazistische Propaganda," *Exilforschung: Ein internationales Jahrbuch* 10 (1992): 162.

35. One may also mention Adorno, who, in an attempt at self-distancing, called himself an "extreme case"; see Fleming and Bailyn, eds., *Intellectual Migration,* 338. There also: "I consider myself European through and through, considered myself as such from the first to the last day abroad, and never denied it."

36. See Giselher Schubert's preface to the *Wiener Urtext Edition* of Paul Hindemith's *Ludus Tonalis* (Vienna: Wiener Urtext Edition / Schott, Universal Edition, 1989), ix–x, where all the pertinent documents are cited.

37. Richard Taruskin, *Defining Russia Musically* (Princeton: Princeton University Press, 1997), 486. Hindemith's and Taruskin's aesthetic verdict is supported by Béla Bartók, who supplied his own ironic compositional commentary on Shostakovich's Seventh in his Concerto for Orchestra of 1944 (mvmt. 3, mm. 95ff.). Hindemith's reaction is not mentioned by Taruskin.

38. Symphonic concert programs in the United States, however, remained surprisingly Germanophile: never during the war was Beethoven's rank as the most frequently played symphonic composer challenged.

39. This is not intended as an aesthetic verdict on *Ludus Tonalis,* a work of artistic and music-historical significance despite, or beyond, its authorial intentions, nor is it a final judgment on Hindemith's complicated relation to Nazi Germany. A few years later, interestingly, Schoenberg voiced similar concerns, though without the political implications and in a comparatively moderate tone: "The tendency is to suppress European influences and encourage nationalistic methods of composition constructed on the pattern adopted in Russia and other such places" (Schoenberg to Rudolf Kolisch, 12 April 1949, in Arnold Schoenberg, *Letters,* ed. Erwin

Stein, trans. Eithne Wilkins and Ernst Kaiser [London: Faber & Faber, 1964], 270). On Hindemith's relationship to Nazi Germany, see the most recent summary by Michael E. Kater, *The Twisted Muse: Musicians and Their Music in the Third Reich* (New York Oxford: Oxford University Press, 1997), passim.

40. See Jay, *German Migration,* passim.

41. See Ernst Loewy, "Zum Paradigmenwechsel in der Exilliteraturforschung," *Exilforschung: Ein internationales Jahrbuch* 9 (1991): 208–27.

42. See above, note 12.

43. The most important French contribution to recent exile studies is Jean-Michel Palmier, *Weimar en exil: Le destin de l'émigration intellectuelle allemande antinazi en Europe aux Etas-Unis* (Paris: Payot, 1988). A remarkable joint editorial effort is the "Internationales Jahrbuch" *Exilforschung,* published by the Gesellschaft für Exilforschung / Society for Exile Studies since 1983 (15 vols. to date). An international cooperative to secure sources was the short-lived Bavaria-Harvard Committee for Twentieth-Century Music History from the 1980s. The Deutsche Forschungsgemeinschaft currently supports a project, directed by Horst Weber, to identify sources in California and in several cultural centers of the American East Coast. Recent international symposia were the related 1991 Essen and the 1994 Harvard conferences; for the former, see Horst Weber, ed., *Musik in der Emigration 1933–45: Verfolgung, Vertreibung, Rückwirkung* (Stuttgart: J. B. Metzler, 1994). The International Musicological Congress held in London in 1997 included a study session on the migration to South America and East Asia; a 1997 New York symposium directed by Hartmut Krones, a joint venture with the Vienna Hochschule für Musik, is advertised by the Goethe Institute of New York City.

44. Cornelius Schnauber, *Spaziergänge durch das Hollywood der Emigranten* (Zurich: Arche, 1992). Dr. Schnauber is a professor of German at the University of Southern California, Los Angeles. The exhibition catalog *Exiles in Paradise,* ed. Carol Merrill-Mirsky (Los Angeles: Hollywood Bowl Museum and Los Angeles Philharmonic Orchestra, 1991), also partly functions as a guide to the places where German émigrés lived.

"We miss our Jews"
The Musical Migration from Nazi Germany

Peter Gay

The story of the great musical migration from Nazi Germany is really two related stories—of impoverishment for Germany and Austria and enrichment for the United States—and it is the second that is the focus of this volume. Walter Cook, in the 1930s the chairman of the Institute of Fine Arts of New York University, used to say, "Hitler is my best friend: he shakes the tree and I collect the apples." This is a lighthearted way of summing up the consequences of one of the most terrible passages in the history of our blood-red century. So this series of essays discusses a serious subject.

It is a large subject as well: students of immigration to the United States have estimated that between 1933 and 1944 some 1,500 musicians entered the United States from Europe. Nor did they all remain in New York—though at first glance it might seem so. They scattered across the country and left their mark as professors in colleges, as performers on tour, as guest conductors. Bruno Walter never had an orchestra of his own, but his direct impact on conductors, players, and audiences was impressive, to say nothing of the legacy he left with his recordings. In December 1935 Kurt Weill told an interviewer, "Lots of the best talents have left Germany, and I hear nothing from the pens of those who remained." Many more would leave after, until it was too late.

To be sure, European musicians working in the United States have long been a familiar phenomenon. They were not the unintended fruit of the Nazi thousand-year-Reich alone. As historians of music in America have fully documented, conductors and performers had been visiting, and occasionally settling in, the United States for many decades. Indeed, the prestige of singers, violinists, and conductors from the Old World among Americans was unsurpassed—and a source of some frustration for the native born. It was quite exceptional for an American-born conductor like Leonard Bernstein to acquire so towering a reputation: exceptional and a subject of much astonished comment. European performers from Jenny Lind on found ecstatic audiences over here, and one can hardly read Jacques Offenbach's triumphant letters to his wife on his American tour without emotion. And of course some Europeans, like Arturo Toscanini, became exiles in America because they chose to be, not because they were forced to be. What set the flood from the early 1930s apart was its concentration, its numbers, and the lasting shaping power of its talents on this country. They certainly justify this volume.

In the mid–1960s I attended a festivity at the New School for Social Research to celebrate some of the aging refugees—mainly sociologists, economists, and political scientists—who had been the lifeblood of what in the 1930s had been called the "University in Exile." The principal speaker was Willy Brandt, chancellor of West Germany. In an emotional address, speaking directly to the elderly social scientists on the platform, he exclaimed: "We miss our Jews." It was an electrifying moment, and I think of it often as I go to Germany these days and note a certain thinness of cultural texture. There are no Jewish composers or conductors of any note, except a few who have been imported.

Certainly Willy Brandt meant well with this sentiment, and it cannot be my intention to criticize it. But I do want to offer two glosses on his remark. In the first place, not all those who fled Hitler were Jews. Paul Hindemith and Adolf Busch, to name only two, were not Jewish. We must not forget the gentiles who left Nazi Germany and, later, Nazified Austria—left it because they were politically undesirable, could not bear the regime, would not divorce their Jewish spouse. For obvious reasons the overwhelming bulk of refugees were Jewish, but it is essential to remember that the elite, who by emigrating impoverished German culture, were a varied lot in many respects, including religious background.

My second gloss is perhaps more important. It has become commonplace, among both Jews and gentiles living in Germany today and when the subject is discussed there, to speak of "Jews" and "Germans" as though they were separate entities. But while this dichotomy accurately characterizes the situation now, when the number of Jews is small and their cultural weight negligible, it did not characterize the years of the Weimar Republic. There were, to be sure, Jews in the 1920s who felt excluded, even if the laws made no distinction on the basis of religious origin, who felt socially excluded, sensing a certain animosity, whether latent among those working with them or overt in right-wing political movements. But by and large the Jews living in Germany were Germans—they certainly thought they were, whatever anti-Semites might say.

This willingness, even eagerness, to be incorporated into the host nation has been severely rebuked again and again. For one by Zionists like Gershom Scholem who consistently argued, from the early 1920s on, that the Jewish-German symbiosis was a sham, the love affair a most one-sided one. The Jews, he said, loved the Germans, but the Germans did not love the Jews. Others who found the Germanness of Germany's Jews unacceptable were East European Jews, who saw this supreme attempt at assimilation as a betrayal of time-honored ideals and time-honored identity. Although I find this reproach unfortunate and unhistorical, what is at issue here is that before Hitler, most of Germany's Jews were thoroughly at home in their country, and not as guests, but as essential ingredients in their culture.

In fact, the part that Germany's Jews played in German high culture was very prominent indeed—and it was something they had had to fight for. For centuries, one might say, the Jews living in ghettos in German cities had little history. Then Moses Mendelssohn, though remaining a devout Jew, urged his people to rejoin history by joining the world around them. And the generations of reformers that followed him, seeking to understand their religious and cultural heritage in the same critical spirit they witnessed growing among gentile scholars, continued his work. Until 1848, in some lands until 1871, certain discriminatory laws and many discriminatory practices were kept alive. Although social discrimination never completely vanished, Germany's Jews learned to speak German, learned to feel at home in their new language and their country, and became loyal and, as the First World War demonstrated, patriotic citizens. They were woven into the texture of Germany—not completely, but filled with the hope that the exceptions would disappear.

In high culture this integration became quite obvious. The celebration of a Goethe anniversary, Schiller's centenary, a new edition of Kant's works, were events in which Jews played an indispensable role. It would be a mistake to think of German Jews as invariably clustered among the cultural revolutionaries; Arnold Schoenberg, surely the most radical of the composers after the turn of the century, was by no means the rule among them. The bulk of Germany's Jews, I would argue, were good bourgeois in the paintings they bought, the furniture they lived with, the music they listened to. In any event, in cultural activity, be it art, literature, theater, or music, no matter on which side of the divide between academic and avant-garde they stood, Jews were active.

When we think from this perspective to the years of Weimar, whose destruction started the avalanche of emigration, there is something poignant about this trusting enthusiasm for great Germans. Having won full civil rights with the launching of the German empire in 1871, German Jews were involved in the 1920s in a precarious experiment—a republic born in defeat and disgrace, little loved and much hated. It matters only to later history that the author of the Weimar constitution, Hugo Preuss, was a Jew, but it was typical of the situation that had arisen with the end of empire. As I put it in the little book I published on Weimar culture in 1968, outsiders had become insiders. And for Germany's Jews, the republic was the outsiders' best, and it seemed only, hope for a peaceful future.

The history of Jews in German music is a complicated one. The most painful episode, it seems to me, involves Jews placing themselves in an unfortunate, exceedingly humiliating position: I am of course referring to Wagner's Jewish acolytes. The Master—spurred on, one should remember, by his wife—mercilessly tormented his Jewish disciples, who almost literally adored him, who ran his errands and spread his message. He would lament the curse under which they were forced to live as Jews, alternately recommending that they be baptized or resign themselves to their racial inferiority. But, ever the supreme manipulator, he did not let them go. He did not let them go because he needed them. King Ludwig II of Bavaria, on whom Wagner had staked his career and who was the most munificent of patrons, may have been mad, but his insanity did not include anti-Semitism. I have often thought it poetic justice that the premiere of Wagner's most Christian work, *Parsifal,* was directed by one of his Jewish slaves, the brilliant Munich conductor Hermann Levi—to which I might add in passing that the centenary performance of *Parsifal* was conducted by James Levine. As a seasoned historian, I have discovered long since that history has a rather perverse sense of humor.

Wagner apart, Jews participating in German high culture faced few such embarrassments. Goethe, Schiller, Kleist were their Fontane; Thomas Mann their novelists; and Bach, Beethoven, Wagner, Brahms—not all of them at once, of course—their composers. Now, these choices matter to my argument because it was precisely their total immersion in German high culture that made refugee musicians so available to the United States. German and American theorists, composers, conductors, and performers had a common ground that made working together easier than it was for, say, refugee lawyers or physicians, let alone businessmen. People have often observed, and rightly, that the language of music is international. Frequently it was difficulties with English that kept so many refugees in general from making a success of it in America. There used to be a joke that among the refugees, the psychoanalysts were best off, because all they had to say was "hmmmm." But the musicians were even better off: they could communicate on instruments, or with notes, if not at first with words. They—the musicians, like their colleagues in the theater, in the arts, and in literature—believed, and with justice, that they had taken the best of German culture with them and yielded their onetime home, Germany, to barbarians. And the culture they imported to America was in no way esoteric to their new hosts.

This is where my second gloss on Willy Brandt comes in again. What did it mean, culturally, to be a civilized Jew in Germany at the time of the Weimar Republic? Was there a distinctive Jewish way of playing or conducting music? Could one identify Bruno Walter's way with Mozart, Beethoven—and Wagner—as in some way Jewish? This rhetorical question has, of course, quite general application. Did Wilhelm Kempff play the Beethoven sonatas with a gentile sound, Artur Schnabel in a Jewish way? Did Siegfried Trebitsch translate Shaw as he did because he was a Jew? Was that energetic left-wing journal of Weimar fame, *Die Weltbühne,* a Jewish magazine under its first editor, Siegfried Jacobsohn, and a gentile magazine under its second editor, Carl von Ossietzky? Was there a recognizably Jewish way in which Fritz Kortner played Hamlet or Elisabeth Bergner played Hedwig in Schiller's *Wilhelm Tell?* To ask an even more absurd question: Was the *Dreigroschenoper* Jewish with Kurt Weill's music and gentile with Bertolt Brecht's text?

On this score the testimony of Erich Leinsdorf is of particular interest. Born in Vienna in 1912, Leinsdorf emigrated from Austria in 1936, a year and a half before Hitler took Austria, alert to what was coming—or, I should say, sensitive to what was already happening. He is an extraordinary witness in more ways than one, not only as a celebrated figure in the musical world but also as a convinced and extreme individualist. In a long interview of 1989, responding to the question of where he thought himself most at home, he replied: "Home is where I feel at home." Asked why there have been so many gifted musicians who are Jewish, he replied with a historical generalization: "If you are thinking of physical constitution—I don't believe in that. I think that Jews have concentrated on fields in which they were permitted to unfold their talents." Even more to the point, the interviewer asked Leinsdorf: "Has your own musical feeling been influenced by the fact that you are a Jew?" His reply was simple: "No. I don't know how that could have influenced me. I have spent my entire life as an individual and never sought support from a group."

One might wish to complicate so straightforward an attitude. Leinsdorf's own thought that Jews entered fields they were allowed to enter suggests a possible sociological ground for their prominence in music—as it does, for not very different reasons, in psychoanalysis. But that says nothing about the way in which Jews theorize, compose, conduct, or play music, and indeed, can say nothing about it. A composer like Max Bruch might specialize in Jewish themes. Even Kurt Weill wrote some explicitly Jewish music, researching traditional Hebrew melodies for *The Eternal Road.* Not long after the war, in 1946, he accepted a commission to compose a short liturgical piece, a Kiddush, for a synagogue in New York. It was a very personal testimony, and unlike anything he ever wrote; a completely irreligious person, he dedicated this composition to his father, who had been a cantor. What, then, of Felix Mendelssohn? But after all, Mendelssohn was a Christian, with a *Reformation* Symphony to his credit. We can call him a Jew only if we are interested in tracing his family history, or if we adopt racial criteria, and they, I trust, have by now been discredited. In any event, how would one identify any sort of Jewish quality in his compositions?

Still, in their eagerness to enlist as many as possible in their catalog of famous Jews, authors of compendia and encyclopedias have included Mendelssohn, while conceding that there was really nothing identifiably Jewish about his music. In a collection of essays on the contribution of Jews to modern civilization (only baseball seems to be missing) Eric Werner lists eight Jewish composers chronologically, and says after the first three—Meyerbeer, Mendelssohn, and Offenbach—that none of these "can be considered as an embodiment of Jewish ideas or ideals." He then sadly adds: "This is certainly regrettable." It is not regrettable to me, but the debate whether it should be or not belongs in a forum other than this one. What matters here is that Werner is documenting the overriding importance of craft—in this case musical craft—for those who practice it, whether they are Catholics, Protestants, or Jews. Music has traditions and styles quite independent of religious origins or allegiances. And it is these traditions and styles, both eminently portable, that mattered most to those who left Nazi Europe to find a new home in the United States.

It would be redundant of me to undertake in these introductory remarks an outline of the impact of Europeans on the American musical scene. What I want to concentrate on instead is a much-neglected topic: the impact not of Europeans on America, but of America on Europeans. And I shall give some instances from fields other than music, though they apply to music as well.

We must see the migration of Germans and Austrians to the United States as a two-way street. Traumatized, anxious for those they had left behind, worrying how they might make a decent living in a foreign country under strange circumstances, a few refugees took to denigrating their new home. These were the notorious "bei-unskis," that is, refugees who kept saying, "Bei uns [back home] was everything better." These unfortunates had, of course, a time-honored European tradition to draw on: the dismissal of American culture as ignorant, grossly provincial, purely materialistic. This denigration goes back to Stendhal and Dickens and flourished across Europe well into the twentieth century. Indeed, it is a snobbery we still encounter, at times in high places. The hunt after the almighty dollar has been taken for almost two centuries as the emblem of American life. The "bei-unskis," though, complained about America mainly because they were frustrated and anxious; it was sad to hear them. But having lived through those years myself as a young refugee, and having tested my impressions on others, I think I am safe in saying that the vast majority of us did not endorse this gloomy appraisal. America took us in—in the best sense of that phrase—and changed us forever.

I have scholarly warrant for this assertion. In the early 1950s a group of five European scholars who had made a new home for themselves in the United States joined in a symposium in Philadelphia to discuss their disciplines and their own contributions to those fields of study since their arrival, and to compare their later impressions with those formed in their early training. It was a distinguished group: the political scientist Franz Neumann (who, I should note, was one of my graduate teachers at Columbia in the late 1940s and early 1950s), the student of French literature Henri Peyre, the art historian Erwin Panofsky, the psychologist Wolfgang Köhler, and the theologian Paul Tillich. One thing they had in common was that they had landed in great centers of learning and were aware of having made a difference in their disciplines. Another thing they had in common was that they had learned much from the United States and were pleased to say so.

This was not just humility, or sheer good manners. It was the truth. In a characteristically lucid exposition, Franz Neumann listed three possible ways in which European exiles could have responded to the American experience. "The exiled scholar may (and sometimes did)," he states, "abandon his previous intellectual position and accept without qualification the new orientation." Or "he may (and sometimes did) retain completely his old thought structure and may either believe himself to have the mission of totally revamping the American pattern, or may withdraw (with disdain and contempt) into an island of his own." Or "he may, finally, attempt an integration of his new experience with old tradition." Not surprisingly, Neumann concludes that this last form of adaptation "is the most difficult, but also the most rewarding, solution."

I can testify that Neumann for one (and many others like him) did succeed in choosing this last alternative. A left-wing Marxist intellectual, he became a most popular guide to graduate students in the Department of Public Law and Government at Columbia University. Even those whose field of specialization was American government went to him for advice. He had never been a professor in Germany, but a trade union lawyer, and after his emigration to London in 1933 he had been a student at the London School of Economics before coming to the United States in 1936. All this no doubt kept him from the typical German professorial manner. In any event he came to appreciate the country that had given him his opportunity. By 1950 he was seriously studying Freud and moving (partly, I must note, under the influence of his students) toward a left/liberal position. He was becoming Americanized without giving up his European roots. Those magic names Wilhelm Dilthey and Max Weber, then almost unknown in this country, continued to appear in his lectures and seminars, and led us to books we had never heard of. As we taught him, he taught us—but we did teach him.

One reason that Neumann gave for his adaptability was one that his four fellow speakers also offered: the openness of American society, the hospitality of American colleagues, the informality of American life. Henri Peyre, who after a migratory career as a teacher came to Yale to accept a distinguished professorship, objected (in an almost self-consciously French way) to certain American culinary habits: he "kept shy of milk and mint sauce and vitamins and mayonnaise and fruits on his salad" but grew tolerant of those who thought of these chemical miracles as food. Yet he too praises the Americans for opening their doors to him.

We now know that the life of the immigrant scholar was not necessarily so blissful. The five speakers at this gathering, after all, had landed at Columbia, Yale, the Institute for Advanced Study, Swarthmore, and Union Theological Seminary. Köhler, though teaching at a college—Swarthmore—was elected president of the American Psychological Association and chosen to give the William James Lectures at Harvard. Other refugees, however, fared less well. The depression affected American academia as it did everything else; there was some wonderment at these strange foreigners; there was even some anti-Semitism. But with some reservations about idealization, we may, like these five, credit Americans in general with making a new life possible for these aliens. There is good evidence that makers of music encountered that welcome too.

I want to pursue what this welcome made possible—leaving aside the performers for a moment, who had, after all, a special relationship with their audiences. Briefly put, Americans pushed the Europeans toward life. Tillich titled his talk "The Conquest of Theological Provincialism." The German academic tradition, he pointed out, had encouraged theorizing remote from reality. It had fostered grand, at times pretentious, syntheses; it had invited the professoriate to give deep reasons, even where a more commonsensical approach would have been more appropriate. It was as though the German intelligentsia had forgotten a splendid little essay of Immanuel Kant's, on the saying "That may be all right in theory, but it won't work in practice." Kant vigorously rejected this statement. If something does not work in practice, there must be something wrong with the theory, since practice is proof of a theory. German theorizing, these refugees came to see, had permitted itself to become alienated from practice.

And they came to see it because the Americans were in principle empiricists, a philosophical orientation not favored in German universities. "I still hear the sneers of my philosophy professor," Neumann recalled, "about Locke, Condillac, and Dewey." The "German scholar," he states,

> generally came under three intellectual influences: German idealism, Marxism, and historicism. All three have in common that they are comprehensive systems of thought claiming to fit every phenomenon into its system. All three express the extraordinary weight of an historical tradition. Thus the thought of German scholars was primarily theoretical and historical—rarely empirical

and pragmatic. It makes for skepticism. To the historically thinking scholar, the historical process is frequently the repetition of a previous pattern. Innovations are thus belittled at the expense of the "great historical trend." It may make for radicalism if—as in the Marxian theory—history is believed to operate in a specific direction; and it always makes for a certain rigidity bordering on dogmatism.

"Hence," Neumann continues, "on the whole, the German exile, bred in the veneration of theory and history, and contempt for empiricism and pragmatism, entered a diametrically opposed intellectual climate: optimistic, empirically oriented, a-historical, but also self-righteous." This view of America (except for that rather surprising qualifier at the end: "self-righteous") was shared by all the other speakers. I might argue that Americans really were not hostile to history. It was only that in the United States history was less burdened with its weight than it was in Germany. But I do not want to belabor the issue. America changed its immigrants, among whom were musicians. In her charming book *Illustrious Immigrants,* Laura Fermi notes that "Schoenberg too benefited from his transplantation to American soil. He became more human, entering into closer contact with the contemporary world."

The most brilliant instance of this musical symbiosis is of course Kurt Weill. Weill surely was one of the most adaptable musical geniuses on record. One has the feeling that nothing he heard was ever wasted. Even as a young composer he had been adept at pastiche and parody, daring to offer banal music without being banal. He emigrated early, in March 1933, and went to Paris. There he began to write French music. In some doubt as to whether he was being considered a serious composer, he shrugged in resignation and threatened, as it were, to write musical comedy. And the model he picked was significant: Offenbach. Then, in a musical, *Marie Galante,* he wrote a hit song, "J'attends un navire," which his biographer Ronald Sanders, to whom I am much indebted, calls "so at home in France that it was later to become a theme song used by the Resistance."

When Weill moved to the United States in mid-1935 this adaptability became if anything more spectacular. As we follow his American years, we see him consulting possible sources that will make his music all the more authentic. For that great success *Knickerbocker Holiday,* done in collaboration with Maxwell Anderson and Ira Gershwin, a musical drama set in seventeenth-century New Amsterdam, he looked into Dutch tunes, American folk music, and jazz. One reason he succeeded was his ear, already mentioned; another was the need to make a living. But one senses, as one reads his comments, yet another reason: the feeling that soon overcame him that he was finally at home. No doubt he continued to weave German music into his American productions, at times borrowing tunes he had written back in Berlin. But his sequence of successes, including *Knickerbocker Holiday, Lady in the Dark,*

A Touch of Venus, and others, testifies that he became more and more authentically American. It seems almost providential that not long after his arrival his new acquaintances, the Gershwins, should take him to a rehearsal of *Porgy and Bess.* This was the kind of music he could understand.

It is not necessary to expound further on Weill's memorable fifteen years in the United States (including the songs, like the "September Song," and "Jenny," and "When My Ship Comes In"), since Weill's musical career is covered in greater depth in other essays in this volume. I want rather to close with the statement Weill is reported to have made in 1943 when he became an American citizen: "It's strange: our family goes back to 1329 to Freiburg and I lived in different parts of Germany till I was thirty-three. Yet I never felt the oneness with my native country that I do with the United States; the moment I landed here I felt as though I'd come home." The statement sounds like one a press agent would dream up. But I believe he made it himself, and that he meant it.

PART TWO

Experiences, Reports, and Reflections

My Vienna Triangle at Washington Square Revisited and Dilated

Milton Babbitt

I have chosen to appropriate, with suitable augmentation, the title of a talk I gave at Washington Square College, New York University, in a series of lectures honoring Professor Martin Bernstein, not because the shared content of that talk and this essay is that extensive but because I need to inform—even warn—the reader and to remind myself that this is a personal, necessarily fragmentary, documentation of a perilous journey that began at Washington Square in early February 1934 and is distinguished, at least by its chronological coextension, with that era during which, first mainly in New York but eventually throughout the country, thinking in and about the total musical environment was transformed by the sudden, unforeseen transplantation of all that were the diverse, often revolutionary modes of contemporary musical creation, re-creation, and explication, from—mainly—Austria and Germany to, mainly, this country, and by—mainly—those very persons, even celebrities, who had invented, molded, and developed those modes. First among them was Arnold Schoenberg, who, as the vanguard of that musical population shift, arrived at the Port of New York (really, Hoboken) with his wife and daughter on the last day of October 1933. Although I was not yet in New York, his disembarkation was the occasion for the first in a chain of (perhaps) fortuities that guided my voyage through the thirties. For greeting Schoenberg at the boat, as a "reporter" for *Musical America,* was the young composer Lehman Engel, who had come to New York to study with Roger Sessions and with whom I had grown up in Jackson, Mississippi. When I arrived in New York three months later Lehman was the first musician I saw, and he told me of his greeting and interviewing Schoenberg on his arrival. Lehman knew no German, and Schoenberg's English was limited and noncolloquial, so when Lehman delivered a formal greeting and Schoenberg responded, in English, with "Thank you," and Lehman further responded, in American, with "You're welcome," Schoenberg apparently took this to mean: "Welcome to this country"; his eyes teared, and he embraced Lehman. A short time later Lehman interviewed Schoenberg at length; the piece he then wrote began: "Schoenberg is in America!"[1]

Schoenberg's further welcome to this country oscillated between what Thomas Mann later characterized as "glorification and neglect." There were social events and a few chamber concerts in New York, an appearance with the Boston Symphony in which he conducted two early works and a Bach transcription, while so ill with his persistent bronchitis that he could not fulfill his promised "first pronouncement on the subject" of twelve-tone composition at Princeton University—in English![2] In 1933 there was no music department at Princeton, and Schoenberg's invitation had been arranged by members of various departments and the university organist. Such was Schoenberg's celebrity. And it was yet primarily as a remote, exotic figure that he was known to the world, even to large sectors of the music world. It was his name, rather than his music, that was celebrated, and his music, particularly his most recent music, was known far less by direct acquaintance than by description—usually secondhand, journalistic, misleading, and always inadequate. There were no recordings and only few readily available scores; one was the Klavierstück, later designated op. 33b, published in 1932 by New Music Edition in California. In that publication, rather than supplying the customary "explanation" by the composer, it was simply stated that "Arnold Schoenberg has requested that we do not publish either biographical notes or musical explanations concerning his work, since both he and his musical viewpoint are well known."

How might he have reacted, here, to an occasion about which I have told at least thrice, but for which I can find no suitable substitute as a didactic tale? Early in my student days in New York I decided to broaden my horizons by attending a series of lectures and discussions on contemporary music given at a loft on Fourteenth Street (near Union Square) that called itself "The Jefferson School." Anyone familiar with the particular political correctness of that time and place should be able to infer the ideological orientation of any institution that involved the name of Jefferson, slaveholder or not. Therefore, the initial attitude toward Schoenberg at the school was ambivalent: there was sympathy for a refugee from Nazism but suspicion of a music that never had been embraced as "the people's music." When the discussion proceeded to "specifics" the urgent, moot question was whether "twelve-tone music" was or was not "democratic." The initial vote was "yes," for wasn't each note in the "row" created free and equal? One note, one vote! But suddenly a querulous, dissenting voice was heard: Was it not the case that each twelve-tone work was founded on an order of notes, and thus that each work was founded on a "new order"! The mere uttering of this ominous expression brought the symposium to a quiet, disquieting conclusion.

It was the presence of examples from actual contemporary music, including *Erwartung* and *Pierrot lunaire,* which I never had heard, that made Marion Bauer's *Twentieth Century Music* a book apart in 1933 and transferred me to Washington Square. Her small, congenial courses extended little beyond such examples, but she went everywhere and knew everyone; although she belonged to the extensive Boulanger, Franco-American, circle (and was no friend of any Viennese Circle) she professed great admiration for and friendship with Schoenberg and kept us in touch with his movements, from Boston, when the cold and good sense drove him south to balmy New York, itself undergoing a frigid winter in the depths of the depression. Although we only occasionally encountered Schoenberg after he moved, with his family, into the Ansonia Hotel on Broadway in March, we constantly monitored his condition—in all its aspects, starting with the summary, forced removal from his position in Europe, from his milieu, from his language. That he was able—apparently exceptionally able—to so survive these physical, professional, and "spiritual" deprivations was remarkably reassuring, but there was the sad realization that at this important stage of his creative career (he was approaching sixty years of age) he had been unable to compose for many months. This circumstance, however, was about to change, before our very eyes.

Martin Bernstein, the junior member of the music department at Washington Square, had studied physics before joining the New York Philharmonic as a double bassist. His broad musical and extramusical culture together with his professional musical experience drew him back to the academic world, where he was a superb teacher, a distinguished scholar, and the instigator of a significant event in the history of music.

Schoenberg spent the summer of 1934 in Chautauqua, New York, in order to pursue, among other activities, the sport of tennis with Martin, who was playing in the Chautauqua orchestra. Although Martin waited fifty years before recounting publicly the story of that summer,[3] I have on several occasions related it orally from the standpoint and knowledge of a student who heard from Martin on his return from Chautauqua the extraordinary news of Schoenberg's enthusiastic desire and, already, plan to compose a work, his first "American" work, for our student string orchestra, conducted by Philip James.

I have reported my excitement, as well as our anticipation both of the prospect of such a Schoenberg premiere and of the further possibility of his presence. The latter was immediately dispelled by Schoenberg's decision to leave for even balmier California. The former suffered the same fate, though slowly and more painfully. While we were attempting to fathom what manner of work Schoenberg might be writing—for he had told Martin only that he wished to write a work that would be didactic, to the extent that it would provide young performers with the technical disciplines necessary to perform demanding contemporary music, but in a relatively familiar, comfortable pitch and rhythmic environment—Martin encountered a succession of practical obstacles that, perhaps, he could have overcome if, in the meantime, Schoenberg were not being convinced, perhaps by Carl Engel of Schirmer's, or by his wife, or by his new California acquaintances, that such an important premiere should not be squandered on a mere student orchestra but rather should be offered to Klemperer, who had become the conductor of the Los Angeles Philharmonic. Schoenberg completed the work in December 1934; Klemperer gave the first performance in Los Angeles in May 1935, and in October he gave the first New York performance with the New York Philharmonic, making the possibility of a performance by our orchestra superfluous and anticlimactic.

It may convey some sense of the times (although the times, in that regard, have not changed that much) if I recall the review of that first New York performance by the "respectable" critic, Lawrence Gilman, of that "respectable" newspaper, the *New York Herald-Tribune*. It begins: "Herr Schoenberg [observe the subtlety of that speech act—M.B.], for some reason that is not quite clear, composed last winter in Hollywood what he referred to as a 'school suite.'" Mr. Gilman then compounded this perhaps willful ignorance with references to Schoenberg's presumably abandoned "twelve-tone scale" and "twelve-note scale." Mr. Gilman ended his review with the considered summation: "Mr. Klemperer played the *Suite* as if he believed in it. All things are possible."

That half century after the event, Martin generously observed that "the critics were confused by the sudden appearance of a clearly tonal work. All of their speculations, some patently ridiculous, might have been laid to rest if the foreword of Schoenberg's autograph had been quoted in the program notes."

The original title of the Suite had been Suite in Olden Style for String Orchestra. Schoenberg's foreword, which was to have been included with the printed score, but was not, begins: "The composition of this piece was suggested to me by the favorable impression and perspectives which Professor Martin Bernstein of New York University gave me concerning the ambitions, achievements, and successes of American college orchestras." The foreword elaborates further, and ends: "This piece represents no repudiation of what I have created up 'till now."

So Martin was responsible for the birth of an extraordinary creation, a little-performed, little-known composition, but not a puzzling one, in the light of not just what Schoenberg offered young performers but what he offered composers, young or not: a compact, exacting vade mecum of what every composer should know, even *must* know. Schoenberg had said: "I had been educated in the spirit of the classical schools, which provided one with the power of control over every step." The principles, the procedures, the craft which provided that power are applied and displayed in the Suite in G.

What for Schoenberg was a multilayered link to the past was for us a multiple, if passive, connection to a tradition that we inherited primarily through its extensions. If the Suite was an edifying compendium for us, it was Schoenberg's bridge between his old and new worlds, and he wasn't about to burn his bridges.

But even without Schoenberg's preface or without attempting to discover the "reason," anyone who believed or wished to believe that the Suite was Schoenberg's palinode had to wait only for his next two "American" compositions, the Fourth String Quartet and the Violin Concerto.

The Fourth String Quartet was presented under modest auspices in a room at the New York Public Library. The Kolisch Quartet performed the work in February 1937, a month after they had premiered it in California, and a decade after they had premiered the Third Quartet in Vienna. The audience at the Fourth Quartet performance was substantial and distinguished; I remember that Roger Sessions, with whom I had been studying composition privately for a year and a half, and Elliott Carter were there. I believe that the Kolisch Quartet did not play the work from memory, as they did the rest of their repertory, and I don't know if they even did so in the last two years remaining of their existence. But I vividly recall this, my first encounter with the work. For those of us who had the opportunity to study, for example, the Orchestral Variations, the Schoenbergian hexachordal communality (his already "common practice"), we were able to find our way immediately into the monumental work, and by the time we had found our way through and out of it we at least had glimpsed the reach and range of instantive reference, the richness of multidimensional relatedness, of dimensional imaging attainable within the formational and transformational syntax of the twelve–pitch-class system (henceforth, "twelve-tone system").

It was anticipated that Schoenberg would return to the East for the premiere of his Violin Concerto in Philadelphia in December 1940. Louis Krasner, the soloist, had been waiting at least three years to perform the work, as it was announced for each successive season and then successfully canceled by the management. Suddenly, Stokowski bravely placed it on a program, paid the soloist's fee himself (though Krasner offered to play it without a fee), and the time had come. Although it was known that Schoenberg could not attend the performance, a caravan was organized from New York and Princeton. For that first performance on Friday afternoon, the program order was announced, in the newspapers and on the poster in front of the Academy of Music, as: Sibelius, Symphony no. 7; Schoenberg,

Violin Concerto; and Stokowski, *Tristan und Isolde* "synthesis." So we took our time crossing Broad Street from a delicatessen across the way, feeling that we could afford to miss at least the first movement of the Sibelius symphony, but as we entered the Academy we spied Krasner standing on the stage, prepared to play. Since we conjectured that he was not there to perform a violin transcription of the Sibelius work, we rushed into the hall just in time to hear those unaccompanied, opening notes of the concerto.

It turns out that when the local radio station that broadcast the Philadelphia Orchestra concerts, which customarily did not air the first work on the program, discovered that the announced order of the program would oblige them to broadcast the Violin Concerto, they demanded that the order of the first two pieces be reversed, so that the broadcast audience could be spared the experience of the Schoenberg work.

Nevertheless, the work inspired two of the classics of journalistic evaluation. In the "liberal" *Philadelphia Record,* one Edwin Schloss wrote: "Yesterday's piece combines the best sound effects of a hen yard at feeding time, a brisk morning in Chinatown, and practice horn at a busy music conservatory. The effect on the vast majority of hearers is that of a lecture on the fourth dimension delivered in Chinese."[4] A less orientally oriented description appeared in the "conservative" *Inquirer,* to wit: "The violinist slithers his bow around, apparently at random, pauses to pluck a string here, and poke at another there. While this is going on, the orchestra is busy playing a game that sounds like every man for himself."[5]

If such vulgar contumely had, in a sense, followed Schoenberg from Europe (as early as 1924 he had written, "In order to save myself all superfluous annoyance, I have long sought to keep any journalistic criticism of myself from entering my house"),[6] by the time of the performance of the Violin Concerto he also had been followed to this country by many—perhaps most—of his close and protective musical colleagues from abroad: Rudolf Kolisch, his brother-in-law, became in 1944, after the demise of the Kolisch Quartet, the first violinist of the other most celebrated European quartet, the Pro Arte (which earlier had performed Schoenberg's Third String Quartet, among other of his works, at the New York Town Hall all-Schoenberg concert soon after Schoenberg's arrival); Eduard Steuermann, his "personal" pianist since, at least, the premiere of *Pierrot lunaire;* Fritz Stiedry, who became the conductor of the New Friends of Music Orchestra; and Felix Galimir, the leader of the "young" quartet that had performed Webern's op. 5 and op. 9 at the celebration of Webern's fiftieth birthday in the house of American composer Mark Brunswick in Vienna, after which many of the celebrants (except, of course, Webern himself) found their way to New York and beyond.[7] Louis Krasner, though an American, had become a member of the inner circle, celebrated for his premiere of the Berg

Violin Concerto in that extraordinary drama at Barcelona in 1933.[8] There were many, many others, and while we could not replicate their hazardous pilgrimages, even as a "thought experiment," or duplicate the formative factors of their informal or formal musical and cultural conditioning, I became a colleague, I hope, and a close acquaintance of many of them, because of yet another (perhaps) fortuity: my decision in 1935 to study with Roger Sessions.

Roger had lived in Europe from 1926 to 1933 and had moved from Italy to Berlin at the urging of Otto Klemperer, who soon was obliged to join Roger in the United States. It is the case, as observed by Claudia Maurer Zenck, the editor of Ernst Krenek's *American Diaries,* that "of the significant American composers of his generation, only Sessions did not study with Nadia Boulanger. Consequently he was practically the only one who related closely to his colleagues exiled from Europe."[9] Indeed, many of the American "advanced" composers, whose musical ideas appeared to have few consequences, both understandably and incomprehensibly resented the influx and—above all—the influence of the émigré musicians, and remained apart from the "European-oriented" Sessions. As I have observed elsewhere, he was (and not only in that sense) the "Lone Roger"; but while I gladly admitted and exposed myself further to the foreign influences, I remained, in the eyes (and probably ears) of those older and surely educationally differently oriented European musicians, a young American, perhaps "clever" and "knowledgeable," but forever doomed by the absence of that *Geist und Seele* which was not acquirable, yet was the necessary attribute of a "real" composer. One felt the chasm between our two cultures symptomatically, even decisively, in what might appear mundane matters of manner and manners, in external manifestations of personal relations. I think of three such anecdotal, yet salient, moments associated with Schoenberg.

When Schoenberg came to New York to conduct *Pierrot lunaire* at Town Hall, I attended (at least) one rehearsal, and there came a moment when Kolisch—playing the violin—said to Schoenberg: "Schoenberg, you have notated the harmonic here in a way less comfortable for me than another way, in which I would prefer to play it. Let me play it my way." Schoenberg answered sternly: "No, play it as I have notated it." Kolisch persisted: "Turn your head, and I will play it both ways. See if you can tell any difference, while my way makes for a less awkward succession of fingerings." "No," Schoenberg insisted, "play it as I have written it." I don't know what Kolisch actually did, but the rehearsal continued without further incident. Later I asked Steuermann, whom by that time I had come to know well: "After all, Kolisch is Schoenberg's brother-in-law, but he addressed him as 'Schoenberg'; does anyone call him Arnold?" Steuermann answered: "Sometimes his wife does, but he doesn't like it."

Around the time of that trip, Carl Engel arranged for Schoenberg to lecture on "text setting" at Schirmer's. At 11:00 A.M. one day, an "invited" audience gathered to hear him speak. I arrived a few minutes early to find Schoenberg instructing the slide operator as to the proper focus for the first example projected on the screen, the vocal line of a Reger song. When the appointed hour of eleven arrived, nothing happened. Schoenberg looked apprehensive, and glanced at the open grand piano to his right, but—as was his wont—he didn't touch it. We waited—and waited. At about ten minutes after the hour, Steuermann burst through the door, tossing off his overcoat. He whispered something to Schoenberg as he ran to the piano. (Later we were told he had apologized for having been stuck on the subway.) Then Schoenberg proceeded to the first example: the Reger. After a few preliminary words, he casually tossed out what obviously had not been prearranged, the remark that the "busy" accompaniment for this relatively simple song reminded him of the last movement of Beethoven's op. 2, no. 2. He turned, not entirely, toward Steuermann and asked: "Steuermann, do you know the opening of that movement?" Steuermann responded with neither word nor gesture but immediately launched into the movement and—after launching—continued to sail through it, while Schoenberg stood, helplessly, until Steuermann had completed the movement, to applause. How dare anyone, even Schoenberg, ask if he knew op. 2, no. 2—or any other Beethoven sonata? The talk then continued without deviations from the script, with Steuermann content to perform the short musical examples required.

Finally, one evening at Steuermann's, after yet another episode in our ongoing, low-key gentleman's disagreement arising from our very different construals of the twelve-tone idea (we were both, for different reasons, not prepared to allow it to go too far or too deep), Steuermann smiled wryly (his smile was usually wry) and confided to me that, years before, he had shown one of his large-scale chamber works to Schoenberg, who examined it carefully and finally asked: "Steuermann, why don't you write piano etudes?" His motive for telling me this was surely complex, but it was clear that, however disappointed, even hurt, he had been, he had been, even more, flattered by a candor that bespoke collegial rapport and even intimacy. Surely Steuermann had been the condign accompanist for the convoluted Karl Kraus.

I confess that I felt obliged constantly to measure my words when I was with these musicians from abroad, even those I came to know well, particularly as the news of the enormousness of the enormities reached us throughout the decade. So, when I finally dared to ask Steuermann why he had never performed Webern's Piano Variations, which was dedicated to him, he answered: "You can play it for yourself." When I reminded Steuermann, as I didn't have to, that I was not a pianist, and that all I could do was find the notes, he replied that was what he could do. I understood—as well as I could.

All of the factors of our very different musical, educational, and worldly experience determined our decisively different construals of the twelve-tone "idea." After all, even the youngest among us could not have been to the twelve-tone manner born. But the need to define our positions in a musical continuity wherein our chronological predecessors were reevaluated as our musical forerunners induced what in word and—necessarily, in some respects—in musical deed can only be termed "historicism." Phrases such as "historical necessity," even "inevitability," as justificatory were, for us, unfortunate, undesirable, and—beyond all else—unnecessary. And while such expressions were being employed in the great debate, in the struggle for the soul of music (Herman Scherchen's multilingual journal *Musica Viva,* for instance, devoted an issue to the responses of Europe's "leading" composers to a questionnaire probing their attitudes toward the twelve-tone system), they also shared that mode of viewing the twelve-tone series as a theme, or a motive, therefore as most appropriately susceptible to the procedures of "motivic saturation," "continuing variation," and "chromatic completion," the techniques of the recent past and, by extension and selective analysis, of the great classical past. But for us, this obscured the extent—the considerable, decisive extent—to which we were thinking in music in a new way, a thinking which yielded the "new" holistic compositional concinnity of Schoenberg's Fourth Quartet and Violin Concerto, with yet its multiple implications of extensions to conceptually even "newer," even more personal compositional contexts. When I dared suggest that Schoenberg could not have been aware of the full extent of those implications, as no creator of a profoundly new, potent conception could be, I was banished from the company of true believers. I countered with the reminder that Schoenberg had asserted that "the twelve-tone system could assure the supremacy of German music for the next hundred years," and since he uttered this when he was about fifty years old, he could not have believed, in all realism— nationalism aside—that he was going to ensure and secure that supremacy entirely by his own hand.

For us the idea of the twelve-tone series was, as the referential norm of a work, pervasively and persistently influential, acting at constantly varying distances from the surface of the composition; if and when it appeared in a surface interpretation, as an instantiation of the series, it then might be viewed as a theme or motive, or concatenation of motive, but perhaps only fleetingly, as but a moment in the structural rhythm of the latent and the explicit.

The series, then, was far more importantly viewed as an ordering than even for its "twelveness," its expression as the ultimate chromaticism. Certainly, the fact of all twelve pitch-classes operated upon by interval-preserving transformations required new criteria of hierarchization, contextually sensitive to the singular ordering of the series. But the revelations of the imposed reexaminations of order in the twelve-tone syntax extended beyond "twelve," to orderings of fewer than twelve pitch-classes, to orderings with pitch-class repetitions at any distances within the orderings: the mutual derivability of transposition (formerly and conventionally regarded as an operation on pitch) and inversion (formerly regarded as exclusively an operation on contour); the relation between inversion and "rhythm," the temporal dimension. This latter realization yielded techniques of multiple temporal counterpoint, of intervallic invariance under temporal interchange of inversionally related lines rather than of spatial interchange—as in traditional multiple counterpoint, but with a crucially significant difference in degree of self-reference, as attends a necessarily more automorphic music.

The other constituent of the "historicism" derived from the then almost universal representation of tonal structure as proceeding from one chordal slice of musical lifelessness to another such slice (even when enlarged à la Riemann or Schoenberg the tonal theorist) and, finally, making the great leap from such incompletely characterized local events to the global, to one of the familiar patterns of dimensionally synchronous recurrences of morphic similarity, which endow the work with "form"; such patterns (including "sonata form") were extractable from, and imposable upon, all compositional phenomena, including tiny Webern works. Such patterns, of course, are discoverable trivially, in defiance of Goodman's strictures on similarity, where no other criteria of dependency or contingency are invoked.

But if one views tonal structure in terms of parallelism of prolongational processes through ever-extending and subsuming temporal spans, those descriptional discontinuities in structural ascent vanish and, at the same time, suggest the comparably satisfactory characterization of a twelve-tone work in terms of parallelism of *transformational* processes—inter- and intradimensional processes. Then, when one looks and listens beyond the minute "harmonic" moment, or the crude similitudes, the essential incomparability of the two musical systems is unmistakable.

Such a view of "tonal" structure is due to Schenker, or to one understanding of one aspect of Schenker's "theory." And Schenker entered our lives at almost exactly the same time as Schoenberg entered our country, and from a most unexpected source: an article in the magazine *Modern Music* (!) by Israel Citkowitz,[10] already well known as one of Nadia Boulanger's protégés, who was even viewed as the possible successor to Aaron Copland in the American compositional hierarchy. His article, "The Role of Heinrich Schenker," was not a detailed exposition of Schenkerian analysis but an understanding, appreciative presentation of what Citkowitz termed "Schenker's lifelong consecration to the music of the Masters." And then the word began to circulate that there was a man named Hans Weisse who had been a student of Schenker's in Vienna and was now teaching at the then-titled David Mannes Music School. There were whispers, even semiofficial announcements, that he would be conducting seminars at Columbia and New York University. That did not happen, but in December 1935 Weisse emerged at the annual meeting in Philadelphia of the Music Teacher's National Association (in its own, very different way, as unlikely a site for a discussion of Schenker as *Modern Music*) with a talk entitled "The Music Teacher's Dilemma." As if documenting Schenker's reference, in the second sentence of *Der freie Satz,* to the "false theory" that had been and still was being taught, Weisse analyzed two traditionally "problematical" passages. The first comprised eleven measures from the second movement of the Mozart F Major Piano Sonata, for which Weisse provided a lengthy, detailed verbal and slightly graphical exegesis—which, to make the matter even more "delicate," was placed in the mouth of Mozart. It begins (Mozart speaking): "Sit down; I shall be your teacher." (Mozart, some were surprised to discover, spoke excellent, if accented, English.) The other passage was the "notorious" counterpoint and voice-leading of the fourth measure of the B Minor Fugue of the *Well-Tempered Clavier,* book 1. Even today, both analyses would be viewed as sophisticated and, in many quarters, baffling. Weisse ended his talk with exalted praise for *Der freie Satz,* which had just appeared—at the expense, I should add, of a widely used American text, whose routine and strangely, sadly self-depreciating analysis of the Mozart sonata had incited Weisse's rebuttal and alternative analyses.

It did not take long for the shock waves to travel from Philadelphia to New York. There were violent reactions, such as that of Paul Lang, *the* musicologist (for all that his graduate degree was in French rather than music) at Columbia University, who asserted that he would fire any number of *his* department who took Schenker seriously, fully aware as he was that in *his* department was William Mitchell, an American student of Schenker's, who was to write the first (of, later, many) harmony textbooks reflecting Schenker's ideas.

I was studying with Roger Sessions privately when Weisse's lecture became the talk of the town. Roger had himself written an extended article on Schenker (in *Modern Music!*)[11] and, in my first lesson with him, had discussed Schenker's analysis of Beethoven's op. 2, no. 1, which had appeared in *Der Tonwille.*[12] He knew Weisse, the only one of Schenker's students who continued to compose, however boldly or futilely, given Schenker's celebrated pronouncement that Brahms was the "last master of German *Tonkunst* [tone-art]." I knew Weisse as a composer; his String Quartet had been published by Universal Edition, the chief publisher of Schoenberg, Webern, and Berg (but also of *Der freie Satz*). I met Weisse just once, thanks to Roger;

he obviously was an extraordinary musician who, when he became aware of my deviant interests and sources, felt obliged to admit that "Schoenberg probably was a genius," but, he was quick to add, "a mad genius."

A few years later Steuermann confided to me that one of the most unexpected conditions he had encountered in this country was that "Schenker was a household word." Although not quite an accurate description of Schenker's position in the musical world at that time, what led Steuermann to this exaggeration was his characterization of Schenker's status in Vienna, where, he said, there was that "funny little man who haunted the back streets exposing his analytical graphs, which no one understood. Webern said that he did, but we all knew that Webern didn't." When I reported this statement of Steuermann's I received angry letters, as if I had made it up, rather than quoting Steuermann. I knew that the tale about Schenker could not have been literally true, but it was pertinent evidence of the deep antagonisms between two sides of my triangle.

I assumed that Steuermann and his friends were aware that Oswald Jonas, one of Schenker's best-known students and the author of the first book on Schenkerian analysis, had circulated (probably in 1936) an extensive, single-spaced, typewritten document that was intended as a legal statement directed against the Viennese journal *23* and its editor, Willi Reich, who had published an article in that journal, the crucial imputation of which was that Brahms was a source, a root (*eine Wurzel*), of Schoenberg's composition. For Jonas—and, presumably, his colleagues and a large sector of the population of Vienna—this was libel, a strong intimation of guilt by association. Jonas's article was intemperate, almost violent, in its attack on Schoenberg, his music, his writings, and anyone associated with him. It didn't help matters that Schoenberg himself had invoked Brahms as a "revolutionary" predecessor. Jonas apparently expected the sympathetic court to rule that Willi Reich should at least apologize publicly, as he had been obliged to do when—again in *23*—he had intimated that the politically powerful critic Julius Korngold had a hand in the compositions of his prodigious son, Erich.

Fortunately, this vicious Viennese chatter did not make its way to our shores, for here the Schenker and Schoenberg circles maintained a discreet, discrete distance. (Schoenberg even placed Schenker's writings at the head of his list of recommended readings, though with the demurral that he "disagreed with almost all of it.") Rather, removal to this country induced a schism within the body of Schenkerians, as Jonas and Felix Salzer, Schenker's most prominent students and the coeditors in Vienna of *Der Dreiklang* went their separate ways. Salzer soon joined the faculty of the Mannes School and, then, Queens College, which became a distinguished stronghold of Schenkerian theory.

Jonas was not so fortunate, but his convictions never wavered. Clemens Sandresky tells of his concern for Jonas's condition, and of his suggesting that Jonas accompany him to his alma mater to meet Walter Piston—whose concern and generosity were well known—in the hope that Piston would be able to find something for Jonas at Harvard. Sandresky took Jonas to Piston's seminar, where, that day, Piston was analyzing a work of Chopin, the nature of which analysis one can easily infer from Piston's writings. When the seminar ended, Sandresky told Jonas that now they would talk to Piston, as had been arranged. Jonas, however, refused, telling Sandresky that he could not shake hands with a man who analyzed Chopin in such a manner.

I met Jonas soon after his arrival here, but I came to know him better after his student from Berlin, Ernst Oster, joined him in New York. I often met with the two of them in Oster's modest apartment on Seventy-second Street, where a large wooden crate, containing the complete Schenker *Nachlaß*, occupied an honored place in the front room. (Mrs. Schenker had succeeded in shipping it to Oster before she perished in a concentration camp.) Usually, I was primarily a witness to the intense dialogue, sometimes arguments, between the two of them. Carl Schacter has observed that Schenkerian analysis demands that one spend a great deal of time with a single composition, and Jonas and Oster did, brilliantly, often getting no farther than a single measure.

I was necessarily an outsider, perhaps even a suspect outsider (even after we became very close friends), although I was one of the few of my generation to travel back and forth across that ideological no-man's-land. No mention ever was made of my composition or its manifest allegiances. Just once Jonas could not resist telling me that he had been obliged to listen to *Pierrot lunaire;* he said he wished the instrumentalists would stop the nonsensical noise so that he could hear the poetry.

I came to be included within their discussions, given their boundary conditions, after I, finally, presumed to confess one day that I found the section on *Übergreifen* in *Der freie Satz* unclear, at the least. Jonas frowned—at me, I think—and went to the bookshelf, took down his beautifully bound volume of *Der freie Satz*, and opened it to that paragraph, beside which, in his hand, was a large question mark. (In the translation of *Der freie Satz*, Oster remarks: "Since Schenker's definition and presentation of 'reaching over' is somewhat lacking in clarity, a few additional editorial comments may be in order.")[13]

I was not successful in parlaying that slight moment of certification into the probing of a question that had concerned me for years: Why did Schenker not notice, or not think it worth noticing or even noting, "details" that I had to regard as significant singularities, events in compositions that had determinative consequences for the work in question? For instance, in one of Schenker's most extensive analyses, that of the Mozart G Minor Symphony, there is no recognition, in the graph of the foreground or in the text, of the high C in measure 15.[14] Granted, it is a token of the prolongational-type "neighboring note" at the most foreground level; nevertheless, it is in the flute the highest note of the work thus far, and it is an "accented" neighbor—that is, it sounds against prominent C-sharps. This C versus C-sharp relation emerges throughout the movement as C versus D-flat, vertically and linearly in measures 34–37, 58–61, etc.

When I asked why the phrasing of the cellos and double basses in measure 56, articulating the E-flat to D (the opening notes of the violin in the work), had not been mentioned or reflected in the graph, Oster—only half jokingly—simply passed this off as an example of the composer's awareness of a practicality: the shortness of the double-bass bow. I felt obliged to point out that the bow must have grown in the course of the movement, for in the corresponding point in the "recapitulation," the corresponding notes C to B-flat are not so isolated.

I wished particularly to discuss Schenker's analysis of Haydn's *Representation of the Chaos,* where, in a welter of programmatic metaphors, pitch presences across the total "movement" remain unmentioned and excluded from the graph.[15] Even if the A-flat is "heard in place of the fifth," that first triad is an A-flat major triad, and in the subsequent "swelling movement," which "occurs above and below," an F-sharp is adjoined, and the A-flat/C/E-flat/F-sharp is reasonably interpretable as a "dominant seventh" of D-flat (particularly as it is arpeggiated in measure 9)—or, if one prefers, as the defining element of the D-flat collection—the D-flat that, in measure 21, is a point of registral, dynamic, and textural emphasis and the referent of the Neapolitan details in measures 54 and 56, the end of the section.

I mentioned (and mention) such "details" not to supplant the Schenker analyses, but to supplement them. I hoped to elicit from Jonas some sense of how Schenker taught and talked privately, whether he discussed such "details" beyond what is in the printed texts. For such "details" as I have noted are most likely to be heard and discovered, and surely to acquire full significance, within the voice-leading framework of the successive, subsuming prolongations, as the communal induces the individuated; such conflations of the analeptic and the proleptic, such instances of particularity, transcend musical systems as syncategorematic processes and disambiguations in the common quest for musical mereology.

When I asked Oster why there were no Schenker or Schenker-derived analyses of symphonic or chamber music movements by Brahms, he threw up his hands and almost cried: "They are so complicated!" I could not resist using this revelation as the point of entry into a crucial aspect of the whole Schenkerian enterprise; so I asked: "If they are so complicated, how do you know they are any good?" Oster didn't answer, but looked at me in a way that suggested he didn't know if I was joking, but if he suspected I wasn't he was probably thinking either "Oh, these American 'positivists'" or (and this is an inclusive "or") "This question would not be asked by anyone with an artist's *Geist und Seele*." I was attempting to discover to what extent, if any, there was an awareness that the Schenkerian cosmos in all its manifestations rested on a normative but fruitful, circularity; lurking behind every analytic diegetic was an intimated disguised evaluative. The verbal components of the analyses are riddled with imperatives and prescriptives, and the very choice of instances rests ultimately on an illicit derivation of a "should" from an "is" or—given that the analyses are exegetic wakes—of a "should" from a "was." This does not diminish the extraordinary accomplishment, the unprecedented achievement of the undertaking, the explanatory scope of the subtle individual analyses, but Schenker's small number of allowed entrants into his pantheon, floating disjunct from one another and on a different plane from all others in the historical continuum (as graphically displayed in his representation of the relation, or the lack of relation, between *Genie* and *Durchschnitt* in the first edition of *Der freie Satz* [fig. 13] but suppressed even by Jonas in his revised German edition and—therefore—absent from the English translation), suggests an enthymemic leap over concealed criteria that are not inferable even from his "counterexample" analysis of the Reger Variations and Fugue on a Theme of Bach and of a small portion of the Stravinsky Piano Concerto. It is this apparently unknowing invocation of a familiar fallacy that led me to wish that Schenker and his students, as well as Schoenberg and *his* students, had been aware that right around the Ringstraße in Vienna was the "Vienna Circle" (which I presume to embrace as the third vertex of my "Vienna triangle"), with its concern for responsibility and clarity of discourse and the techniques of rational reconstruction. But when the leading members of that circle—among them Carnap, Feigl, and Hempel—came to this country, and I was able to meet Carnap when he spent the years 1952–54 in Princeton, he appeared to be only vaguely aware of the existence of Schoenberg, and seemed surprised that anyone was *that* interested in him, particularly an American boy or man. Carnap was then teaching at UCLA, where there was a Schoenberg Hall to honor the composer's past presence at that university. Carnap also appeared never to have heard of Schenker. So the ignorance and lack of interest were mutual.

When Ernst Krenek arrived here in 1938 he was the public celebrity of all the "transplanted composers" (to cite the term he used for his first published article in this country). He had traveled in the United States the year before as a glamorous appendage to the Salzburg Opera Guild, but now that he had emigrated, he could be treated as should the composer of *Jonny spielt auf*, for even newspaper readers were aware that *Jonny*, in 1927 alone, had played in forty-two different opera houses, receiving 421 performances in its first season. Even the New York Metropolitan Opera felt obliged to take notice and produced it as its first "modern" opera in 1929. Even its failure there attracted public notice, so that it was as the composer of that putative "jazz-opera" that Krenek was welcomed in this country. That Krenek disclaimed its "jazziness" was of no consequence, for, what few knew, Krenek had since *Jonny* composed through a "Schubert" period, and in 1932 he embraced the "system" whose nature and products he had violently reviled, entering the camp of the enemy to the degree that he was in that chosen company that celebrated Webern's fiftieth birthday at Mark Brunswick's house.

In 1937 he published *Über neue Musik,* the first book on "the twelve-tone system," with chapters ranging from "Music and Mathematics" to "Music and Humanity."[16] The volume was reviewed in *Modern Music* by Roger Sessions. There were sections on "harmonic zones in the twelve-tone domain" and on "the all-interval row." This latter was still very much on his mind when I met him for the first time, at Christmas dinner at the Sessionses' home in 1938. Above all, he wished to know the number of (independent) all-interval twelve-tone series. In his book he had invoked, thanks to Willi Reich (!), the device of the clock for its modular arithmetic; this was not an advisable method for securing the computable, but not otherwise trivial, answer to the all-interval question. Such "technical" concerns led to the projected translation of *Über neue Musik*'s being abandoned, and the more general, yet ideologically consonant, *Music Here and Now*'s appearing instead. When, in 1940, his *Studies in Counterpoint* ("based on the Twelve-Tone Technique") appeared, he became the didactic twelve-tone authority. His *Studies* were an importantly characteristic instance of that early twelve-tone thinking, grounded in the "motivic" view of the series, with, even, a grading of the "tension degrees" of chords, as context-independent universals, unrelated to any specific series—not too unlike Hindemith's Series II.

Krenek's pre–twelve-tone celebrity was so great as to secure an engagement for him to perform his Second Piano Concerto with the Boston Symphony. But when Serge Koussevitzky received the score of the surely not jazzy, "serial" work from the camp of his enemies, he developed a "sore arm"; Richard Burgin conducted. The work was "coldly" received, and Krenek, perforce, retired from the public arena to a teaching position at Vassar College. He has documented those first American years in fascinating detail, from the "glamorous" days of visits to Hollywood to the difficult days at Vassar, which culminated in his being denied a third year of teaching by the Vassar department, in spite of the "plea" of the president of the college and the recommendation of the Advisory Committee.[17] I recall Roger Sessions's great concern, and I remember that, soon after Pearl Harbor, he wrote a strong letter to the president of the college on Krenek's behalf. Krenek lived in what he termed "perpetual fear and tremble." He joined the distinguished group that, over the years, had and have been denied Guggenheim Fellowships. And he was particularly disturbed by an article sent to *Modern Music*, written by a tenured (as Krenek was not) professor of music history at Stanford University, Warren Allen, in which—according to Krenek—it was asserted that "the German twelve-tone composers were not really driven out by the Nazis; they were, in his opinion, sent by Hitler to America in order to corrupt the spirit of American youth. They only *believed* they were persecuted."[18] Allen's article was not published, but the fact of its existence was widely known, and its scurrilous contents were quoted in various forms. And even though Krenek continued to compose at virtually his usual pace and delivered a carefully prepared paper entitled "A Study of Cadential Formations in Atonal Music" to the New York Section of the American Musical Society (where he was "heckled" by Joseph Schillinger), the Allen article was still on his mind when I saw him for the last time in Princeton after he had been purged by the Vassar Department and before he left for a position in Hamline University. As we walked around the campus, his manifestly deep depression, intensified by the state of the war and the world, dissolved for a moment when he asked, surely rhetorically: "Hindemith teaches in a place like this, doesn't he?" I answered: "Well, not exactly. It's called Yale, but he does teach there." "Then," Krenek observed, "I'm not worried about my future. I may not be the greatest composer in the world, but I'm certainly better than Hindemith!" I didn't then know, and probably wouldn't have told him had I known, that Hindemith was appointed at Yale only after the dean of the Yale School of Music had assured the president of the university that "Hindemith had lately softened his style considerably, so that now it is acceptable to the average listener. He could now be trusted not to proselyte [*sic*] among, students in favor of modernistic [*sic*] music!!"

Hindemith himself, unlike Krenek, took no part in the New York contemporary music scene; he spent his time traveling between his position in New Haven and his public appearances as a performer. Nevertheless, one titillating circumstance falls within the purview of my triangle. When the first volume of Hindemith's *Unterweisung im Tonsatz* arrived in this country in 1937, it contained an interesting introductory acknowledgment of the "valuable assistance" of Hermann Roth, who was known in this country as the author of *Elemente der Stimmführung*, explicitly influenced by Schenker, an influence acknowledged in the foreword. When the translation of *Unterweisung* appeared in 1942, however, Roth's name was missing. When I asked the translator, Arthur Mendel, about this omission, he was surprised, for he had been unaware of it. On consulting his notes, he discovered that Hindemith had given him a "revised" typescript from which to make the translation: the revised version made no reference to Roth. Did Hindemith, who had engaged in private correspondence with Schenker, wish to avoid any suggestions of affinity or derivation, perhaps with respect to "step-progressions," perhaps not?

When Stefan Wolpe arrived in the United States the same year as Krenek, he was as little known as Krenek was celebrated. Where his name was at all familiar it was associated with his "worker" songs that he had composed in Berlin before his odyssey to Vienna, where he studied for a short time with Webern, and then to Palestine, and, finally, to New York. Marion Bauer introduced him to the world with an article in *Modern Music,* and to me at the same time. Although his music and training suggested that he belonged within or near the ambit of the "Second Viennese School," he distanced himself from the twelve-tone system (as the thematic "twelve-tone rows" of his *Passacaglia* surely confirmed) by proclaiming early on his dissatisfaction with what he perceived as the constant circulation of all twelve pitch-classes, a strangely limited, rudimentary view of twelve-tone compositions as a succession of series "forms." His analysis instruction was heavily and completely motivic, as was his music, often in highly attenuated and sophisticated ways. One of his major articles, "Any Bunch of Notes," in its title and intricate content represents the highly context-dependent, autonomous properties of his compositional thought, which became, with time, both more rarefied and, superficially, "simpler."[19] Although his period of great influence as a composer and teacher came after World War II, his underground influence began to spread when he began teaching in Philadelphia in 1939.

In those worst of times—the time of the Great Depression, of a terrifyingly increasing awareness of the spread of the demonology, of, finally, war—and with the displaced musicians' professional and personal perplexities, crises, and often inscrutable dispositions coloring our own personal and professional lives, we still could be stimulated and informed by what was the best of those times, as our milieu and music changed profoundly and permanently, and not only by the "great names" of music. There was Karol Rathaus, who, after a celebrated career in Germany as the composer of the music for the film *The Brothers Karamazov* and other films in Germany, France, and England, immediately went to Hollywood, where he composed the score for the film *Let Us Live,* directed by a colleague from Germany. But he was obliged to return to the East Coast and, eventually, took a teaching position at Queens College, where he maintained a position of considerable prestige and influence as a teacher and of respectable prestige as a composer. I met him on his return from the West Coast when Roger Sessions invited him to teach as a "fill-in" in an undergraduate theory course at Princeton; he was therefore my associate. His teaching reflected the traditional (untouched by recent heads) "chordal" instruction of middle Europe, but it was done with elegance and cultivation and even cynicism.

There were the "Viennese Conservatives," men of great musical culture and post-Regerian skill, such as Karl Weigl, or of singular ideology, such as Hugo Kauder, who, after having at least rubbed elbows with the Schoenberg group, underwent a prelapsarian epiphany and—over here—advocated, taught, and composed so unsullied and consonantial a music as to shame the sinful nineteenth-century Cecilians. He irrationalized his dissent from Schoenberg by appeals to "the moving and shaping forces of music itself . . . the primordial source of music . . . the order of the universe."[20]

And there was, very much on the other two hands, Erich Itor Kahn, who came to New York from Germany by way of Paris (where he was associated with Stravinsky) and immediately, with the greatest modesty and sensitivity, became a force, as a composer, as a performer, being a soloist and member of a celebrated trio, and as one with a considerable knowledge of analytical theory. He coached recalcitrant divas in the songs of Schoenberg and younger performers in the unwritten traditions of performance.

Perhaps the most unlikely colleague was a star performer whose repertory suggested allegiances similar to Schenker's. But Artur Schnabel, even in the early compositions of his that we knew, a string quartet published by Universal and a movement from his solo violin sonata (published as a "horrible example" by Carl Flesch in his book *The Art of Violin Playing*), hardly suggested such limited horizons. When, in this country, both his chamber and orchestral music became better known and his admirations were revealed, it was not surprising that Roger Sessions, his close friend, finally should ask him, in my presence, why, since he was such an avowed admirer of Schoenberg's music, he never performed it. Schnabel responded: "I play only music which is problematical for me. Schoenberg's is not problematical."

We became conscious that the influence of the émigré composer was reaching the part of our country between the two coasts when Marcel Dick, the last violist of the Rose Quartet (which, in the early days, had given the premieres of Schoenberg's first two quartets), passed through New York to an influential career at the Cleveland Institute of Music, and when Paul Fisk, a Schoenberg student from Vienna, eventually settled at the University of Texas.

The many who joined Schoenberg, Stravinsky, Toch, and others at Hollywood and Wien require their own chronicling, but one who returned for a short visit demands a presence here. Paul Dessau came to New York in 1934, but joined his friend Brecht in California in 1937. In May 1941 he returned to New York for the performance of his work *Les voix de Paul Verlaine et Anatole France* in the ISCM Festival. At the rehearsal of that intricate work for two pianos, percussion, and voice, Dessau suddenly grabbed Roger Sessions by the arm and forced him to walk (or, more accurately, pace) up and down the corridors of the Forty-second Street Library while he shouted and gesticulated: "Do I have a right to compose music like this at a time like this?" Shades of the Jefferson School! Krenek, in his diary, reported of that occasion that Dessau "behaved in a rather crazy way. . . . Yet he got the most convincing performance, worthy of his outstanding composition." Dessau resolved his dilemma, presumably to his own satisfaction and surely to his own profit, by returning with Brecht, in 1947, to East Germany, where he joined Hanns Eisler and Wagner-Regeny as honored composers of that country. And so were we sadly reminded, as we did not have to be, that the same music which the Nazis condemned as "Bolshevik modernism" was proscribed by Communist Russia as "bourgeois, formalist modernism."

This report, as well as the more extensive report it could have been, should be taken as testimony to the insufficiently documented and heralded intercontinental achievement of Mark Brunswick. Personally and as the chairman of the National Committee for Refugee Musicians, this American composer was responsible for saving and transporting to this country a larger part of a musical culture than we ever shall be able to know.

NOTES

1. A. Lehman Engel, "Schoenberg Speaks Out His Mind on Art of Today," *Musical America* 53 (25 Nov. 1933): 5, 34.

2. Claudio Spies, "Vortrag/12 T K/Princeton," *Perspectives of New Music* 13 (1974): 58–136.

3. Martin Bernstein, "On the Genesis of Schoenberg's Suite for String Orchestra," *Institute for Studies in American Music Newsletter* 14 (Nov. 1984): 1,2, and 11.

4. *Philadelphia Record*, 7 Dec. 1940.

5. *Philadelphia Inquirer*, 7 Dec. 1940.

6. Arnold Schoenberg, in a letter to the chairman of the Committee, Austrian Association of Teachers of Music, 11 Dec. 1924; in *Arnold Schoenberg Letters*, ed. Erwin Stein (New York: St. Martin's, 1965), 112.

7. Hans Moldenhauer, *Anton von Webern* (New York: Knopf, 1979), 402–3.

8. On this incident, see, for example, Louis Krasner, "Some Memories of Anton Webern, the Berg Concerto, and Vienna in the 1930s," *Fanfare*, Nov.–Dec. 1987, 335–47.

9. Ernst Krenek, *Die amerikanischen Tagebücher, 1937–1942: Dokumente aus dem Exil*, ed. Claudia Maurer Zenck (Vienna: Böhlau, 1992), 28n.76.

10. Israel Citkowitz, "The Role of Heinrich Schenker," *Modern Music* 11, no. 1 (1937): 18–33.

11. Roger Sessions, "Heinrich Schenker's Contribution," *Modern Music* 12, no. 4 (1935): 170–78.

12. *Der Tonwille* 2 (1922): 25–48.

13. Heinrich Schenker, *Free Composition*, ed. and trans. Ernst Oster (New York: Longman, 1979), 48–49, 83.

14. Heinrich Schenker, *Das Meisterwerk in der Musik*, vol. 2 (Munich: Drei Masken, 1926), 107–57.

15. Ibid., 161–70.

16. Ernst Krenek, *Über neue Musik* (Vienna: Ringbuchhandlung, 1937).

17. Krenek, *Amerikanische Tagebücher.*

18. Ernst Krenek, *Horizons Circled* (Berkeley: University of California Press, 1974), 65. See also Alan P. Lessem, "Teaching Americans Music," *Journal of the Arnold Schoenberg Institute* 11 (June 1988): 7.

19. Stefan Wolpe, "Any Bunch of Notes," ed. Austin Clarkson, *Perspectives of New Music* 21 (spring–summer 1983): 295–310.

20. Hugo Kauder, *Counterpoint* (New York: Macmillan, 1960), viii.

Displaced Musics
and Immigrant Musicologists
Ethnomusicological and
Biographical Perspectives

Bruno Nettl

In this volume we are confronting a musical migration, from Germany and Austria—and perhaps associated regions, such as the Czech Republic—that took place between 1930 and 1950. My parents took part in this migration, and so did I as a young boy. The events that led to this migration, and to the Holocaust, were unique in human history. But migrations of peoples, and of their musics, are almost a commonplace in history, and ethnomusicologists have for some time been engaged in investigating the processes, results, regularities, and patterns of music migrations from a comparative perspective. In what follows I will be undertaking two tasks: to recall some personal aspects of this migration as my parents and I experienced it; and to write a bit about the study of the music of displaced peoples in the ethnomusicological literature. To conclude, I will try to see what these two tasks have to do with each other. I will thus alternate being autobiographical, biographical, and bibliographical.

When comparative musicology began around 1900 its practitioners conceived of themselves mainly as students of static cultures that had not changed since the Stone Age. Even as a student around 1950, I was taught to pay attention to that kind of "authentic" music and to avoid musical phenomena that had in some sense moved: changed in style, social context, or function; moved from rural to urban, or from Old World to New. Largely, this attitude has in the meantime been replaced. Ethnomusicologists now concentrate on the study of change, process, motion. One of the main questions they habitually ask concerns the ways in which population movement and cultural evolution have affected music and musical life. Musicians have migrated, and music has been displaced; what has been the effect of the migration on the music, and the effect of migrants on the music of their new home?[1]

One approach to surveying the large body of literature dealing with these questions is to distinguish different kinds of migrants, and the different motivations people have for leaving, deciding where to go, and staying there once they've arrived. For one thing, we should distinguish the migration of individuals and families from the movement of large social units. In this regard (as well as others), the experiences of German musicologists coming to the United States in the 1930s and 1940s, Indian villagers traveling to Trinidad in the 1800s, and Africans brought as slaves to Brazil from the 1600s well into the 1800s are very different. Once the migration has taken place, there are generational differences in attitudes toward the homeland as well. Doing research in Detroit in the 1950s, for example, we found that immigrants from Poland, their children, and the grandchildren had quite different attitudes toward their Polish folk heritage.[2]

There is always some kind of pressure to leave—no one just does it on a lark. Most migrants to North America at least, whether they arrived voluntarily or because of forces outside their control, have seen themselves, so it seems to me, for a time as refugees.[3] Let me, however, call *refugees* specifically those people who have been forced to leave home, who upon their arrival are sometimes maintained in segregated living arrangements such as camps, who at first have no defined relationship to the culture of their new home, and who use the culture they brought with them as a means of survival. After a while they may become *exiles,* people who expect to return home when conditions have improved and who try to maintain certain central aspects of their traditional culture in the new home. I will reserve the term *immigrants* for people who come to another country to find work and a higher standard of living and who, expecting to stay, nurture particular conceptions of their original home. There is a last category, *abductees,* who were forced to leave their home not because it was in some way unsatisfactory, but because another country wanted them and brought them by force. The most obvious example is African slaves. Each of these classes (which are not mutually exclusive but for many migrants may at times overlap) has its own configuration of cultural and musical relationships. I want to try to identify some patterns.

Let me mention first the collecting of European folk music in strange places. Using the theory of marginal survival as a guide, collectors sought traditions in North America and elsewhere that had been lost or irretrievably changed in Europe. Like the paradigmatic study of Cecil Sharp in Appalachia, much of this work centered on the assumption that immigrant populations may often maintain their culture in an especially pure form.

The study of English folk music in North America, and eventually of everything from Czech songs in Florida to Amish hymns in the Midwest, became a centerpiece of American folkloristics; studies of German folk song in Russia by Georg Schünemann and in Argentina by Marius Schneider indicate a wider scope for this work, even before World War II.[4]

The search for purity was eventually supplemented by analyses of the changed functions of music in immigrant communities. Studies of North American cities, seen as combinations of ethnic groups who drew boundaries in various ways, became the model for what is sometimes called "urban ethnomusicology," a field that came to include studies of European cities—such as Turkish music in Berlin—and the third world.[5] In North America, urban ethnomusicology began with European cultures but began to include Asians in the 1970s.[6] Many authors—among them Robert Klymasz, Stephen Erdely, the venerable Marius Barbeau, and, more recently, Ronald Riddle, Isabel Wong, and Kay Shelemay—looked at changes in music: songs and performance practices, the institutions that produced them, and the conceptions and values that governed them, including a society's view of its place in America as well as its memory of its original home.[7] It turned out that the traditional music of these societies played a special role in cultural integration. Indeed, among the cultural domains that could provide coherence for an immigrant group, music appears to be in the forefront. Although the venue, performance practice, and function may change greatly, the content—the identity of songs and pieces—is likely to remain. At the same time the migrant people's view of the old country becomes more synthesized; regionalism declines, and national or ethnic identity in a larger sense may come to dominate. Italian choirs and Polish folk-singing groups in Chicago, for example, find music from all parts of the home country. V. S. Naipaul, visiting India after growing up in an Indian community in Trinidad, found that his Trinidadian village had a comprehensive and holistic conception of India that was not shared by people actually living in that country.[8]

The large body of musicological research in Israel exhibits a combination of the search for survivals and analysis of processes of change. There are numerous studies of immigrant groups in Israel—Yemenites, Turks, Moroccans, Persians, Indians, Eastern Europeans, and Germans—beginning with the pioneer studies of Robert Lachmann and Edith Gerson-Kiwi and continuing through the work of Philip Bohlman.[9] In these studies we see the complexity of the concept of displacement. In a small project I once did with Amnon Shiloah, Persian Jews in Israel described themselves in part as displaced musicians who had been serving Islamic societies, but in other respects their self-view was not of going into but of returning from exile.[10]

Musical studies of displaced people have found their richest ground in the music history of abductees. I speak, of course, of Africans who were brought as slaves to North and South America and the Caribbean, though another example might be Native Americans who were moved to reservations. The main question here was how these people preserved aspects of their traditional musical culture while at the same time creating a new one through combination with what they found in the new venue.[11] In other words, how and why did the members of independent, and often disparate, cultures combine into a single, broadly African American or Native American culture unit?[12] Concepts united under the old label of syncretism have been used to explain retention, change, combination, and synthesis, as factors of cultural cohesion and compatibility among cultures and musics.

What then of the people I've called exiles, who are temporarily displaced but who fully expect to return home? This group has not constituted a separate category in the ethnomusicological literature. But some of the migrants to whose music this conference is dedicated were exiles who expected to return to Europe. A few did. In my experience, and as documented in the work of Craig Macrae, the Iranians who came to the United States in the 1970s and 1980s have tended to remain, in their minds, exiles; that is, they fully plan to return.[13] Whether they will depends on political events of the future, but my impression is that they want to return, just as did many of those who fled the Nazi menace. Largely members of the professional and business classes, these Iranian exiles exhibit some similarities to the Central Europeans I knew in the 1940s. Their lifestyle is reminiscent of that of Tehran in the 1960s, except that they are far more attached to Persian music than they were back home. Active concert attendance among Iranians in America seems to me to exceed, per capita, that of Tehran. Macrae and I have heard many statements to the effect, "I didn't get interested in Persian music until I came here, but now I want to learn as much as I can." I am reminded of Philip Bohlman's findings among Jews of German origin in Israel, for whom the German classical and romantic repertoire became a special sort of ethnic music.[14] For the Iranians, it's a matter of discovering their culture in exile; for the Israelis of German origin, it was a matter of finding a cultural focus of their home that was not tied to the forces close to the Holocaust.

In addition to the abductees, the refugees, the exiles, and the willing immigrants, we must also consider those who move not as part of a group but as individuals, bringing, presenting, and teaching their culture from a personal point of view. In many cases, these visitors come specifically—perhaps by invitation—to share their culture, and although often they stay, their initial intention is simply to pay a visit. In North America, in the field of music, such immigrants range from Antonín Dvořák from the Czech lands, to countless conductors, to scholars such as J. H. Kwabena Nketia from Ghana. Their purpose was not to find accommodation with the new environment but to affect it. Such immigrants have long been a facet of history. The Mughal emperors, for example, brought Persian musicians to India, presumably to present and teach their music.[15] In the 1960s one Jewish Persian musician I knew in Israel kept going back to Iran, to soak up, as it were, the proper music in order to present it effectively to his Iranian-Israeli compatriots.[16] These cultural mediators—or, as anthropologists call them, culture brokers—perform a valuable function in this era of heightened cultural interaction. One thing that has not been widely noted is the tendency for individuals to move from one category of migrant to another and even to a third, all the while perhaps seeing themselves as representatives of a fourth.

I want to suggest, therefore, that, however unique the individual experiences of World War II migrants and exiles, we may derive insight from looking at them in the contexts I've mentioned. I am particularly interested in seeing whether similar patterns—social, intellectual, musical—can be discerned in the lives and works of the musicologists who came to the United States. Although ethnomusicologists haven't often explicitly investigated the musical scholars of the societies they study, Alan Merriam's well-known tripartite model of the anthropology of music suggests that this should be essential, since musicologists are among the principal bearers of systems of ideas about music.[17]

Unfortunately I don't have systematic data about musicologists as a group. I can, however, provide a personal view of the subject—in the form, as well as I can from such a close perspective, of a case study of my father, Paul Nettl (whom I have no need to introduce to a musicological audience), with mention also of my mother, Gertrud Hutter-Nettl, who worked both in Europe and in the United States as a piano recitalist and teacher, and a few others briefly as well. How did their attitudes, in their musical and scholarly work, change as a result of the political and social events of their lives after 1930, and how did they affect the American musical scene?

My father actually never considered himself an American, despite his treasured U.S. citizenship papers. Once, in about 1950, when asked outright about his inner ethnicity, he said that he was really an Austrian; but he hadn't lived in Austria since 1927, and in any case, he clearly meant a pre-1914 Austrian. Having come from Prague to America yet feeling Austrian may seem strange, but I think he would have felt quite at home with the concept of mutliculturalism. To him, the ideal milieu was always the Prague of the time before World War II, when it was rather explicitly multicultural, and in his writings and conversations he reveled in the contrastive contributions of Czechs and Germans, Jews and Christians, Catholics and the descendants of the Hussites, of Hungarians, Poles, Italians, and yes, even the Swedes of the remote Thirty Years War.

Born in the Sudeten mountains, in the area known as Riesengebirge or, in Czech, Krkonose, he studied at the German university of Prague, went on to postdoctoral study in Vienna with Guido Adler, worked as his assistant and did local arrangements for the 1927 Beethoven congress, and the same year moved back to Prague to be a lecturer under his thesis advisor, Heinrich Rietsch.[18] His troubles as a member of the wrong ethnic groups had already begun, and in retrospect it is surprising that he made no move to leave an obviously inhospitable environment. Even before 1930, while a young assistant, he perceived Robert Lach, whose scholarship he admired, and many others in Prague—even Rietsch, despite his partially Jewish descent—to be strongly anti-Semitic. After Rietsch died, his position went to Gustav Becking, though in 1955 a German court decreed that it would have gone to my father were it not for his Jewish background. At the same time, in the mid-1930s, Czech resentment of Germans was on the rise, and it was embarrassing to be heard speaking German on the street. Despite all this and worse, my parents did nothing to try to leave Central Europe until 1938, when my father tried to visit England to ascertain the chances for later immigration. There he was twice turned back by immigration officers—something that confirmed his characteristically Austro-Hungarian anglophobia.

I am convinced that my father put up with these problems because he felt that Prague, as a multicultural city, was the world's ideal place to live.[19] Only about the time of the German annexation of the Sudetenland, in September 1938, did he send his vita to several institutions in the United States, while also investigating emigration to Palestine aboard a ship sailing down the Danube.

On someone's advice he had sent his vita to Westminster Choir College; as fortune would have it, he received a telegram from its president on the very day of the Nazi invasion of Prague, saying, "WE HOPE TO HELP YOU," and he eventually received an academic contract that made a special visa possible. After a half year of considerable effort, with some financial help from my father's good friend Alfred Einstein, then already at Smith, the family left the German Protectorate—legally, but three weeks after World War II had officially begun—and, encountering only a few minor obstacles, found its way to Princeton and the home of Westminster president John Finley Williamson. It turned out that the college didn't really have a job for my father, but with a characteristically American combination of charity and enterprise had assessed each student five dollars to make possible a long-term and technically formal association.

My parents felt hugely liberated. After a period of feeling like disoriented refugees, they came throughout World War II to think of themselves essentially as exiles, keeping alive the possibility of returning to Europe. Let me mention a few things that characterized their attitudes. My father continued to think of Prague as a great multicultural center and, ironically, perceived American culture as hopelessly homogeneous. I was warned against joining this homogeneous crowd too readily; indeed, I was obliged to speak German at home, and my father never worked too hard at perfecting his English.

As I look back at my parents' social circle, I note that it was almost entirely European; in fact, it was made up almost exclusively of Austrians and Swiss, German-speaking Czechs, and, importantly, Hungarians. There developed a large network of immigrants, some living in Princeton, others in New York and Philadelphia. These were the people who, one might say, "understood." Very few Americans could enter this circle: mainly those who spoke German well, such as my father's old friend Carleton Sprague Smith, and others who had lived in Europe—well, Central Europe or Germany—for substantial periods.

Otherwise, Americans were seen as kind, generous, helpful people who, however, were both childlike and unpredictable. My parents seemed to regard them as helpers in getting through the years of exile, but also as members of a society essentially lacking in culture. These attitudes were shared by many in my parents' social circle.

Early on in his quest for employment and professional advancement, my father, somewhat like his earlier compatriot Dvořák, mounted a quest for the truly American music. In the 1940s he felt that European music, however much performed in America, could not really be understood here. He ran into African American and Native American musics, into the Moravians, MacDowell, and Menotti, into jazz (which he couldn't distinguish from ordinary pop), John Philip Sousa, even barbershop music. But none of these satisfied his need to find a proper national music, and so he decided, as had others, that what was required was for Americans to acquire the great music of Europe and learn truly to understand it. He once wrote, "Man muß die Amerikaner musifizieren," and was amazed that editors of a translation didn't accept "musify" as a proper English verb.

So he and my mother proceeded to musify America—or at least sections of New Jersey and New York, and later southern Indiana. They gave lecture-recitals on Czech music, my father introducing Smetana and Dvořák, Fibich and Vitězslav Novák, Tomášek, Voříšek, and Viktor Ullmann to American audiences—at colleges, ladies' clubs, even high schools—while my mother played; the event always ended with a rousing rendition of a couple of Dvořák's Slavonic Dances with four hands. This was music in which they had not been very interested in Europe. Their musical relationship to the homeland had obviously been affected by their state of exile.

But much more important, my father wanted Americans to understand the music of the great German and Austrian composers, and some of the not so great as well. As World War II progressed, and as at the end the extent of the Holocaust began to be known, he seemed to me to increase his focus on making German music known. In this he was not alone among immigrant scholars. I am reminded of Professor Gerhard Herz, whom I observed over the decades bringing German music—particularly Bach, but also the chamber works of everyone from Mozart to Wolf—to the population of Louisville, Kentucky, tirelessly organizing concerts, giving lectures at public libraries, encouraging the formation of clubs, writing program notes. He, like my father, felt somewhat like a prophet in the wilderness—a bit like Theodore Thomas, the nineteenth-century conductor, or Dvořák during his three years here. Why this focus? Well, for one thing, he clearly would have liked to show that the Nazis and their depredations were an aberration, that proper German culture was to be found in Goethe and Schiller, Prague's Kafka, and the great composers. He didn't want to let the Nazis have any of that good German culture. But a more interesting reason, it seems to me, was the notion that he began to develop that music—proper music—was quintessentially a German phenomenon. In Prague that attitude was part of the general atmosphere, but over here it began to be made explicit. Americans (or Indians, or Japanese) could understand Western music only if they learned the German language. Classical music was a kind of German domain in American culture. After the war, at Indiana University, my father tried to associate principally with German-speaking faculty and always assumed that they—even the mathematicians, chemists, and literary scholars among them—understood things about music, any music, that were not really intelligible to others.

As an American teenager, I thought this was totally unreasonable. Recently, however, I found a quotation in a 1993 lecture by Albrecht Riethmüller, a professor in the sciences who sought reassurance for his beliefs from the musicologist.[20] What he said was: "Die Musik ist doch deutsch, oder etwa nicht?" (Music is surely a *German* thing, isn't it?). Illogical as it may seem to us (and, indeed, to Riethmüller), there is a strong tradition in German thought which holds that although each culture may have its own musical ideas and practice, music in its loftiest sense is essentially a German product. Unconsciously, my father shared this view, I think, and extended it to musicology. Thus teaching Americans about music meant, ipso facto, teaching them about German music.

As I said, through World War II my parents were true exiles who would probably have returned home if they could. In 1946 my father took a trip to Europe, to survey the situation for himself. He didn't return to Czechoslovakia, then not yet in the Warsaw Pact, and I think he avoided Prague because he couldn't face the idea of his home city now bereft of its German-speaking population, despite their Nazi tendencies. Indeed, although he made many later trips to Western Europe, he never did return to Prague. At the end of this first trip, in any event, it had become clear to him that he

couldn't go home again, and there was no longer any question of returning—to my great relief, I must tell you. Whatever reservations my parents
had, I felt that I wanted to be an American from my first day here.

Meanwhile, my father's musicological and musical attitudes became not
less, but rather more, German-oriented. Having decided to stay, he took an
even greater interest in his ethnic German-ness or Austrian-ness.

I don't know to what extent this attitude was shared by other migrant
musicologists of the 1930s—Einstein, Gombosi, Apel, Sachs, Schrade, and
the others—but it may be interesting to compare briefly the background
and eventual contributions of an immigrant scholar of earlier times, my own
teacher, George Herzog.[21] A Jewish Hungarian, he studied in Budapest and
then with Hornbostel in Berlin, then came to the States in 1925, at the age
of twenty-four, ostensibly to study with Franz Boas. Although this was not
a time when young scholars were fleeing Central Europe, I doubt that he
came to America only to get his Ph.D., intending to return to Hungary or
Germany. In my years of acquaintance with him, I never heard him mention a desire to return. He had been married to an American woman, was
proud of his membership in a distinctively American school of anthropo-
logical thinking, and was scathingly critical of German and English diffu-
sionist schools. In fact, he developed an emblematically American approach
to ethnomusicology, fashioning a synthesis of Hornbostel's and Bartók's
methods of research and analysis, Franz Boas's historically oriented anthropology, the linguistic techniques of Leonard Bloomfield and Edward Sapir,
and the so-called Finnish method of folklorists as developed in America by
Stith Thompson—an approach reminiscent of the syncretism described for
African Americans by Melville Herskovits and Richard Waterman. Herzog
considered himself, despite his thick accent, a true American, and a leader
of American comparative musicology. A refugee of sorts, he quickly became
a true immigrant, not an exile, and although he was a culture broker like
the later musicological immigrants, his brokering had a different flavor. If
you compare his contributions to those of the quintessentially American
Charles Seeger, you might think that Herzog was saying, in effect, "There is
a European way to become a real American."

But to return to my father, Paul Nettl, the subject of my main case study:
Starting out as a refugee, he tried early on to accommodate the American
scene, to learn what was truly American in music. Perhaps he was too old to
do this very well; as the war years continued, in any case, he settled into the
role of exile, trying to find ways of holding on to Central European culture,
particularly Bohemian and even Czech, while at the same time trying to integrate his life and his associations with recent arrivals as well as Americans.
Then, giving up the self-image of an exile, he became a full-fledged immigrant, and I think it was at this point that he withdrew to his older roots,
concentrating on German language and culture, and perhaps developing a

holistic conception of German culture analogous to Naipaul's Trinidadian vision of India. But he also saw himself, throughout his thirty-three years in America, as a culture broker, a missionary whose job it was to bring his culture to American students. It was perhaps for this reason that, to the end of his teaching days, he affected certain Central European professorial manners, working at home and having students visit him in his study there, playing down the accomplishments of English and American scholarship, trying hard to avoid idiomatic English, and striving to present a portrait of European erudition that his students were supposed to admire but could never hope to achieve. Yet despite these changes in attitude, his scholarship seemed to me to maintain its focus on the unitary historical method developed by Adler, and his broadly interpretive approach as music critic and writer for a general public was well honed. Although he was largely removed from the primary sources of his earlier research, in its fundamentals his approach to musicology didn't change as a result of the American experience, and in this respect he may not have been typical.

I don't know to what extent Paul Nettl was representative of the many music scholars who went into exile, or of the twenty or forty senior scholars who found themselves in the United States. Perhaps the change from refugee to exile to immigrant, accompanied by the culture broker's role, characterized the lives of other scholars as well. And I don't know whether Herzog's synthetic approach to scholarship was shared by anyone, whether there is anyone to whom he could meaningfully be compared. My categories are loose and they overlap, but the suggestive notion that a person or a community might move from one category of migrant to another, thus taking on a new self-view and new role in the immediate cultural environment, may help ethnomusicologists in their study of other displaced societies and their music. And I hope I am right in thinking that understanding the contributions of scholars who were driven to emigrate in the 1930s and 1940s can be enhanced by looking at the accomplishments of other displaced societies.

NOTES

1. Publications in which the issues raised here are synthesized include James Porter, "The Traditional Music of Europeans in America," *Selected Reports in Ethnomusicology* 3 (1978): 1–23; and Adelaida Reyes Schramm, "Music and Tradition: From Native to Adopted Land through the Refugee Experience," *Yearbook for Traditional Music* 21 (1989): 25–35.

2. Bruno Nettl, "Aspects of Folk Music in North American Cities," in *Music in the*

Americas (Bloomington: Indiana University Research Center in Anthropology, Folklore, and Linguistics, 1967), 142–43.

3. Adelaida Reyes Schramm, "Music and the Refugee Experience," *World of Music* 32 (1990): 6–7. See also the classification of immigrant populations in Jehoash Hirschberg, "Radical Displacement, Post-Migration Conditions, and Traditional Music," *World of Music* 32 (1990): 68–69.

4. Some examples of early studies are Svatava Pirkova-Jakobson, "Harvest Festivals among Czechs and Slovaks in America," in *Slavic Folklore: A Symposium,* ed. Albert B. Lord (Philadelphia: American Folklore Society, 1956); Rupert Karl Hohmann, "The Church Music of the Old Order Amish in the United States" (Ph.D. diss., Northwestern University, 1959); Stephen Erdely, "Folksinging of the American Hungarians in Cleveland," *Ethnomusicology* 8 (1964): 14–27; and Cecil J. Sharp, *English Folk Songs from the Southern Appalachians* (London: Oxford University Press, 1932). A special issue of *Selected Reports in Ethnomusicology* 3 (1978), edited by James Porter, is devoted entirely to European traditional music as it exists in North America. See also Georg Schünemann, *Das Lied der deutschen Kolonisten in Rußland* (Munich: Drei Masken, 1923); and Marius Schneider, "Volksdeutsche Lieder aus Argentinien," *Archiv für Musikforschung* 4 (1939): 190–201.

5. Max Peter Baumann, ed., *Musik der Türken in Deutschland* (Kassel: Yvonne Landeck, 1985); Bruno Nettl, ed., *Eight Urban Musical Cultures* (Urbana: University of Illinois Press, 1978); Adelaida Reyes Schramm, "Explorations in Urban Ethnomusicology: Hard Lessons from the Spectacularly Ordinary," *Yearbook for Traditional Music* 14 (1982): 1–14.

6. See "Asian Music in North America," ed. Nazir A. Jairazbhoy and Sue Carole DeVale, a special issue of *Selected Reports in Ethnomusicology* 6 (1985).

7. See, for instance, Robert Klymasz and James Porter, "Traditional Ukrainian Balladry in Canada," *Western Folklore* 33 (1974): 89–132; Stephen Erdely, "Research on Traditional Music of Nationality Groups in Cleveland and Vicinity," *Ethnomusicology* 12 (1968): 245–50; Kay Kaufman Shelemay, "Together in the Field: Team Research among Syrian Jews in Brooklyn, New York," *Ethnomusicology* 32 (1988): 369–84; Ronald Riddle, *Flying Dragons, Flowing Streams: Music in the Life of San Francisco's Chinese* (Westport, Conn.: Greenwood Press, 1983); Isabel K. F. Wong, "The Many Roles of Peking Opera in San Francisco in the 1980s," *Selected Reports in Ethnomusicology* 6 (1985): 173–88; and innumerable publications by Marius Barbeau, for example, "How Folk-Songs Traveled," *Music and Letters* 14 (1934): 306–23.

8. Vidiadar Surajprasad Naipul, *India: A Million Mutinies Now!* (New York: Penguin Books, 1990), 6–7.

9. For a comprehensive account of such studies, see Edith Gerson-Kiwi, "Musicology in Israel," *Acta Musicologica* 30 (1958): 17–26; and Edith Gerson-Kiwi and Amnon Shiloah, "Musicology in Israel, 1960–1980," *Acta Musicologica* 52, no. 2 (1981), 200–216. Also of special interest are Philip V. Bohlman, *The Land Where Two Streams Flow* (Urbana: University of Illinois Press, 1989); and Amnon Shiloah, *Jewish Musical Traditions* (Detroit: Wayne State University Press, 1992).

10. Bruno Nettl and Amnon Shiloah, "Persian Classical Music in Israel: A Preliminary Report," *Israel Studies in Musicology* 1 (1978): 145–58.

11. The central figure in the history of this direction of inquiry was Melville J. Heskovits; see his *Myth of the Negro Past* (New York: Harper, 1941), esp. 262–68; also

his "Problem, Method, and Theory in Afroamerican Studies," *Afroamerica* 1 (1945): 5–24.

12. See John Storm Roberts, *Black Music in Two Worlds* (New York: Praeger, 1972). In the case of Native American cultures, of special relevance here is the development of the so-called "pan-Indian" movement. The seminal publication in this area of study is James H. Howard, "Pan-Indian Culture of Oklahoma," *Scientific Monthly* 81, no. 5 (1955): 215–20. See also William K. Powers, *War Dance* (Tuscon: University of Arizona Press, 1990).

13. Craig Macrae, "Integrating a Society: Persian Music in the Iranian Community," in *Community of Music: An Ethnographic Seminar in Champaign-Urbana,* ed. Tamara Livingston et al. (Champaign, Ill.: Elephant & Cat, 1993), 180–201.

14. Philip V. Bohlman, "Of Yekkes and Chamber Music in Israel: Ethnomusicological Meaning and Western Music History," in *Ethnomusicology and Modern Music History,* ed. Stephen Blum, Philip V. Bohlman, and Daniel M. Neuman (Urbana: University of Illinois Press, 1991), 254–67.

15. Daniel M. Neuman, *The Life of Music in North India* (Detroit: Wayne State University Press, 1980), 88–89; Bonnie C. Wade, *Music in India: The Classical Traditions* (Englewood Cliffs, N.J.: Prentice-Hall, 1979), 94–95.

16. Nettl and Shiloah, "Persian Classical Music in Israel"; Bruno Nettl, "Emigration: The Radif in Israel," in *The Radif of Persian Music,* rev. ed. (Champaign, Ill.: Elephant & Cat, 1992), 177–80.

17. Alan P. Merriam, *The Anthropology of Music* (Evanston, Ill.: Northwestern University Press, 1964), 32–33.

18. The biographical material on Paul Nettl comes largely from personal accounts orally transmitted. A short autobiographical publication appears, however, in Thomas Atcherson, ed., *Ein Musikwissenschaftler zweier Welten* (Vienna: Schönborn, 1962), 5–19.

19. Bruno Nettl, "Paul Nettl and the Musicological Study of Culture Contact," *Bulletin of the Czechoslovak Music Society* (St. Louis), spring 1993, 1–4, 9.

20. Albrecht Riethmüller, *Die Walhalla und ihre Musiker* (Laaber, Ger.: Laaber-Verlag, 1993), 23.

21. For information on Herzog, see David P. McAllester, "In Memoriam George Herzog," *Ethnomusicology* 29 (1985): 86–87; Edgar E. Siskin, "George Herzog: A Peerless Musicologist Remembered," *American Jewish Archives* 4 (1989): 77–83; and Bruno Nettl, "The Dual Nature of Ethnomusicology in North America: The Contributions of Charles Seeger and George Herzog," in *Comparative Musicology and Anthropology of Music: Essays on the History of Ethnomusicology,* ed. Bruno Nettl and Philip V. Bohlman (Chicago: University of Chicago Press, 1991), 266–74.

Music and Musicians in Exile
The Romantic Legacy of a Double Life

Lydia Goehr

Difficult as it must always appear to the thinker, to satisfactorily define the true relation of a great artist to his nation, that difficulty is enormously increased when the subject is neither a poet nor a painter, but a musician. . . . Neither through language, nor through any form wherein his country or his people greets the eye, does the musician reveal his origin. It has generally been assumed, therefore, that tone-speech belongs to the whole human race alike, that melody is an absolute tongue, in power whereof the musician speaks to every heart. However, upon closer examination . . . we recognize that it is possible to talk of a German . . . music.

RICHARD WAGNER, "BEETHOVEN," IN *PROSE WORKS*

During the Second World War my grandfather assumed a double identity. He even went by two names. Under the safe English-sounding name George Walter he composed film music, light music, and music for the Allied war effort, specifically for the BBC's propaganda newsreels. Under his German birth name, Walter Goehr, he continued the career he had pursued in Berlin, predominantly as symphonic conductor but also as composer. He regarded as more self-authenticating not only his birth name but also the musical activity the name symbolized. "I have worked very hard for many years," he wrote in wartime correspondence to his former teacher Arnold Schoenberg, who was now in America, "and lately I am happy to say I find more time for composing. . . . This is the only thing in life I feel is worthwhile. . . . Whenever I try to compose . . . old times appear clearly before me."[1]

For my grandfather, as for others in my family who have lived in countries different from those of their birth, his musical activity was one of his strongest connections to home. Unreflectively, "home" simply names a place and a life once lived; reflectively, it names a continually transforming set of bonds organized by activities, conversations, and relationships that trace memories of past, establish patterns of present significance, and suggest desires for the future. "Home" is largely synonymous with "family": when a family feels more no place than a place in particular, the bonds (musical or otherwise) holding them together carry the significance of home.

The constant questioning about the soil of a family's significance is no different for those who emigrate in freedom than for those who emigrate for political reasons, even if the urgency of the questioning is.[2] In contrast to the relative comfort of the freely moving immigrant, the often indescribable suffering of political exile links the questioning to extreme emotions: melancholy mixed with relief in leaving, happiness mixed with guilt for surviving, excitement mixed with trepidation for the new life to be lived. Indeed, the principal reason my grandfather had written to Schoenberg was to thank him for all he had done for his brother Rudolf. "I hope he will be able to get to the U.S.A.," he wrote. "At the moment it seems very difficult to accomplish."

My great-uncle did eventually reach the United States, but the journey was agonizing. Exiled from Germany and interned in France, Rudi himself wrote to Schoenberg with a desperate request: could his former teacher help him obtain a visa or work permit for entry into America? His writing traveled across the languages of German, French, and English as he described the camps of his internment, his places of hiding and refuge. "I hope you received my postcards," he wrote after the occupation of France. "Unfortunately, I am always in a camp, but I hope to be free soon and to see my wife." He continued:

> It was really a miracle. The German army stopped its advance just 5 miles before the village. So I escaped them. But now, know all is very sad. There will not be any chance for me to work again in France and I don't know what to do. Could you help me? I am very sorry to disturb you, but my situation is very serious. Otherwise I know, after a week in America, all could be so easy—I mean, I could perhaps try my chance.

Rudi did try his chance. "Life is very hard in New York," he wrote to Schoenberg after his arrival.

> Weather and thinking, thinking and weather. It is a terrible conflict, but I have always the impression that somehow it will work out. . . . These days I make music with Rudi Kolisch. We've been playing the Bartók violin concerto, and it's great fun. . . . But besides this, one hears only Shostakovich, Sh. and more Shostakovich.

Rudi joined the army. "Three months in the Army and already an American citizen," he told Schoenberg on 4 February 1944.

> I write you again. The infantry never did like much musicians, so I have to wait and see what is going to happen. . . . I got wonderful news from my brother, always conducting concerts with very interesting programs. I was—before I came here—arranger and musical director of the Eastman Kodak Show on NBC.

Apparently the purpose of having music on the Eastman Show was unapologetically commercial: it was used to encourage new Kodak customers to take snapshots with their cameras on picnic outings.[3] "The musical direction of the programming is not very interesting," Rudi wrote on 13 December 1942 while commuting between Rochester and New York. "Beethoven is far less appreciated than Sousa!" Apparently, some of Rudi's early musical activities in America were not so different in style from those of his brother, known in Britain as George.

It is clear from Schoenberg's replies to Walter and Rudi that he wanted to help his former students, and sometimes succeeded in doing so, but was not confident at any point that he *could* do so. Schoenberg had surmised early on that his position in America would not be exactly what it had been in Europe: "I'd like to know too if I can do anything for you in America," he had written in 1933, before his own departure, responding to a plea for help from Alban Berg—but he added, "always supposing that I should have the power. . . . For there's no knowing how disregarded, slighted, and without influence I may be there."[4] Had his students not been facing quite desperate circumstances, they too would have recognized that, in exile, as every other kind of family is transformed, so also is a family of musicians.

This essay investigates the transformations that occur to a musical family in exile, specifically the mass move of European composers to America prompted by Germany's National Socialism. It investigates the tensions that arose in musical practice when a powerful nineteenth-century metaphysical thesis about music and musicians was converted into the most extreme of ideological terms, when, more specifically, purportedly universal ideals were converted into racially bounded ideals. However, the ultimate concern of this essay is less historical than philosophical.

Thus, by "a musical family" I shall not mean just a historical family of persons who were musicians, or the relations holding between composition teachers and their pupils who in turn became composers and teachers. I shall also include a family of views about music. The kind of views I include are those invoking what I like to call the condition of *doubleness*. Bonding the family will be the view that composers, who because of exile were propelled into foreignness, began to live what the philosopher Ernst Bloch called in 1939 the double rather than divided life of frontier men. I shall show, first through a detailed description of composers' responses to exile and later through conceptual clarification, that the doubleness involved in this frontier life has had numerous expressions of a musical, historical, aesthetic, and metaphysical sort. In general, doubleness exists in practices of thought and activity that invoke two-sided, mediating, or conflicting ideals, productions, and conditions. In particular, doubleness has been expressed in, for example, music-text mergers of languages and idioms, strategies of adaptation and resistance, articulations of insider and outsider positions, and, finally, in romantic-modernist theorists invoking limits. These diverse expressions of doubleness do not, however, together form a neatly unified picture, nor do they always mesh exactly with one another, even though they are often employed as if they do. Nor do they together refer to a single way of conceiving of doubleness. Rather, they stand to one another, at best and appropriately, as "family resemblant."

Doubleness pervades this century's thinking about the exile of artists and intellectuals generally. Thus, this thinking tends to take the two notions of language and creativity as constitutive within artistic and intellectual practices and the sociopolitical notions of expression and freedom as regulative. Its theorists then ask whether living on foreign soil affects a person's freedom of expression or whether being forced to speak a foreign language renders an artist more or less creative.

In historical mode, theorists answer these two questions by determining whether or not artists and intellectuals were exiled to places that provided them with adequate living conditions so that they could continue to create and write in comfort and freedom. They also study the impact of exile on the quality and quantity of the exiles' artistic and intellectual creation. But theorists also investigate exile as an existential or psychological condition. "Being an exile is not a matter of needing a passport," Henry Pachter once wrote; "it is a state of mind."[5] An exile is any artist or intellectual who maintains a critical distance from what Adorno called the "administered world." Thus, even if artists are not living in political exile, they may live in a state of psychological or inner exile. Some theorists even claim that this inner exile is required for creative work because it marks the free human subject. Political or outer exile may be just the thing to shock the artist out of a comfortable complacency, but, by itself, it is neither necessary nor sufficient for creative work.

This highly positive view of the state of exile is countered by an equally positive view of the state of rootedness in home. Some argue that exile (in either its inner or outer form) is deadening, not awakening. Exile from one's culture, losing the use of a native language, does not quicken the fancy but places it far out of reach. "To be rooted," wrote Simone Weil, "is perhaps the most important and least recognized need of the human soul."[6] Creativity and the language of free artistic expression requires more the sense of belonging, more a native or saturated cultural understanding, than it does the purportedly alienating and empty condition of political or social freedom. In this view, rootedness rather than exile is the true condition of the creative spirit.[7]

To complicate matters, the two opposing views are not always presented as such. In paradoxical flourish, some theorists play with the meaning of "home." The artist is truly at home when not at home. Home for an artist is a place that allows her to feel constructively alienated from home—for truth is better grasped at a distance. If paradox (irony and laughter) once fueled Groucho Marx's rejection of belonging to a club, it has also fueled the artist's position more generally.

Yet it is just this complication of paradox that allows us to see the duality of home and estrangement less in mutually excluding than in doubling terms. Estrangement (linked to freedom, reflectiveness, and openness) and home (linked to understanding, identity, and involvement) capture in their mutual mediation a complex and constructive modernist attitude that persons may take in relation to the society in which they live. The cosmopolitan wants to be both estranged and at home in the modern metropolis. Of course, in times of intense social and political upheaval the terms are usually employed in excluding and not in mediating ways, so that the duality between home and estrangement prompts negative claims of opposition, rigidity, and purity. Such terms are encouraged by a society's different groups—by those "at home" *and* those "estranged"—according to their respective advantage. In the history of mass and individual exile we should not be surprised to find, therefore, the home/estrangement duality being used in wiser moments in its doubling or mediating form, and in more extreme moments in its most dividing and polarizing form.

The polarization that negatively conditions a particular practice under certain historical circumstances may disrupt without permanently destroying the practice's ability to accommodate the constructive condition of doubleness. When investigating a given practice it is necessary to view it from both descriptive and normative perspectives, to see how it is conditioned at any given time and how it could be conditioned, and to see how the practice is being described and how in fact it is working. This dual perspective, in other terms, allows us to see past a polarization that forces us to conclude either that creativity demands estrangement or that it demands home, and allows us to conclude instead that, if it demands either, then it most likely demands both.

The dual perspective also suits a musical practice whose specific modernist character is captured precisely in a myriad of "doubling" views. For example, one view describes music's otherworldly or aesthetic status on the one hand, and its worldly or historical character on the other. Another view describes the play between inner and outer exile, that is, between the psychological exile musicians experienced "at home" in Europe and the actual exile they experienced in their move to America. In what follows, we will see that these distinct doubling views are connected.

The philosophy of music has thrived on claims about the language of music as bound or not bound to a nation, as free, expressive, and creative. But exiled musicians challenged two basic views: that music is a language and, relatedly, that creativity is causally or otherwise connected to the condition either of exile or of home. However, their challenge consisted less in a rejection of these views than in showing their limits. Chiefly, their experiences revealed the limits of describing music monologically, as one might an ordinary, conceptual or cognitive, language, because the description failed to capture the full significance of music, notably its creative moment. A resemblant claim was contemporaneously made that music could not be reduced to its social conditioning or embodiment insofar as that reduction would fail to recognize music's resisting (purely musical) aspects. In general, the romantic-modernist legacy in the philosophy of music has been exemplary in showing the need for recognizing limits and doubleness, and thus the dangers of reductionism, in both our theories and our practices.

The double life of the exiled musician makes explicit the double-sided character of music that the sometimes more comfortable life of the musician at home leaves implicit. Accordingly, my cast of characters is chosen for the manifold ways each character lived both "homed" and "foreign" lives. The primary cast comprises composers. All moved to a country with a different spoken language. Most were Jewish (by birth, or by force or choice of return) and thus already had some understanding of the condition of religious exile. Some had experienced exile or inner emigration at home for their political views. All had experienced historical or psychological exile en masse or as individual targets. The philosophical chorus comprises thinkers closely connected to the aforementioned composers, to issues of musical composition and creativity, and who themselves experienced exile or emigration. The doubly destructive and inspirational spirit of Richard Wagner will burst at least once onto the stage to overshadow the entire proceedings.

EXPERIENCES OF EXILE

In 1950 Albert Goldberg of the *Los Angeles Times* asked several exiled composers to respond to a claim made by a composer of European birth who, despite being "distinguished," remained nameless. The claim was that "European composers had changed since they lost contact with their native countries and the music the majority of them had written [in the United States] did not equal that . . . previously composed."[8] Of the many responses given, Schoenberg's statement that he was unconscious that his exile had changed him has been the most frequently cited by theorists to characterize him as the composer who most resisted Americanization.[9] Taken in isolation, Schoenberg's statement fails to capture what was, as one would expect, a much more complex reaction.

Drawing on a range of documents, I shall show that responses to exile were usually too varied to allow us to characterize the composers as merely resisting or adapting to Americanization. To be sure, some variation within and across individual cases is due to context of utterance: whether, say, the responses were politically strategic or guided by particular emotions. But some variation reflects the conflicting views composers often held regarding the need for their creativity and use of the musical language to be positioned sometimes at a distance from, and sometimes as rooted in, home. Following conventional discursive patterns, composers responded to exile dichotomously. They distinguished between inner and outer lives and between music's transcendence and its situatedness. They gave flesh to these distinctions by distinguishing high from low art, the quality from the quantity of their work, and their resisting from their conceding to market pressures. Precisely because there is no perfect fit between these different distinctions, and because composers often wanted to endorse both sides, we find constructive conflicts in the overall picture of music as a language and of conditions of creativity. In other words, in mixing the particular exigencies of their exile with the musical aesthetic they brought with them, composers' responses to exile became deeply conflicted. My claim is that these conflicts are better interpreted in doubling terms rather than in dividing terms.

Schoenberg attached his famed response to a question a Spanish musician once asked him about the effect a country's climate or character could have on his compositional style. He replied rhetorically at first—should my style be cold in Alaska, but hot near the equator?—but then more soberly. He surmised that, whereas the quantity of his compositional output might be affected, the quality would not be, for quality comes from within.[10] Schoenberg was not the only one to answer this way. Quoting the exile Albert Einstein, Mario Castelnuovo-Tedesco wrote to Goldberg: "The bitter and the sweet come from the outside, the hard from within, from one's own efforts. For the most part I do the thing which my own nature drives me to." And of Béla Bartók, Yehudi Menuhin recalled: "Exile made of him [an] unaccommodated man, solitary, intense, requiring for material support only a bed, a table to write at and—but this might be considered a luxury— absolute quiet in which his inner concentration might bear fruit."[11]

Many exiles believed that the reliance upon their "inner natures" had grown in proportion to the decline they experienced in external support. Although some composers admitted that they were just too old to adapt to new conditions ("I was a finished product of the old world," wrote Eric Zeisl), others blamed the conditions of America's musical life. Something is "missing in America's musical scene," complained Miklós Rózsa, "the bubbling, fertile, and germinating artistic atmosphere of prewar Europe that gave inspiration to many masterpieces." Composers are isolated in America, the protesters continued; concert audiences only want to hear the old warhorses; there is a "critical lack of demand for contemporary music" and a lack of performance opportunities; performers are vain, conductors are temperamental. Comparing himself to Schoenberg, Stravinsky commented with some irony: "We shared a common exile to the same alien culture," and there "we wrote some of our best works (his *Fourth Quartet,* my *Abraham and Isaac*)," but "we are still played far less [here] than in the Europe that exiled us."[12]

The moderate conclusion drawn from these complaints was that relying on one's inner nature was a contingent consequence of one's exile: one may not be able to *overlook* external conditions, Castelnuovo-Tedesco remarked, but one must try to *overlive* them. Some composers drew a stronger conclusion: since exile reveals the true relation between creativity and the inner life, exile is a necessary or optimum condition. Zeisl thus explained that the artist

> is always unhappy and maladjusted to his society and that it is this [condition] . . . which prompts him to dig so deeply into the hidden resources of his soul. . . . The more harassed he is, the stronger the medicines with which he will come up for his own benefit and the benefit of mankind. (See Beethoven, Mozart, Wagner, etc.) Longing, nostalgia, loneliness, and strife. I . . . know of no better nourishment for the artist's soul, and we have in proof the fact that the world's most beautiful works of art and music have frequently been created in exile and far from home (Wagner, Chopin, Stravinsky, Hindemith, etc.).

Stravinsky agreed with the last sentiment at least. Despite his warning against generalities and dismissing Goldberg's subject as "not worth a column of [his] pen," he still felt obliged to comment that the Soviets had tried to intimidate artists by warning them that their creativity would be impoverished by exile. However, the Soviet's claim had been "brilliantly refuted" throughout history—"by Handel, Gogol, Chopin, Picasso." Strategically, said Stravinsky, composers should never admit defeat; fortunately, they rarely, if ever, had had to.

Some composers were skeptical of the advantages of exile. Having bitingly attributed his creativity in exile to the "torment of boredom," Hanns Eisler dismissed the glorification of the "masochistic suffering of exile."[13] (Virgil Thomson commented similarly when he wrote that one does not have to be poor to be an artist.)[14] If exile was inspiring, it was not because of the suffering involved, but because exile has the positive effect of making one see the world anew. Seeing distant lands, Eisler wrote in 1935, "tests our methods of reasoning." Exiles "are never absolutists." Eisler was seeing a link that others would see too, a link between thinking differently and being creative.[15]

Ernst Krenek expressed his skepticism regarding the link between exile and creativity more strongly than Eisler.[16] Exile, he said, is an external condition; it is simply the condition of composing away from home. Although some exiles' works followed in the tradition of "the European output" and some "were written for American opportunities," because we do not know how composers would have composed had they stayed in Europe, we cannot determine whether exile made them more or less creative. External conditions affect composition wherever you live; the safest conclusion, therefore, is not to consider them. "It is amazing that the pattern of one's [creative] life does not change," Krenek reflected autobiographically in 1941, "in spite of the most comprehensive outward changes."[17]

Many exiled composers enjoyed reminding one another that external conditions in their native lands had not always been so good. Modern (dissonant) music was already alienated in Europe; even European audiences preferred their warhorses. That conditions before and after exile could be more similar than different was a point made by one composer who simply reminded his fellow exiles that they were now ten or fifteen years older and, if their creativity were lessened, it might simply be because they had "not discovered the pills which Wagner took to write his *Parsifal* and Verdi to write his *Falstaff.*"

Still, composers generally agreed that dismissing the impact of exile altogether was untenable. Krenek remarked that a total disregard would probably be motivated by defensiveness, even though he retained his skepticism.[18] Describing his composition as always having been guided by two contradictory tendencies—the pure and the situated, or the purely musical and the socially influenced—he maintained that he had never been able to tell which tendency had made his work better.[19]

Some composers used the pure/situated dichotomy to draw precisely the same conclusions as was done with the inner/outer one. Having already asserted that "nothing comes out, [that wasn't already] in," Schoenberg, for example, unhesitatingly moved from "inside" to "beyond." A musical idea or style, he said, is like a mathematical truth, and "two times two equals four in every climate." He then used this claim to stake out a position of artistic integrity: "Maybe I had four times four times harder to work for a living. But I made no concessions to the market." And then he used the implied distinction between loyalty to a pure musical tradition and concession to market pressures to support the traditional distinction between autonomous "high" art and dependent "low" art—although to the latter he refused even to give the name art. "No serious composer in this country is capable of living from his *art,*" he had written in a letter in 1945: "only popular composers earn enough." But then, he proclaimed, they are not producing "*art.*"[20]

Exiled composers generally agreed that they could not live from composition alone and that they were having to spend their energy on teaching or writing film music. ("The only way to escape Hollywood is to live in it," snapped Stravinsky.)[21] If composers were living by composition alone, it must be because they were compromising. Rózsa thus warned of the dangers of writing down to the American public and of diluting one's art, and, like Schoenberg, concluded that real art is produced only with full conviction. Compromise, he said, is "synonymous with the ruin of all artistic endeavor." "'Adjustment,'" Castelnuovo-Tedesco wrote similarly, "shouldn't mean 'opportunism' or obedience to transitory fashions. I believe that only by following sincerely and honestly my natural trend can I bring some contribution . . . to musical art."

Expressing resistance to external pressures in terms of a retreat into one's private inner world enabled exiled composers to articulate the continuity they needed to feel across the radical rupture they had experienced. What would have been the point of conceding that their life's work, their creative inspiration, had been inhibited by exile? Most frighteningly, it would have been to admit the triumph of National Socialism. Composers *had* to believe that they could compose anywhere.

On the other hand, the sense of a composer's belonging to a place captures another side of exile experience. Sixteen years before Schoenberg spoke to the *L.A. Times,* he wrote:

> It is perhaps [to be] expected that now I am in [the] new world I should feel its amenities ample compensation for the loss I have sustained and which I had foreseen for more than a decade. Indeed, I parted from the old world not without feeling the wrench in my very bones, for I was not prepared for the fact that it would render me not only homeless but speechless, languageless.[22]

"Languageless"? Surely Schoenberg hadn't lost his music? To make sense of his statement, perhaps we have to assume that he was referring only to speech and language associated with nation and tongue. The idea that music (at least purely instrumental music) is not nation bound, and the related idea that if music is a language then it is not an ordinary one, are familiar ideas in the history of music. They are familiar also in exile theory. Jarrell C. Jackman has written recently that the "great advantage the émigré composers and musicians had over writers and actors was not being bound to language for economic survival."[23] In this claim, music is apparently not even classified as a language. Günter Berghaus writes comparably that "those artists who relied in their profession on verbal language and linguistic skills had to overcome considerably greater difficulties than those who worked in [arts which were] more international in their general outlook."[24] At least Berghaus assumes that the difference between nation-bound and international arts is one of degree. Only the exiled musician Boris Schwarz tempers his account appropriately: "On the surface," he writes, "the fate of a musician forced to emigrate seems less onerous than that of an actor, writer, or scientist. Music is an international language; a musician—with his instrument in hand—can play and be understood in Paris, New York, or Rio, without the need to communicate through spoken works." However, composers are "more difficult to transplant: there are subtle national differences in musical tastes and customs."[25]

The appeal to music as abstract, unbounded, or international clearly provided composers a way to resist the impact of exile, but it could only be used so far. For exiled composers also had a very strong sense of themselves as carrying a national musical identity with them into their new and foreign lives. Thus, within their responses to exile there arose a conflict between two claims: on the one hand, that music was an abstract language, and on the other, that it was nation bound. (This conflict was already embroiled in Krenek's distinction between pure and situated tendencies.)[26]

"As much as I have an accent in my language," a painter exiled to Britain would remark, "I have an accent in my painting."[27] Could not the same be said about music? Apparently Schoenberg sometimes thought so: "Artistically speaking," he had written as early as 1928, "it is all the same whether someone paints, writes, or composes; his style is anchored in his time."[28] Later, after his exile, he may well have added: "And his style is anchored also in his place." Maybe he really did feel that he had lost his musical language.

Certainly he used the conflict between music's abstraction and its being culture or nation bound to strategic ends. It allowed him to retreat from explicit involvement in war and politics. "I did not come into this marvelous country to speak about terrors," he announced, "but to forget them."[29] He had long ago motivated this act of forgetting: "There are . . . reasons," he had written in 1928, "why one cannot seriously believe that the arts influence political happenings. . . . By what chord would one diagnose the Marxist confession in a piece of music, and by what colour the Fascist one in a picture?"[30] Schoenberg wasn't being naive. Music, he knew, could be a powerful language: "Composers speak symbolically of philosophy, morals, etc.," he wrote in 1943; it is just that their music speaks "without a defined vocabulary."[31] As a symbolic language, music could function without such a vocabulary but convey values nonetheless. Schoenberg was adapting here the traditional romantic strategy of claiming that music, unable to mean in ordinary referential or conceptual terms, resists description as a language yet, precisely in this act of negation, succeeds in communicating, in its unique musical and transcendental terms, philosophical, moral, and social value.

Describing music this way gave composers the confidence to maintain both that in exile nothing had changed (because the musical language is abstract or universal), and that they had brought with them a language thoroughly permeated by value, and when it suited a national value. But to sustain their confidence, they had to employ yet another distinction. To conserve a musical culture or tradition abroad required that the idea of music's being, for example, German should be separated from the idea that it had to be situated in Germany. This separation was already a staple of exile discourse. Many German-speaking artists and intellectuals were simply proclaiming that it was they who defined German culture; it was not the geography or social/political condition of a country that did so. "German culture," Thomas Mann apparently announced, "is where I am."[32] German culture was being maintained abroad because it no longer existed in Nazi Germany. If one could found a "university in exile," why not also a culture?[33]

For many musicians, therefore, composition in exile was an act not merely of personal survival, but also of cultural survival. Composers were, as Berghaus describes them, *Kulturvermittler* ("cultural ambassadors"), keepers of a tradition abroad, because the country in which this musical tradition originated had expelled its proponents.[34] Krenek thus spoke of the political necessity of continuing to use the twelve-tone technique, despite its often negative reception, simply because the Nazis had banned it.[35] Darius Milhaud commented that even in exile the "profound impulses of race endure. . . . You cannot make a mistake as to the nature of a creative artist," he continues: "It is idle to pretend that any great composer fails to demonstrate the racial origins of his expression."[36] Eugene Zador likewise denied "the hypothesis that a composer must live in the country of his birth, even," he said, "when his musical style is based on native folk-lore. Stravinsky's ballets, written in Paris, are Russian, just as Bartók's 'Concerto,' written in America, is Hungarian." Stravinsky agreed: "A man has one birth place, one fatherland, one country—he *can* only have one country—and the place of his birth is the most important fact of his life."[37] Castelnuovo-Tedesco, finally, spoke of his having never felt "cut off" in exile from either his Jewish ancestry or Latin culture, because, as he said, they were "a wealth which I had acquired once and for all: which were in me forever."

In these responses, exiled composers were now asserting a continuity between their personal and their cultural or national selves, rather than a severance. Looking back at this period, Elliott Carter duly explained that the maintenance of the European culture of serious music was one of the things that made composers "who and what they [were]."[38] Further sense to this identification was again given by Thomas Mann when he described his own work as requiring "long roots in my life, secret connections must lead from it to earliest childhood dreams if I am to consider myself entitled to it. . . . The arbitrary reaching for a subject to which one does not have traditional claims of sympathy and knowledge, seems senseless and amateurish to me."[39]

If one could separate a tradition from its originating country, one could similarly separate a language. Thus Brecht distinguished the language spoken in Nazi Germany from the "true" German language, and claimed to take the latter wherever he went.[40] Profoundly skeptical, moreover, of the possibility of being creative in a foreign language, Brecht asked in song: "Wozu in einer fremden Grammatik blättern? / Die Nachricht, die dich heimruft / Ist in bekannter Sprache geschrieben" (Why turn the pages of a strange grammar? / The news that calls you home / Is written in a familiar language).[41]

If Brecht held passionately on to his familiar/native language, other exiles just as passionately gave it up. Bartók refused to speak or write German because it was the language of the enemy; he did not, however, feel obliged, according to György Sándor, to reject the "German" tradition of music. Bartók, Sándor wrote, was "strongly anti-German in all his activities, except [in] his musical work."[42] Bartók thus sought continuity in his musical language (Hungarian/German) but discontinuity in his spoken language. The same was true in the case of Brecht's former collaborator Kurt Weill—but with a twist.

Weill sometimes described himself as having given up speaking German, as being "the same composer as before," but denied that he was any longer a "German composer."[43] Of course, it wasn't clear that Weill had been a German composer for a long time. Stephen Hinton records Constant Lambert's prophetic, if incongruous, description of Weill as an American composer even before exile.[44] What seemed to motivate this description was the fact that the musical tradition Weill had been developing since the mid-1920s, and which he transported from Germany to America, was, according to contemporary views, more "American" than "German" to begin with. It was a tradition that, as Weill described it himself, saw music as composed not for posterity but, unlike the tradition of "serious" music, for contemporary lives and times. Its techniques and material were, therefore, of a "popular" sort.[45]

Contrary to the crude assessment of Weill as the great assimilator, or as a "popular" composer who "sold out" to commercial pressures, a more subtle assessment recognizes that although he composed in a "popular" vein, he not only saw himself as doing what he had always done, but he saw that what he had always done was resistant as much as it was adaptive. "My position in America has become so secure," Weill once explained, "that I am able to contemplate making my earlier works better known here than they have been up to now. . . . I have now completely settled down and feel absolutely at home." However, he continued, "it is heavy going in America, especially for someone who speaks his own musical language, but in the theatre the situation is still better and more favorable here than anywhere else, and I am sure that I shall reach the point where I can carry forward here what I began in Europe."[46] Apparently, although Weill conceived of his music as thoroughly situated in the world, he did not believe that it thereby had to be dictated by the world. To borrow a distinction from the philosophy of law, music as immanent is different from it being merely in-

strumental (that is, in service): immanent music still has the freedom to resist. In this matter of resistance and continuity Weill, moreover, was no different from Schoenberg; it is just that they did not seem always to agree on
how and in what ways music should be anchored in time and place. Of
course, that was for the exiles precisely the matter in dispute.

If Weill was not, crudely, an adapter, then Schoenberg was not, crudely,
a resister. Consider this description Schoenberg once gave of his expatriation. Contrasting his experience to that of the snake who "was driven out of
paradise" and "sentenced to go on its belly and to eat dust all the days of its
life," Schoenberg experienced, he said, a new freedom: "I . . . came from
one country into another, where neither dust nor better food is rationed
and where I am allowed to go on my feet, where my head can be erect,
where kindness and cheerfulness is dominating, and where to live is a joy
and to be an expatriate of another country is the grace of God." In sum, he
wrote: "I was driven into paradise."[47]

Other composers would also see the promise of paradise—or at least
freedom—at the end of their tunnel of complaints. Having fully detailed
the utter physical and mental torment of exile, Castelnuovo-Tedesco concluded his interview with Goldberg by saying: "On the other hand, America
gave me something I didn't have before or perhaps I hadn't fully developed: a greater sense of freedom and a better understanding of social conditions and of community life."

Nowadays, the "on the one hand/on the other hand" style of argument
is often dismissed as unappealing intellectualization or academese; nonetheless, it serves to capture the often conflicting aspects of human experience.
We have seen this style employed constantly by exiled composers to convey
a range of different distinctions, distinctions which demonstrated, overall,
that in the matter of musical creativity composers saw both the advantages
and disadvantages of exile, doubly conceived as an inner and outer condition, even though in claiming a given side they often spoke as if they were
dismissing another. To see constructive doubleness emerging from their
distinctions, rather than polarized one-sidedness, one simply must be cog-
nizant of the hand with which any composer is speaking at any given time.

CONCEPTUAL CLARIFICATION

Let me now fortify with conceptual clarification the historical construction
of the double-sided discourse of music and musicians in exile. Certain philosophical claims and distinctions need to be detached from their particular historical expression. For example, the palatable claim that music and
musicians are bounded to nation, tradition, or culture must be separated
from the more difficult and disturbing historical fact that they were once so
bounded according to a racial criterion.

As is well known, Wagner psychologically exiled many composers from the tradition of German music long before Hitler geographically exiled them, and he did so with thoughts that would pervade exile discourse far into the future. In his sinister essay "Judaism in Music," Wagner conflated his broad metaphysical concept of Judaism (which he used synonymously with his negative concept of the rootless, wandering, modern cosmopolite) with a more local and racial criterion to demarcate a class of living persons—the Jews.[48] He spoke accordingly of "the effect the Jews produce on us through [their] speech; and [of] . . . the Jewish influence upon music," charging that "the Jew speaks the language of the nation in whose midst he dwells from generation to generation, but he speaks it always as an alien." He described this alienation first in terms of the "violent severance" of Jews from "Christian Civilization," and then in terms relating to language use: "the Jew talks the modern European languages merely as learned, and not as mother tongues." This fact, he continued at length,

> must necessarily debar him from all capability of therein expressing himself idiomatically, independently, and conformably to his nature. A language, with its expression and its evolution, is not the work of scattered units, but of a historical community; only he who has unconsciously grown up within the bonds of this community takes also any share in its creations. . . . To make poetry in a foreign tongue has hitherto been impossible, even to geniuses of the highest rank. . . . The Jew can only after-speak . . . not truly make a poem of his words, an artwork of his doings. . . . Now if the aforesaid qualities . . . make the Jew almost incapable of giving artistic enunciation to his feelings . . . through *talk,* [they make his aptitude for] enunciation through *song* . . . [even] smaller, [for] song is just talk aroused to highest passion.

Wagner went on to describe what he saw to be the apparent success but real failure of Jews in the musical world. He attributed their apparent success to their ability to deceive, to present the appearance of being German; their real failure he attributed to their lack of ability to express themselves as "purely human." Combining the appearance and the reality, he wrote: "If we hear a jew speak, we are unconsciously offended by the entire lack of purely-human expression."[49] From this, Wagner's main conclusion duly followed: Despite external appearances to the contrary, Jews can participate in the German musical tradition only as second-hand thinkers.

Wagner's reading of Jewish second-handedness was reread along the path of its pervasive influence. In remarks that might well have been gathered together for "friends . . . scattered throughout the corners of the globe," Ludwig Wittgenstein once described, with Wagner's essay in mind, how the Jew had been measured in Western civilization "on scales which [did] not fit him"; consequently, the Jews had been either over- or underestimated but, the suggestion is, never judged aright.[50] Wittgenstein reminded his readers that Jews believe that "'genius' is found only in the holy man" and thus that "even the greatest of Jewish thinkers" takes himself to be "no more than talented." "Myself for instance," Wittgenstein wrote, and then added: "There is some truth in my idea that I only think reproductively." In this context, being second-hand is not a negative quality: following Jewish law, to think reproductively is to think in truthfulness; it is to think (albeit imperfectly) in the image of G-d.

For Wittgenstein, however, truthfulness was also linked to one's being "at home" in a language. Prima facie—and certainly Nazi doctrine supposed this—"being at home in Jewish tradition" was incompatible with "being at home in German tradition." But upon reflection, this incompatibility proved at most contingent. For it is false that belonging to one tradition automatically precludes one from belonging to another.

Wittgenstein spoke of the need for an expression sometimes "to be withdrawn from language and sent for cleaning." My purpose in comparing Wagner's remarks with Wittgenstein's is to show how the latter withdrew Wagner's judgment on the alienation of the Jews and tried to clean it. Schoenberg tried the same thing. In the second of his two speeches on the Jewish situation, given in 1935, he recalled young Austrian-Jewish artists growing up in circumstances in which their "self-esteem suffered very much."[51] It was a time (the late nineteenth century), he wrote, when Wagner's "victorious career" was beginning to have its impact. Wagner, according to Schoenberg, had challenged the Jews to try to become true Germans, but racism had interfered. Camp followers, Schoenberg wrote forgivingly, had distorted Wagner's views by turning his "mild" pronouncements into "harsh and excessive" ones.[52] (Wagner had not made the distortion so difficult.) The impact on young artists was severe: How could one create if one was not convinced of one's creative capacity? Schoenberg went on to describe the resistance that Jewish artists and intellectuals were able to muster against this destructive view, but commented sadly that Jewish audiences had been more compliant: Aryans were more appreciative of his music, he wrote, than the Jews. Schoenberg, however, concluded positively: We should not pity Jews for being second-hand, but celebrate the fact that they are G-d's chosen people. "He is only a Jew. No, he is a Jew and therefore is probably of great importance," Schoenberg wrote, to turn the anti-Semitic propaganda on its head.

Now, both Schoenberg and Wittgenstein could have concluded their remarks by identifying a special quality not of a racial or religious group (although we can understand why they did the contrary), but of a particular condition, namely that of being second-hand. For this condition by itself may foster qualities in persons that contradict outright the judgment that they are second-rate.

This possibility was given its first steps toward credibility in Bloch's brief but insightful article of 1939 entitled "Disrupted Language, Disrupted Culture" in which he dismissed an exile's suffering from *divided* loyalties and embraced an exile's celebrating his *double* loyalties.[53] Bloch generated his doubleness thesis specifically as a response to the conflict that arises when exiles or refugees (and he was thinking here explicitly of writers) recognize that they are bound to the language of their home but are forced to fulfill their cultural task in a foreign place. He described the difficulties of translation and of trying to create art in an alien or second language, and then described the role of language in the shaping and maintaining of "the culture-world," a world that results from the mediation between subject and object. Where the mediation is disrupted, where the "I" meets the "Other" in shock, where the language does not mediate through a feeling of belonging, the cultural task is temporarily arrested. What, Bloch asked, is the exile to do?

Bloch narrated, as I stated above, the exile's temptation to drift toward the extreme either of resistance or of adaptation, but argued that both temptations are incorrect. The correct attitude, he wrote, is "as far from insipid intrusion as it is from introverted foreignness." The exile, he explained, "brings his roots with him . . . to America" but "remains faithful to them not by making museum-pieces of them, but by testing and quickening his powers of expression on the new stuff of life." The point is not to produce "travel-books about America," but to produce an American literature in the German language. Crying out to be translated, this literature will reach a multilingual audience, but insofar as it succeeds this literature will remain a "deeply original creation," for it will have been "fostered by double but not divided loyalties—by memory and a vigorous faith in the future." He wrote in conclusion: "We are creating on the frontier of two epochs. We, German writers in America, are frontier-men in a doubly legitimate sense—both temporally and spatially—and we are working at the one necessary task: the realization of the rights of man."

Bloch thus showed how the transition from divided to double loyalties demanded a twofold account, of doubleness itself and of the creativity or originality of composition issuing therefrom. But what he left more implicit than explicit in this demand was the many forms of doubleness supporting the construction of exile discourse. The rest of this essay attends to making these forms explicit.

Bloch's thesis derived from an exile's attempt to use his native language in a new country. But the same thesis could be derived were the exile to adopt the new language as well. Given the many elements involved—languages, genres, styles, customs, traditions, cultures, and countries—and the fact that these elements are not related by simple one-to-one correspondences, the ways of mixing the so-called old with the new are countless: one may change country but retain the customs, change the style but retain the language, and so on.

Essential to the exile's experience is the feeling of doubled kinship. Exiles always have two elements in mind—broadly referred to as the old and the new—that share a common function. If exiles always experienced the old and the new as mutually exclusive, their decisions would be straightforward. But because they more often experience the old and the new as interpenetrating or mediating one another, their tasks are complex. For mediation allows symmetric and asymmetric processes of transfiguration to occur in the relata when, say, the use of a secondary language in a new country brings changes to the dominant primary language, and vice versa, or when the mixing of two musical traditions or styles brings changes to one or both.

These processes are capable, furthermore, of generating different creative outcomes. One outcome recognizes new products arising straight out of the doubleness, where the "two-tone" character is preserved. Another outcome rests upon the doubleness's being overcome: when aspects of continuity overshadow aspects of discontinuity, a synthesis or a "supervenient unity" may be formed (for example, a new or third language) on the basis of which new products may then be created.

Recall now Bloch's recommendation that exiled writers express their double rather than divided loyalties by producing an American literature in the German language. This production might involve the use of American themes and content and a foreign literary form or genre, or the form or genre may be American too and only the language foreign. But the recommendation could be extended to allow authors to write of German concerns in the language(s) of America. Extending this recommendation now to the other arts, one soon sees that there are myriad ways in which exiled artists may match the old with the new and thereby demonstrate the many creative possibilities available to them.[54]

Against this background, consider some musical works composed in exile in America of which one might judge that they could only have been composed by foreigners. Many composers set American or new-life lyrics or themes to what was still generally regarded a German or European (old-world) language of music: Eisler's exile lieder (the *Hollywood Songbook*), Stravinsky's a cappella arrangement of "The Star-Spangled Banner," Weill's "Down in the Valley" or Four Walt Whitman Songs, Schoenberg's (mixed-language) *A Survivor from Warsaw*, and finally Krenek's orchestral composition based on the South Carolina song "I Wonder as I Wander."[55] (Perhaps we should also include the Britten/Auden opera *Paul Bunyan*.) What is shared by these and other examples—whether the compositions end up being purely instrumental or not—is the dialogical play between the words (or themes) and music, where the presence of the foreign music transfigures or subverts the conventional, expressive significance of the text or theme, and/or vice versa.[56]

These transfigurative possibilities illustrate the creative possibilities of doubleness. They illustrate not only the very general principle that changing the context may change the meaning, but also the more specific principle that setting the familiar against the unfamiliar, the new against the old, the native against the foreign, may result in a changed understanding of the two sides. These musical examples also attest to the possibility of there being different kinds of creative or expressive outcomes. Composers who imagined their "old world" language transforming into a future "American" language were imagining, in relative terms, a synthetic "third" language. Composers, however, who still saw their compositions as embodying "unlovely," parodistic, or Aesopian antagonisms generated through the mixing of languages would not have been so desirous of eventual synthesis—at least "not yet." Recall Eisler's bitter song "Under the Green Pepper Trees."[57]

So far, I have extended Bloch's thesis of doubleness to accommodate, first, the production of different mixes of German-American literatures and, then, comparable production in the other arts. I have also allowed for the creative possibilities to be twofold, depending on whether doubleness is maintained or synthesis attempted. But another extension is possible, for the doubleness pervasive in exile discourse also describes the position of artists as artists rather than as exiles. Hence, the doubleness entailed in the desire of exiles to hold on to the old as they negotiate the new is guided by the same ideal of creativity as the doubleness entailed in the long-standing claim that artists, from their position of difference or distance—from their position, as it were, at the limits of the world (another frontier)—undertake to transfigure the familiar. For artists, the doubleness is conventionally expressed in the vertical distinction between the transcendent and the ordinary; for exiles it is expressed horizontally between the old and the new. But what exiles and artists share is their experience of being both insiders and outsiders. In doubling terms, by seeing outside, beyond, or above, they both claim to see more truthfully the "here and now" within. Ironically, Wagner played on the advantages of this shared double positioning as explicitly as any composer ever has.

This shared position can also be seen as infusing European artistic culture before the war. Recall the sense of newness, linked increasingly to a sense of outsiderness or psychological exile, that composers were cultivating as they experimented with compositions mixing familiar and unfamiliar themes. Looking back, it seems tragically prophetic that they often voiced their desired doubleness by contrasting the European "old world" and an Amerikan "new world." However, it was not the European-influenced American establishment to which they looked, but the music of alienated "black" America, because there they found similarities with their experience of alienation at home. Of course, the practice of fusing "American" motifs of jazz, folk song, and poetry with European idioms to suggest idealistic, utopian, or avant-garde visions had already been developed by Puccini, Ravel, and Dvořák, but it was given increasing political urgency in the music of Milhaud, Chavez, Krenek, Hindemith, Zemlinsky, and Weill. (It was also being developed in America itself by Ives, Copland, and, of course, Gershwin.) Probably, however, the best doubling examples from Europe were the unofficially (but appropriately) named "zonks" emerging out of the Brecht/Weill collaboration.[58] But another telling example is found in Zemlinsky's *Symphonische Gesänge* of 1929 (especially the "Afrikanischer Tanz"), in which he mixed tonal and atonal idioms with Dixieland and African idioms. This piece gave urgent expression to the message he had already conveyed in the opening of his *Lyric* Symphony of 1924, in which he used the words of the Bengali poet Tagore to cry: "I am a stranger in a strange land" and "am athirst for far-away things."

The visionary or revolutionary moment captured in the doubled compositional style of the doubled exiled artist prompts us to extend Bloch's thesis a step further. For this moment has also been invoked in modernist and more recent descriptions of the condition and progressive potential of migrating, marginal, and minority social groups. These descriptions have forced us to think with dynamic models and traveling terms. They have stressed the importance of difference and duality in opening up spaces for multiple and new voices, and have stressed mediation to overcome static dichotomies. They have spoken of borders and frontiers as sites for constructive displacings of the center. James Clifford has thus recently written of Diaspora cultures as mediating, "in a lived tension, the experiences of separation and entanglement, of living here and remembering/desiring another place," and of diaspora consciousness as a product of "cultures and histories in collision and dialogue."[59]

The doubling thesis so extended allows us to see that it is less the "twoness" than the "more-than-oneness," the lack of sameness or fixity, or, in Adorno's terms, the excess, that is considered the positive moment. A multiply situated person, in proceeding beyond the limits of the familiar, sees that there is more than one way to view the world. The doubleness thesis is compatible, in other words, with a fundamental openness or a purposive ambivalence to the world ("Let's see what the world is like"). When exiles thus spoke of their losing their absolutism (Eisler), of America's deprovincializing them, of their learning not to take things for granted or "regard as natural the circumstances that had developed in Europe" (Adorno), they were suggesting not that these new conditions were leading them all to think the same new thing, but that, in seeing the world anew, each had a genuine option about how they would shape their home in permanent exile or eventual return.[60] Santayana made the point earlier and most poetically: "Migration," he wrote, "like birth is heroic: the soul is signing away her safety for a blank cheque."[61] Edward Said made the point more recently when he talked about the painfulness, but also the benefits, of an exile's contrapuntal awareness.[62] (Neither for this essay nor for Said's is the musical term accidental.)

Neither openness nor the condition of doubleness, however, carries progressive value by itself; rather, according to most exile theorists, each must connect to the integrity of the self, albeit now nonintegrated. For in this connection, the condition becomes linked also to a person's deeds. In other words, whether exiles described themselves as feeling at home, or as estranged, or as oscillating between the two, they believed—rightly, I think—that they would be judged less on the condition itself than on the outcome of their condition, that is, on their human deeds. Victor Hugo once wrote that "an exile is a decent man who persists in decency," but for the exiled composer the concern was also whether, as a creative person, he had persisted in creativity.[63] Of course, the two concerns were not necessarily unconnected.

I have suggested that Bloch's thesis of doubleness with my extensions establishes a link between the condition in which exiles and artists found themselves, on the one hand, and their creative products, on the other. But it would be wrong to think that the link is one of either a necessary or sufficient condition. Even were a composer to be "ideally" saturated in a culture and critically estranged from it, there would be no guarantee that his products would be creative. That the link is not one of guarantee, however, does not mean that there is no link at all. Rather, the link is one of "opening up a space"—an autonomous or critical gap that allows us to make assessments of creativity by looking not at the conditions of production but at the productions or exemplars—the works themselves. Describing the link this way is intended to help forestall reductionist arguments, assertions of causal links, or specifications of necessary and sufficient conditions, all of which close the gap between the conditions of musical practice and its creative productions. The attempt to preserve this gap is an attempt, in other words, to recognize through philosophical theory music's aesthetic moment or, otherwise put, its double quality of being at once purely musical and socially conditioned.

Using doubleness as a technique of philosophical description, however, requires that we extend Bloch's thesis one last time. This extension asks us to see the limits of conditions and of philosophical descriptions in a positive light. It asks us to follow Nietzsche in seeing philosophy and language as approximating to the condition of music and not vice versa. For "compared with music," Nietzsche wrote, "communication by means of words is a shameless mode of procedure; words reduce and stultify; words make impersonal; words make common that which is uncommon."[64] It has long been claimed that the true significance of music—its creative or aesthetic moment—is ineffable and inexpressible, and that it fails to be accounted for even in the most complete description not only of its conditions of production but also of its own forms and contents. Such a view we saw invoked by exiled composers when they spoke of music as partially surpassing its situatedness, and it was this characterization that led them to conclude that music was not wholly, even if it were in part, an ordinary, nation- or culture-bound language. But suppose exiled composers had focused more than they did on these so-called ordinary or common languages and had noticed the extent to which they, too, are capable of being taken abroad and transfigured. What they might then have seen is that "ordinary" language is much more like the "nonordinary" language of music than the "nonordinary" language of music is like an "ordinary" language.

Recall Alfred Schutz's explanation of William James's "fringes" in the former's germane discussion of *The Stranger:* "Every word and every sentence is surrounded by 'fringes' connecting them, on the one hand, with past and future elements of the universe of discourse to which they pertain and surrounding them, on the other hand, with a halo of emotional values and irrational implications which themselves remain ineffable." He concluded: "The fringes are the stuff poetry is made of; they are capable of being set to music but they are not translatable."[65] In this picture, ordinary language has a double identity: it has "ordinary" conceptual significance and it has its fringes. As such, it seems to approximate to the condition of suggestiveness or expressiveness that we find in lyric poetry or music, or paradigmatically in song.

Following James and Schutz, and then not accidentally (the Tractarian) Wittgenstein, one may likewise say of philosophical theory itself that its full meaning fails to be grasped in what it tries ordinarily, that is by means of reason and logic, to say. For its meaning is captured as well in what a theory suggests or shows "between the lines," or even in what it fails to say in its spaces and silences. In other terms, meaning is captured in the doubling condition of a philosophical theory, in, that is to say, a theory's allowing what it says to be weathered and/or defied by what it shows. Thus, just as the doubling condition of the exiled composer opened up a space without fully accounting for any creativity that might follow, so the apparent failure or limits of a philosophical theory to account for everything is precisely the positive condition in which it is able to suggest the polysemous nature of its meaning. Music, in broader terms, teaches language and philosophy to see their limits as positive.

In this essay, I drew a philosophical picture out of an exemplary instance, that instance being the fact of my grandfather's having once adopted a double identity. Like an aphorism, the instance opened up a world of significance. But it was a world that revealed much more constructive conflict or contrapuntal doubleness than it did either simple logical opposition or harmonious theory. It was a world, moreover, that challenged two claims prevalent in exile theory: the rigid "Wagnerian" line that exile precludes creativity, and the diminishing line, articulated most recently by Edward Said, that an exile "exists in a median state, beset by half-involvements and half-detachments." For, as an exile and as an artist, alienated at home or living abroad, an exiled composer, I have tried to show, may live constructively in a condition of doubleness, as opposed to division. Suffice it to conclude on an ironic note: that my grandfather would surely have been surprised to know that his double identity, once adopted in a period of crisis, would one day spawn so much philosophy.

NOTES

I would like to thank many colleagues and friends who offered useful comments, my Summer Institute colleagues in Rochester, and the NEH.

1. Letter of 17 July 1941. All quotations from the correspondence between Schoenberg and the Goehr family originate in documents collected at the Arnold Schoenberg Archive at the University of Southern California. I am grateful to Lawence Schoenberg for permission to use them. I have corrected spelling and grammar in these letters where appropriate, for the sake of readability.

2. I have borrowed here from Eva Hoffman's autobiographical *Lost in Translation: A Life in a New Language* (New York: E. P. Dutton, 1989). "Pattern," she writes, "is the soil of significance; and it is surely one of the hazards of emigration, and exile, and extreme mobility, that one is uprooted from that soil" (278).

3. I am grateful to an Eastman House archivist for giving me this information.

4. *Arnold Schoenberg Letters,* ed. Erwin Stein, trans. Eithne Wilkins and Ernst Kaiser (London: Faber & Faber, 1958), 184.

5. Henry Pachter, "On Being an Exile," in *The Legacy of the German Refugee Intellectuals,* ed. Robert Boyers (New York: Schocken, 1972), 16. Cf. Louis Wirth's comment that "intellectuals are always nomads in the universe of the mind and should feel at home anywhere," quoted by Claus-Dieter Krohn in *Intellectuals in Exile: Refugee Scholars and the New School for Social Research,* trans. Riba Kimber and Robert Kimber (Amherst: University of Massachusetts Press, 1993), 179.

6. Quoted in Edward W. Said, "Reflections on Exile," in *Altogether Elsewhere: Writers on Exile,* ed. Marc Robinson (Boston: Faber & Faber, 1994), 146.

7. Cf. Pachter ("On Being an Exile," 17) again: "The myth that exile produces Dantes, Marxes, Bartóks, and Avicennas certainly is not justified in the mass. More often exile destroys talent, or it means the loss of the environment that nourished the talent morally, socially, and physically."

8. The interviews are printed in section 4 in the issues of 14, 21, and 28 May.

9. See Günter Berghaus, ed., *Theatre and Film in Exile: German Artists in Britain, 1933–45* (New York: Oswald Wolff Books, 1989), 19; Jarrell C. Jackman, "German Émigrés in Southern California," in *The Muses Flee Hitler: Cultural Transfer and Adaptation,* ed. Jarrell C. Jackman and Carla M. Borden (Washington D.C.: Smithsonian Institution Press, 1983), 98; and Walter Rubsamen, "Schönberg in America," *Musical Quarterly* 37 (Oct. 1951): 485–86.

10. Unless otherwise noted, all views recorded in this section are taken from Goldberg's interviews in the *Los Angeles Times.*

11. Malcolr Gillies, ed., *Bartók Remembered* (New York: Faber & Faber, 1990), 186.

12. Igor Stravinsky and Robert Craft, *Dialogues and a Diary* (London: Faber & Faber, 1968), 108.

13. *Hanns Eisler: A Rebel in Music—Selected Writings,* ed. Manfred Grabs (New York: Seven Seas, 1978), 14. See also Albrecht Betz, *Hanns Eisler: Political Musician,* trans. Bill Hopkins (Cambridge: Cambridge University Press, 1982), 14 and 153.

14. *Virgil Thomson* (London: Weidenfeld & Nicolson, 1967), 346, ending his chapter "Europe in America."

15. "A Musical Journey through America," in *Eisler: Rebel in Music,* 82.

16. See Ernst Krenek, "America's Influence on Its Émigré Composers," trans. Don Harran, *Perspectives of New Music* 8 (spring–summer 1970): 112.

17. Ernst Krenek, *Die amerikanischen Tagebücher, 1937–1942: Dokumente aus dem Exil,* ed. Claudia Maurer Zenck (Vienna: Böhlau, 1992), 192.

18. Krenek, "America's Influence," 112.

19. Ernst Krenek, "Self-Analysis," *New Mexico Quarterly* 23 (spring 1953): 7.

20. *Schoenberg Letters,* 233.

21. Vera Stravinsky and Robert Craft, *Stravinsky in Pictures and Documents* (New York: Simon & Schuster, 1978), 347.

22. *Schoenberg Letters,* 191–92. Cf. Hannah Arendt's observation in "We Refugees" (in Robinson, ed., *Altogether Elsewhere,* 10): "We lost our language . . . the naturalness of reactions, the simplicity of gestures, the unaffected expression of feelings."

23. Jackman, "German Émigrés," 101.

24. Berghaus, ed., *Theatre and Film in Exile,* iv. He discusses this point further on page 18, but in a different context. There he acknowledges the languages difficulties faced by all artists.

25. Boris Schwarz, "The Music World in Migration," in Jackman and Borden, eds., *Muses Flee Hitler,* 137.

26. The dichotomy is also related to Aron Gurwitsch's description of the refugee's life as coming, in one sense, out of a void and, in another sense, out of a three-thousand-year past; see *Philosophers in Exile: The Correspondence of Alfred Schutz and Aron Gurwitsch, 1939–1959,* trans. J. Claude Evans (Bloomington: Indiana University Press, 1989), xvi.

27. Quoted in Berghaus, *Theatre and Film in Exile,* 18. The painter's name is not given.

28. Arnold Schoenberg, "Does the World Lack a Peace-Hymn?" in *Style and Idea: Selected Writings of Arnold Schoenberg,* ed. Leonard Stein (Berkeley: University of California Press, 1985), 500.

29. Arnold Schoenberg, "Two Speeches on the Jewish Situation," ibid., 502.

30. Schoenberg, "Does the World Lack a Peace-Hymn?" 500.

31. *Schoenberg Letters,* 217.

32. Brecht ascribed these words to Mann, as James K. Lyon explains in *Bertolt Brecht in America* (Princeton: Princeton University Press, 1980), 252. For more on Mann's conflicting attitudes toward exile, see Henry Hatfield's "Thomas Mann and America," in Boyers, ed., *Legacy of the German Refugee Intellectuals,* 174–85.

33. For more on the "University in Exile" or New School for Social Research, see Krohn, *Intellectuals in Exile.*

34. Berghaus, *Theatre and Film in Exile,* xvi and 33.

35. Krenek, "Self-Analysis," 32.

36. See David Josephson's essay in this volume.

37. Quoted by John Warrack in his comments on Stravinsky as a Russian, *Tempo* (1967): 9, to confirm his general point that theorists have underestimated the fact of Stravinsky's Russianness and have tried to denationalize him.

38. In Allen Edwards, *Flawed Words and Stubborn Sounds: A Conversation with Elliott Carter* (New York: W. W. Norton, 1971), 13.

39. Quoted in Jackman, "German Émigrés," 103.

40. For further details, see Lyon, *Bertolt Brecht in America,* 30, 109, 251–62, who describes Brecht's position here as being directly influenced by Ernst Bloch. Of Bloch, more later.

41. Bertolt Brecht, "Thoughts Concerning the Duration of Exile," in *Selected Poems,* trans. Hoffman Reynolds Hays (New York: Regnal & Hitchcock, 1947), 30, set to music by Hanns Eisler.

42. Gillies, ed., *Bartók Remembered,* 201.

43. See Ronald Taylor, *Kurt Weill: Composer in a Divided World* (Boston: Northeastern University Press, 1991), 227; also Kim Kowalke, "Formerly German: Kurt Weill in America," in *A Stranger Here Myself: Kurt Weill Studien,* ed. Kim Kowalke and Horst Edler (Hildesheim: Georg Olms, 1993), 35–57.

44. Hinton, ed., *The Threepenny Opera* (Cambridge: Cambridge University Press, 1990), 70.

45. Quoted in Taylor, *Kurt Weill,* 251.

46. Ibid., 233.

47. Schoenberg, "Two Speeches on the Jewish Situation," 502. Boris Schwarz comments on Schoenberg's dual position this way: "Although Schönberg is known to have been rather uncompromising in his musical views, he did make some concessions so that his writing would be more accessible to the American public, particularly to young American musicians" ("Musical World in Migration," 141).

48. Richard Wagner [writing as "K. Freigedank"], "Judaism in Music" (1850), in *Richard Wagner's Prose Works,* trans. William Ashton Ellis (Lincoln: University of Nebraska Press, 1995), 3:75–122. The following quotations, unless otherwise specified, are also from this essay.

49. Quoted in Paul Lawrence Rose, *Wagner: Race and Revolution* (New Haven: Yale University Press, 1992), 70.

50. The reference to "friends around the globe" is from Wittgenstein's "Sketch for a Foreword," printed originally as a foreword to *Philosophical Remarks* (ed. Rush Rhees), and in *Culture and Value,* trans. Peter Winch, ed. Georg Henrik von Wright (Oxford: Oxford University Press, 1980). All quotations from Wittgenstein, unless specified otherwise, are from this book, remarks 16, 18, 35, 39, 49, and 50.

51. Schoenberg, "Two Speeches on the Jewish Situation," 501–5.

52. Cf. the Nazi statement that "when a Jew speaks writes or thinks as a German he lies"; quoted by Herbert Peyser in the *New York Times,* 10 Dec. 1933, X-8, in an article on the Cultural League of German Jews. See David Josephson's documentation in this volume.

53. Ernst Bloch, "Disrupted Language, Disrupted Culture," *Direction,* Dec. 1939, 16–19 (a special issue entitled "Exiled German Writers: Art, Fiction, Documentary Material").

54. Note that although the identification of nations is not a necessary feature of this mixed production, linked as the mixing often is with experiences of travel and exile, such identification is very common. And note that "German" and "American" already stand for complex and historically constructed unities and are neither related nor opposed to one another as pure elements.

55. Boris Schwarz, "Musical World in Migration," discusses many more examples of what he calls the "Americana" compositions to demonstrate the mutual and immeasurable enrichment of American music by European musicians.

56. Cf. Hinton, *Threepenny Opera,* 5, 102, and 118.

57. For more on "unlovely" antagonisms, see Hatfield, "Thomas Mann and America," 175.

58. For more on "zonks," see Taylor, *Kurt Weill,* 107.

59. James Clifford, "Diasporas," *Cultural Anthropology* 9, no. 3 (1994): 311, 319.

60. Thedor W. Adorno, "Scientific Experiences of a European Scholar in America," in *The Intellectual Migration: Europe and America, 1930–1960,* ed. Donald Fleming and Bernard Bailyn (Cambridge, Mass.: Harvard University Press, Belknap Press, 1969), 367.

61. George Santayana, "The Philosophy of Travel," in Robinson, ed., *Altogether Elsewhere,* 44.

62. Said, "Reflections on Exile," 148.

63. Victor Hugo, "What Exile Is," in Robinson, ed., *Altogether Elsewhere,* 79.

64. Friedrich Nietzsche, *The Will to Power,* sec. 810, in *Complete Works,* trans. and ed. Walter Kaufmann (New York, 1968), 15:254; quoted in Robert P. Morgan's "Secret Languages: The Roots of Musical Modernism," in *Modernism: Challenges and Perspectives,* ed. Monique Chefdor, Ricardo Quinones, and Albert Wachtel (Urbana: University of Illinois Press, 1986), 33–53.

65. Alfred Schutz, "The Stranger: An Essay in Social Psychology," *American Journal of Sociology* 49, no. 6 (1944): 504.

The Exile of European Music
Documentation of Upheaval and Immigration in the *New York Times*

David Josephson

The great drama of the exile of European music in the 1930s played itself out in countless individual stories, some of them told, more waiting to be unearthed, most to remain lost forever. This essay treats of one scene in that drama: the upheaval in Germany, the flight of its disenfranchised musicians and others from countries swallowed by the German leviathan, the response of their colleagues abroad, and the arrival of those who came to the United States, as these events were set forth in the pages of the *New York Times*, the American newspaper of record.

Five weeks after Hitler's accession to power, readers of the *New York Times* learned of the early impact of his government on musical life in Germany, when the ouster of Fritz Busch as conductor of the Dresden State Opera was reported. In a news miscellany cabled from Berlin on 7 March, they read of the funeral of a Nazi storm trooper in Düsseldorf, the hoisting of the swastika over a synagogue in Bochum and a department store in Allsberg, the bombing of a synagogue in Königsberg, the closing of a Woolworth store in Duisburg, and then the humiliation of Fritz Busch, the distinguished general music director of the Dresden State Opera.

> When Fritz Busch, the conductor, took his place in the Dresden Opera House orchestra tonight for a performance of "Rigoletto" there were shouts, "Out with Busch," from front rows, occupied by Nazis. After several minutes of uproar Herr Busch left and his place was taken by Kurt Striegler. The performance then took place without further trouble.
>
> After conducting a rehearsal of "Rigoletto" early today, Herr Busch was called to the stage and informed by a Nazi storm troop detachment that executive control of the Saxon State theatres had passed to the Nazis and that Herr Striegler would take over the musical direction in Herr Busch's place. The ousted director is believed to be a Socialist.[1]

The following day, a second cable filled in the details. The Nazis had charged that Busch, the highest salaried official of the Saxon state government, had taken frequent leaves of absence in order to earn money elsewhere, leaving substitutes to fill in for him. Busch countered that he had attended to his responsibilities faithfully, conducting more rehearsals and performances than his two assistants together, and had rejected more lucrative invitations in order to stay at Dresden. Still, he offered to accept a salary reduction of 20 percent. Moreover, he was a patriot who had won the Iron Cross and kept away from politics. The Saxon authorities were to take up the case on 9 March.[2]

By mid-March, *Times* readers learned from an account by Herbert Peyser, the *Times* music correspondent in Berlin, that the issue was neither Busch's salary nor his absences, but that he and Dresden Opera House general director Alfred Reucker were targets in a rapidly spreading national campaign that placed Jews, foreigners, Social Democrats, and other theater personnel on the left at risk:

> Musical circles in Germany are acutely feeling repercussions of recent political developments. Opera houses, which are State or municipal institutions, have been increasingly subjected to pressure with respect to their administrative staffs and artistic personnel, and rumors point to even more extensive changes. In the past few days the State Opera of Dresden and the Civic Opera of Berlin were compelled to discharge some of their principal functionaries and replace them with National Socialists.

Carl Ebert, intendant of the Berlin Civic Opera and a Social Democrat, had been thrown out of his theater on the night of Saturday 11 March along with four members of his senior staff: conductors Fritz Stiedry and Paul Breisach and artistic directors Rudolf Bing and Jürgen Fehling. As in Dresden, the firing had taken place in the theater and under physical threat by an S.A. (*Sturmabteilung*) mob. Jews, foreigners, Social Democrats, and others on the left were at risk. The Berlin State Opera was thought to be next, with Otto Klemperer and Leo Blech among its conductors and Alexander Kipnis, Frida Leider, Emanuel List, and Lauritz Melchior among its leading singers. Its intendant, Heinz Tietjen, was rumored to have threatened his resignation in the event of the firings of those musicians. The *Deutsche Allgemeine Zeitung* had weighed in against the dismissals, or at least against the way they were handled. So great was the turmoil that the premiere of Richard Strauss's *Arabella,* scheduled for Dresden in July, was now open to question. In Dresden, General Director Hartmann was obliged to work with a Nazi committee, while in Leipzig Gustav Brecher, the conductor "who for a number of years directed the first performances of numerous modernistic works," was thrown out.[3]

Two days later, on 17 March, the cautious tone of the reporting changed perceptibly, bending now with irony as the outrages grew more transparent, as unrelated firings in far-flung cities of the Reich under the jurisdictions of different states came to be seen as elements of a coordinated purge, and as they suddenly came to touch on a musician lionized in New York. Like the 8 March report, this one was a miscellany; now, though, music captured the headline, in the person of Bruno Walter, who had just returned from his second season with the New York Philharmonic-Symphony Orchestra. The reporting betrayed continuing confusion: there seemed to be no national leader of the national "purging process," though its center clearly lay in the Berlin government.

> The daily newsreel from Germany is compelled to depend upon a medley of happenings in all corners of the Reich, for while Berlin is the official domicile of the Hitler–von Papen government and the centre of this "national revolution," it is the happenings in the provinces that supply the patches of color needed to fill in the general picture.

The reporter, though he noted a tightening federal grip on the states, seemed incredulous that no opposition had arisen to the dismissals. This time a concert of the Leipzig Gewandhaus Orchestra that was to have been led by Walter on 16 March was canceled. Although officials attributed the cancellation to fear of public disorder, Walter's friends were cited as having attributed it to his Jewish blood. His Berlin Philharmonic concert planned for 20 March was still scheduled, but the soprano Jarmila Novotna was removed from its roster, presumably because she was Czech.

Other items in the miscellany included the renaming of streets and public squares in Thuringia named for Marxists or Jews, the removal from Saxon prisons of Marxist and pacifist writings, the arrest in Schleswig of General Paul von Schoenaich, chairman of the German Peace League, the first flag parade in Kiel since the Great War, the announced Socialist boycott of the forthcoming services in the Garrison Church at Potsdam dedicating the new government, and the banning of "Negro jazz" at Berlin's radio station by its new director. This time the *Deutsche Allgemeine Zeitung* sided with the authorities on the grounds that such a ban met "an old demand in those sections of the public where the sense for morals and good taste has not 'gone to sleep.' "[4]

The first critical response to the news by Olin Downes, chief music critic of the *Times,* was published in a Sunday column two days later, on 19 March. Trying to make sense of, and draw meaning from, conflicting signals emanating from Germany, he addressed the issue of nationalism, which he saw as a fundamental and positive quality in music, "the inspired expression of heredity and environment, of race and soil," a quality now being twisted by the Nazis into a chauvinism in which the political status of a musician counted for all. A culturally immature America swung between the extremes of imitation of foreign models on the one hand and chauvinism on the other, he believed; it could not yet find a middle road. In a few years' time, as the flow of skilled immigrants turned into a desperate flood, the issue would be framed as a debate among musicians and the communities that supported them—directors of institutional boards, judges in competitions, administrators and teachers in colleges, universities, and conservatories; and it would find its way into the pages of the *New York Times*. But in 1933, with the flight from Germany still in an early, uncertain stage, Downes felt secure prescribing a reasonable national policy for what could be seen as either boon or threat to the American musical landscape:

> Each country should strive to stimulate its creative artists. Special assistance can be given them, but they should not be encouraged in erroneous ways by pampering mediocrity or excusing incompetence. Criticism of artistic effort should be unsparing. Give the native musician . . . opportunity for self-development. Then examine his offerings and estimate them for what they are and not what we would like them to be.[5]

By the beginning of April the musical turmoil had made its way to the front page, with a report that Toscanini and ten other musicians had sent Hitler a cable the previous day in "protest against the persecution of their colleagues in that country for political or religious reasons." The cable had been drafted by Berthold Neuer, vice president of the Knabe Piano Company, at the suggestion of Artur Bodanzky, conductor of German opera at the Metropolitan Opera, after he heard that the outrages against Busch and Walter had been followed by an assault by storm troops on Klemperer. The article was oddly vague about the chronology of events regarding the cable. On the one hand, it quoted Toscanini's request that his name head the list of signatories; on the other, it quoted from a letter of Ossip Gabrilowitsch, conductor of the Detroit Symphony, to Toscanini asking him to support the protest to Hitler, for without his support no protest to Hitler would be effective. Gabrilowitsch, who was openly contemptuous of the courtly tone of the protest letter as drafted by Neuer, wrote a separate letter to Toscanini in unusually strong language—language that might have been unnecessary had he been certain of Toscanini's stance—urging him to cancel his Bayreuth contract. In the event, Toscanini signed the protest. At his request, his name appeared first, followed by those of the conductors Walter Damrosch, Gabrilowitsch, Alfred Hertz, Serge Koussevitzky, and Fritz Reiner, the composers Rubin Goldmark and Charles Martin Loeffler, the pianist Harold Bauer, and Frank Damrosch, director of the Institute of Musical Art.[6]

One noted musician who did not sign the cable was Fritz Kreisler, an Austrian citizen and a Jew, on tour at the time in the United States. On the contrary, in a statement issued on 4 April and printed in full in the *New York Times* the next day he urged Toscanini to honor his contract with the Wagner festival. The German government, he stated, could not control the passions of Germany's masses and especially of her youth, passions attributable entirely to the exhaustion of German resources in the Great War and to what followed: social collapse, starvation, revolution, the humiliation of Versailles, a hyperinflation that had decimated the middle class, civil war, economic depression, and unemployment. Once the violence had run its course, Germans would "settle down to face their domestic and external problems with their traditional sobriety and sense of order." But Germany would have to be left alone, especially by artists, who had to remain above politics. "I believe," wrote Kreisler,

> that the artists who are responsible for the moral pressure put on Maestro Toscanini are acting in defiance of the very principle which they purpose to defend. Namely: inviolability of artistic utterance under all circumstances and its removal above the sphere of political and racial strife. Moreover, they are performing a poor service to their colleagues.
>
> Bayreuth is an institution cherished in Germany and admired all over the world. Maestro Toscanini's coming there is earegly [*sic*] anticipated and his [*sic*] gratitude of the many who will be privileged to hear Maestro Toscanini's recreation of the German master's works will constitute a more favorable atmosphere for intercession on behalf of his colleagues than a formal protest or a willful absentation.
>
> I believe that no other interpretation could be put on the Maestro's decision to go to Bayreuth than that o[f] his manly and courageous determination to carry out his artistic obligation under all circumstances and his desire to uphold the artist's most glorious prerogative of being a herald of love and a messenger of good will from men to men and nation to nation. I solemnly urge Maestro Toscanini to go to Bayreuth. We can not dispense with such a powerful ambassador of peace and harbinger of good will when the nerves of all nations are on edge and sinister grumblings of war are heard again.
>
> Let these harbingers of good will increase and there may be less need for protests.[7]

Although Kreisler's historical analysis and prognosis were common enough, by the time he returned to his Berlin home that summer he recognized that his position was untenable, and joined Toscanini in refusing to play in Germany.[8]

In a dispatch from Berlin dated 7 April and published two days later, the *Times* reported the new Nazi policy of party control of the nation's cultural life, and the removal of Jews from official positions in theaters and opera houses. Hans Hinkel, a member of the Reichstag, leader of the Militant League for the Promotion of Defense of German Culture (the reporter's translation of Kampfbund für deutsche Kultur), and member of the Prussian Culture Ministry, announced the policy in response to the protests against the Nazi prohibitions on the activities of Walter, Max Reinhardt, and other Jews in the theater and the opera. No longer did one read of appeals for public order in the cancellation of concerts and opera performances led by Jews. The *Times* noted:

This edit is of far-reaching significance in Germany, where all the leading theatres, operas and orchestras are either government-owned or supported out of the public exchequer.

Such foreign artists as will be tolerated under the new dispensation must not do anything that might injure the interests and welfare of the German people, Herr Hinkel said, and free-lance Jewish artists must conform with the duties of citizens of the new State. Jewish performers, he added, will receive every opportunity to show what they can do.

"It is natural that the National Socialist program implies that National Socialists must be in charge of all organizations having to do with national cultural life," Herr Hinkel declared, adding that the stamp of party membership would not, however, be made a condition for employment, since it was not thought desirable to narrow the work of creative artists.

The new bare-fisted policy barring Jews notwithstanding, Hinkel asserted that Walter's concert had had to be canceled for lack of police protection. He protested American support for Walter and complained of threats against Richard Strauss, who had replaced Walter in Berlin. The status of a second Jewish conductor, Klemperer, remained uncertain; until it was resolved, he would not be permitted to conduct in Germany:

for reasons of discipline and the artistic development of Germany his concerts have had to be postponed for the same reason as the concerts of Herr Walter. Our storm troops have more important functions than providing protection for concerts.

In any case, Jews would no longer dominate German music any more than they would German courts, medicine, or education, through the authority of their official positions.[9]

Three days later the *Times* reported that Wilhelm Furtwängler, conductor of the Berlin Philharmonic, had appealed to Propaganda Minister Joseph Goebbels for complete artistic freedom and criticized the growing official discrimination against Jews; and that Goebbels had thrown the conductor a bone while laying down the law: he would always protect "true artists," and he didn't approve of what he called "certain events during recent weeks," but what had happened to Walter, Klemperer, and Max Reinhardt counted for little in the face of the silence forced on "many true German artists" since Versailles.[10]

On 21 April came news that Adolf Busch had resigned from the Brahms centennial celebration in Hamburg after Rudolf Serkin was denied permission as a Jew to play with the Busch Quartet, and that the Prussian minister of culture had canceled a series of Brahms concerts at the Berlin Singakademie scheduled by Artur Schnabel, Bronislaw Huberman, Gregor Piatigorsky, and Paul Hindemith.[11]

Nine days later came the first set piece on music in the new Germany, written by Peyser on 14 April. No longer the cautious journalist, Peyser began in a tone of disgust with the Kampfbund für deutsche Kultur (now translated as the Fighting League for German Culture), which had "acquired a preponderating influence in German artistic and cultural life and gives promise of wielding this influence without mercy." It had created an orchestra of Nazis led by Gustav Havemann, with rude and mediocre musicians forced on the Berlin Philharmonic as substitutes for regular members; and it had proposed testing procedures whereby musicians had to be licensed before they could perform, teach, or write in journals and newspapers, their licensing being tied to race and their support of the government. Now a union of music critics was proposed under Fritz Stege, editor of the "venomously reactionary and anti-Semitic" *Zeitschrift für Musik.* Apart from the outrages, but tied to them by a leadership he would not name, Peyser noted a growing conservatism in Berlin's musical life, into which Furtwängler was allowing himself to be drawn, and the concomitant sugarcoating of the repertory of the once-adventurous City Opera:

> In the recent Furtwängler-Goebbels correspondence, which threw the entire community into a ferment, both disputants agreed on one point of musical esthetics—namely, that "experiments" are no longer desirable and, in the present state of national grace, should be done away with. It is not altogether clear what the two gentlemen understand by "experiments" or just what kind of experiments are accursed. Ever since the war the German stage has, in one way or another, been "experimenting." Some of these experiments have been offensive and preposterous (such as certain stylizations and modernizations of standard operas), others highly fruitful, suggestive and stimulating. Exactly how and why Mr. Furtwängler would restrict "experiment" in so far as it affects musical creation, I do not know. At present jazz is under an official ban here (it may not be broadcast in some places and in others it may not be played publicly); but the new State pilots, though they have taken no official cognizance of it, are none too friendly, I understand, to atonality, polytonality and such like processes. Atonality, for example, has a bad press these days. It is alleged to be an invention of Jews and Marxists. For the weal of the folk, things like Lortzing's "Der Waffenschmied" and Nessler's "Trompeter von Säckingen" (which it is now proposed to dust off and revive in Leipzig) are presumably better. The Lortzing "Singspiel" was resurrected at the Städtische Oper lately amid great rejoicings, accompanied by assurances that its restoration indicated the return of a sounder taste than prevailed under a more liberal dispensation. Be all of which as it may, the strictly artistic value of "Der Waffenschmied" is about on a par with that of "Abie's Irish Rose."[12]

On 21 May came the first report of the flight under way from Germany. Written by Henry Prunières, the founding editor of the *Revue musicale* and Paris music correspondent of the *Times,* it described the plight of exiles relying on charity that would soon be exhausted and unable to find work at a time when survival was difficult even for French musicians.

The exodus of German Jews or liberal suspects continues. They reach Paris in great numbers and are given a good reception. The Israelite Alliance and the Painlev committee are constantly distributing aid, and the government has waived the restrictions concerning passport visas for foreigners. It now remains for these exiles to find work—no easy matter in these times, when so many French are barely able to survive. The situation is particularly sad and difficult for the exiled musicians. France is actually gorged with conductors, pianists, violinists and teachers of harmony with no work. How [to] find employment for the hundreds of Jewish musicians who continue to arrive? With the best will in the world, the situation is too vast to be coped with, and people are asking themselves anxiously what will become of these refugees in a few months, when the emergency funds raised in their behalf have been exhausted.

Public indignation is at a high pitch. All Frenchmen learned in school to hate the revocation of the Edict of Nantes as one of the most detestable facts of history. The exile of the German Jews awakens and renews this sentiment.

Many non-Jewish German artists have also come to Paris seeking refuge from the persecution leveled against those considered guilty of "Musical bolshevism"—that is to say, the composition of modern music. One is no longer permitted, for example, to play the works of Paul Hindemith. Alas, for Germany, reduced to the compositions of a Pfitzner! The noble protests of Toscanini and Furtwängler have been echoed loudly in Paris, where public opinion is preparing a triumphal welcome for the latter, who has refused to dismiss a single Jewish musician from the Philharmonic Orchestra.[13]

On the last day of the month came news that Franz Schreker and Arnold Schoenberg had been fired from their posts in Berlin as director of the Hochschule für Musik and professor at the Prussian Academy of Arts, respectively.[14] On 6 June, on the front page, the *Times* announced that Toscanini had canceled his Bayreuth contract, and on the next day, that Klemperer had been fired from his position at the State Opera (he had fled Germany two months earlier) along with nine other musicians on the house staff.[15]

A few days later, the composer Roger Sessions and the pianist Leopold Godowsky, returning from Berlin, confirmed Peyser's reports. Sessions, who had seen the violence first-hand and knew of ongoing covert outrages, called the damage caused by them and by the firings of Jewish musicians "irreparable." Nothing he had witnessed in his six years in fascist Italy compared with "the crude and intolerant spirit of Germany." Every opera house in Germany had suffered. Godowsky, for his part, spoke of "the fury and rage of the German nation," an anger beyond the imagining of Americans: "The natural Teutonic hatred of the Jews had full outlet, as the German is nothing if not thorough. You can imagine the consequences."[16]

With summer now at hand, musical news shifted to reports from the two great Central European festivals: Bayreuth, which opened on 21 July with a performance, attended by Hitler, of *Die Meistersinger* conducted by Karl

Elmendorff, who had replaced Toscanini; and Salzburg, which opened at the beginning of August, its second concert conducted by Bruno Walter.[17] With the contrasting treatment of the two festivals the *Times* laid bare its policies. While it printed Peyser's report on Bayreuth on page 14,[18] it placed Frederick Birchall's report on Salzburg on the front page. It had waited until the second performance, ignoring the opening night, in order to focus on Walter, then gave him a hero's headline and assured readers that "he has never shown himself in better form." Birchall, a political reporter apparently innocent of musical training, limited his musical evaluation of the concert to the phrase "a little masterpiece of interpretation," then continued in a report that shuttled between propaganda and hagiography:

> Applause greeted Herr Walter the moment he entered and walked to the conductor's desk. He had seemed to hesitate just a trifle, as if he wondered how he would be received. From his native Germany in the last few months there had come to him mostly abuse. Last night, when applause from every part of the Mozart Auditorium met him, it seemed almost to surprise him.
>
> But from the moment that he raised his baton there was no doubt as to the effect, upon the conductor, the orchestra or the audience, of the situation created by the propaganda that has sacrificed German art to German politics. Never in Salzburg has a conductor performed his task with greater inspiration, never has an orchestra responded more nobly and never has an audience received the result with greater acclaim.
>
> After each number there was long and fervent applause. At the end of the concert Herr Walter had to return again to the platform and bow his thanks. He brought with him [the singer] Frau [Lotte] Schoene to share it, for she, too, had sacrificed a brilliant career on the German concert stage to the Aryan shibboleth of National Socialism. Bouquets were carried to her and the crowd pelted the singer and the conductor with roses.
>
> Herr Walter spread out his hands in deprecation, but it was useless. A Salzburg Festival crowd knows no politics—only art. It lingered almost half an hour after the concert had closed, expressing its enthusiasm.[19]

Other dispatches from Bayreuth and Salzburg in the summer of 1933 continued the pattern, Peyser's work tough and musically engaged, Birchall's adulatory. Aside from the festivals, little of musical interest was reported; the most notable events were Karl Muck's resignation from his post as conductor of the Hamburg Philharmonic Orchestra late in July and the spreading boycott of Germany by musicians, who by early August included Pablo Casals, Kreisler, Schnabel, Adolf Busch, Vladimir Horowitz, and Bronislaw Huberman.[20] A stinging letter written by Huberman refusing an invitation from Furtwängler was printed on 14 September.[21] By 31 October the American composer and conductor Werner Janssen, pianists Alfred Cortot and Josef Hofmann, and violinist Jacques Thibaud were added to the list.

On 12 November the *Times* printed, without comment, the translation of an article from the *Vossische Zeitung* of 23 September whose "announced intention" was to clear up the confusion following the Nazi reorganization of musical life into a myriad of associations, unions, leagues, and cartels.[22] A month later came its mirror image, a moving dispatch from Peyser dated 26 November on the establishment and activities a few months earlier of the Kulturbund deutscher Juden, a cultural ghetto of some thirty to forty thousand dues-paying members, a crumb thrown by the same government that had forcibly separated Jews from their fellow Germans. Its activities were barely tolerated, harshly controlled, minutely regulated, and stringently hidden from the society at large.[23] Everyone associated with it, from directors to coat room attendants and audience, had to be Jewish. It owed its existence, Peyser believed, to Furtwängler's support. The general population, which in any case was not informed of its activities, was strictly forbidden to attend its lectures, concerts, and opera and theater productions. As Peyser observed, "by a paradoxical reversal of the usual Nazi process, only the non-Aryan is here looked upon with favor. For once, racial 'impurity' becomes a sort of asset." What was so poignant, and Peyser caught it precisely, was that the league's purpose was to serve the intellectual and psychological needs of Germans suddenly stripped of their national identity, rights, and status by their government simply because they were Jewish, Germans who struggled to assert and maintain their dignity and position in society even as they were driven ever closer to its margins. Through the Kulturbund,

> artists who vanished from the theatres, the opera houses and the concert halls of Germany because they were racially suspect may suddenly return to notice under these singular auspices.
>
> Take for instance Joseph Rosenstock, of wistful New York memory, who was cast out of Mannheim at the first onslaught of triumphant Hitlerism. He has become operatic conductor of the "Kulturbund." Then there is Michael Taube, whose little orchestra, giving concerts of eighteenth century music, was long a feature of Berlin musical life. He is now to conduct Bach, Handel, Vivaldi and the rest of them for this community of music-loving Jews. Herman Schey, the admirable oratorio baritone, until recently in constant demand from one end of Germany to the other, will sing recitals for the league.
>
> Others employed in its sheltering fold include Fritzi Jokl, one time leading coloratura [*sic*] soprano in Munich; Marcel Noe, a utility baritone ejected on racial grounds from the Berlin Staatsoper; and Dr. Kurt Singer, prominent physician, choral conductor and not so long ago Intendant of nothing less than the Städtische Oper in Berlin.[24]

The final musical notice of the year, coming on its last day, reported the emigration "on political grounds" of Curt Sachs, "one of the greatest musical scholars of the century."[25] The *Times* would see fit to cover his arrival in the United States four years later.

The year 1933 was decisive. German musicians experienced, as did all their countrymen outside the Nazi party, an upheaval for which they were utterly unprepared. Neither Jews nor any German of liberal habit and affiliation could breathe freely any longer. They sought patterns in the unpredictable, seemingly undirected, occasionally contradictory early stages of what was not yet seen as an irreversible catastrophe; from the evidence of what happened later, many failed in that task. As one edict after another eroded their political liberties, social position, professional status, and economic opportunity, they had only two choices: to remain and hope for stabilization of the social order, no matter how reduced their place in it, or to leave. The vast majority who remained in Germany adapted as they could to the chaos, violence, legal restrictions, and petty harassments. As the victims gradually awoke to the horror of what was being engineered, so foreign correspondents and editors watched in disbelief, struggled too to find patterns, and reacted with growing indignation and, one senses, discomfort in their role as journalists. The drama was thoughtfully played out on the pages of the *Times*.[26]

While shock followed shock in the first year of the Nazi takeover, the reporting in the *Times* from 1934 gradually assumed a repetitive, predictable quality, as did events, for the most part, until 1938. Not that those events were anything but ugly; but there were now few surprises as the government tightened the screws. Until its waning weeks, 1934 saw, aside from the obligatory Bayreuth reports, only two miscellanies from Peyser in Vienna. One concerned the shelving of Ernst Krenek's *Karl V* and other Nazi attempts to disrupt musical life there.[27] The other concerned Furtwängler's hero's reception in the Austrian capital and Strauss's intention as head of the Reichsmusikkammer to make "a clean sweep" of Hindemith's music.[28] A brief front-page item on Alfred Rosenberg's commissioning of music to replace Mendelssohn's *Midsummer Night's Dream* appeared, followed a month later by a story on Pfitzner's and Strauss's refusal to write that music.[29] The last weeks of the year and early months of 1935 saw a flurry of articles covering the Nazi denunciation of Hindemith, Furtwängler's defense of him in the *Deutsche Allgemeine Zeitung,* the conductor's resignation from the Berlin State Opera, the Philharmonic, and the Reichsmusikkammer, and the eventual collapse of his position and moral leadership in the German musical world. The headlines of these and other reports of interest, notably Peyser's miscellany on 4 August 1935 with its discussion of conductorial musical chairs, and of articles documenting the musical fallout from the annexation of Austria in March 1938, are found in the appendix to this essay. The musical impact of the Anschluß, though incomparably swifter and more decisive than that of the Nazi assumption of power in Germany in 1933, received limited coverage. As the storm gathered in Central Europe in 1938 and 1939, the fate of Austria's and Czechoslovakia's musicians would earn hardly more than a footnote.

The great emigration had begun in the wake of the Nazi accession to power in 1933. Its second phase can be traced to the catastrophic year of 1938, in panic-stricken Austria after its annexation to Germany in March, in fascist Italy upon the promulgation of anti-Jewish laws under German pressure, in Czechoslovakia after the Sudeten debacle in September, and in Germany itself following the Kristallnacht in November. That phase continued into 1939, with the final German dismemberment of Czechoslovakia in March and its invasion of Poland in September, provoking pan-European war. A third phrase can be traced to the devastating spring of 1940, when France, the Low Countries, Denmark, and Norway fell with lightning speed under German control.

As our attention moves from the calamity in Europe to the exodus from its shores, we pass to the *Times*'s reporting of the arrival in America of the émigré musicians between 1933 and June 1941, when Germany's invasion of Russia shut the last escape route from the continent, aside from Spain and Portugal, and emigration came to a virtual standstill. Only the best known had their arrivals recorded in the *Times,* and even a few of them slipped through the net of its attention. As for the men and women below the top rung—the lesser successes and the failures in whose stories the complex texture of the émigré experience is richly and delicately caught—they escaped public notice entirely. One might note, for example, Felix Gatz, founder with Artur Nikisch of the Berlin Bruckner Vereinigung and teacher at the Vienna Academy of Music and Dramatic Art in the early 1930s, who died at age fifty in obscurity in Scranton, Pennsylvania, in 1942. Or Ludwig Landshoff, who, after the demise of his Bach Verein in Munich in 1928, struggled in Berlin, fled to Italy in 1936 and Paris in 1938, made his way to the Pyrenees after the fall of France in 1940, and landed in New York in 1941, where after one summer he died suddenly at age sixty-seven.[30] Or Heinrich Schalit, a student of Theodor Leschetizky and Robert Fuchs in Vienna, organist of the Great Synagogues in Munich and Rome and composer of significant liturgical music, a difficult and unhappy man who ended his days in the small Jewish communities of Providence and Denver. Or the anonymous scholar whose story was told by Stephen Duggan and Betty Drury, two American heroes in the effort to rescue European academics from the Nazi tide:

> There was a musicologist who carried on research for several years at a Western institution until his job folded up; answering an advertisement placed in

the newspapers by a great industrial concern, he was employed as a day la-
borer at $6.00 a day. "When I met him," the field representative of the Emer-
gency Committee wrote, "he had finished his first week of work there and was
able to sit in his friend's house, smoke his pipe, admit his muscles were rather
sore, and smile about it."

He may have smiled, but as Duggan and Drury noted, working as a ma-
chinist in a defense plant at the cost of blunting "his sensitive pianist's fin-
gers" was not the mark of a successful professional adjustment.[31] We shall
have to search for the stories of such people in memoirs, correspondence,
interviews, and local papers; they are not in the *Times*. But the public figures,
the successes in the field, were covered well in our newspaper of record.

The patterns of the *Times* reports are varied. They can be divided according to two criteria: the extent of the coverage, and its nature. The first criterion, the extent of the coverage, would seem straightforward. The arrival
of famous émigré composers and writers on music represented by major
American publishers, and of performers who had regularly toured in this
country and were backed by powerful managers or institutions, would be
covered thoroughly; the arrival of musicians familiar mostly to the narrower
professional musical community would be covered briefly; and those who
were little known here would not be covered at all. That is generally what
we find. The arrivals of Schoenberg,[32] Klemperer, Lotte Lehmann, Jaromir
Weinberger, Darius Milhaud, and Ignace Paderewski received thorough
coverage.

Among those whose arrivals as émigrés were not reported in the *Times*
were Rudolph Benatzky, Paul Dessau, Hanns Eisler, Max Graf, Ernst Krenek, Artur Schnabel, George Szell, Bruno Walter, and Kurt Weill. Most of
them were well known in the American musical community; the absence of
an arrival notice had to do with the circumstances of their arrivals. For example, Walter's regular visits were well covered; the *Times* could not be expected to know which of them would result in immigration. Szell had developed a promising career in Europe, first at the Berlin State Opera and
Hochschule für Musik, then as general music director of the New German
Theater and Czech Philharmonic Orchestra in Prague, before his appointment as conductor of the Scottish National Orchestra in 1937. His reputation in the United States was modest, his conducting experience here limited. He had stopped over in New York on his way back to Scotland after a
summer tour of Australia as director of the Celebrity Concerts of the Aus-
tralian Broadcasting Commission when war broke out. Shortly afterward his
orchestra was disbanded, and he decided to remain in the United States.
There had been no tour, no planned immigration for the *Times* to cover.
He was first mentioned in its pages in 1941, and only with his engagement
by the Metropolitan Opera did he figure significantly in the newspaper (21
and 27 September 1942 and thereafter).

The second criterion, the nature of the coverage, can be divided into several categories: (1) reports of departures from Europe or arrivals in America as émigrés; (2) announcements of appointments to academic or musical positions; (3) announcements of appointments to administrative positions; (4) reports of arrivals for visits; (5) announcements of musical performances, recital series, or tours; and (6) reviews of musical performances. The reports do not always fit the classifications neatly. The story on 11 October 1933 reporting Klemperer's flight from Germany and arrival in New York, for instance, also covered his dismissal from the Berlin State Opera, flight from Germany, and appointment to the conductorship of the Los Angeles Philharmonic Orchestra; since his arrival in the United States was the occasion for the report, I include it in the first classification. An earlier story, published on 17 June 1933, focused on the Los Angeles appointment, however, and so belongs in the second classification. The fourth classification is problematic; entries assigned to it must be checked closely against other reports and documents. The announcements and reviews in the fifth and sixth categories range from recognition that a performance was the first public American appearance of an emigrant musician to silence on the subject. Performances announced beforehand and reviewed afterward appear in the fifth classification.

1. REPORTS OF DEPARTURES FROM EUROPE OR ARRIVALS IN THE UNITED STATES AS ÉMIGRÉS

The arrivals of three émigrés were reported in the fall of 1933: Erich von Hornbostel in September,[33] Klemperer in October,[34] and Schoenberg in November.[35] Lehmann's immigration after fleeing Austria following the Anschluß was reported in August 1938,[36] Peter Herman Adler's after fleeing occupied Czechoslovakia, in April 1939,[37] and Robert Stolz's a year later.[38] The report on Adler's arrival was unusually succinct and straightforward: Adler asserted that he was a refugee and planned to settle in the United States, having fled Germany when Hitler assumed power there. Stolz, in contrast, insisted that he was not a refugee.

Six who came to America after the fall of France in spring 1940 were covered: Milhaud in July,[39] Oskar Straus in October and November,[40] Paderewski and Nadia Boulanger in November,[41] Bohuslav Martinů; in February 1941,[42] and Wanda Landowska that December.[43] Milhaud's arrival was noted in a piece on the docking of the American Export liner *Excambion*. On his way to Mills College, he confined his remarks to his opera *Medée* and the other members of Les Six, and in an interview with Downes spoke confidently of his future in America.[44] The *Excambion* also brought Paderewski and Boulanger to the United States. Paderewski, identified as a pianist but speaking as a statesman, issued a prepared statement pleading for American intervention in Europe, while Boulanger cautiously declared her loyalty to Marshal Pétain and insisted that "obedience and discipline are necessary," adding cryptically that they had to be "freely chosen and not imposed." The Martinů; and Landowska entries are more personal than most, the former referring to the composer's sudden and "dramatic flight from Paris" to Aix-en-Provence, part of it on foot, the latter to the harpsi-chordist's terrible losses.

A variant of these reports comprised articles on application for citizen-ship, for example those on Lehmann in September 1938,[45] the opera con-ductor Frederic Zweig in flight from France in May 1940,[46] and Szell in July 1941.[47] Another variant is the article on Weinberger, based on an interview given a few days after his arrival in late January 1939.[48] It presents his so-journ as a visit, his first to America in more than ten years. Although the word "visit" could be used to slip out of its meaning as a short stay or so-journ, the interview does not mislead. Cut off from royalties from his sensa-tionally successful opera *Schwanda* and other music because his publisher was German, and with his music banned in Nazi Europe, the Jewish Czech composer could no longer live off the earnings of his music, and after a failed year of exile in Paris he had come here to start over. He set his sights on a symphony on the life of Lincoln—his *Eroica*. While he would produce the *Lincoln* Symphony in 1941 and many other works in America, especially for synagogues, churches, and schools, his sad exile marked an inexorable decline of a once promising career. Following his suicide in St. Petersburg, Florida, in 1967, the *Times* obituary reported simply: "Jaromir Weinberger, the composer of the opera 'Schwanda, der Dudelsackpfeifer,' died in his home here on Tuesday night at the age of 71. The police listed the possible cause of death as an overdose of pills."[49]

2. ANNOUNCEMENTS OF APPOINTMENTS TO ACADEMIC OR MUSICAL POSITIONS

Like the first class of reports, this one includes straightforward and reliable documents of the arrivals of émigrés, which must have been brought to the attention of the *Times* by the institutions or organizations involved in the appointments. Subjects of these reports were Klemperer at the Los An-geles Philharmonic, in June 1933;[50] Hornbostel at the University in Exile of the New School for Social Research,[51] Schoenberg at the Malkin Conserva-tory,[52] and Hugo Leichtentritt at Harvard, all in September 1933;[53] Ernst Toch at the New School for Social Research one year later;[54] Sachs at New York University in June 1937;[55] Fritz Stiedry at the New Friends of Music in March 1938;[56] William Steinberg at the NBC Orchestra the following month;[57] Rudolf Serkin at the Curtis Institute of Music in February 1939;[58]

Alfred Einstein at Smith College that April;[59] Igor Stravinsky at Harvard that October;[60] Walter Olitzki at the Metropolitan Opera that November;[61] Hindemith at Buffalo, Cornell, and Wells College in February 1940;[62] Milhaud at Mills College that July;[63] and Karl Geiringer at Hamilton College that November.[64]

In Einstein's case, the arrival notice in early February 1939 was the announcement not of his Smith position, but of his having brought to America five middle-period Haydn symphonies that he had "exhumed and edited" and that were to be performed by the Orchestra of the New Friends of Music under Stiedry. He received a short biography:

> Dr. Einstein, a distant relative and close friend of Professor Albert Einstein, was the music critic of the recently discontinued Berliner Tageblatt in the pre-Nazi days in Germany. He is a distinguished musicologist and has written and edited many books and scores. A native of Munich, he has lived since 1933 in London and Florence.[65]

3. ANNOUNCEMENTS OF APPOINTMENTS TO ADMINISTRATIVE POSITIONS

This group constitutes a small but interesting class, all connected with the Metropolitan Opera. The announcement in April 1938 of Felix Wolfes's appointment as assistant conductor there states in a straightforward manner that "as a non-Aryan, [he] found it advisable to leave that country at the start of the present Hitler regime."[66] The report on Maurice Abravanel in September 1936 gives the conductor's recent professional history blandly, in a manner befitting a young man who had dealt so successfully with an exile undertaken almost four years earlier.[67] After getting out of Berlin two weeks after the cancellation of Walter's Leipzig concert, Abravanel had spent a year in Paris as his assistant, Kurt Weill's collaborator, and George Balanchine's music director, then two successful years in Australia. Now he was coming to the Metropolitan Opera on recommendations from Walter and Furtwängler.[68] A third such announcement, that of the appointment of Friedrich Schorr as "vocal adviser of the Wagner department" of the Metropolitan Opera in September 1938, tells nothing, surely because he had been coming from Europe to sing here for fifteen years.[69]

4. REPORTS OF ARRIVALS FOR VISITS

This is an ambiguous class, one difficult to read. Some visits seem to have been only that, although given the deteriorating political climate in Europe, surely none was undertaken without some consideration of preparing for an eventual departure from that continent. Thus at the end of October

1934 the *Times* reported the arrival of Paul Wittgenstein for his first American concert tour, at the conclusion of which he returned to a battered Austria.[70] He emigrated in 1938 and settled permanently in the United States early the following year, and this time the newspaper alerted its readers to his new status in the context of a report on a concert.[71]

In the case of Bruno Walter, the *Times* reported his arrival in early March 1939 for a five-week concert series with the NBC Orchestra, the series itself, and notice of his return to Europe on 15 April to open the opera season at Covent Garden and go on to The Hague, Paris, and Lucerne.[72] When the *Times* reported his return to the United States in February 1940, it would have been simply another visit by the peripatetic conductor had the German invasion of France that May not turned Walter's stay in America into a permanent exile.[73]

Other visits turned out to be long-term or permanent. Erich Wolfgang Korngold shared the 31 October 1934 *Times* article with Wittgenstein. Here from Austria, like the one-armed pianist, for his first visit, he had come to discuss a new opera for the Metropolitan Opera and a Max Reinhardt production for Hollywood. Unlike Wittgenstein, Korngold remained in the United States, although he returned to Austria each summer, and was in Vienna during the winter of 1938; but circumstances that he called miraculous brought him back to America just before the Anschluß, and he remained here until after the war's end.[74] When the seventy-three-year-old pianist Moriz Rosenthal arrived on the French liner *Normandie* in November 1936, the *Times* noted only that he had been away for seven years, and that this was his tenth visit.[75] In fact, his stay was to be permanent.

A third such visitor was Kurt Weill, who, having fled Berlin for Paris in March 1933, arrived with Lotte Lenya aboard the SS *Majestic* in New York on 10 September 1935 to prepare for the production of Franz Werfel's *The Eternal Road,* for which he was composing the music. He never returned to Europe. Instead, in August 1937 he went briefly to Canada so that he could reenter the United States on an immigrant visa, and crossed over the border into Buffalo as an immigrant on 27 August.[76]

Some visits were exploratory, among them Béla Bartók's in spring 1940, his first trip to the United States in twelve years.[77] The *Times* covered it thoroughly. On 14 April Howard Taubman had reported on a chamber music concert given by Bartók and Joseph Szigeti at the Library of Congress under the headline "Bela Bartok Plays Own Compositions." He opened his review with the encomium, "Bela Bartok, who has not been in this country for more than a decade, was the bright adornment of this morning's concert, the second in the ninth festival of chamber music being presented here by the Elizabeth Sprague Coolidge Foundation," and went on to describe the composer:

Mr. Bartok, a frail little man with a sharp, tense face, proved to be an accomplished pianist. Aside from an occasional swollen tone—probably because he underestimated the carrying qualities and the excellent acoustics of the auditorium—he played with a musician's imagination. It may be assumed that he knew just what he wanted in his own compositions. Mr. Szigeti, who was at the top of his form, gave Mr. Bartok's music vibrant interpretations as if a measure of his affection for the gray, straight, little man beside him heightened his usual concentration.[78]

A week later, a caption under a large portrait of the composer announced that he would perform at a concert of his music presented by the League of Composers at the Museum of Modern Art, and Olin Downes reviewed the concert.[79] In early May the *Times* published an extended appreciation of Bartók by the young Hungarian émigré scholar Otto Gombosi,[80] and on 19 May his picture appeared again in conjunction with an article on the sailing of the American liner *Manhattan* for Italy; the caption read, "Professor Bela Bartok, Hungarian composer, also sailed on the Manhattan after participating in several concerts here." Although the *Times* did not cover his arrival in New York as a permanent immigrant on 30 October of that year, it announced his Town Hall concert with the New Friends of Music four days later and then reviewed it,[81] and went on to cover his remaining years in America richly.

In the case of Krenek, the *Times* caught the end of a visit, not its start. Krenek had arrived in New York on 17 October 1937 for a cross-country tour with a company called the Salzburg Opera Guild,[82] founded and led by the Hungarian opera director and conductor Paul Czonka, on whose commission he had adapted and abridged Monteverdi's *Coronation of Poppea*. Krenek had come along because Sol Hurok, the guild's American manager, had insisted that as the only recognized name in the group he accompany it for public relations purposes; the cover was that he would oversee performances of the opera. During the California segment of the cross-country tour he was enchanted by Los Angeles and comfortable in its émigré community, and saw it as a possible domicile. At the end of February, back in New York preparing to return to Europe, he was given a tribute by the League of Composers, and it was that event that the *Times* covered.[83] He embarked for the trip home from New York on 2 March 1938, and while in Brussels on the day of the Anschluß he decided to emigrate. On the strength of affidavits from Carl Engel, president of the music publisher G. Schirmer, and Mark Brunswick, an American composer who had lived in Vienna for most of the 1930s and in 1938 became chairman of the National Committee for Refugee Musicians,[84] he and his wife acquired visas on 12 May, sailed to Montreal in mid-August, and entered the United States on 29 August, where they settled for a few weeks in New Hampshire before moving to Boston so that he could assume his teaching appointment at the Malkin Conservatory.[85] No doubt the *Times* missed his immigration because it took place not in the usual manner, with him disembarking from a boat in New York harbor, but rather at a remote border crossing somewhere between Montreal and the New Hampshire village that was his immediate American destination.

One *Times* story did not indicate any reason at all for the arrival in question, though in fact it was for the purpose of settling in the United States. Hidden away toward the end of a report (with a headline beginning "New Zoo Inmates Here from Africa") of the docking on 6 September 1940 of the liner *City of New York,* with fifty-three human passengers, fifty snakes, ten antelopes, three zebras, two cranes, and one Cape buffalo, was mention of Bronislaw Huberman. The violinist gave the reporter an interview that seems to have focused on his dream of a federal Europe, a dream that he acknowledged as "remote and even fantastic under present circumstances" but one about which he remained "not pessimistic."[86] He must have had a stout heart.

5. ANNOUNCEMENTS OF MUSICAL PERFORMANCES, RECITAL SERIES, OR TOURS

Brief and dry, these announcements were almost invariably nothing more than captions accompanying a photograph. They were often, though not always, followed by a review of the performance or the first recital of the projected series or tour. They signaled the arrival of Erich Leinsdorf in January 1938,[87] Alice Ehlers[88] and Gisa Bergmann in May,[89] Nikolai and Joanna Graudan that December,[90] Adolf Busch in February 1939,[91] Mario Castelnuovo-Tedesco in September,[92] the Budapest String Quartet a month later,[93] Robert Goldsand in April 1940,[94] and Emmerich Kalman in February 1941,[95] among others. They told nothing of the larger purpose usually underlying the concerts or recitals, which was to introduce the New York audience to a musician about to settle in the United States—though when a musician or ensemble was already well known in America, as was the case with the Budapest Quartet, Elisabeth Schumann,[96] and Artur Schnabel,[97] the concert served no such purpose.

In the case of Schnabel, in fact, the *Times* announcement, the first since his permanent settlement in the United States, came more than six months after his arrival as an immigrant. An Austrian citizen, he was in Berlin at the time of Hitler's accession to power. He lingered in the German capital in order to complete a seven-recital traversal of the Beethoven sonatas he had begun the previous November. On 29 April, the day after the last recital, he left Germany permanently, making his home now in Italy. His career continued to flourish; the center of its gravity merely shifted westward and across the Atlantic. He was in St. Louis on an American tour in March

1938, when the German annexation of Austria deprived him of his citizenship. On reaching New York, he began to plan his immigration to America. Because of complications in both the American quota system and his professional schedule, however, he did not arrive as a petitioning immigrant with resident alien status until February 1939. After a tour of Australia and New Zealand that spring and summer, he returned to the United States via Honolulu on 2 September, the day after the German invasion of Poland. "After September 1939 I did not leave the United States again. In the meantime, we all became American citizens."[98] The *Times* thus missed his arrival as a permanent U.S. resident, as it did most of the arrivals of those who did not pass through New York, and its notices of him in March 1940 dealt only with his first concert appearance, not with his immigration.

One recital announcement, that for Egon Petri in January 1940, told the story of the pianist's recent life, his dramatic last-minute flight from Poland, the abandonment of his home, library, and career in Cracow, and his uncertain status in the United States. That summer, he would settle in Ithaca and teach at Cornell.[99]

6. REVIEWS OF MUSICAL PERFORMANCES

Reviews signaled the arrival of the Kolisch Quartet in April 1935,[100] Vronsky and Babin in February 1937,[101] Felix Wolfes[102] and Eduard Steuermann in April 1938,[103] Emanuel Feuermann that October,[104] Elisabeth Schumann a month later,[105] Paul Wittgenstein in March 1939,[106] Alexander Kipnis and Jarmila Novotna in January 1940,[107] and Artur Schnabel that March.[108]

These six classes of entries range from the straightforward through varying levels of suggestiveness, including silence. Only a quarter of the entries, as we have noted, give the fact of an émigré's arrival directly. For the rest, and for those whose immigration received no mention at all, we can posit many reasons. The *Times* could depend on the major wire services only for the most famous émigrés, had a limited number of reporters to cover the arrival of others, and relied on agents, managers, publishers, and institutions to bring news of their clients and employees to its attention. It could not be expected to cover émigrés who slipped quietly through New York on their way to other destinations or, like Krenek and Schnabel, arrived in the United States through some other point of entry. Many émigrés, for their part, had reasons for not bringing attention to their arrival. Some, no doubt, hid the intention to immigrate for reasons similar to those noted in the report on Hornbostel dated 2 September 1933, in which six scholars hired by the New School for Social Research withheld their names from public view so that they might "wind up their affairs in Germany and . . . take such precautions as were necessary for the protection of their friends and relatives pending their official acceptance of their posts in this country." Some may have had problems with their legal papers. Many had family and friends at home to protect. Most lacked the business or institutional connections to prepare the ground for their arrival. Few had certain plans or firm offers of long-term employment. Among those who arrived in the early 1930s, some entertained the hope that the madness would contain itself, perhaps even end, and they could return. After passage of the Nuremberg Laws that hope became far more difficult to entertain; in the panic attendant on the terrible events of 1938 it vanished. All these emigrants had to feed, house, and clothe themselves and their families; those who had left property behind would have to return to Europe if they wished to claim it.[109] Many of them, such as Darius Milhaud, wanted to put the entire matter behind them. None wanted to appear as a helpless refugee, stripped of dignity and worth, victim of forces beyond rational comprehension; for the vast majority who were German or Austrian, robbed of their national identity, having their citizenship revoked and suffering humiliation and expulsion at the hands of their fellow countrymen must have been trauma enough.

While the *New York Times* covered the immigration richly, it rarely addressed the impact of the émigrés on musical life in this country. An article on performance in the summer of 1938 reported on the efforts of an unnamed artists' manager to place émigré conductors: having identified cities and towns that lacked orchestras, he wrote asking whether those communities had musicians, whether those musicians would want to create orchestras from among their number, whether the communities would support concerts, and whether they could raise the money to hire a conductor. The responses had, according to the *Times* article, so far been encouraging.[110]

Two articles on musicology are noteworthy. One of them, by David Ewen on 8 September 1940, introduced readers of the *Times* to Einstein, Leichtentritt, Nettl, Paul Pisk, Sachs, and, more briefly, to the composer-teachers: Krenek at Vassar, Karol Rathaus at Queens College, Toch at the University of Southern California, and Milhaud at Mills College. These men would be vital to the development of a generation of American musical scholars and to the creation of an American musicology "destined to achieve new and unparalleled significance." Whatever their mother tongue, they were starting to write in English, and through their work and influence, one day the English language would become "the favored tongue of musicology."[111]

A year and a half later, in May 1942, Einstein introduced the subject of musicology to *Times* readers, giving its dictionary definition, explaining that its concern is "with the understanding of music as a function of life, as related to the culture of its time," and tracing its bloodline from eighteenth-century Europe, then placing it squarely in the Anglo-Saxon democracies of the twentieth century:

> But when the Library of Congress built its tremendous wing for old and new music, when the unforgettable O. G. Sonneck, Otto Kinkeldey, Carl Engel and others, published their first articles and books, musicology had found a home in the United States. Since then many other good names, American and foreign, have been added to those mentioned above. For America, besides England, is now the refuge for free and true research—untainted by racism, nationalism, by fear or toadying to the government—in musicology as in other fields.[112]

Fascinating articles on the subject of émigré adaptation, opportunities, and influence—on the place the émigré would be given by his colleagues in the land of his exile and possible adoption—are clustered in a four-week period in January and February 1941. The exchange was set off by a request by Howard Hanson, a leader in the musical establishment and director of the Eastman School of Music, to use Downes's column, "Music of the Times," to air an issue that had arisen at the annual convention of the National Association of Schools of Music. Downes consented, and in his first column devoted to the subject he published Hanson's letter, quoted from a letter from Guy Maier and from Maier's recent column in *Etude,* and referred at length to a letter from Roger Sessions.[113] Downes introduced the issue:

> Several letters received within a few hours of each other from American musicians of prominence show the concern the writers feel at one of the gravest problems of adjustment which has confronted the American musical community. It is the problem of the refugee musician from overseas and the place that he takes among his colleagues in the land of his adoption.

Hanson argued that Americans had the twofold duty of assuming responsibility for the "creative musical development" that had been abandoned in much of Europe, and at the same time of encouraging the "musical creative processes" at home. These tasks, he insisted, were "in one sense mutually inclusive, while at the same time in the working out of details they may be mutually conflicting." The émigrés should be given not only asylum, but also opportunities to work and to have their music performed. It was in the American tradition to do so. Beyond that, their assimilation would enrich America's cultural life. However, he warned,

> we must not solve the problem of providing opportunities for our foreign guests by curtailing the already meager opportunities for the young American. There is some evidence that exactly this situation is occurring. This is particularly unfortunate at the present time when American music is showing enormous vitality. It is also particularly unfair at a time when we are asking

young Americans to assume important responsibilities, and in some cases to make definite sacrifices for the welfare of their country. . . . [The problem] must be solved . . . by an increase of opportunity for greater artistic productivity. It must not be solved at the expense of the native American.

Maier railed against what he called the "marked preference" given the foreign musician for no apparent reason other than that he was foreign:

We have carried him on our shoulders, we have glamored him, we have enriched him—and how! Now as a result of the tragic world conditions, we have five hundred foreign pianists, violinists, conductors, musicologists, instead of fifty. The half dozen truly great musical personalities do not concern us. They are not only welcome but are necessary for our inspiration and development. But what of the other hundreds of lesser lights, the not so great who menace our own young artists, many of them not so able or so well equipped as the native product? Shall we stir up prejudice against them, shall we prevent them from earning an honest living? Not at all. By all means give them their chance. But in considering their problem we must not deprive our own young Americans of their rightful chance. For once, let's give our talent a square deal, let's put the matter on a fifty-fifty basis.

While Hanson used lofty language to avoid dealing squarely with the challenge of balancing the demands of Americans and refugees, Maier injected venom by describing refugees as "non-Americans or Americans of such recent vintage that only in the letter, not the spirit, can they be called citizens"; complaining that universities were "training dozens of American musicologists only to give away their jobs to foreigners"; and comparing "honest-to-goodness American[s]" with hapless aliens who could not speak or understand English, refused to adopt American values, and scorned American musical training.

Downes, declining to quote from Sessions's letter on the grounds that it is "too long to include here," characterized it as "a strong protest" against Maier's position and noted that it appealed to America's tradition of hospitality; it "opposes," he said, "preference being given Americans, on nationalist grounds, in matters of art, and disapproves of such expression as might increase rather than decrease misunderstandings arising from the present situation, as being against the very spirit of the artist and the beauty that he tries to communicate, regardless of political or social or economic barriers, in his art." Patently uncomfortable with the staking out of these positions and the seeming impossibility of reconciling them, Downes suggested that Maier probably agreed with the principles Sessions espoused, "but sees their practical working out in a different proportion." Most refugees, he surmised, wanted to integrate themselves into this nation and were grateful for whatever work they might find for whatever pay—a fact that, ironically, threatened American workers. Urging against ill will and flag-waving by

American-borns and underselling of the market by refugees, he limped to his anodyne conclusion that "Americans must guard their artists—and not be un-American!"

Downes's column elicited so many letters that the following week he was reduced to excerpting paragraphs from the longer ones.[114] In the 26 January column, under pressure from H. S. Pinson of Queens College, he quoted at length from the Sessions letter that he had paraphrased the week before. Its language is so strong that one cannot imagine how Downes could have reconciled its principles with Maier's argument. Sessions had attacked Maier's position passionately on both moral and musical grounds:

> For many years the undersigned has noted with concern a movement among certain musicians and "music lovers" towards a kind of chauvinism which is neither musical nor American. This trend of thought, in its most vicious form, has recently been brought to his attention in the form of an article by Guy Maier, which appeared in last month's Etude. Mr. Maier whines once more that the American is neglected in favor of his foreign colleague, aided and abetted often by the latter's government; that owing to insidious prejudice and policy he does not stand even an "equal chance" with the foreigner. He takes a fling at "refugee" musicians who, he intimates, should in most cases not have come here, being, he writes, "not regarded as undesirables" in their homelands.

Then Sessions took his own cheap shots. American musicians valued the personal too greatly, the professional too little, confusing intention with achievement. Such standards worked against the refugee, who was better trained than his native-born counterpart. He established a straw man of "master craftsman," then compared him invidiously to the "artist":

> If an American composer . . . can write counterpoint fairly correctly, or can put together a playable orchestra score, he may easily find himself hailed as a master craftsman—a title which itself is hardly a matter of credit, since it is the minimum to be expected of a serious artist. If he shows the rudiments of originality or even expresses a striking intention, he is heard very seriously and given every benefit of the doubt; with some luck he will be written up in our musical magazines with solemn sentences and neat phrases regarding his "style."

What applied to composers applied equally to performers and teachers. Sessions knew many foreigners denied positions or engagements simply because they were foreign. It was "only natural" that American musicians would try to keep at bay Europeans

> possessed of the inevitable advantages which result from the more intensive routine, the greater abundance of musical activity, and the security of an older tradition, which prevailed until recent years almost everywhere in Europe. It

is natural that such a state of affairs should aggravate the hypersensitivity of that large class of American musicians who already for years have nourished a feeling of inferiority and the self-pity that goes with it.

If the occasional foreigner who saw himself as "a prophet in the cultural wilderness" refused to adapt to America—invariably a second-rate foreigner—Americans who appealed to "blood and soil" and feared free exchange and open competition posed a far more serious problem. The United States, after all, was built largely by refugees. Americanism is "a dream of a society somehow better than any yet achieved on earth, and . . . the true patriotism is fidelity to that dream, wherever it may lead."

Sessions's abridged letter was followed by several others, all written in the period 19–21 January, that is, within three days of the publication of Downes's first column on the subject. A Norwegian immigrant living in Brooklyn, a carpenter who cared enough about music to have read the column, had experienced "the loneliness and the degradation of immigrant life" yet felt he had to reconcile himself to "a humdrum life" in return for being permitted to begin life anew here. Nevertheless, he argued that

> we hear entirely too much about the artistic and other contribution which the refugees are going to make, are making. But if this country is to develop an indigenous art (is that the word for it?) this art must not get into the hands of newly arrived refugees; it must not even be dominated by second-generation foreigners.

One Arthur Austin vented his frustration with the policies of two government-supported organizations, the National Youth Administration (NYA) and the Works Project Administration (WPA):

> Here in New York City the NYA Radio Work Shop Symphony Orchestra is conducted by a "citizen" of some four years. The New York City Music Project is currently running a series of concerts in Carnegie Hall conducted by another such person. Last Summer a man whose speech could hardly be understood was brought from a WPA project in California to conduct a series of concerts with the New York City Project orchestras. All the time young American conductors are at their wits' ends attempting to get even a "guest," no pay, appearance with a United States Government supported orchestra.

That attitude, evident also at the Lewisohn Stadium concerts and the Metropolitan Opera, was unfair, Austin asserted, not only to native conductors but also to native composers, whose music was ignored in favor of that of "Bruckner, Mahler, and other assorted 'alien corn.' If we must have 'corn,' let it be American!"

Lazare Saminsky, a composer of Jewish liturgical music, founding director of the League of Composers, and director of music at Temple Emanu-El in New York City, challenged Maier's suggestion that restrictions be placed on naturalized citizens. Saminsky carefully identified himself as an immigrant, not a refugee, who had lived in the United States for more than twenty years. His experience was the opposite of Maier's (and Austin's):

> As to the refugee musicians overwhelming our musical labor, I do not know how much Mr. Maier's position permits him to see. My own forces me to observe and to deal with a triple stream of refugee musicians, composers, singers, organists. And this is what, as a rule, they get out of musical life here:
>
> A first-rate composer and former conductor of a famous opera house in Europe has lived for two years here, on a few dollars earned from teaching piano.
>
> An operatic prima donna and brilliant musician, no more than 34, is forced, after three years' [*sic*] of abject want, to a scanty livlihood [*sic*] by bookbinding and other and lower paid work.
>
> I know excellent soloists, cantors, men who have occupied fine positions abroad who are given nothing better than washing dishes in restaurants.
>
> It is this valuable kind of musician which Mr. Maier's lament may, perhaps, help to restrict and prevent finding employment useful to the nation—not the clever and pushing mediocrities with strong elbows who have broken their way to a few positions.
>
> Finally, there was a brief letter from an American-born and -trained musician, who found all positions closed to him, and had been told in two or three instances that under ordinary circumstances I could easily be placed in my rightful position as an artist, but the "refugee" situation has made it impossible. Others have even been unwilling to grant me an interview. . . .
>
> Perhaps there is some hope of an adjustment whereby the refugee musicians may await their turn instead of forcing out the American artists.
>
> In the final analysis of the situation, the Americans deserve first consideration, and then we shall be very happy to help the refugee musicians.

The following week, on 2 February, Downes spoke his mind.[115] There was more than one side to the subject, and it had generated both misunderstanding and misinformation. The central issue, he stated in his lumbering English, was "whether America can protect her cultural identity and the expression of her own spirit in her music, in the years before us, and in spite of foreign artistic ideas, weakening to creative development, from the Old World." American musicians lacked technique and experience, skill and tradition. A commercial environment denied them the time to grow. As a result, American composers failed to reflect their society, their music failed to express their national identity:

> Not all the refugees in the world can overwhelm the spirit of a native expression if it once takes form among us. This must be if we are to reflect in tones the spirit born of fresh and great traditions and the strength of our soil, and the temper of a young people with the power, if we can understand it, to unfold new horizons and to take part in the re-shaping of the world.

On the same page as Downes's column, the *Times* printed a letter dated 26 January from Horace Johnson, director of the New York City WPA Music Project, rebuking Austin, who, far from being the victim of prejudice toward nonnatives, had himself benefited from government largesse:

> Mr. Austin has officiated as a guest conductor and also as a permanent payroll conductor with the New York City WPA Music Project during the past three years. He was auditioned in June, 1937, and subsequently had ten performances as guest conductor of three of our major units—one orchestra and two bands. Because of the excellent work that he did with us, he was assigned to our payroll on May 2, 1939, and conducted many concerts of the Opera Chorus during the period when it gave concerts in and about the five boroughs of New York City and at the World's Fair. Mr. Austin resigned from the project on Sept. 22, 1939, to accept a position as conductor of Princeton University Band.

Nor, Johnson pointed out, was Austin alone as an American-born guest conductor in the program. In the previous two years the New York City project had had forty other American-born conductors lead ninety-two performances. Furthermore, native-born Americans were permanent conductors of three of its five orchestras and bands, while the other two permanent conductors had been citizens for more than a decade. Native-born musicians, citizens, and those holding first citizenship papers could apply on an equal footing to appear with any of the project's musical groups, and would be auditioned before a strictly impartial board.[116]

Two more letters appeared on 9 February. The first, from Stanley L. Stevens, director of the NYA Radio Workshop, asserted that every citizen was entitled to equal consideration by the workshop; the sole standard in hiring staff members was technical and supervisory ability. Fritz Mahler, whom Stevens identified carefully as "an American citizen,"[117] had done more in the twelve weeks he had led the NYA Symphony Orchestra to advance American composers and music than any organization in the nation during the same period: among those whose music he supported, some with world premieres, were Henry Brant, Aaron Copland, Henry Cowell, Paul Creston, Roy Harris, Frederick Jacobi, Oscar Levant, Daniel Gregory Mason, Douglas Moore, Earl Robinson, Albert Stoessel, and Virgil Thomson. A forthcoming gala concert at the Brooklyn Museum to be given on 22 February, capping ten days of the Second Annual American Music Festival broadcast on radio station WNYC, would be offering first performances of works by five native-born American composers.

The second letter published on 9 February was from a student of Hindemith's at Tanglewood the previous summer, Robert Strassburg, attesting to Hindemith's encouragement of his American students. The great lesson he taught, Strassburg wrote, was

Be true to yourselves! If your talent is such that you can only draw from your inner being simple and undistinguished music, then that unpretentious music is more honest and truly spoken than if you tried to assume the technical and musical mannerisms of a Stravinsky, a Bartók or a Hindemith. The usages of these artists arise from an inner necessity.

The American composer who lagged behind his colleagues in the other arts and literature did so because he lacked insight into his art and knowledge of his nation's folk music. The sooner he absorbed it, "the sooner will we arrive at a distinctive art unfolding new horizons."[118]

The following Sunday saw the skewering of the unfortunate Strassburg by David Diamond, writing from Yaddo in Saratoga Springs.[119] If Strassburg's paraphrase of Hindemith's "great lesson" was accurate, it reflected little glory on Hindemith and less on Strassburg. Surely, though, Hindemith could not have offered such a lesson. In any case,

> there is a very dangerous and non-creative tendency on the part of young Americans studying with European musicians to swallow, hook, line and sinker, all the philosophical and theoretical dogma with a kind of stoic insensibility. A genuine creative talent does not have to be warned of mannerisms. It instinctively creates an intelligent method which warrants clarity as well as an integrated musical speech. Today, as in the past, the composer who develops his craft most completely will not trouble himself with the danger of mannerisms, but will rebuff pontifical authority in teaching, above all.

A second letter that week, from George Newton, a voice teacher in Indianapolis, offered a practical suggestion in dealing with the challenge of the refugee musicians:[120]

> The more these people can be scattered over the country the more quickly will they be absorbed. No one will deny that. The most efficient way of doing that is to find or, if necessary, form an organization which can make contact with smaller communities to discover whether they are lacking competent musical instruction of one sort or another. It would seem that the local chamber of commerce, or Rotary, or some other similar group, could be interested in such a project and could be induced to invite, and stand sponsor for, a musician who would not be competing with any one already established. . . . I know of no organization of teachers equipped to carry out such work, but surely there is some group which would be willing to lend a hand to these strangers and thereby help ourselves. Possibly the ladies with their many clubs could be interested. As a last resort, there are one or two government agencies which might help.
>
> From my own experience . . . I can say that many towns in Indiana need vocal instructors. I do not refer to those in which the teaching is mediocre or worse, but to those in which there is no professional singer or teacher. I have many students who must come from as far away as fifty miles for their lessons. . . .

I do not pretend that success would be easy for any one in such a place, or that many of the refugees are not deserving of better places; but I do say that it would provide a home and an opportunity better than that afforded their cousins who have been coming to our country for the past century. If, by reason of superior skill, they could move into more important circles, they would be progressing, not as refugees, but as Americans.

After Maier's mean-spirited frustration, Sessions's indifference, Downes's placebos, Austin's self-serving complaints, and Strassburg's abject hero-worship, Newton's thoughtful letter seems, almost fifty-five years later, a breath of fresh air. It led nowhere, however, for with it the exchange in the *Times* petered out. The refugees' reception and adjustment would play itself out neither on the pages of the nation's newspapers and magazines nor within the framework of grand social strategies and government programs, but in the community and the workplace, in a thousand individual dramas of adaptation, success, and failure, some leaving indelible marks on American culture, others relegated to footnotes, archives, and attics.

APPENDIX

Headlines of Uncited Articles on Music in Nazi Europe in the New York Times, *1933–38, in Chronological Order*

"Nazis Hunt Arms in [Albert] Einstein Home; Only a Bread Knife Rewards Brown Shirts' Search for Alleged Huge Cache. Ousting of Jews Goes On; Physicians Are Removed from Hospitals and Judges from the Criminal Courts. Bruno Walter Departs; Philharmonic Conductor Cancels Frankfurt Concert—Will Return Here in Fall," 21 Mar. 1933, 10.

"Hail French Conductor. Berliners Acclaim Monteux, Replacing Walter, Who Was Banned," 6 Apr. 1933, 9.

"Wagner's Birthday Celebrated by Nazis; Composer's 'Fight' against 'All the World for German Culture' Noted at Baireuth," 23 May 1933, 22.

"Toscanini Refuses to Go to Baireuth; Won't Conduct at Wagnerian Festival Because of Persecution of Jews. Athletes Also Protest; 20 Olympic Champions Here Ask Committee to Bar 1936 Games from Berlin," 6 June 1933, 1.

"Snub by Toscanini Worries Germans; Refusal to Conduct Festival Brings Realization of Force of World Condemnation. Radio Ban on Him Ended; Barring of His Works from the Air Laid to False Report Anti-Nazi Protest," 8 June 1933, 8.

"Germany's Nationalistic Revival; Pfitzner, Attacking Verdi as 'Insipid,' Advocates Operas of Marschner, Lortzing and Bruch," 18 June 1933, 8:4.

"Hitler Provides Audience for Baireuth Music Fete," 11 July 1933, 15.

"Kreisler Is Firm on Reich Concerts; Says He Will Refuse to Appear Until Deeds Follow Pledge of Artistic Freedom. Receives Many Offers; But Rejects Them Till Musicians Are Not Only Tolerated but Welcome, Regardless of Faith," 21 July 1933, 5.

"Wagner Festival in Baireuth Today; Chancellor Hitler Expected to Attend Lavish Production of 'Die Meistersinger.' Town Is Much Changed; Festspielhaus Has Been Newly Decorated—Nazis Due to Take Part in Ceremonies," 21 July 1933, 20.

"Musicians Rebuff Reich. Furtwaengler Gets Refusals by Artists to Perform in Germany," 2 Aug. 1933, 6.

"Refugee Singers Meet in Salzburg; 'Non-Aryan' and 'Semi-Aryan' of Nazi Code Find Haven in Austrian Music Centre. Agents Bid for Services; Lotte Schoene, Ousted from State Opera in Berlin, Wins New Laurels as an Exile," 6 Aug. 1933, 2:1.

"Nazis Fear Press on Salzburg Fete; Journalists Had Gathered from All Over World, Anticipating Overt Acts. Protest Talk Effective; Hitlerites Now Make Artists from Germany Break Their Contracts at the Last Moment," 7 Aug. 1933, 5.

"Festival at Baireuth; Mediocrity of Performances—Attempt to Identify Wagner with the Nazis," 13 Aug. 1933, 9:4.

"Hubermann [*sic*] Bars German Concerts; Violinist Rejects an Appeal by Furtwaengler to Play with Berlin Philharmonic Again. Stresses Nazi Race Bias; Declares That the Elementary Preconditions of European Culture Are at Stake," 14 Sept. 1933, 11.

"[Werner] Janssen Refuses to Conduct in Germany; Displeased Management Warns American," 31 Oct. 1933, 11.

"Nazi Plea Spurned by Violin Prodigy; Yehudi Menuhin, Back from Europe, Tells of Request to Help Pacify Musicians. Balks at Ban on Jews; Warned He Would Be Blamed If German Art 'Goes to Dogs'—Toscanini Also Arrives," 5 Jan. 1934, 10.

"Nazis Coordinate Vaudeville World; All Performers and Employers Are Brought into a League with Circus People," 5 Apr. 1934, 11.

"Klemperer Loses Property in Reich; German Orchestra Conductor, an Exile, Is Accused of Evasion of Taxes. Action Is Laid to Malice; Los Angeles Friends of the Musician, Well Known Here, Cite Previous Acts," 12 July 1934, 4.

"Hitler Expected at Wagner Fete; Due at Baireuth for Festival Opening Tomorrow—May Be Guest of Frau Wagner. Visit to Aid Tourist Drive; Registered Marks Forbidden for Ship Fares, Germany Now Offers Low Rail Rates," 21 July 1934, 5.

"Baireuth Is Filled by Nazi Troopers; Hitlerites Arrive on Eve of the Wagner Festival to Unveil a Huge Bronze Fist. Theatre's Sales Large; All

Performances Till Aug. 13 Are Said to Be Sold Out, but Visitors Are Fewer," 22 July 1934, 7.

"Hitler Eclipses Opera in Baireuth; Chancellor Centre of Interest at Opening of Festival of Wagner's Works. Crowds Applaud Leader; 'Parsifal' Is Disappointing—New Scenery Less Attractive Than Old Settings," 23 July 1934, 18.

"Nazis Fail to Harm Salzburg Festival; Town Is Quiet and 'Tristan und Isolde' Is Success Despite Reich Ban on Noted Tenor. Strauss Is Kept Away; Composer Is Unable to Attend, Even after Talking with Hitler at Baireuth," 1 August 1934, 2.

"Wagner Today at Baireuth; German Political Interests Dominate Festival—Small Attendance by Foreigners—Elmendorf's 'Meistersinger' Spirited," 19 Aug. 1934, 4.

"Toscanini Declines New Bid to Baireuth; Conductor Is Reported to Have Maintained Decision Not to Appear in Reich," 4 Sept. 1934, 23.

"Hindemith Defended From Nazi Criticism; Furtwaengler Denies Composer Is Jewish and Assails the 'Political Zealots,'" 26 Nov. 1934, 6.

"Hindemith Centre of Nazi Music Row; Furtwaengler Makes Fervent Defense of Composer Who Faces Official Ban. Plea Made in the Press; Conductor in Two-Column Letter Says Attempt to 'Defame' Modernist Is 'a Crime,'" 3 Dec. 1934, 15.

"Dr. Furtwaengler Quits Reich Posts; Resigns All Musical Positions after Storm Raised by His Defense of Hindemith. Kleiber to Follow Him; Conductor Says Two Promised to 'Stick Together' and Now It Is 'Matter of Honor,'" 5 Dec. 1934, 28.

"Kleiber Is Unable to Resign in Reich; Goering Refuses to Permit Opera Musical Head to Quit His Post. Furtwaengler Is Hailed; Withdrawal from Berlin Opera and Orchestra Directorship Causes Wide Approval," 6 Dec. 1934, 27.

"Rebukes Furtwaengler. Goebbels Says Nazism Is Cultural Conscience of Nation," 7 Dec. 1934, 27.

"Nazi Papers Score Dr. Furtwaengler; But the Conductor Is Not Put in Prison Camp—Audience at Opera Calls for Him," 8 Dec. 1934, 18.

"Music in Germany Is Now at Low Ebb; Withdrawal of Furtwaengler Leaves Modern Music with No Defenders. Nazi Standards Supreme; Repudiation of Many Classics Likely—Restrictions Expected for Performing Artists," 9 Dec. 1934, 6.

"German Music Critic [Hans Heinz Stuckenschmidt] Expelled from Post; Championing of Modern Works Called Intolerable—Krauss Leaves Vienna Saturday," 13 Dec. 1934, 25.

"Kleiber Again Resigns Post with Prussian Opera," 2 Jan. 1935, 15.

"Mengelberg Shuns Reich; Conductor Rejects Conditions for Leading Berlin Philharmonic," 7 Feb. 1935, 8.

"Nazis May End Ban on Furtwaengler; Propaganda Minister Says the Orchestra Director Admits Hitler's Control of Art," 1 Mar. 1935, 17.

"Furtwaengler to Direct; He Will Appear in Berlin after Making Peace with Nazis," 18 Apr. 1935, 18.

"Jewish Concert Banned," 28 May 1935, 5.

"Negro Singer [Marian Anderson] Says Nazis Bar Concerts in Austria," 9 July 1935, 24.

"Strauss Resigns from Reich Post; Music Chamber Head Quits after Nazi Opposition to His Jewish Librettist. Issue Split Party Ranks; Composer Lays Action to His 'Advanced Age'—Supplanted in Composers' League Also," 14 July 1935, 11.

"What Next in Berlin? The Resignation of Strauss and Its Possible Effects on Krauss," 4 Aug. 1935, 9:4.

" 'Change' in German Music. Martial Songs Replace Tuneful Old Ballads, Dr. Dykema Reports," 17 Sept. 1935, 25.[121]

"Reich Bars Radio Jazz to Safeguard 'Culture,' " 13 Oct. 1935, 2:3.

"Furtwaengler Drops Mendelssohn Opus; Deletion from Budapest Program Explained on Ground Time for Rehearsal Was Short," 14 Jan. 1936, 25.

"Nazis Said to Curb Opera Conductor; Knappertsbusch of Munich Is Reported to Have Been Deprived of Passport. Has Opposed Hitlerites; Month's Sick Leave Extended—Friends Fear He Will Be Unable to Make Tour," 28 Jan. 1936, 11.

"Year's Leave Set for Furtwaengler; Hitler Relieves Him of Duties as Conductor in Reich and He Will Not Appear Abroad. Nazis Got Him to Resign; Now Regime Wants Him Back at Berlin Opera, but Krauss, Successor, Won't Quit," 3 May 1936, 38.

"Reich Orders Delayed Dramatic Criticism; New Rule Allows a More Rigid Censorship," 14 May 1936, 1.

"Toscanini Bars Salzburg Broadcast to Reich; Refuses to Conduct Unless Plan Is Dropped," 30 July 1936, 23.

" 'German' Text [for *Judas Maccabeus*] Replaces Handel's Biblical One," 24 Oct. 1936, 2.[122]

"Leipzig Nazis Destroy Statue of Mendelssohn," 15 Nov. 1936, 12.

"Items from Foreign Music Field" [on Hans Stieber's arrangement of music from Purcell's *Fairy Queen* to replace Mendelssohn's music for *A Midsummer Night's Dream*], 4 Apr. 1937, 10:6.

"Bar Jewish Music Pupils; German Teachers Told in Decree Not to Instruct Them," 8 Oct. 1937, 6.

"Berlin Outlines Policy for Austria; Sees a Reorganized Central Europe. Gloom Pervades Vienna; Nazis Freed. Toscanini Breaks with Salzburg Because of Nazi Victory in Austria; Maestro, Perturbed, Announces He

Will Not Conduct at Music Festival—Will Divert Proceeds of March 4 Concert Here," 17 Feb. 1938, 1.

"Salzburg Concert Canceled by [Emanuel] List; Metropolitan Opera Basso Follows Toscanini in Refusal to Attend; Others Expected to Act; Artists, Perturbed over Recent Nazi Victory in Austria, to Miss Summer Festival," 18 Feb. 1938, 3.

"Walter in Amsterdam; Guest Conductor Says He Has No Idea of Quitting Austria," 2 Mar. 1938, 16.

"Salzburg Mourns Loss of Toscanini; Followers Fear That through His Decision Conductor Has Played into Nazi Hands; Four Suggested for Post; Stokowski or Furtwaengler May Succeed as Director in Forthcoming Festival," 5 Mar. 1938, 11.

"Bruno Walter Resigns Vienna Opera Post; Dr. Roebbeling Ousted from the Burgtheater," 15 Mar. 1938, 3.[123]

"Bruno Walter's Daughter Is Arrested in Vienna," 21 Mar. 1938, 2.

"Changes in Austria; New Musical Situation with Nazi Control—Americans Develop Festivals," 3 Apr. 1938, 11:5.

"Vienna Press Scorns Toscanini," 8 May 1938, 5.

"Reich City [Osnabrück] Bars 'Hot' Music," 19 Nov. 1938, 2.

"Nazis Ban Swing Music as Not Fit for Germans," 27 Nov. 1938, 45.

NOTES

1. "One Dies in Attack on Funeral of Nazi; National Socialists Oust Busch as Orchestra Conductor of Dresden Opera House," *New York Times*, 8 Mar. 1933, 10. [In what follows, all unattributed articles are from the *New York Times;* paragraph breaks have been omitted in the interests of saving space.] Busch recounted the incident and its aftermath in *Pages from a Musician's Life,* trans. Marjorie Strachey (London: Hogarth Press, 1953; repr. Westport, Conn.: Greenwood Press, 1971), 198–211. Using the disorder at his rehearsal as a pretext, the Saxon state government determined that any musical event that threatened to provoke similar demonstrations could be banned; Bruno Walter's experience at the Leipzig Gewandhaus nine days later was the result. See Eric Levi, *Music in the Third Reich* (New York: St. Martin's Press, 1994), 42.

2. "Take Up Case of Opera Head," 9 Mar. 1933, 10. None of Busch's arguments made a difference; nor did the fact that he was under the protection of Hermann Goering, whose mistress Emmy Sonneman had informed him in February that Goering, who controlled the Prussian State Theaters, wanted him to replace Wilhelm Furtwängler as director of the Berlin State Opera (Busch, *Pages from a Musician's Life,* 198). Following his ouster, the position at Dresden remained vacant until January 1934, when the Saxon authorities appointed Karl Böhm to replace him.

3. "Nazis Are Feared by German Operas; Discharges of Some Directors and Conductors Expected to Be Followed by More. Strauss Work Involved; Premiere of 'Arabella' Is Uncertain Because Composer Dedicated It to Men Hitlerites Ousted,"

15 Mar. 1933, 10. Despite the fact that its libretto was the work of Hugo von Hof-mannsthal, who was half-Jewish, the premiere of *Arabella* took place in Dresden as scheduled, on 1 July, conducted by Clemens Krauss in place of Busch. As for Brecher, among whose many premieres was Kurt Weill's *Mahagonny*, he and his wife would commit suicide on the Belgian coast in 1940 while in flight from German forces.

4. As reported in the *Times* article "Nazis Ban Concert by Bruno Walter; Leipzig Police Forbid It on the Ground It Threatens Public Order and Security; 'Negro Jazz' Prohibited; Thuringia to Redesignate Streets Named for marxists or jews; General, a Pacifist, Arrested," 17 Mar. 1993, 9.

5. "Racial Spirit vs. Chauvinism in Art; Hitlerism and Politics in Music Con-trasted with Honor Extended Toscanini by the Town of Baireuth," 19 Mar. 1933, 10:5.

6. "Toscanini Heads Protest to Hitler; He and Ten Other Musicians of World Fame Ask End of Persecution of Colleagues; Likely to Quit Baireuth; Gabrilowitsch Urges Him to Stay Away as Disapproval of 'Brutal' Regime," 2 Apr. 1933, 1. In re-sponse to the cable, German Radio banned broadcasts of the concerts and record-ings by its signatories on 4 April (Levi, *Music in the Third Reich*, 268). In reference to the pressure on Toscanini, Berlin newspapers reported on the morning of 6 April that "Kreisler . . . had heard that a group of American musicians had tried, by dint of fairly intensive persuasion, to get Toscanini to cancel his duties at the Bayreuth festival. They had even, so it was said, threatened to cease performing with him if he did not withdraw" (Fred K. Prieberg, *Trial of Strength*, trans. Christopher Dolan [Boston: Northeastern University Press, 1994], 50).

7. "Kreisler Deplores Plea to Toscanini; Urges Him to Go to Bayreuth Despite Pressure of Some Fellow-Musicians; Says They Defeat Aim; Violinist Holds Conduc-tor Will Do More Good as 'Herald of Love' Than by Protest Gesture," 5 Apr. 1933, 11. Prieberg cites a slightly different version of Kreisler's statement from the *Börsen-Zeitung* of 6 April in *Trial of Strength*, 50–51, 339n.26.

8. Kreisler's later statement, in a letter of 1 July to Furtwängler, who had invited him to perform with the Berlin Philharmonic in the 1933–34 season, is cited in Louis P. Lochner, *Fritz Kreisler*, rev. ed. (Neptune City, N.J.: Paganiniana Publica-tions, 1981), 281; and Prieberg, *Trial of Strength*, 89.

9. "Nazis to Control All Cultural Life; Jews Will Be Wholly Barred from Execu-tive Positions in Theatre and Opera. To Get Chance as Artists Foreign Performers Are to Be Welcomed, but They Must Not Injure Interests of Germans," 9 Apr. 1933, 4:1.

10. "Plea for Art Made by Furtwaengler; Orchestra Conductor in Berlin De-plores Discrimination Against Jews," 12 Apr. 1933, 24. The full text of the Furtwän-gler-Goebbels correspondence was published in Frederick Birchall's article "'Alien Experimental Mania' in Art Attacked by Nazis; Goebbels, Answering Protest of Furt-waengler on Discrimination, Says the Principles of State and Society Take Prece-dence," 16 Apr. 1933, 4:1.

11. "Adolf Busch Quits Brahms Fete in Hamburg Because Serkin, Jewish Pianist, Is Barred," 21 Apr. 1933, 10.

12. "'Artistic Reforms' in Germany; Militant League for Culture Gains Power— Effect on Orchestras and Programs—Unionizing the Critics," 30 Apr. 1933, 9:5. Levi discusses the Kampfbund für deutsche Kultur and the *Zeitschrift für Musik* in

the 1920s and early 1930s in *Music in the Third Reich,* chapters 1 and 2: "Conservative Musical Reaction in the Weimar Republic, 1919–33" and "Music and State Control."

13. "Events in Paris; Plight of Numerous German Exiles; New Ballets by [Sergei] Lifar and [Kurt] Joos [*sic*]," 21 May 1933, 10:5.

14. "Prussia Ousts Musicians; Profs. Schreker and Schoenberg Get Indefinite Academy Leaves," 31 May 1933, 8: "Berlin, May 30.—Professor Franz Schreker, for twelve years director of the High School of Music, and Professor Arnold Schoenberg, Austro-German composer, have received indefinite leaves of absence as directors of the master composition classes of the Prussian Academy of Arts. Both have long-term contracts, the disposition of which will be decided by Bernhard Rust, Prussian Minister of Education. Schreker was dismissed on May 17, Schoenberg six days later."

15. "Klemperer Ousted from Berlin Opera; Conductor, a Jew, Dismissed as a Non-Aryan Despite Contract Till 1937. Modern Views a Factor; His 'Culture Bolshevism' a Target of Attack—Nine Others of Musical Staff Out," 7 June 1933, 10: "Berlin, June 6.—Otto Klemperer, one of the principal conductors of the Berlin State Opera, has received notice of cancellation of his contract under the 'non-Aryan section' of the Civil Service Act. The contract was to have run until 1937, but Herr Klemperer must retire at the end of the current season early in July. Simultaneously dismissed from the State Opera, also as non-Aryans, were the concertmaster, Fritz Zweig, and his wife Tilly de Garmo, soprano; two other singers, Lottie Schone [*sic*] and Marcel Noe; and five lesser members of the musical staff. Leo Blech, a conductor, who is also a 'non-Aryan' and who has been with the Berlin State Opera for a quarter of a century, has been retained on the ground, it is said, that if he was acceptable to former Kaiser Wilhelm, who appointed him, he should not be objected to by the new régime. The news of Herr Klemperer's dismissal comes on the heels of reports leaking in from outside Germany that Arturo Toscanini has notified Frau Winifred Wagner he will not conduct the Baireuth festival performances this season. No word of this was printed in any German paper. This correspondent's telephoned inquiry to the Baireuth festival management elicited hardly more, apart from unconcealed disappointment over Signor Toscanini's decision, than the statement that 'it is bad news.' It was also said that Frau Wagner could not make public the contents of Signor Toscanini's communication, but it was said his motives for withdrawing were of a political nature. Herr Klemperer was a target for attack right after 'the revolution,' not only because he was a 'non-Aryan' but also because of his Leftist tendencies—he jokingly avowed himself 'a culture Bolshevist.' He will be on tour in the United States this Autumn. 'There is no denying,' says a Hugenberg newspaper commenting on his dismissal, 'that Klemperer has great musical talent, but it is equally undeniable that his whole attitude runs counter to German ways and feeling.' Herr Klemperer, who is a Jew, was guest conductor of the New York Symphony Orchestra here in the seasons of 1925–26 and 1926–27, and assumed the post of director of the Berlin State Opera in the Fall of 1927, making it impossible for him to return to New York. . . . While Herr Klemperer has paid all the expected attention to the classics at all times in his career, he has revealed marked sympathy for modern composers, whose works he frequently performs. This is probably not the least of his defects in the eyes of the Nazis. In addition, his

efforts to modernize stage settings and scrap traditional mountings of classics have caused considerable stir. In 1927, when he made a restudy of Wagner's 'The Flying Dutchman,' he even received threatening letters from those who refused to tolerate his experiments."

16. "Music Hurt by Nazis, Two Composers Say; Godowsky and Sessions, Back from Europe, See Irreparable Damage to Their Art," 12 June 1933, 20.

17. General music director of the Hesse State Theaters in Kassel and Wiesbaden, Elmendorff had conducted performances of Wagner's *Ring* at Bayreuth since 1927, and was responsible for the two performances of the cycle at the 1933 festival. Alfred Einstein, reviewing the performance for the *Christian Science Monitor* on 11 September, called it "the outstanding event of this year's festival." Working with producer Heinz Tietjen and scenic artist Emil Preetorius to produce "a united and effective performance," Elmendorff "hovered, as usual, between mechanicalness and sensitivity, robustness and delicacy, although he undoubtedly knows more than anyone else about the acoustic properties of the Festival House" (reprinted in *Alfred Einstein on Music: Selected Music Criticisms,* ed. Catherine Dower [Westport, Conn.: Greenwood Press, 1991], 148).

18. "Baireuth Honors Hitler, Wagner; But Chancellor Forestalls Nazi Demonstration by Order to 'Respect the Master.' 'Die Meistersinger' Sung; Toscanini's Failure to Conduct Is Lamented As Elmendorf's Work Is Called Uninspired," 22 July 1933, 14: "Baireuth, Germany, July 21.—With the swastika banner floating from the roof of Richard Wagner's theatre, and with Adolf Hitler, Joseph Goebbels, Wilhelm Frick and other high officials of the Nazi Government sitting as guests in the box of the Wagner family while a guard of honor stood at rigid attention before the Festspielhaus and Brown Shirts guarded the entrance with scowling looks and menacing rifles, the Baireuth festival got under way today with the performance of 'Die Meistersinger.' . . . Although the foreigners present were few tonight compared with their numbers in recent years, let alone earlier days, the Festspielhaus was completely filled, even if the reports were true that the house had been considerably 'papered,' and although it was possible to purchase tickets twenty minutes before curtain time, despite the resolute assurance that the first performance has been sold out for months. Many distinguished visitors were to be seen on the terrace between acts. Among them were Lucrezia Bori of the Metropolitan Opera Company, on her first visit to Baireuth, Mr. and Mrs. Cornelius Bliss, Arthur Honegger, Ernest Newman, Olga Samaroff and Mr. and Mrs. Richard Hagemann. Tonight's production of 'Die Meistersinger' was an entirely new one. . . . The leading singers were Maria Mueller, Rudolf Bockelmann, Alexander Kipnis and Max Lorenz. The conductor was Karl Elmendorf [*sic*], to whom Frau Winifred Wagner assigned the opera when Arturo Toscanini, for reasons of his conscience, decided he would wash his hands of Baireuth. It proved to be a most unlucky choice, for Herr Elmendorf's treatment of the score was so lumbering, uninspired and dull and most of the tempi were so distressingly slow that the greater part of the opera lost most of its vitality and grandeur and the singers found themselves more than once in difficulties."

19. "Salzburg Idolizes Bruno Walter, Ousted by Nazis as 'Non-Aryan'; Festival Audience Pelts Him with Roses after He Conducts in Inspired Manner—German Hitlerites Cease Efforts to Mar the Austrian Musical Fete," 4 Aug. 1933, 1. Birchall

was a news editor on the *Times* who, on reaching retirement age in 1931, had gone to Europe to report on political events for the next eight years as a *Times* correspondent, then returned home and wrote *The Storm Breaks: A Panorama of Europe and the Forces That Have Wrecked Its Peace* (New York: Viking Press, 1940). One of the few references to music in the book was to Willi Schmidt, a music critic for the *Münchner Neueste Nachrichten* murdered in the purge of 30 June 1934 when he was mistaken for an eponymous local storm-troop leader (207). Another account, which traced the story to a "whispered revelation" following the purge, had Schmid (without the "t") arrested in his apartment while playing the cello, then murdered; see John Toland, *Adolf Hitler*, vol. 1 (Garden City, N.Y.: Doubleday, 1976), 365.

20. "Foreign Musicians Spurn Reich Bids; 'Regrets' Answer Persistent Efforts of Furtwaengler to Get Artists to Appear; Muck Resigns in Hamburg; Veteran Conductor Unwilling to Acquiesce in Nazy Plans for Musical Reorganization," 26 July 1993, 9: "The [Berlin Philharmonic] Orchestra, Germany's most celebrated one, has been making persistent efforts to obtain the appearance in the next musical season of the usual representative 'foreign artists,' but without success. 'Regrets' from the foreign musicians invited follow each other, and the same applies to those German musicians who because they are Jews or otherwise regarded as undesirable by the Third Reich have left the Fatherland and are sojourning abroad. Although Herr Furtwaengler dared to protest publicly, in a letter to Dr. Paul Joseph Goebbels, Minister of Propaganda, against the elimination of German artists like Bruno Walter and Max Reinhardt as 'nonAryans' [*sic*], he is not only countenanced by the Nazi régime but has even been promoted to 'first Staatskapellmeister' and has been named a member of the Prussian State Council. Meanwhile, the scrapping of eminent German musicians continues. The veteran Karl Muck, in his seventy-fifth year, has resigned from the conductorship of the Hamburg Philharmonic Orchestra, finding himself unable to acquiesce in the ideas of the new Nazi holders of power concerning the musical consolidation of the Hamburg Philharmonic with the Hamburg Opera and the political 'coordination' of both. The Senate of Hamburg begged Dr. Muck at least to conduct the first five orchestral concerts on the program for the Autumn, but he emphatically declined and requested to be relieved of all his official duties forthwith. He is not Jewish."

21. Prieberg, characterizing the letter sent from Vienna on 31 August as "offensive," notes that it was "a barely altered version of his first refusal" (*Trial of Strength*, 107).

22. "Music Notes from Lands Overseas," 9:7.

23. "Germany's Jewish Cultural League; Organization Tolerated by Government to Afford Jews Artistic Expression Gives Moving 'Figaro,'" 10 Dec. 1933, 10:8. The Kulturbund was established by the Prussian Education Ministry at the suggestion of the intellectual and cultural leadership of the Jewish community in Berlin, in response to the exclusion of Jews from German cultural life as mandated by the Civil Service laws of 7 April 1933; it served not only the Jewish community but also the government, which used it as a tool of its propaganda. Its activities were regulated and monitored by Hans Hinkel, state commissar and president of the Prussian Theater Commission. For a summary of its history, see Levi, *Music in the Third Reich*, 49–57; and the volume of essays and documents *Geschlossene Vorstellung: Der Jüdische*

Kulturbund in Deutschland, 1933–1941 (Berlin: Edition Hentrich, 1992), published by the Berlin Akademie der Künste on the occasion of the eponymous exhibit from 27 January to 26 April 1992.

24. Among the musicians named in the *Times* dispatch, Rosenstock, who had been general music director at Darmstadt and Wiesbaden before going to Mannheim in 1930 and was a founder of the Kulturbund, left Berlin in 1936 for Tokyo as conductor of the Nippon Philharmonic, suffered internment during the Pacific war, reorganized musical life in postwar Tokyo, and finally settled in New York, where he directed the City Opera and later conducted at the Metropolitan Opera until his retirement in 1969; he died in 1985 at the age of ninety. Taube, formerly assistant conductor at the Berlin City Opera under Bruno Walter, left for Palestine in 1935, where he founded a short-lived conservatory in Tel Aviv, helped build the Palestine Orchestra and was one of its regular conductors, and organized and conducted other orchestras during a long and active career; he died in 1972 at eighty-one years of age. Schey, a singer and vocal coach, emigrated to Holland in 1934, becoming a professor at the Amsterdam Conservatory until his internment by the Germans during the war, resumed his career after the war, and retired to Switzerland; he died in 1981 at age eighty-five. Singer, deputy intendant at the Berlin City Opera from 1927 until fired by the Nazis, was the principal organizer of the Kulturbund; he perished in a German death camp. Jokl, first coloratura soprano at the Munich State Opera, emigrated to the United States in 1936, where she had a minor career; she died in New York in 1974 at seventy-nine years of age. Noe, a tenor who sang comprimario parts at the Berlin State Opera until 1933, emigrated to Palestine, where he worked as a cantor and taught; he died in Jerusalem at age sixty-four.

25. "Overseas Music Notes," 31 Dec. 1933, 10:7: "Curt Sachs, formerly Professor of Musicology in Berlin University, has left Germany on political grounds, according to foreign news dispatches, and has recently been in London. Professor Sachs is rated in Europe as one of the greatest musical scholars of the century. Instruments, old and new, archaic and primitive, are his special subject, on which he has written an imposing array of monographs. Germany's loss will be the gain of whichever country Professor Sachs chooses as his home. 'Will that country be England?' asks The London Telegraph. 'It would be a capital thing if a suitable post could be found for him here. The R.A.M. and R.C.M. might join in an invitation, which would honor them, to persuade him to settle in London.' Professor Sachs, who is 52, was a pupil of Kretzschmar and Johannes Wolf. His posts in Berlin included that of keeper of the collection of instruments at the High School for Music."

26. Thoughtfully, but not fully. For a chronology of significant musical events and political decisions impinging on music in Germany from Hitler's accession to power on 30 January 1933 through the end of the year, and continuing until Goebbels's order closing all musical venues except the Berlin Philharmonic on 25 August 1944, see Levi, *Music in the Third Reich,* 267–80.

27. "Vienna Revisited; Contrasts of Artistic Activities in Days before Internal Strife," 18 Feb. 1934, 9:6. The premiere of *Karl V,* to have been conducted by Clemens Krauss, was scheduled for the State Opera on 26 February. While Oliver Daniel in *The New Grove Dictionary of Music and Musicians* (London: Macmillan, 1980) attributes cancellation of the performance to "the implied political nature of the

work" (10:254), the story of the conspiracy (for that was what it was) demonstrates how fluid were the lines dividing hero from villain. One villain was the Nazi critic Joseph Rinaldini, who was responsible for a scurrilous article published on 9 January in the *Österreichische Abendzeitung,* the newspaper of the paramilitary Heimwehr on which the government of Chancellor Dollfuss depended, attacking the opera on political grounds. Another was Hugo Burghauser, first bassoonist and manager of the State Opera Orchestra and, like Rinaldini, a cultural director of the Heimwehr. A third was Josef Krips, who had been brought to the State Opera by Krauss as his assistant after being fired from Karlsruhe as a part-Jew. Playing a lesser role in the abandonment of the opera were two great ladies of the stage, Lotte Lehmann and Elisabeth Schumann: unhappy at having to learn new roles for *Karl V* but annoyed that Krauss was replacing them with younger singers, they reported to Vice-Chancellor Kurt von Schuschnigg, who as minister of culture had ultimate authority over the State Opera, that Krauss was a Nazi. Emil Schippers, a house baritone whom Krauss had tried to fire, also used his membership in the Heimwehr to undermine the hapless conductor. Burghauser, Krips, Lehmann, and Schumann would eventually find themselves victims of the Nazis. Krauss, vilified for his later role in Nazi Germany, seems to have been the only hero of this episode, as told in John L. Stewart, *Ernst Krenek* (Berkeley and Los Angeles: University of California Press, 1991), 174–77. The opera was first performed at the German Theater in Prague on 22 June 1938, and finally reached the Vienna stage in a performance at the State Opera under the direction of Lorin Maazel on 18 October 1984. See also Claudia Maurer Zenck, *Ernst Krenek—Ein Komponist im Exil* (Vienna: Lafite, 1980), 77–85.

28. "Furtwaengler in Vienna; Earns Ovation at Special Concert, but Forgoes Appearance at Salzburg Festival," 8 July 1934, 9:4.

29. "Nazis Now Order New Score to Replace Mendelssohn's 'Midsummer Night's Dream,'" 3 Nov. 1934, 1; and "Mendelssohn in Germany; Pfitzner and Strauss Refuse to Replace His Music for 'The Dream,'" 2 Dec. 1934, 10:7.

30. For his biography and an assessment of his work, see Alfred Einstein's obituary in *Musical Quarterly* 28 (1942): 241–47.

31. Stephen Duggan and Betty Drury, *The Rescue of Science and Learning: The Story of the Emergency Committee in Aid of Displaced Foreign Scholars* (New York: Macmillan, 1948), 21–22.

32. Schoenberg's case was well documented in the *Times.* It began with an article on his firing from his Berlin post on 31 May 1933 (see above, note 14), his return to Judaism ("Schoenberg Returns to the Jewish Faith; Composer Readmitted in Paris Ceremony to the Religion He Abandoned in 1921," 25 July 1933, 6), and his appointment at the Malkin Conservatory in Boston (see below, note 52). There followed a long biographical entry, "Schoenberg Coming to America; Composer, an Exile from Germany, to Teach in Boston—May Influence American Music and Students of Composition," 17 Sept. 1933, 10:5: "Germany's loss is this country's gain. Arnold Schönberg has agreed to come to Boston next month to teach harmony and composition at the newly organized Malkin Conservatory of Music. One of the outstanding figures in the world of music, Schönberg is known here only from a portion of his works. This will be his first visit to these shores. Whatever the critical evaluation of Schönberg's creative powers may ultimately be, there can be no dispute that his has been one of the most daring and inquiring minds that

have devoted themselves to music in our time. Schönberg's coming here, then, is a matter of vital importance."

Next came an announcement of the establishment of a scholarship fund at the conservatory, "Schoenberg Scholarship Fund," 1 Oct. 1933, 9:6: "The news of the approaching arrival of Arnold Schönberg . . . to teach at the Malkin Conservatory of Music in Boston, has brought an instantaneous response from patrons and friends of music. Their desire is to have as many young American composers as possible study under this great modern master, who is no longer permitted to live or teach in Berlin, where he stimulated and helped develop many talented composers. . . . Among others, George Gershwin has sent a sum of money to be added to the scholarship fund [established by Mrs. A. Lincoln Filene]. His hope was that this 'might help some worthy American composer avail himself of the rare opportunity to study with a great musician and teacher.' Mr. Gershwin's name has been added to the list of distinguished musicians who make up the institution's advisory board: Harold Bauer, Ernest Bloch, Artur Bodanzky, Dr. Archibald T. Davison, Arthur Fiedler, Ossip Gabrilowitsch and Frederick Stock."

Olin Downes then addressed the questions of Schoenberg's impact on American music and the impact of America on Schoenberg in a discursive column, "Schoenberg's Impending Visit; The Possible Effects of His Sojourn Here on One of the Great Figures in Modern Music," 22 Oct. 1933, 9:6: "One of the most striking examples of post-war conditions as they affect music is the arrival, now near, of Arnold Schönberg, about to make his first American visit, to teach in Boston. This proceeding appears singularly at variance with Schönberg's past and with his position in modern music. But the American visit may not be so much at variance with Schönberg's creative career as it seems. Two questions can be asked: (1) What will be the effect of Schönberg's teaching in America? and (2) What effect will America have on Schönberg? . . . Schönberg, whom we have considered the quintessence of an old, perhaps too old, culture; a master of prodigious knowledge and also of unquestionable and searching sincerity; one who has been a leading influence in all European music of the last thirty years, and who counts among those who deeply esteem his mastery composers as far distant as the young Ernst Toch and the elderly Sibelius—this man comes to America. He comes to new frontiers, to the home of a new civilization which might use him roughly, to try not only his material but his artistic fortune. . . . Schönberg will come, probably with a degree of personal trepidation, to these shores, but probably also with a very considerable degree of curiosity and susceptibility to new impressions. It is to be hoped that his stay will be an extensive one, and one duly recorded in his music. The man has annoyed his audiences the world over by works that set minds and ears on edge. But he has never stood still or remained for many years immune to change. He has always been progressive from one phase to another of what is actually a logical and coordinated process of development. No doubt circumstances have been a primary factor in determining his coming to America. For Schönberg, exiled from Germany, has been deprived of nearly all his means. But there is more than necessity, one hopes, in the mind of this musician. Schönberg will be at least as willing to experiment and as curious about America as America will be about him. How will he function here as a teacher?"

Schoenberg's arrival was reported on 1 November (see below, note 35).

33. "3 Professors Here for Exile College; Wertheimer to Lecture on His Thought System—Hornboste [*sic*] and Son Arrive," 4 Sept. 1933, 10: "Max Wertheimer, exiled professor of psychology at the University of Frankfort, Germany, and founder of the Gestalt School of Thought, arrived yesterday on the White Star Liner Majestic with his wife and two children for an indefinite stay in the United States. . . . Two other members of the Exile University staff also arrived yesterday. Professor Ernest von Hornboste, formerly head of the department of music in the University of Berlin, came on the French liner Champlain with his wife and their son. . . . Both father and son lost their posts in Germany several months ago. They said they had not been expelled from Germany but had left for Zurich when deprived of their means of livelihood."

34. "Klemperer Is Here; Dropped by Nazis. Former Conductor at Berlin State Opera to Direct Los Angeles Concerts," 11 Oct. 1933, 33: "Among the passengers who arrived yesterday on the Ile de France of the French Line was Otto Klemperer, whose contract as conductor at the Berlin State Opera was broken last June by the Hitler government. He has come to this country to conduct the Los Angeles Philharmonic Orchestra. Speaking of his recent experience with the Nazi Government, Mr. Klemperer said: 'My contract with the State Opera was to have run until 1937. On June 1 I received a polite note from the Minister of Education telling me to quit by July 1. I protested, and thereafter my name was left off the programs and I was replaced as conductor. I consulted lawyers and was told that my contract was good even under the new laws. Though the government is not obliged to let me conduct, my salary is due until 1937. The law provides that any man employed as I was since Aug. 1, 1914, does not come under the non-Aryan section of the law. I have been employed there since 1913.' The noted conductor's last visit to the United States was in 1927, when he was guest conductor of the New York Philharmonic-Symphony Orchestra."

35. "Arnold Schoenberg, Composer, Arrives; Left Berlin Because Jews Were Oppressed. To Make His Home in Boston," 1 Nov. 1933, 21: "Arnold Schoenberg, composer, who was for eight years a member of the faculty of the Berlin Academy of Arts, arrived yesterday on the Ile de France, accompanied by his wife and child, to make his home in Boston. He is 59 years old and has been composing and teaching for the last thirty years. The composer, who speaks English fairly well, said he had left Germany of his own accord in May because of the oppression of the Jews. Since then he had resided in Paris. He has been engaged by the Malkin Conservatory of Music in Boston to be a member of its staff and he expressed his pleasure at the prospect of living in this country. . . . The League of Composers has arranged to give a concert and reception for Mr. Schoenberg in this city at the Town Hall on the night of Saturday, Nov. 11. The composer was met at the pier by Joseph Malkin, director of the Malkin Conservatory, and Manfred Malkin, its dean."

36. "Lotte Lehmann to Become a 'Real American Citizen,'" 5 Aug. 1938, 10: "Paris, Aug. 4.—Friends of Lotte Lehmann, German-born opera singer, said today she had told them as she left for the United States that she would 'do everything possible to be a real American citizen.' Austrian friends said she had called herself 'a woman without a country' since the Nazis took power in Germany in 1933. The singer sailed from Havre for New York yesterday aboard the liner Champlain. The singer was born in Perleberg, Germany, but after the Nazi assumption of power

she adopted Austria as her home. Austria in turn was annexed by Germany last March 13."

37. "Conductors Who Arrived Here Yesterday: Jerzy Bojanowski, left, of the Tulsa Symphony Orchestra, and Hermann Adler, Former Director of the Prague Symphony Orchestra [with photograph]," 24 Apr. 1939, 12: "Two symphony orchestra conductors, who arrived yesterday from Europe on the steamship President Roosevelt of the United States Lines, played deck games with each other all the way across from the Channel without knowing each other's name. After they landed at the pier at West Eighteenth Street and were waiting for their baggage to be examined their identities were disclosed. One was Jerzy Bojanowski, conductor of the Symphony Orchestra of Tulsa, Okla., here to direct the Polish ballet at the Metropolitan Opera House in connection with the World's Fair, and the other was Hermann Adler, conductor of the Prague Symphony Orchestra. Mr. Adler said he is a refugee and plans to make his permanent home in the United States. He was conducting the orchestra at rehearsals for the Janacek Festival in Prague, which was to have opened Sept. 25, when he was informed that a mobilization of troops had been ordered and that the festival was to be canceled. When Hitler took over the country he fled."

38. "500 Refugees Aboard Washington Met by Crying, Cheering Crowd; Relatives and Friends Jam Pier and Give Arrivals a Picture of 'Promised Land'—Woman Photographer Tells of Arrest," 2 Apr. 1940, 27: "When the United States liner Washington arrived yesterday from Naples and Genoa with 817 passengers, including 500 refugees fleeing from the terrors of Central Europe, the scene was one of happy reunions. . . . Robert Stolz, a 53-year-old Viennese composer, was a passenger en route to Hollywood where, he said, he would compose the score for a forthcoming Deanne Durbin picture now entitled 'Spring Parade.' He explained that he was an 'Aryan' and not a refugee, but had been living in Paris for the past few years. Mr. Stolz is the composer of many light operas and popular songs, among them 'Two Hearts in Three-Quarters Time.' He said that while he is in the United States he plans to complete an opera to be entitled 'Viennese Cavalcade.'"

39. "Celebrities Forced to Flee France Arrive Here by Way of Lisbon; Jules Romains, Author, Doubts Fascist Rule Will Last—Mme. de Fontnouvelle, Darius Milhaud and Julian Green on Liner," 16 July 1940, 19: "The 9,360-ton American Export liner Excambion, which in normal times carries tourists, commercial men and missionaries to Mediterranean ports, arrived here yesterday after her first round trip in the company's new service between Lisbon and New York with a group of celebrities rivaling those that used to come in on the Queen Mary and the Normandie. Included were Jules Romains, author of the series of novels known collectively as 'Men of Good Will'; Darius Milhaud, modernist composer; Julien Duvivier, French film director; Mme. Josef Beck, wife of the former Foreign Minister of Poland; Mme. Charles de Ferry de Fontnouvelle, wife of the French consul general here; Julian Green, novelist; and Dr. Alexander Bruno, American surgeon—all refugees from France. The small ship docked at 9:20 A.M. at Exchange Place in Jersey City. 'It is impossible that France should go fascist,' M. Romains said. 'The immense majority of France is against fascism. There is no basis in the country for it. It will be materially impossible to establish anything comparable to a fascist regime.' The other passengers from France preferred to remain silent on the subject. They also were reluctant to discuss their difficulties in getting safely on board the ship. They all spoke

fairly confidently of returning to France—even Mr. Green and Dr. Bruno, Americans who have made their homes there. But they indicated they would not return while the Germans are in control. . . . M. Milhaud said he was last in Paris in May when his latest opera, 'Medée,' was produced at the Paris Opera House. It was beautifully done, he said, and at that time, when new operas still were being produced, no one suspected France would be conquered in little more than a month. He was one of a group known as 'The Six.' He said he did not know where Durey was, but Auric and Germaine Taillerer [*sic*] were in the south of France, Honegger was in Switzerland and Poulenc had been mobilized into the French Army just before the armistice. M. Milhaud was accompanied by his wife and their 10-year-old son Daniel. They will go to Mills College, Oakland, Calif."

40. "Oskar Straus Coming; Composer of 'Chocolate Soldier' to Tour U.S. with a Ballet Group," 3 Oct. 1940, 30: "Oskar Straus, composer of 'The Chocolate Soldier,' is on his way to this country. The composer, who was born in Austria but is now a French citizen, left ten days ago for Lisbon to take a clipper, his son, Walter Straus, now living at the Hotel St. Moritz, said yesterday. Father and son hope to make a tour across the United States with a ballet company that will perform 'The Princess Tragant,' one of the composer's early ballets." "Oscar Strauss [*sic*] Sails for U.S.," 23 Nov. 1940, 15: "Lisbon, Portugal, Nov. 22—Oscar Strauss, Vienna composer of light operas, and his family were among the 320 passengers who sailed today for the United States aboard the American Export Lines' chartered steamship Siboney."

41. "Paderewski Here, Pleads for Britain; Summarizes His Concern for Threat to Civilization with a Six-Word Appeal; Liberty His Goal in U.S. Virtuoso, Who Has Not Touched Piano since Invasion, Calls Europe 'Unbearable,'" 7 Nov. 1940, 30: "Ignace Jan Paderewski, the noted Polish pianist, arrived in New York yesterday after a ten-day voyage to escape what he termed 'the unbearable moral atmosphere' abroad. Accompanied by his sister, Mrs. Antonina Wilkonska, and a party of five others, Mr. Paderewski landed in Jersey City from the American Export liner Excambion and was met by representatives of the United States Government and others. . . . Yesterday was the pianist's eightieth birthday anniversary. He told reporters on the ship that because of his age he was unable to take an active part in the struggle raging today, and that he had decided to leave Europe to avoid possible interference with his rights and his duty in the 'sacred' service of humanity. The pianist said that he was feeling 'fine' and members of his party said that he had stood the trip well, although he did not leave his cabin during the entire voyage. His secretary revealed that Mr. Paderewski had not touched a piano since Poland was invaded. In a prepared statement the pianist declared that his love of all that is 'noble and lofty in human nature' gave him strength to speak his mind on the present world crisis. Then he added: 'Help Great Britain—save the world.' When Mr. Paderewski traveled from his home in Switzerland to Lisbon he was held by the Spanish police at Saragossa, and he said yesterday the police had pretended that he and his party had left Barcelona without properly notifying the authorities. He was released from police supervision through the efforts of President Roosevelt and United States Ambassador Alexander Weddell. . . . Others on the liner, which brought 179 passengers and a cargo including more than $3,000,000 in gold, included Mme. Nadia Boulanger, the French music teacher, composer and conductor, who has visited

here several times in former years to lecture and conduct. She said she would conduct Gabriel Fauré's Requiem in Washington and later go to Cambridge to teach in the Longy School. Mme. Boulanger spoke guardedly of France and the government in Vichy, where she has been living. She said she gave her 'total devotion' to Marshal Pétain. Obedience and discipline are necessary, she declared, adding, however, that they must be 'freely chosen and not imposed.'"

42. "Martinů Works," 23 Feb. 1941, 9:6: "Bohuslav Martinů, Czech composer, is on his way to New York, and will arrive in the next few days. He comes from unoccupied France, where he has spent the last seven months following a dramatic flight from Paris, his adopted home for the last eighteen years. In spite of the upheaval around him since last June, when he left Paris so suddenly, briefcase in hand, arriving at Aix-en-Provence, having walked part of the distance, Martinů did not stop composing. At Aix he finished two new scores in the six months that he waited for his French and Spanish visas. One was 'Phantasy and Rondo for Piano,' dedicated to the Czech pianist, Rudolf Firkusny, and an important work for piano and orchestra, 'Sinfonia,' dedicated to Germaine Leroux. Both have preceded Martinů and they have to tell us of the tragic last days of his stay in France. Martinů brings with him new projects to work out in America. 'On my arrival in America,' he wrote from Lisbon, 'I wish to begin work at once on a comic opera. I have some ideas of my own about it, but I'll have to have an American collaborator for the libretto.'" Sick, exhausted, and impoverished, Martinů arrived with his wife on the Exeter on 31 March 1941, their passage from Lisbon underwritten by the Swiss conductor Paul Sacher. They were taken to a Manhattan hotel, where they were met by Firkusny and others, and were later guests of honor at a League of Composers reception. See Brian Large, *Martinů;* (London: Gerald Duckworth, 1975), 82; and Milos Šafránek, *Bohuslav Martinů: The Man and His Music* (New York: Alfred A. Knopf, 1944), 81–82.

43. "Pianist a Refugee; Wanda Landowska, the Polish Artist, to Arrive Here Monday," 5 Dec. 1941, 24: "Wanda Landowska, eminent Polish harpsichordist and pianist, who lost her estate at St. Leu-le Foret, near Paris, under the German occupation of France, will arrive here Monday on the Exeter of the American Export Line. Mme. Landowska was in the unoccupied zone in Southern France until her departure for the United States. She came to this country as a refugee, having been deprived of all her property. The artist made frequent visits to this country from 1923 to 1932, giving many recitals. She also made many appearances as soloist with major orchestras." Landowska's first recital after her arrival was reviewed by Noel Strauss, 22 Feb. 1942, 19: "Wanda Landowska Plays Bach Work; Eminent Harpsichordist Heard in the 'Goldberg' Variations at the Town Hall; Returns after 14 years. Artist, Acclaimed by Audience, Offers Purcell and Rameau Compositions and Encores."

44. "Milhaud Arrives to Teach; French Composer Describes Evolution of 'Groupe des Six'—Affirms Racial Impulse in Art Inextinguishable / by Olin Downes," 21 July 1940, 9:8: "[Milhaud] had left France shortly after the Nazi invasion. He will teach next season at Mills College in California. He is in no sense nonplused by catastrophic change. He looks to the future, not the past. Some European musicians are incapable of blending with the American scene. Mr. Milhaud meets it without the batting of an eye, on its own terms, and, one imagines, finds stimulus and invigoration in its dynamism and many challenges. His opera 'Médée,' a one-act work,

was elaborately produced, with an excellent cast, at the Paris Opéra on the 8th of last June, six days before the German Army entered the city. Three performances of the opera were given there in all, including performances on the 15th and 25th. A good press, a brilliant interpretation—and there was an end on't. In the meantime Mr. Milhaud has completed a symphony which will be given its first public performances next season as a feature of the programs of the fiftieth anniversary of the Chicago Symphony Orchestra, which will change places for two weeks with the Philharmonic-Symphony Orchestra in New York giving programs of works old and new. There is also a Tenth quartet, written at the behest of Mrs. [Elizabeth Sprague] Coolidge, which doubtless will be heard here in the course of the coming months. It will be seen that Mr. Milhaud's well-known productivity has not deserted him. He remarked that recent events abroad, when most Frenchmen who were not directly under fire at the front, or under aerial bombardment back of the lines, spent the greater part of their hours at the radio and wherever there was to be found any reliable news of what transpired in the hours so fateful for France and her people, were not precisely propitious for composition."

45. "Opera Star Seeks to Become Citizen; Lotte Lehmann, 'Eager to Forget Germany and Europe,' Files Her First Application; Voices Her Happiness. Her Husband and His Four Children Will Follow Her Example Soon," 16 Sept. 1938, 23: "In fine spirits, observing gayly that she felt 'happy, just happy,' Mme. Lotte Lehmann, Metropolitan Opera singer, took the initial step yesterday toward becoming an American citizen when she filed application for her first papers at the Naturalization Bureau, 641 Washington Street. Expressing a desire to forget 'everything I know about Germany and the rest of Europe,' Mme. Lehmann, who is in this country for the seventh—and she hopes final—visit, remarked that she could 'hardly wait' to become a full-fledged citizen of this country. A native of Germany, and by marriage a citizen of Austria, the famous singer did not conceal her delight at the step she was taking. 'I'll probably look like a criminal,' she complained good naturedly as her official picture was taken by the bureau authorities. 'But I'm happy.' Then she arose and began to march around the room, as pleased as a high school girl with a new dress. 'I'd like to take the American flag and wave it,' she said in high glee. Mme. Lehmann wasn't interested in politics. You can't mix politics and music, she insisted; to sing, an artist must have peace and quiet. She expected to find both here. As for Germany and Austria, both nations, now one, were filled with trouble and unrest; but, she observed, she was not banned from her native land. She came to this country voluntarily. . . . Now that she had taken out first citizenship papers would the German public welcome her back with the acclaim formerly accorded her? a reporter asked. Mme. Lehmann thought so. . . . Mme. Lehmann plans to make New York her home. Her husband, Otto Krause, a former major in the Austrian Army, also intends to file his citizenship intentions soon. Her four stepchildren, Manon, Hans, Ludwig and Peter, now live in this country and will follow suit in becoming citizens as soon as possible."

46. "Czech Conductor Settles Here" (notice), 19 May 1940, 28: "Frederic Zweig, who has just settled in the United States with his wife, the singer Tilly di Garmo, may be counted among the few conductors who have worked on a permanent basis in the opera houses of Europe's most important capitals—Berlin, Paris, Prague and

London. His long stay in Berlin at the Staedtische Oper and at the Staats Oper was marked by his presentation of little-known works. . . . The husband of an American citizen, Mr. Zweig has now taken out his own first citizenship papers."

47. "Szell to Conduct for New Friends; He Will Be the Guest Leader of Orchestra for Next Season—Stiedry Head of Group; Concerts at Town Hall. Large Choral Work and Varied Programs Are to Be Given in Annual Series and Tour," 23 July 1941, 15: "Georg Szell, Hungarian conductor, who has taken out first citizenship papers in this country, has been engaged as guest conductor of the New Friends of Music Orchestra for next season, I. A. Hirschmann, founder of the organization, announced yesterday. . . . Mr. Szell will conduct one large choral work and several other concerts during the Town Hall series and many of the concerts on tour. Fritz Stiedry, who has been the orchestra's regular conductor since it was founded in 1938, will continue as head of the ensemble and conduct the majority of its concerts."

48. "Weinberger Seeks Time to Compose / by H. Howard Taubman," 29 Jan. 1939, 9:7: "A paradox, a paradox! A grim, ingenious paradox! One of the most successful composers of the past two decades needs help if he is to do the creative work that he has outlined in his mind. His music has earned, and continues to earn, enough to provide him with a decent living and with the time and tranquillity he requires for composition. Yet the full earnings do not reach him, and unless some kind guardian angel comes to his aid he will be obliged to resume the hack work which has perforce occupied his time in recent months, leaving his larger creative designs unrealized. The composer is Jaromir Weinberger, the man who penned 'Svanda Dudák,' or 'Schwanda, der Dudelsackpfeifer,' as it is known in German, or 'Schwanda, the Bagpiper,' as it is called in English. He arrived here some days ago, his first visit to America in more than a decade. He talked freely and eagerly about his music, past and present and future, but was reluctant to discuss his personal problems and difficulties. Nevertheless they are worth examination, for they emphasize the plight of many artists who have lived and had their being in totalitarianized Central Europe. It should be borne in mind that Mr. Weinberger himself refused to talk politics. But politics are implicit in the activities even of artists in Europe today, and the story of Mr. Weinberger's music and his personal life was shadowed by the thing which he would not discuss. For the proper perspective on Mr. Weinberger's problems let us go back to his 'Schwanda,' which had its first performance in Prague, the composer's native city, in 1927. 'Schwanda' is perhaps the work that has received the most performances of all operas written since the war. . . . Then there is the Polka and Fugue, that deliciously wry and laughing music which Schwanda extracted from his Dudelsack and which bewitched the devil and his minions into a memorably amusing dance. . . . Mr. Weinberger was asked how many times the Polka and Fugue had been played all told. The composer shrugged his shoulders as if to say that no answer was possible. 'All I can say,' he smiled, 'is X times.' How was he paid his royalties for X performances? Mr. Weinberger's face and eyes, which express his feelings eloquently, grew serious. There was the rub. Royalties had come in properly and regularly before 1933. Some time after Hitler's rise to power performances of 'Schwanda' ceased in Germany, but the composer's work continued in popular favor throughout the other opera houses of Europe. Lately, of course, it has ceased to be presented in Austria; other countries within the Nazi orbit may follow suit. The

publisher of 'Schwanda' and Mr. Weinberger's other music is German. Royalties for performance and rental rights are paid to the original publisher. Like other composers whose music was published in Germany and who are now persona non grata in that land, Mr. Weinberger receives spasmodic accountings. He did not charge that these accountings were inaccurate; he did not know. All he did know was that until recently he was able to make a reasonable livelihood out of the earnings of his music, and now he cannot. During the past year the composer has lived in Paris, and he confessed, rather unwillingly, that he had done arranging and writing of little things for which there was an immediate demand and price. 'After all,' he said, 'a man must live, I have plans for new scores. For example, I have in mind a symphony based on the life of your Abraham Lincoln. I would call it a symphony on the life of a hero. Perhaps you Americans do not realize what Lincoln means to some of us Europeans and how he stands out as a man who lived and died for a great idea. The figure of Lincoln has always fascinated me, and I would make my symphony with a final choral movement using the words of Longfellow's 'Excelsior.' 'To tell the truth,' and Mr. Weinberger's eyes shone as he spoke of this project, 'I have the symphony all worked out in my head. I need at least six months and peace of mind to set it down on paper and to orchestrate it.' Mr. Weinberger had no idea how he could achieve that happy state, unless some foundation or some rich man chose to help him during the period required for the writing of the work. He had other scores for orchestra in prospect, but it was the same story."

49. 11 Aug. 1967, 21.

50. "Klemperer Gets Los Angeles Post; Conductor Ousted from Berlin Opera by Nazis Will Direct Philharmonic on Coast. Was Here Two Seasons; Busch Rejects Bid to Return to Germany for Wagner Festival—Will Go to Buenos Aires," 17 June 1933, 16: "Vienna, June 16.—Otto Klemperer, who was one of the candidates for the post of conductor of the Vienna State Opera, has accepted an invitation to conduct eighty-four concerts by the Los Angeles Philharmonic Orchestra from October, 1933, to the end of April, 1934. Before his departure he will conduct in August a concert in Salzburg, Mozart's opera, 'Cosi Fan Tute' [*sic*], at Fiesole, near Florence, and in September a concert of the Vienna Philharmonic Orchestra. Several prominent German singers, expelled from German opera houses, plan to give performances of Janacek's opera 'Jenufa' in Austria, Czechoslovakia and Hungary. Their first performance will take place in September in Vienna at the Volkoper [*sic*]. Herr Klemperer will conduct."

51. "10 Named to Staff of Exiles' College; Faculty of Ousted German Leaders Nearly Completed for Session Opening October 1. 300 Educators Hail Plan; Dr. Johnson Says Selections Were Based on Scholarship Only—$60,000 Raised," 2 Sept. 1933, 13: "Nearly 300 American educators, including twenty-seven college presidents, endorsed yesterday the University in Exile of the New School for Social Research to be opened Oct. 1, with a faculty of German scholars dismissed or 'furloughed' from German universities by the Hitler government. The list of American scholars endorsing the project was made public by Dr. Alvin Johnson, director of the New School for Social Research, together with a list of ten of the German scholars who are to form the faculty of the University in Exile. The names of six of those on the list had been withheld, to permit them to wind up their affairs in Germany and to take such precautions as were necessary for the protection of their friends

and relatives pending their official acceptance of their posts in this country. The total number of German scholars who are to join the University in Exile is fifteen. The names of the remaining five will be made public shortly. All have been chosen entirely on the basis of scholarship and not of race, Dr. Johnson said. Most of them are Jews. They are divided about equally between Social-Democrats and Liberals. [Dr. Johnson:] ' . . . We picked the names from German periodicals which carried lists of the 800 scholars driven from German universities and we selected those who have to their credit the highest attainments in their respective fields.' Of the 800 scholars 150 are non-Jews. 'Those who suited best the purpose of our enterprise were invited to come. It so happens that a majority of them are Jews.' " Among the ten German scholars named is "E. von Hornbostel—Field, musicology, psychology and ethnology. One of the leading authorities on comparative musicology."

52. "Schoenberg, Exile, to Teach in Boston; Eminent Modern Composer, Barred from Germany, to Pay Us First Visit. His Music Familiar Here; Long a Storm Centre in Creative Field—Opera 'Wozzeck' the Work of His Pupil, Berg," 8 Sept. 1933, 11: "Arnold Schoenberg, one of the world's foremost composers and teachers of music, who is an exile now from Germany, will come to this country next month to teach harmony and composition at the Malkin Conservatory of Music in Boston. . . . The name of Schönberg has been associated with bold experimentation and as a result has been the centre of many violent controversies in the musical world during the last three decades. He has had many ardent supporters and as many ardent opponents. Schönberg's pupils have attained significant stature in the field of modern music. Foremost among them are Alban Berg, Anton von Webern, Egon Wellesz, Paul Pisk, Hans [*sic*] Eisler, Heinrich Javlovetz [*sic*] and Erwin Stein. Berg, the best known here, is the composer of 'Wozzeck,' which received its American premiere three years ago under the direction of Leopold Stokowski." Of the seven pupils listed in the last paragraph, five (all but Berg, who died in 1935, and Webern) were to emigrate, and four of them were to achieve eminence in exile. The fifth, the pianist and conductor Heinrich Jalowetz, is barely remembered. A saintly man who fled Europe in 1938 and ended his years as a beloved teacher at Black Mountain College, he entirely escaped notice in the *Times*. The last hours of his life were recounted by Richard Lockwood, a colleague of his at Black Mountain, in a poignant memorial to a man and his embattled culture: "Jalowetz played a program of Beethoven sonatas one evening, acknowledged the applause, walked out on the porch, sat down and died. Johanna [his wife], my wife and I sat most of the night together, talking and listening to music that we loved, the Saint Matthew Passion, the Brahms Clarinet Quintet, Mozart Concerti, and the Bach Sonatas for Unaccompanied Cello" (Martin Duberman, *Black Mountain: An Exploration in Community* [New York: W. W. Norton, 1993], 497n.87).

53. "To Teach Music at Harvard," 26 Sept. 1933, 22: "Cambridge, Mass., Sept. 25.—Dr. Hugh [*sic*] Leichtentritt, noted German authority on music, will join the teaching staff at Harvard University for the first half year and give several courses to students of music."

54. "Ernst Toch, Noted Composer-Pianist, Who Has Been Engaged to Lecture Next Season at the New School [with photograph]," 9 Sept. 1934, 9:5: "Ernst Toch, well-known composer-pianist, will give a series of lectures on musical theory at the New School for Social Research next season. These seminars will embrace work for

professional students, for amateurs and for laymen." On a postcard written aboard the Cunard liner RMS *Laconia* and postmarked 25 August 1934, Toch's wife Lilly informed Alfred and Hertha Einstein (then in London) that they would be landing in New York the following day. The card is in the Ernst Toch Archive at the University of California, Los Angeles.

55. "Gets N.Y.U. Music Post; Dr. Curt Sachs Is Appointed to a Visiting Professorship," 27 June 1937, 2:5: "Dr. Harry Woodburn Chase, chancellor of New York University, announced yesterday the appointment of Dr. Curt Sachs, European music authority, as visiting Professor of Music for the coming year in the Graduate School of Liberal Arts. The appointment of Dr. Sachs, whose services will be shared by the university with the Metropolitan Museum of Art and the New York Public Library, was made possible by grants from the Emergency Committee in Aid of Displaced German Scholars and the Rockefeller Foundation. Professor Philip James, chairman of the Department of Music, said Dr. Sachs would present three graduate courses during the academic year, one on the history of musical instruments, another on primitive music and a third on music and the dance."

56. "Orchestra Formed for Chamber Music; Organization of Ensemble is Announced by New Friends for Next Season; Fritz Stiedry to Direct. Austrian Conductor to Give Concerts at the Town Hall Beginning Oct. 23," 17 Mar. 1938, 16: "The formation of a chamber orchestra of thirty-six men which will be heard during the next season's subscription series of sixteen concerts of the New Friends of Music at Town hall was announced yesterday by I. A. Hirschmann, founder and president of the New Friends. Fritz Stiedry, Austrian conductor, will be musical director of the new ensemble and Richard Moses, manager of the New Friends, will act as manager. Mr. Stiedry, now making his first visit to this country, was a pupil and assistant of Gustav Mahler. He was the former director of the Vienna Volksoper and the general music director of the Berlin City Opera, following Bruno Walter, from 1929–33. During the last four years he has been conductor of the Leningrad Philharmonic, and he conducted an annual series of concerts in Moscow as well as operatic performances in both Leningrad and Moscow."

57. "Toscanini Aide Is Named; Steinberg Engaged to Prepare NBC Orchestra for Concerts," 8 Apr. 1938, 16: "Negotiations were completed yesterday by the National Broadcasting Company for the engagement of Hans W. Steinberg, one of the conductors of the Palestine Orchestra Association and a Jewish exile from Germany, to aid Arturo Toscanini next season in preparing the NBC Symphony Orchestra for the Italian maestro's broadcasts, it was announced. A native of Cologne, Herr Steinberg began his career as an assistant conductor to Otto Klemperer at the Cologne Opera. From there he went to Prague as assistant conductor of the Germany Theatre, and soon afterward was promoted to the post of conductor. From 1929 until 1933 he was first conductor at the Frankfort Opera, where he gained distinction. In 1939 he went to Palestine as one of the conductors of the Orchestral Association. It was Herr Steinberg who prepared that orchestra for Mr. Toscanini, and the Italian maestro is expected to begin a series of concerts with it in Palestine about the middle of this month." Olin Downes reviewed Steinberg's first performance with the NBC Orchestra under the headline "Steinberg Directs Bruckner 'Fourth.' Ex-Conductor of Palestine Symphony Leads Concert of the NBC Orchestra; His Work Is Impressive. Stravinsky's 'Fireworks' and Works of Dukas and Jo-

hann Strauss Also Are Heard," 5 Mar. 1939, 48. He found Steinberg "a conductor of unmistakable gifts . . . a substantial and gifted interpreter."

58. "Notes Here and Afield; Rudolf Serkin Joins Faculty of the Curtis Institute Next Fall," 19 Feb. 1939, 9:8: "Rudolf Serkin, the eminent Austrian pianist, has been added to the faculty of the Curtis Institute of Music, according to an announcement just made by Mrs. Mary Louise Curtis Bok. Mr. Serkin will begin his new duties next October. Auditions will be held during the first week in May for students desiring to receive his instruction." Serkin was delayed in taking up the Curtis position, as indicated by the following story in the *Times* under the headline "Effects of War," 8 Oct. 1939, 9:7: "Rudolf Serkin, who was to have opened this season's Town Hall Endowment Fund Series on Nov. 8, will be unable to appear. According to his managers, who heard from him about a fortnight ago, he has had some 'slight trouble' obtaining papers from his native Switzerland, but it is only a 'delay' and the rest of Mr. Serkin's American tour is expected to proceed as scheduled."

59. "Smith to Hear Alfred Einstein," 21 Apr. 1939, 28: "Northampton, Mass., April 20.—Dr. Alfred Einstein, German music scholar and writer, has been appointed visiting Professor of Music on the William Allan Neilson Foundation for the first semester of 1939–40. He will give his first lecture at Smith during the Haydn festival, April 28 to 30. He will be heard on April 29. In the Fall he will conduct a graduate seminar."

60. "Stravinsky to Lecture; Russian Composer to Give 12th Norton Series at Harvard," 15 Oct. 1939, 48: "Igor Stravinsky, noted Russian composer, will give the twelfth annual serieis [*sic*] of Charles Eliot Norton lectures at Harvard University beginning Wednesday, it was announced yesterday. The lectures will take place in the New Lecture Hall, and will be given in French. . . . Stravinsky went to Cambridge immediately after arriving in New York on 30 September 1939." The *Times* listed the lecture dates as 25 October, 1 November, 13 and 20 March, and 10 April.

61. "Olitzki Will Bow at Metropolitan; Wagnerian Basso-Buffo Sings in 'Meistersinger' in Debut at First Saturday Matinee," 18 Nov. 1940, 22: "Walter Olitzki, Wagnerian basso-buffo, has been engaged by the Metropolitan Opera and will make his debut during the opening week of the season. He will appear as Beckmesser in the Saturday matinee of 'Die Meistersinger' on Dec. 2. . . . Mr. Olitzki . . . was born in 1903. His first engagement was at the City Opera in Koenigsberg where he sang under Richard Strauss, Max von Schillings, Hans Pfitzner and Hermann Scherchen. He sang leading roles for this company for ten years. He has also made guest appearances at the Berlin State Opera and in Monte Carlo and Amsterdam. . . . Among the other cast members in that performance conducted by Erich Leinsdorf were Irene Jessner as Eva, Charles Kullmann as Walther von Stolzing, Friedrich Schorr as Hans Sachs, and Emanuel List as Pogner. Downes wrote about Olitzki: He interpreted the part with scrupulous care for detail and with considerable felicity and vocal interest. The serenade has not often been given such meticulous treatment. What the part lacked . . . was the snap and the bite, the sardonic vigor and maliciousness of the character. This Beckmesser was a little tame, and rather older than the man who, after all, desired to marry Eva. In details of business, diction, song, Mr. Olitzki proved himself an artist."

62. Notice of 25 Feb. 1940, 7: "Paul Hindemith has been engaged as visiting lecturer by Buffalo University, Cornell University and Wells College for their second

terms. As already announced, he will head the advanced composition department at the Berkshire Academy during July and August. His new violin concerto will receive its premiere by the Boston Symphony Orchestra, under Dr. Serge Koussevitzky, with Richard Burgin, the orchestra's concertmaster as soloist." Hindemith's emigration from Germany and arrival in New York City on a boat from Genoa on 15 February 1940 are recounted in Luther Noss, *Paul Hindemith in the United States* (Urbana: University of Illinois Press, 1989), 60–62.

63. See above, note 44.

64. Notice of 17 Nov. 1940, 9:5: "Dr. Karl Geiringer, Austrian musicologist, who from 1930 to 1938 was the curator of the archives of the Society of the Friends of Music in Vienna, has been engaged as visiting professor in the music department of Hamilton College, Clinton, N.Y. Dr. Geiringer also has been invited to lecture on Dec. 6 at Harvard University." According to his vita, a copy of which is found in the Toch Archive at the University of California, Los Angeles, Geiringer and his family arrived in New York in August 1940.

65. "Haydn Symphonies in Rehearsal Here; Dr. Alfred Einstein Brings Five Works Never Yet Heard in This Country; Fritz Stiedry to Direct. Orchestra of New Friends of Music to Play Scores at Sunday Concert Series," 4 Feb. 1939, 11. Einstein and his wife had arrived in New York on 5 January 1939. The story of his exile is told in Dower, *Alfred Einstein on Music,* 9–19. He and Albert Einstein were acquaintances but not cousins.

66. "Engaged for Metropolitan," 24 Apr. 1938, 10:6: "Felix Wolfes, widely experienced German director of opera, has been engaged as assistant conductor of the Metropolitan Opera Association. Following an uninterrupted career as opera leader in Germany from 1912, Mr. Wolfes, as a non-Aryan, found it advisable to leave that country at the start of the present Hitler regime. He went to Paris, where he remained until five months ago, when he came to America as accompanist and musical coach of Marjorie Lawrence, the Metropolitan dramatic soprano. Mr. Wolfes is a native of Hanover. He studied piano with Robert Teichmueller, composition with Max Reger and Hans Pfitzner and conducting with Otto Klemperer and Hans Brecher. His first conductorial post was an assistantship to Pfitzner and Brecher, from 1912 to 1915, at the Strasbourg Opera. He continued his activities as assistant conductor in Cologne, under Brecher (1915–16), in Mannheim, under Furtwaengler (1916–17), and [in] Frankfurt, under Brecher (1917–18). Thereafter he became chief conductor of the Operas of Elberfeld (1918–19), Halle (1919–23), Breslau (1923–24), Essen (1924–31) and Dortmund (1931–33). From Dortmund Mr. Wolfes went to Paris. During his four-year sojourn in France, where he was busied principally as coach and accompanist, he was chief conductor at the Monte Carlo Opera for the seasons of 1935–36 and 1936–37. He was engaged again for this year's season at that house, but decided to remain in the United States, where he intends to stay permanently and become an American citizen."

67. "Opera and Concert Activities," 20 Sept. 1936, 9:7: "Principal addition to the staff of conductors during the coming Metropolitan Opera season will be Maurice de Abravanel. He will take over at least a portion of the duties assigned in recent years to Louis Hasselmans, who has left the Metropolitan. It is understood that the newcomer and Wilfred Pelletier will divide the French repertoire. How the divi-

sion will be fixed remains to be determined. Mr. de Abravanel will be the youngest of the opera's first line conductors. He was born in 1903. The newcomer is one of Edward Johnson's answers to the demand for new and youthful blood. A Portuguese by birth, Mr. de Abravanel studied medicine at the University of Lausanne, where he assembled an orchestra of students and became its conductor. He decided to abandon medicine and devote himself entirely to music. He went to work as conductor in some of the smaller German theatres and then became chorus master and conductor at the Zwickau City Theatre. Then came engagements at the Stadt Theater in Altenburg, an interval of operetta and concerts in smaller centers in Germany and appointment as opera conductor in Cassel. The Berlin State Opera, concerts, opera and ballet in Paris, and engagements in Rome and Australia have been recent occupations."

68. Lowell Durham, *Abravanel!* (Salt Lake City: University of Utah Press, 1989), 11–21. His Metropolitan debut was in Saint-Saëns's *Samson et Dalila* on 6 December 1936.

69. "Friedrich Schorr Operative Adviser; Will Supervise Training of Gifted Youths in Wagner Roles," 15 Sept. 1938, 28: "Friedrich Schorr, distinguished Wagnerian baritone, has been appointed vocal adviser of the Wagner department of the Metropolitan Opera Association by the board of directors, upon the recommendation of Edward Johnson, general manager, it was announced yesterday. After this appointment, the Juilliard Musical Foundation established two scholarships for young American students whose training will be entrusted to the care of Mr. Schorr. The baritone's new position was created to give gifted American students an opportunity to receive training in Wagnerian style and tradition from an artist who has been an outstanding exponent of some of the greatest roles of the music-dramas. Mr. Schorr will continue to sing at the Metropolitan. This season will be his sixteenth as the leading Wagnerian baritone of the company."

70. "Korngold, Composer, Here from Austria; Will Discuss New Opera with Mr. Gatti—Wittgenstein, Pianist, Also Arrives," 31 Oct. 1934, 14: "Two noted European musicians, Erich Wolfgang Korngold, the Viennese composer, and Paul Wittgenstein, one-armed pianist, also an Austrian, arrived here last night on the Majestic for their first American visits. Mr. Korngold plans to leave in a few days for Hollywood, where he will join Max Reinhardt for the latter's production of 'A Midsummer Night's Dream,' for which Mr. Korngold has written music. The composer said that while in New York he plans to consult Giulio Gatti-Casazza about a new opera for possible production at the Metropolitan, as well as in Vienna. He was pleased to hear that 'The Great Waltz,' for which he adapted the music, had made a success here. Two of his operas, 'Die Todt [*sic*] Stadt,' in which Maria Jeritza made her New York début, and 'Violanta,' in which Mme. Jeritza also appeared, have been given at the Metropolitan. Mr. Wittgenstein, who lost his right arm in the World War, while in service on the Russian front, will begin his first American concert tour in Montreal in five days, he said. His first appearances in the United States will be at Boston on Nov. 9 and 10 with the Boston Symphony Orchestra. He will play in Carnegie Hall here on Nov. 17."

71. "Wittgenstein Is Soloist," 20 Mar. 1939, 12: "Paul Wittgenstein, celebrated one-armed Austrian pianist now resident in this country, was the soloist with the

New York Federal Civic Orchestra, under Eugene Plotnikoff, at its concert given before a large and appreciative audience last night at the Federal Music Theatre. Mr. Wittgenstein was heard in Ravel's concerto for left hand alone on a program also containing Arthur Gutman's First Suite for String Orchestra and Sibelius's Second symphony."

72. "Dr. Bruno Walter Here; Conductor, Who Banned Concerts in Hitler Area, on Delayed Liner," 4 Mar. 1939, 19: "Dr. Bruno Walter, the conductor, was among the 748 passengers who arrived on the Cunard White Star liner Aquitania, which docked here last night a little after 11 o'clock. The vessel was twelve hours behind schedule as the result of what was described as one of the roughest crossings this Winter. Dr. Walter, who will conduct the National Broadcasting Company Orchestra for a five-week engagement beginning March 11, said he would not conduct again in Salzburg or Vienna as long as Chancellor Hitler was in power. He added that he was 'gratified' that other conductors and vocalists had refused to appear at Salzburg this year. The Aquitania brought about $5,000,000, in gold and 4,000 bags of mail." "Barbirolli Signs for 2 More Years; Philharmonic Re-engages Him as Conductor for 22 Weeks of 30-Week Season; Walter Will Be Guest; Dimitri Mitropoulos Also to Direct in 14 Concerts, First Time with the Orchestra," 18 Feb. 1940, 1:40: "Mr. Walter, who has been associated with the Philharmonic for many years in the past, will conduct fourteen concerts, from Jan. 13 through Feb. 9. Mr. Walter directed the old New York Symphony for three consecutive seasons from 1922, and in 1932 he appeared for the first time with the Philharmonic-Symphony. He returned for several years thereafter. Mr. Walter's reputation is international. Before the Anschluss he was Arturo Toscanini's associate in the Salzburg Festivals. Later he became active in the musical life of Paris, and he was soon honored by the French Government with the title of commander of the Legion of Honor. Mr. Walter opened the current season of the Los Angeles Symphony and will appear as guest conductor of the National Broadcasting Symphony Orchestra on Saturday night."

73. Reviews of the concerts are found on 12, 19, and 26 March and 2 and 9 April, in every case in sec. 3, p. 6. In an interview with Orrin E. Dunlap Jr. published on 26 March 1939, 3:10, Walter limited his political remarks to his pleasure at being in the United States: "I'm happy to breathe the American air; it's bracing, so invigorating." His return to Europe, where he made his home in Paris, was reported on 16 April 1939, 3:6. The next article on him, 5 Feb. 1940, 12, stated that he had "opened the current season of the Los Angeles Symphony and will appear as guest conductor of the National Broadcasting Symphony Orchestra on Saturday night."

74. For notice of his arrival in 1934, see above, note 70. Korngold was in Vienna in 1938 to prepare for the premiere of his opera *Kathrine* at the State Opera that March. He told the rest of the story to *Times* reporter Ross Parmenter during an interview in fall 1942 while preparing to conduct a production of Johann Strauss's *Die Fledermaus* by the New Opera Company at the Broadway Theater. The interview was printed under the headline "Famous at 13: Erich Korngold, Who Has Had Success as Composer for a Long Time," 25 Oct. 1942, 8:6: "Eight weeks before the performance [of *Kathrine*], Warner Brothers cabled to ask if he could come immediately to Hollywood. He decided to postpone the premiere and left for America. 'Six

weeks later, no more Austria,' he said. 'It was a miracle.' After the Anschluss the premiere was arranged for Stockholm for October, 1939. The composer bought his tickets for Sweden, but the war had broken out, and he decided to remain in this country. He plans to remain here permanently, for he took out his first papers for his wife and two sons in 1937 and is now waiting for his final papers. 'I'm grateful that I haven't seen the swastika in Vienna,' he said. 'I have no bad memory. I can still dream of Vienna as it was. I am not a refugee and I am happy I had here a new country before I lost my own.' "

75. "Rosenthal, Pianist, Here; Polish Artist Here on Concert Tour after 60-Year Career," 24 Nov. 1936, 24: "Moriz Rosenthal, Polish pianist, who has been on the concert stage for sixty years and will be 74 next month, arrived yesterday on the French liner Normandie after an absence of seven years. This is his tenth visit to the United States."

76. See Ronald Taylor, *Kurt Weill: Composer in a Divided World* (Boston: Northeastern University Press, 1991), chap. 13: "The New World." The *Times* took note of Weill in an interview printed some six weeks after his arrival, "Kurt Weill's New Score; Music for 'Road of Promise' Written in Modern Contemporary Style," 27 Oct. 1935, 9:7: "Although traditional Hebrew music of the synagogue has been drawn upon to a certain extent for the score of 'The Road of Promise,' the elaborate Jewish morality play scheduled to be presented here by Max Reinhardt in December, modernism will be rampant in the tonal investiture given the spectacle by Kurt Weill, the modernist German opera composer. He is now in New York completing the orchestration of his setting of the text by Franz Werfel. . . . Mr. Weill went on to say that he supposed he could be called, as he was called before his expulsion from Germany, a 'Kultur-Bolshevist.' To express human emotions 'I demand a certain freedom. If you find Beethoven's "Fidelio" political, because it deals with a struggle against injustice, then my music is political, too. But I don't know. I sympathize with the ideas in vogue in Russia and America. I like the development of thought going on in both countries. Yet I am not in the slightest interested in communism as a political creed. What appeals to me most is the idea of brotherhood as set forth in the works of Tolstoy.' " On 18 December 1935 the *Times* reviewed a concert of Weill's music sponsored by the League of Composers, under the headline "Weill Works Are Given; Compositions from His Operas Sung at Cosmopolitan Club," 33. On 27 December 1936, anticipating the endlessly delayed opening of *The Eternal Road*, the *Times* published a second interview with him ("Score For 'The Eternal Road,' " 10:7), noting that in the meantime he had written the score for Paul Green's play *Johnny Johnson*. After a final preproduction article written by Bosley Crowther ("Building 'The Eternal Road'; Some of the Obstacles Encountered in the Formative Career of That Epic Drama," 3 Jan. 1937, 10:1), Brooks Atkinson reviewed the play, calling it "a deeply moving experience in the theatre. Although the event may have had a political motive originally, it is now the story of the ages, told with great dignity, power and beauty" ("The Play; 'The Eternal Road,' Produced by Max Reinhardt, at the Manhattan Opera House," 8 Jan. 1937, 14). Given the circumstances of Weill's immigration almost two years after he had entered and established himself in America, the *Times* had neither reason nor opportunity to note it.

77. It had been planned well in advance, and was first noted in a letter from his

countryman Erno Balogh to the *Times* published on 9 July 1939 (8:6): "Next February Bartók will come for a two-month concert tour on his first visit to this country since 1928."

78. "Bela Bartok Plays Own Compositions; Hungarian Pianist Heard in Second Concert of Capital's Chamber Music Festival; Joseph Szigeti Assists; The Beethoven Sonata, Op. 47, Opens Program—Debussy Work Also Presented," 14 Apr. 1940, 44.

79. 21 Apr. 1940, 9:7 (photograph and announcement of concert); 25 Apr. 1940, 27 (review).

80. "The Art of the Hungarian Composer Bartok; An Estimate of the Music of a Contemporary Who Is on a Visit Here," 10:7. Gombosi had arrived in the United States in 1939.

81. "Bela Bartok, the Hungarian composer and pianist, and his wife, Ditta Pasztory, also a pianist, appear with New Friends of Music today [with photograph]," 3 Nov. 1940, 9:8; and "Bela Bartok Work in Premiere Here; Composer and Wife Heard in 'Music for Two Pianos and Percussion Instruments' at 'New Friends' Concert; Dynamism and Vitality Noted in Number Using 'Hitherto Unexploited Tonal Effects,'" 4 Nov. 1940, 23. The performance of the Music for Two Pianos and Percussion Instruments was its American premiere. The review said nothing about the circumstances of the composer's return to America so soon after his previous visit.

82. So named only because of the musical appeal of the city's name, not because of any connection between the organization and the city.

83. "Ernst Krenek Honored," 28 Feb. 1938, 18: "Ernst Krenek, Austrian composer, whose 'Jonny Spielt Auf' was presented at the Metropolitan Opera House about a decade ago, was the guest of honor at a musicale and reception given by the League of Composers at the Cosmopolitan Club last night. A program of Mr. Krenek's works was presented."

84. Brunswick played a vital role in bringing emigré musicians in that capacity. After resigning from the committee in 1943, he taught briefly at Black Mountain College, home to several emigré musicians and scholars, and Kenyon College; presided over the American section of the International Society for Contemporary Music from 1941 to 1950; and led the Department of Music at the City College of New York from 1946 to 1967.

85. The story of the tour and then the emigration is told in Stewart, *Krenek*, 205–13.

86. "New Zoo Inmates Here from Africa; Liner City of New York Brings Animals and 53 Passengers," 6 Sept. 1940, 15: "The liner City of New York of the American–South African Line docked at the foot of West Forty-fourth Street yesterday morning with fifty-three passengers from twelve ports in Africa, Trinidad and the British West Indies. Dr. James B. McCord, an American medical missionary in South Africa for the last forty years; Bronislaw Huberman, Polish concert violinist and founder of the Palestine Symphony Orchestra, and R. Austin Acly, United States consul at Johannesburg, South Africa, accompanied by his wife and children, were among the passengers. The vessel also brought a consignment of African animals for local zoos, including three zebras, ten antelopes, fifty snakes, a Cape buffalo and two cranes. . . . Mr. Huberman has been in South Africa for three months."

87. "Erich Leinsdorf, who makes his debut as conductor at the Metropolitan

Friday night in 'Walkuere' [with photograph]," 16 Jan. 1938, 10:7. The review appeared six days later, under the headline "Leinsdorf Directs in 'Die Walkuere'; Young Viennese, 26, Makes His New York Debut as Batonist at the Metropolitan. Kirsten Flagstad in Cast; She and Hofmann Sing Roles—Miss Rethberg in Supporting Part/by Noel Straus," 22 Jan. 1938, 19: "The fourth performance this season of Wagner's 'Die Walkuere,' given at the Metropolitan Opera House last night, was the ocassion [*sic*] of the debut of a talented young conductor, Erich Leinsdorf. Although but 26 years old, the new director from Vienna led his forces with a sure hand and in general made a favorable impression. If there was nothing startling about his work it evidenced solid musicianship and was ripe with exceptional promise. Mr. Leinsdorf's principal activities as batonist in the past have been in Italy, where he has directed both operas and concerts at Bologna, Trieste and San Remo. He was engaged for the Salzburg Festival in 1934 and since 1935 has prepared all the operas and choral works led there by Arturo Toscanini. At the Metropolitan he will share the German repertoire with Artur Bodanzky and Maurice de Abravanel. . . . Mr. Leinsdorf's interpretation was one evidencing the arrival of a leader of fine gifts whose future here will be watched with great interest." Leinsdorf had left Vienna for Italy in October 1936 after being told by Erwin Kerber, administrator of the State Opera, that a position at the house was available only, in Kerber's words, "if the rosary hung down from your fly." In December he was invited to join the conducting staff at the Metropolitan. After conducting in Italy that winter and spring and assisting Toscanini at the summer festival in Salzburg, he sailed from Europe on 3 November 1937 and arrived in New York five days later, on a visitor's visa valid for six months, to take up his position. The Anschluß closed Austria to him permanently. Following rejection of his petition to extend his visa for six more months, and with the help of the young Lyndon Johnson, then a newly elected congressman from Texas, he went to Havana in spring 1938 to acquire a permanent visa, and quickly reentered the United States as an immigrant. Leinsdorf recounted the story in his autobiography, *Cadenza: A Musical Career* (Boston: Houghton Mifflin, 1976), 47, 50–51, and 57–79.

88. "Alice Ehlers, harpsichord soloist, Tuesday night with the Philadelphia Orchestra at Carnegie Hall [with photograph]," 1 May 1938, 10:6. Downes's review of the concert, published 4 May 1938, 27, under the headline "Ormandy Directs Closing Concert; Philadelphia Orchestra Ends Season Here—Beethoven and Bach Offered; Alice Ehlers a Soloist; Alexander Hilsberg Heard on Violin—William Kincaid Appears as Flautist," noted simply: "The harpsichordist in the performance of the [Bach Fifth Brandenburg] concerto was the accomplished Alice Ehlers, who long since had proved her gifts in this city."

89. "Gisa Bergmann's Debut; Viennese Soprano Will Appear Tonight at Ambassador Hotel," 4 May 1938, 27: "Mme. Gisa Bergmann, Viennese soprano and former member of the Theater An Der Wien, will give her American debut recital this evening in the Embassy Room of the Ambassador Hotel. She will be accompanied by Fritz Kitzinger."

90. "Joanna Graudan, who appears in sonata recital on Saturday [with photograph]," 11 Dec. 1938, 10:8. The couple's recital was reviewed on 18 Dec., 48: "Nikolai Graudan, Russian 'cellist, and his wife, Joanna Graudan, pianist, made their first American appearance in a program of ensemble works yesterday afternoon at

Town Hall. . . . The couple impressed by the intelligence and feeling for style disclosed, their highly perfected phrasing, and the absolute precision and rhythmic life of their performances."

91. "Adolf Busch and Rudolf Serkin, Who Begin a Series of Three Sonata Recitals at Town Hall Tomorrow Evening [with photograph]," 26 Feb. 1939, 9:7.

92. "Three artists who will make their first local appearances: in the usual order, Dorothy Maynor, soprano; Jarmila Novotna, Czech soprano, who has joined the Metropolitan Opera; and Mario Castelnuovo-Tedesco, Italian composer, who will appear with the Philharmonic-Symphony as pianist in the American premiere of one of his own works [with photograph]," 3 Sept. 1939, 9:5. In anticipation of the world premiere of his second piano concerto, the *Times* had Castelnuovo-Tedesco write a substantial column, "A Composer on Writing Concertos," 29 Oct. 1939, 9:7. Downes reviewed the performance under the headline "Composer-Pianist in Own Concerto; Mario Castelnuovo-Tedesco Is Heard with Philharmonic-Symphony Orchestra; Elgar Music Is Played; The Tschaikovsky Overture, 'Romeo and Juliet,' Included in Barbirolli Program," 3 Nov. 1939, 16. He found the concerto pleasing but slight, preferring the composer's overture to Shakespeare's *Twelfth Night*, which had its first American performance at the same concert.

93. "Beethoven Cycle," 15 Oct. 1939, 9:6: "The Budapest String Quartet will give the complete cycle of Beethoven quartets in a series consisting of four Wednesday night concerts, Nov. 8, 15, 22 and 19, and one Saturday night concert, Dec. 2, at the Ninety-second Street Y.M.H.A. A similar series was presented there by the ensemble two years ago." In the United States at the outbreak of the war, the quartet decided to remain in this country. Their first concert in their new, if unpublicized, personal status was reviewed by Downes under the headline "New Friends [of Music] Open Fourth Year Here; Present the Budapest String Quartet at Town Hall in a Mozart, Brahms Program; Three Quintets Played; William Primrose, Violist, and Ellen Stone, Horn Player, the Guest Soloists," 30 Oct. 1939, 13. Downes wrote about them in terms of familiar approval, for he knew their work well. There is no reason to believe that he knew about their changed status in America.

94. "Among the week's performers: Robert Goldsand, piano recitalist, at Town Hall, and Helen Marshall, soprano soloist with the Bell Chorus of New York [with photograph]," 21 Apr. 1940, 9:8. Howard Taubman reviewed the recital under the headline "Goldsand, Pianist, Has Recital Here; One-Time Boy Prodigy of Vienna Gives Program of Contrasts at the Town Hall; Retired in '35 to Study; Compositions of Bach, Chopin, Schubert, Hummel, Scriabin Reveal His Artistry," 24 Apr. 1940, 18: "Robert Goldsand, Viennese pianist, made his first American appearance in 1927 as a lad of 16, and his last in February, 1935. He returned last night in a recital at the Town Hall, an artist with an extraordinary command of virtually all facets of piano playing. On the basis of some of last night's performances, he deserves to take rank with the elite of the piano world."

95. "Viennese composers who will conduct their own music in a program of the art of Vienna at Carnegie Hall on Wednesday: Robert Stolz, Emmerich Kalman and Oskar Strauss [with photograph]," 9 Feb. 1941, 9:8.

96. "Elisabeth Schumann, right, who will appear here in song recital tonight [with photograph]," 13 Nov. 1938, 9:7.

97. "The orchestra of the New Friends of Music begins a series at Carnegie Hall

today. Here is Fritz Stiedry, the conductor, rehearsing the orchestra, and, at left, Artur Schnabel, today's piano soloist [with photograph]," 17 Mar. 1940, 10:7.

98. *Artur Schnabel: My Life and Music* (New York: St. Martin's Press, 1963), 105–7, 111–14.

99. Notice of 21 Jan. 1940, 9:7: "When Egon Petri, the Dutch pianist, appears at Town Hall on Feb. 24, it will be his first local recital in four years. During that time he had been living in Poland, concertizing in the main seasons and conducting a master class in Cracow in the Summers. This season he had planned to come to America for a short tour, not to include this city. But in August, 1939, the Dutch Consul warned him to leave Poland and return to his native land. Overnight, Mr. Petri fled the country with his wife and three American pupils on one of the last available trains. He left behind him a large library of books, printed music and several manuscripts. The books were particularly dear to him because many of them had been hand-bound by Mrs. Petri, whose bookbinding has won prizes in Europe. Within a week of his arrival in Holland, friends had arranged three concerts for him, which put some ready cash in his hands. Still other friends hastened to extend his tour in America, and decided to include New York. Whether Mr. Petri will make his home in this country is not certain, but it seems likely. He remarked that his own teacher, Ferruccio Busoni, had found sanctuary in Chicago during the last war."

100. "Festival Featured by Kolisch Quartet; Viennese Musicians Received Warmly in Debut—The Paris Quintet Gives Program/by Olin Downes," 9 Apr. 1935, 25: "Washington, April 8.—The second day of the Library of Congress Festival of Music presented as its most notable feature the American début of the Kolisch Quartet of Vienna, which had an immense success." "The Kolisch Quartet; Debut in Washington Is Outstanding Event of Coolidge Festival/by Olin Downes," 14 Apr. 1935, 9:5: "The outstanding event, from the standpoint of musical news, of the Library of Congress Festival of Chamber Music held last Sunday, Monday and Tuesday in Washington was the triumphant American début of the Kolisch String Quartet of Vienna. This took place on the morning of the 8th. Flattering reports of the Kolisch players had preceded them, but it is easy to be skeptical of advance reports of music from Europe. European standards of performance are not ours. Critical reviews can be stripped of all fault-findings or reservations, and the emasculated review, containing only phrases which are complimentary, can come by cable from overseas. Artists with impressive European reputations are often coldly received here, while others who have not reached success overseas come to America and make their fortune. A quartet long famous in Europe, whose success was anticipated when they came in a former season to Washington, fell far short of expectations when they made an initial appearance at one of the very chamber music festivals which represent Mrs. Elizabeth Sprague Coolidge's gift to the nation. It was then shown that the quartet in question had outlived its great period and that its honors were those of its past. The Kolisch Quartet is a young organization which has not yet attained its tenth year. The players are young—Rudolf Kolisch and Felix Khuner, violins; Eugene Lehner, viola; Benar Heifetz (not a relative of the violinist), 'cello. They have youth and also knowledge. . . . They have an uncannily finished, flexible and brilliant ensemble. The most exceptional finish and adjustment of technical detail is supplemented by the warmth and vividness of their playing."

101. "Chavez Conducts Beethoven Work; That and 'Anacreon' Overture Added

to Previous Bills with Philharmonic; Pianists Heard in Debut; Vitya Vronsky and Victor Babin, Russian Artists, Perform at the Town Hall / by H. Howard Taubman," 15 Feb. 1937, 12: "At the Town Hall at the same time two young Russians, Vitya Vronsky and Victor Babin—they are Mr. and Mrs. Babin—made their American début as a two piano team. . . . It appears that Miss Vronsky and Mr. Babin are known to American audiences through their records, which have underlined their accomplishments. In their appearance in the flesh they lived up to the advance notices, which is rare among débutantes."

102. Beethoven Group Closes Its Season; Marjorie Lawrence and the Roth Quartet on Program at Town Hall; Dvorak Music Included; Works by Mussorgsky, Mozart and Wolf Also Are Heard—Felix Wolfes Pianist / by H. Howard Taubman," 12 Apr. 1938, 27: "The Beethoven Association closed its nineteenth season of concerts, which are presented annually "in a spirit of artistic fraternity," with one of the most attractive programs of the year at the Town Hall last night. The artists were Marjorie Lawrence, Metropolitan Opera soprano, who had the assistance of Felix Wolfes at the piano, and the Roth Quartet, consisting of Feri Roth, Jeno Antal, Ferenc Molnar and Janos Scholz. . . . Mr. Wolfes, an expert musician, made the piano an integral part of the interpretation both in the Wolf and Mussorgsky songs."

103. "Busoni Society Gives Concert," 21 Apr. 1938, 17: "The first concert of the newly formed Busoni Society, whose purpose is to stimulate an interest in the work of this composer, took place last night at Steinway Hall, with Eduard Steuermann and Michael Zadora giving a recital of music for two pianos. . . . There was a good-sized, well-disposed audience."

104. "Toscanini Directs Score by Strauss; He Leads the NBC Symphony Orchestra in Performance of 'Don Quixote'; Two Soloists are Heard; Feuermann Is the 'Cellist and Cooley Violist—Beethoven Music Also Played / by Olin Downes," 23 Oct. 1938, 1:40: "The concert given last night in Radio City by Toscanini and the NBC Symphony Orchestra began with a performance of Rossini's 'Cenerentola' overture . . . and proceeded with one of the most subtle and moving interpretations that Toscanini has ever given in this city. The composition so presented by him was Richard Strauss's 'Don Quixote.' The audience was fortunate in more than one respect. For it is seldom indeed that an interpretation of this score can count on such a solo 'cellist as Emanuel Feuermann, reinforced by a violist of the quality of Carlton Cooley." Feuermann, a Swiss resident since the end of 1936, had undertaken several tours in America, the last of them in February and March 1938. He returned to Zurich in April, performed Strauss's *Don Quixote* with Toscanini and the BBC Orchestra in London on 23 May, and that summer decided to settle in the United States. After extricating his parents from Nazi-occupied Vienna in September and settling them in Palestine with Huberman's help, he and his family left for New York. See Seymour W. Itzkoff, *Emanuel Feuermann, Virtuoso* (University: University of Alabama Press, 1979), 176–81. Following the 22 October reprise in New York of Feuermann's partnership with Toscanini in *Don Quixote,* and a second concert in November, he and his wife took out first citizenship papers, as reported in "Noted Exiles Turn to U.S. Citizenship; George Grosz Gets His Final Papers in Brooklyn— Emanuel Feuermann Files Plea; Both Escaped the Nazis; German Artist Departed in '33—Austrian Musician Fled to Switzerland 4 Years Ago," 30 Nov. 1938, 17: "Two leading exponents of German art and German music who left Nazi Germany as

exiles, adopted the United States yesterday as their new homeland. George Groz [*sic*], painter and caricaturist, was admitted to citizenship by Judge Marcus B. Campbell in Federal court, Brooklyn, and Emanuel Feuermann, considered one of the world's greatest 'cellists, applied for citizenship papers at the Federal Building in Manhattan. . . . Mr. Feuermann, a native of Austria, left Germany four years ago and has since been living in Switzerland. He was a child prodigy, making his debut as a 'cellist in Vienna at the age of 11, and was later the head of the 'cello department of the famous Hochschuler Fur Musik [*sic*] in Berlin. He owns the last 'cello made by Stradivarius, an instrument insured by Lloyds of London for $35,000. Mr. Feuermann, now 35, has appeared in many concerts in this country in recent years. His most recent appearance was on Monday night at Carnegie Hall. His wife, Eva, accompanied him to the Federal Building to take out first citizenship papers for herself. They live at 100 Pelham Road, New Rochelle, and have one child, Monica, who was born eight months ago while Mr. Feuermann was appearing in a concert at Carnegie Hall."

105. "Elisabeth Schumann Recital," 14 Nov. 1938, 14: "Elisabeth Schumann, the eminent Viennese soprano, who recently returned to this country with the intention of making her permanent home here, was fervently welcomed by a large gathering at her annual recital last night in Town Hall."

106. See above, note 71.

107. "Kipnis Has Debut at Metropolitan; Basso Appears as Gurnemanz in Season's Second 'Parsifal'—Melchior in Title Role; Flagstad Again Kundry; Walter Olitzki and Friedrich Schorr Are Also in Cast—Leinsdorf Conducts/by Olin Downes," 6 Jan. 1940, 8: "The season's second 'Parsifal,' given yesterday afternoon in the Metropolitan Opera House for the benefit of the Girl Scout Federation of New York, presented Alexander Kipnis, basso, who then made his first appearance with the Metropolitan Opera Association as Gurnemanz. Mr. Kipnis immediately won the favor of his audience. . . . The Klingsor was Walter Olitzki, who did not have very much dramatic force, or, despite cleanness of diction, vocal distinction. Friedrich Schorr's Amfortas was authoritative and moving, as ever. Mr. Leinsdorf does not seem to have penetrated deeply to the essence of the score, nor was the orchestral performance, on the technical side, faultless. For all that, the opera was heard with absorbed attention and, save for the end of the second act, without applause. 'La Boheme' at Metropolitan[:] Another Metropolitan début of highly unusual interest was that of Jarmila Novotna, yesterday evening, as Mimi in 'La Boheme.' . . . Mme. Novotna presented her character with charming simplicity, feeling and high artistic intelligence. The voice is not remarkable for opulence or sheer beauty, but it was expressively employed. It has ample range and is capable both of brilliancy and emotional expression. . . . By the end of [the first] act there was a special demonstration for Mme. Novotna, whose name was called repeatedly by the audience and was heard through the tumult and acclaim."

108. "Schnabel Soloist in Mozart Works; Plays the D Minor and C Major Piano Concertos at Concert of New Friends of Music," 18 Mar. 1940, 2: "The New Friends of Music, an organization that is living up to its name, began its Carnegie Hall series yesterday afternoon. . . . Mr. Schnabel played enchantingly, with a blend of pulsing vitality and affecting tenderness."

109. Thus, for example Artur Holde, a conductor, composer, and critic active in

Frankfurt, and his wife, the pianist Heida Hermanns, fled to Belgium in summer 1934, then soon returned and became active in the Frankfurt branch of the Jüdische Kulturbund. After passage of the Nuremberg Laws they planned a second flight, this one permanent. Purporting to undertake a concert tour of the United States, the couple obtained American tourist visas, booked round-trip passage to New York, and left Germany in 1937 with only the bags they could carry. They never used their return tickets. Instead, on arriving in the United States they applied for citizenship, which they received in 1943, and Holde recreated in New York the multifaceted musical career that he had abandoned in Frankfurt. His biography is found in the preface to the revised edition of his *Jews in Music: From the Age of Enlightenment to the Mid–Twentieth Century*, ed. Irene Heskes (New York: Bloch, 1974).

110. "Concert and Opera; Effort Made to Place Refugee Conductors—Development of Local Orchestras," 14 Aug. 1938, 9:5.

111. "Musicologists in U.S.; Eminent Scholars of Europe Working and Writing in America Now," 8 Sept. 1940, 9:5.

112. "Smith Expands Summer Music; Joins Other Colleges by Adding Musicology to Its Courses," 17 May 1942, 2:7.

113. "Problem of Adjustment; Clashing Interests between Native Musicians and Refugees Come to America from Overseas," 19 Jan. 1941, 9:7.

114. "Refugee Problem; Debate Continues on Question of Place of Musicians from Abroad," 26 Jan. 1941, 9:7.

115. "Invasion of Ideas; Need Not Be Feared in Music If the Nation Retains Cultural Identity," 2 Feb. 1941, 9:7.

116. "Record of WPA Project," 2 Feb. 1941, 9:7.

117. Mahler (1901–73), a student of Schoenberg, Berg, Webern, and Guido Adler at the University of Vienna, had conducted in Vienna, various German cities, and Copenhagen before emigrating in 1936 to America, where he became a citizen three years later. The National Youth Administration Orchestra was his first conducting position here; in later years he led the Erie (1947–53) and Hartford (1953–64) orchestras, and taught at the Juilliard School and, in his later years, at Tokyo University (1967–70).

118. "Points of View Culled from the Mail Pouch; NYA Workshop's American Performances—The Problem of Native Composers," 9 Feb. 1941, 9:8.

119. "From the Mail Pouch," 16 Feb. 1941, 9:6.

120. Ibid.

121. Peter Dykema, professor of Musical Education at Teachers College, Columbia University, had just returned from a tour of Europe with fifty-five students and "an extra month alone in Germany studying music trends and the effects of music on the national life."

122. "The new text, which was written by Herman Burte, South German poet and dramatist, at the request of the National Socialist Kultur Community, is entitled 'Hero and Work for Peace' and is based on 'the distress and resurgence of the German people.'"

123. Hermann Roebbeling had been director of the Burgtheater since 1931.

PART THREE

Acculturation and Identity

Composers in Exile
The Question of Musical Identity

Hermann Danuser

There is much talk about identity these days. This is particularly true in Germany, where since the fall of the Berlin Wall in 1989 and the reunification of the two German states into a larger Federal Republic a year later the question of political or national identity has been intensively posed.[1]

Strangely enough, musicology has rarely addressed the issue of identity head on. Is it because we automatically presuppose a strong identity already to be in place whenever a famous composer is mentioned? Whatever the answer, it seems certain that an explicit interest in "identity" arises only in the moment when it is no longer assumed to be intact: when it is—and is perceived as—endangered.

Within the context of this collection of essays, problems of artistic and personal identity gain a very special relevance. For the emigration or exile of musicians from Central Europe (or more precisely, from all the territories under the influence of Nazi Germany) as a result of political persecution by the National Socialists, and their subsequent integration within U.S. society, raises many questions concerning the loss, reconstruction, and maintenance of identity. In this essay I will concentrate on composers, though similar questions could and ought to be asked about performers, teachers, and musicologists as well. After posing some remarks on identity as a general category, I will attempt to apply this category to the music-historical period of the 1930s and 1940s by constructing an "ideal type"; I will end my discussion of musical identity by considering in some detail the cases of several composers and a few selected works.

The theory of identity, as developed in the history of philosophy, has produced many meanings, from Plato down to Heidegger and Adorno. Hegel, in the second part of his *Wissenschaft der Logik,* on the doctrine of the essence (*Lehre vom Wesen*), emphatically rejected what we might call a philosophy of identity based on the laws of mere rationality. He speaks out against what he terms purely reflective definitions of essentialism ("reine Wesensbestimmungen [der] Wesensphilosophie"), such that "The principle of identity [is that] All is identical with itself; A = A; or—negatively—A cannot be both A and not A." This principle, instead of being a true principle of philosophical thinking, is nothing but the law of the abstract rational mind.[2] Hegel probably argues against this premise so strongly because his own dialectical philosophy, with its *Bewegung des Begriffs* (movement of the concept), relies on the *Aufhebung* (suspension—which implies both annihilation and preservation) of this principle of abstract identity.

Indeed, "identity" without its counternotion, "difference," is meaningless. Only when both are considered together can fruitful questions be asked. In music history too, and especially in its modern phase, true artistic identity is inconceivable without difference—that is, without discontinuities, crises, and development. I will therefore use the term "identity" not as a logical category (being identical with itself), but rather as a historical category (remaining identical with itself), thus encompassing both the different and new. Only then can we ask questions about artistic identity in times of far-reaching changes; only then does it make sense to question the possible validity of the category for composers in exile. Otherwise we would be deploring the emigration or exile from Germany only as a loss of identity.

Nevertheless, one might ask whether the idea of identity is not linked to a questionable philosophy of reconciliation, one that follows Hegel's premise that truth is the whole ("Das Wahre ist das Ganze"), which again implies as elements both identity and difference.[3] Theodor W. Adorno, himself an exiled philosopher and musician (large parts of his *Philosophy of New Music* and his contribution to Thomas Mann's novel *Doktor Faustus* were written in the United States),[4] formulated his theory of the "non-identical" in explicit opposition to the Western tradition of the philosophy of identity.[5] In his *Minima Moralia* one reads, "Das Ganze ist das Unwahre" (the whole is falsehood), which reverses Hegel's formula doubly, and it might well be that Adorno's insistence on this central point (right up until the end of his life in 1969) was motivated by his having experienced the barbarism of Hitler and been expelled from his native Germany.[6] Remembering Adorno's philosophy, therefore, we are warned against the danger of explaining even the deepest deviations, the broadest reorientations, the biggest changes in the biographies of exiles as simply a fulfillment of a dialectical principle of identity, however positive the impact of the immigrants on the music culture of America and especially on the development of an American modernism might have been.[7]

It is well known that the decisive premises for the formation of identity are language and culture. Thus, the migration from one sphere of language and culture into another triggers a pressure of assimilation on the part of immigrants, who feel forced into changing an earlier identity. Following Martin Heidegger, who defined language as one's *Heimat* (homeland), migration into a foreign land might be understood as a loss of *Heimat.*[8] Humans, however, have the capacity of learning foreign languages, and of adapting to new cultures. The loss of identity, therefore, might well have as its counterpart the gaining of a new identity, produced by successful assimilation, or "acculturation," to an initially foreign land. Yet some of the émigrés—Thomas Mann being the most famous example—wished to preserve their own cultural tradition in exile rather than accommodate to the foreign society and culture.

Musicians and to a certain extent composers had better chances of successful professional integration into their chosen land of exile than did most other refugees from Nazi Germany. Given their special competence, musicians could adapt more easily than writers, who were confronted with the dilemma of either working in the unfamiliar language of their new home or, after having chosen to continue working in their native language, of becoming even more isolated in the new society. However, music too is bound to specific cultural contexts; it cannot be looked at simply as a "universal language in tones."[9] Differences of pragmatic references, of audiences, of performance styles, as well as institutional and aesthetic bases, are significant, even when the repertoire in question, as during the 1930s and 1940s, is in a sense international. To acknowledge these differences, however, does not mean that a maintenance of identity through adaptation to changed circumstances was impossible; on the contrary, it is precisely the capacity to change (as personified paradigmatically by Goethe's figure Faust) that forms an essential prerequisite for human life in general, and in a more specific sense, for modern art and music.

If the period of music history in question were not the twentieth century but an earlier period, problems of musical identity could possibly be dealt with by referring to style. (As is well known, the investigation of this category was established and fostered by the Viennese musicological school of Guido Adler, many of whose disciples belonged to the group of persecuted musicians who sought refuge in the English-speaking world before and during World War II.)[10] During the twentieth century, however, the category of style has become almost irrelevant in music history. To understand why, we should, as I propose in *Die Musik des 20. Jahrhunderts,* distinguish between two opposed ideals of music: "autonomous music" and "artful functional music" (*artifizielle Funktionsmusik* or as I also call it, *mittlere Musik;* that is, functional music that reflects the tradition of art music by both deliberately continuing and violating it).[11]

In the historiography of twentieth-century music, the paradigm of autonomous music is the older ideal, taken over directly from the nineteenth century.[12] It is based on the premise that art music should be composed,

performed, and listened to for its own sake, and that wherever it seems
to serve other purposes, these purposes are alien to the music itself. Composers of the older generation, especially Schoenberg, Stravinsky, and Bartók, felt bound to this ideal. The paradigm of artful functional music, by
contrast—which over the centuries (until the nineteenth, that is) was the
accepted ideal—was embraced by the younger generation of composers,
most of whom were born around 1900.[13] This approach became prominent
shortly after World War I when there was a burst of creative energy and a
seemingly infinite and easy flow of new musical ideas emerged. Kurt Weill,
Paul Hindemith, Ernst Krenek, and Hanns Eisler among others formed this
generation. Leaving aside the many differences among them, all these composers were convinced that the aesthetic ideas of the nineteenth century, especially the notion of "Weltanschauungsmusik," were a thing of the past and
irrelevant for their own creative thinking. Instead, they focused their energy on the diversity that could be discovered in all fields of musical life—
not only, and indeed not primarily, in the high concert culture—and it was
their aim to react as quickly, flexibly, and ingeniously as possible to the specific needs of a variety of audiences.[14]

Obviously, such a broad dichotomy indicates no more than a trend, albeit a significant one, in the history of music. It does not mark a bipartite
scheme in which all composers can be encompassed without further differentiation. Even within the oeuvres of certain composers, as we shall see
when we compare Paul Hindemith's attitude of the 1940s with that of the
1920s, both paradigms may be represented. However, to returning to the
theme of musical migration—of composers in exile—I would claim that
both paradigms played a similar role in a certain respect: they allowed the
preservation of musical identity.

For an artist whose creation was oriented toward the realization of permanent (*dauerhaft*) music in the Brahmsian sense, that is, following the autonomous musical ideal, the particular conditions of composition were un-
important.[15] Indeed, the work of art, which was the sole aim and goal, was
defined by its very independence from the circumstances of its genesis.
Therefore (assuming, of course, that the economic situation was satisfactory), an artist who was inclined toward this ideal felt elevated above the circumstances of everyday life and able to produce musical works virtually
anywhere. An example of this attitude is provided by Paul Hindemith, who
wrote to his publisher, Willy Strecker, in 1947:

> In one's young years landscape, atmosphere, education, and personal attach-
> ment to matters and events can prove to be an important stimulus for artistic
> work. Now, however, I find that the history of persons, events, and experi-
> ences as well as their interpretation and arrangement by artistic means is less
> strongly connected with these externalities. What matters is how someone uses
> and assimilates his experiences; it is far less significant to always assemble them

anew on the spot. If this were different, then one's desire to deal with a German subject matter should have definitively evaporated during the course of the last twelve years. As far as people with a sedate disposition are concerned, the Rhine does not appear to be more important than the Mississippi, the Connecticut Valley, or the Gobi Desert for the working out of profoundly sound plans.[16]

Under the premises of the artful-functional musical ideal, in contrast, preservation of identity in the context of migration was possible for opposite reasons. In this case, an artist could prevail because he was able to respond to the changing needs of production, a requirement that lay at the heart of this paradigm. The composer who was bound to this ideal in Europe before emigration could rightly consider accommodation of his creative fantasy to the musical life of 1930s and 1940s America as an essential part of his musical identity and, indeed, the greatest challenge of his life.

A preservation of musical identity would have been virtually impossible if one paradigm had been dominant in European culture while the other paradigm drove musical creation in the United States. In that case, a composer would have been compelled to reorient his creativity suddenly, completely, and without any preparation toward an ideal that until the moment of migration was alien to his artistic experience. Such a dramatic and profound move, and the extreme tension thereby engendered, would likely have destroyed artistic, or musical, identity.

Fortunately, the historical reality was less sinister than this extreme and abstractly sketched case. I will now proceed to the closer consideration of some case studies. In this context, of course, the focus must be on categorization rather than on the detailed analysis of works. I will follow a scheme of "double parallel biography," looking simultaneously at a composer of the "autonomous" orientation and one of the "functional" orientation.

The first two composers to be compared and contrasted are Weill and Stravinsky. Perhaps the most obvious—certainly the most discussed—case of a problematical artistic identity is that of Kurt Weill. The question is: Are there *two* Weills—a German and an American one—or is there only *one* Weill? The composer who wrote chamber music, two symphonies, operas, and other works in various genres for music institutions in Weimar Germany, and the composer who after 1935 made a successful career as a Broadway composer in New York: are they one and the same artistic person or should we think of Weill in terms of two distinct personalities? Does a man who, after having immigrated to the United States in 1935, tried to replace his native German tongue as completely as possible by the newly acquired American language have one or two linguistic identities?

From a musicological standpoint, which stresses the differences between, broadly speaking, autonomous works and a heteronomous production, the gap between the German and the American phase in Weill's career seems irreconcilable, and therefore the hypothesis of "two Weills" is probable.[17] However, recent research has caused the emphasis to be shifted more and more toward the thesis of "one Weill."[18]

This shift is made with good reason. For however strongly the musical genres cultivated by Weill in Germany and the United States differed, the fact that Weill belonged to the aforementioned generation of younger composers striving toward the ideal of artful functional music provided an artistic basis for a continued identity. No matter whether Weill, with the *Threepenny Opera* and *The Rise and Fall of the City of Mahagonny*, was producing a critical music theater in Germany in collaboration with Brecht, or whether he was contributing, with works as different as *Lady in the Dark* and *Street Scene*, to the Broadway musical theater, the basic artistic ideal of a functional, though highly artful and refined, music remained the same in both periods.[19] Consideration of the audience, the public, was a central premise of Weill's artistic production throughout his career. Furthermore, many elements of Weill's European works were incorporated into his American works, so that it is possible to speak of common links between his European and American phases, not only as far as the constancy of the basic aesthetic ideal is concerned, but also with regard to compositional techniques and musical characteristics.[20]

Weill's radical break with the German tradition was presumably his way of mastering the past. The thesis of the German philosopher Odo Marquard, that a man has not just one single identity but several different identities, in the sense of roles, proves to be valid for Weill, an immigrant as opposed to an exile, in a very special way.[21] Weill's capacity for adaptation was a key to his success, not only of his person but also of his musical ideals, which proved to be fertile even under such dramatically different circumstances.

In contrast to Weill, Igor Stravinsky is as an example of a composer whose identity rested on the opposite ideal, that of autonomous music. What does this mean in regard to Stravinsky's postmigration musical identity?

It is well known that Stravinsky composed his works on the basis of commissions. In the fall of 1939, when he entered the United States as a voluntary immigrant in order to give the Charles Eliot Norton lectures at Harvard University on musical poetics, he was not on the threshold to a new world. He already knew the United States through visits and several previous commissions, including that for the *Symphony of Psalms,* which was commissioned by Serge Koussevitzky to celebrate the fiftieth anniversary of the Boston Symphony Orchestra in 1930. The work, notably, was composed in France in Latin, and conveys a special spiritual or religious, even Russian, sensibility.[22]

In terms of musical style, I believe that it is impossible to identify any specific American influence in Stravinsky's works. The Symphony in Three Movements, for example, composed between 1942 and 1945 (the latter year being the year he became a naturalized U.S. citizen, is a work constructed entirely in the manner of modern classicism, which had been Stravinsky's idiom since about 1920.[23]

Of course, historiography does not necessarily see his musical identity in this way. The article on Stravinsky—who is described as an "American composer of Russian origin"—in the fifth edition of the *Grove Dictionary of Music and Musicians* (1954) describes his permanent settlement in the United States as a positive step, a kind of turning point toward new achievements:

> On the outbreak of the second world war Stravinsky retired to the U.S.A., where he has lived ever since, having acquired American nationality. There is no doubt that the change of *milieu* has been on the whole beneficial to his development, although for most artists the contrary is usually the case. The cosmopolitan environment of Paris during the 1920s and 1930s may have proved a too distracting influence; at all events his American or "third" period has proved to be one of the most fruitful.[24]

One is hardly surprised that Michail Druskin, on the other hand, in his otherwise valuable monograph on the composer, considered the 1940s a low point in the creative career of Stravinsky, an interpretation perhaps understandable from a Soviet perspective:

> After he had lost his closest relatives, had been deprived of his normal circumstances and separated from his friends and acquaintances, he once again found himself condemned—on the eve of his sixtieth birthday—to rearrange his life (at the side of his second wife) under social and cultural conditions which would remain alien to his nature until the very last day. In his actions one can detect confusion and bewilderment, as well as in his unintentional concessions to the "American taste"; this confusion in Stravinsky's creativity reached its climax at the beginning of the 1940s.[25]

Stravinsky, regardless how his American period is viewed, can serve as an example of a composer bound to an ideal of autonomy, one that grounded him artistically throughout the various periods, countries, and stylistic phases of his life: Russian, French, American; or Russian folk–like, (neo)classical, serial. To write on the basis of commissions did not mean that Stravinsky abrogated his independence. He was certainly shrewd enough to maintain his very own, very personal artistic ideal no matter how the composition process was initiated.

Next I should like to explore the question of musical identity with regard to Arnold Schoenberg and Hanns Eisler, who had, as teacher and student, a rather special relationship, one that was at once very close and very distant. And here again, we find one composer adhering to the ideal of autonomous music, while the other worked in the realm of artful (or at least not artless) functional music.

Schoenberg was forced to flee from Germany for two reasons: he was

Jewish and he was a leading exponent of modern music. Eisler had to flee
for three reasons: in addition to being Jewish and a modern composer, he
was politically affiliated with the Marxist Communist movement.

It is well known that the initially very close relationship between the
teacher and the student broke apart in the middle of the 1920s, when Eisler
forswore the aesthetics of musical autonomy and moved toward the left, politically as well as musically.[26] His *Kampflieder,* his ballads, his compositions
for film and theater after the late 1920s had nothing to do with the severe
musical constructivism and modern classicism of the early dodecaphonic
works of Schoenberg—unless, following Carl Dahlhaus, one subsumes both
under the category of functionalism.[27]

Their common origins notwithstanding, the musical identities of Schoenberg and Eisler, who both lived in Berlin in the late 1920s, were vastly different, in aesthetic orientation, in compositional style, and even in matters
of performance practice, all in accord with the deep contrast between their
basic musical ideals. A comparison of the compositional developments of
these two composers after exile is informative.

In the United States, Arnold Schoenberg disregarded the tenets of an
assimilated Jew in Europe and returned, as Alexander Ringer has shown, to
his Jewish identity, studying Judaism and Zionism intensively.[28] During this
process, which had in fact begun long before he reached America, he was
able to maintain his artistic identity through a process of transformation.
The ideal of the great tradition of German music since J. S. Bach, which
was the basis of his artistic self and the root of his modernism—a basis still
stressed emphatically while he was developing his dodecaphonic compositional procedures—was, in his view, hopelessly corrupted by the Nazis, who
relentlessly emphasized the term "deutsche Musik," though, of course, in a
very different sense. Schoenberg did not question his adherence to this tradition of musical culture since Bach—to renounce it would probably have
destroyed his musical identity—but he made a clever terminological twist.[29]
Once in the United States, he did not speak any longer of the tradition of
"German music," but referred simply to "classical music," a term that also
included romantic music as well as Viennese classicism. In his creative output, Schoenberg maintained his ideal of autonomous music and continued
the series of dodecaphonic works begun in Europe. Works like the Fourth
String Quartet and the Violin and Piano Concertos, though composed in
this country, betray nothing of his situation as an émigré. These works could
as easily have been written in a non-Nazi Germany.

Schoenberg did, however, write a series of other, more involved (*enga-
giert*) compositions. Indeed, they nudge the concept of autonomy in the
direction of political or religious involvement, though without altogether
breaking with the ideal of autonomous art. These works include the English text–based *Kol Nidre, Ode to Napoleon,* and *A Survivor from Warsaw.* All
these works are "weltanschaulich," but in a different sense than is true of the

great *Weltanschauungsmusik* from the period before and around the First World War (the chorus *Friede auf Erden,* for example, or the *Gurrelieder,* or even the oratorio *Die Jakobsleiter*). Conceived as part of the protest against Hitler and Schoenberg's own fight for the Jewish cause, these works differ significantly in musical form from the earlier classicist instrumental works; the form is more individual, with the English texts reflecting Schoenberg's situation in the United States and underlining his new linguistic identity. By loosening the models of neoclassicism, Schoenberg was able to create works that convey the specific substance with which he was involved more fully than if he had remained closer to his tradition.

Nevertheless, we cannot speak, in the case of Schoenberg, of an abandonment of the previous ideal of autonomy, but rather of a transformation in the artistic identity of this composer, the transformation being his own response to the problem of preserving identity. The transformation points in the direction of the ideal toward which Schoenberg's student Eisler had moved: that of an artful, well-constructed—even superbly constructed— functional music.

Although Hanns Eisler also secured his artistic identity during his American exile by means of transformation, he did so by proceeding in quite the opposite direction. In leaving Europe, Eisler lost the possibility of making an immediate political impact through functional music; in his American, particularly his Californian, exile, therefore, he partly turned his back on the strictly functional approach, writing several works that appeal instead to the autonomous tradition of the Schoenberg School. In Eisler's case, then, one could speak of a sentimental perseverance of musical identity. In his Third Piano Sonata (1943), the hard Eislerian idiom is complemented by passages in a late-romantic harmonic style reminiscent of Alban Berg's Piano Sonata. It is as if Eisler's memory were taking him back to his native Vienna. Of course, the music—and it is great music, by the way—still resides in an aesthetics of discontinuity, clarity, and distance.[30] Is it not possible to hear the unusual expressiveness of this music as a reference to Eisler's changed situation as a composer in exile? Although autonomous, the music mirrors the condition of exile through a melancholy tone, a melancholy that marked the broken, even shattered artistic identity of this composer following his emigration from his homeland.

Although the situation of emigration through which these two men avoided physical annihilation in Nazi Germany indeed had an influence on the musical style of their works, interestingly, this influence worked in opposite ways. Because the practical opportunity for realizing Eisler's particular ideal of functional music was lacking in America, he turned to rather autonomous works (among others, of course)—music for hibernation, so to speak. Schoenberg, in contrast, called into question his thus far unchallenged ideal of an autonomous music separated from life, in a time when he was engaged in the political-religious struggle in favor of Judaism.

Artistic identity in the modern age is only conceivable, as I pointed out earlier, as a concept that entails change—but change within certain limits. In adapting to their changed circumstances, these composers did not abandon their identities, but rather reinforced them—reinforced them in the sense that both men reactivated earlier foundations of their artistic lives through an act of modification. Schoenberg, in turning to the idea of functionalism and musical involvement, reactivated aspects of his artistic youth in the workers' culture of Vienna; Eisler, in creating more autonomous works, reactivated his heritage in the Schoenberg School, which as an added benefit led to a better personal relationship with his former teacher in America.[31]

The examples provided by Weill and Stravinsky, Schoenberg and Eisler, respectively, open up a broader spectrum for the category of musical identity in the historical period of the 1930s and 1940s. Returning to Adorno's philosophy of the "nonidentical," we see why nothing could be harmonized, nothing smoothed out. Wounds, wounds of the deepest kind, remained for nearly every person involved, whatever the personal experience might have been. But the will to survive these wounds helped these artists to bring their works to life.

Identity and identities: the singular and the plural are relevant, relevant to the biographies of our composers no less than to their music. By assuming the nonidentical, we are no longer forced to look to the old-fashioned category of personal style as marking a composer's musical identity. Although that category may have been useful in earlier times, it is of little or no use when modern music is at stake.

Bearing in mind Karol Berger's arguments against the proclaimed death of the author, I would like, finally, to turn from the notion of "musical identity" to that of "personal identity" in order to place our discussion in a somewhat different light.[32] Ever since George Herbert Meads and Anselm Leonard Strauss, sociologists have stressed the importance of social background and environment for the formation of personal identity. According to such theories, self-consciousness—that is, a person's consciousness of his individuality, his *Sich-Selbstgleichheit,* or the state of being identical with himself—is not to be regarded as an outcome of self-definition, but rather as arising from his interaction with institutionally predetermined role models, including the manner in which they are perceived, fulfilled, renounced, or modified. Strauss emphasizes the "unfinished, tentative, explorative, hypothetical, deviating, malleable and only partly unified character of human actions."[33] Likewise, Jürgen Habermas draws a distinction between "personal" and "social identity": "Personal identity has its manifestation in the unity of an unmistakable biography, social identity [is manifested] in an individual's longing to belong to different social groups. Personal identity assures the consistency of biographical continuity in a 'vertical' manner; social identity, by contrast, guarantees the possibility of fulfilling the demands of all role-systems to which a person belongs in a 'horizontal' fashion."[34] Let us remind ourselves that "crisis" not only refers to an event with negative connotations, it is also one of the fundamental preconditions for the constitution of identity. According to Erik H. Erikson, childhood and adolescence are characterized by a "phase-specific succession of psycho-sociological crises," so that one can speak of self-identity proper only when a person is mature.[35] These positive (or at least ambivalent aspects) of crises within the context of identity and development also have a strong bearing on musical biography.[36]

The dynamic character of the notion of identity in modern times strikes a sharp contrast with medieval life, where "the complete fulfillment of the general norm was regarded as the highest form of individuality."[37] In the twentieth century, modernity in a general sense, and exile or emigration more specifically, require recourse to mobility and adaptability if the identity of a personal existence is to be secured within ever-changing surroundings and life situations. In conditions of exile and emigration in particular, flight, departure, and uprooting inevitably come to dominate personal experience, at least temporarily, if not permanently. Generally speaking, then, personal identity is affected in one of two ways: either it reverts to a retrospective ideal, which it draws from the past and possibly seeks to regain in the future; or it turns to a current or future ideal, through which life can be dealt with in the new context. The one response leads to an exile that is indissolubly embedded in a blurred and lost past and that, while disregarding the difficult, barely manageable present, hopes for a happy future in the abandoned country; the other leads to an emigration in which every attempt is made to erase all ties with the home country and the relinquished past, with the goal of gaining a new life in a new country and social context.

In real life, of course, these two extremes are linked by numerous intermediate "identity types,"[38] as exemplified by the biographies of numerous exiled artists and scientists.[39] Even if such biographies can be classified according to certain similarities or differences, the complicated range of personal motivating factors, developments, actions, and outcomes in each case really requires individual examination if we are to begin to understand these people's identities. In this sense, all aspects of a person's life history play an important role, as do such aspects as group allegiances within the social world of exiles, the different reasons for and courses of expulsion, including self-chosen emigration, and individual memories of the past. I wish to stress that it would simply not make sense to apply a transcendental "category of identity" in the logical sense (i.e., A = A) to musicological problems because the kind of identity I have outlined in the foregoing displays totally different dimensions: that is, it involves history, society, and context. Furthermore, if the notion of musical identity is to remain viable, it is important to acknowledge the possibility of failure in an attempted search for said identity.[40] When, for example, the Kolisch Quartet had to be disbanded as a result of financial difficulties in 1939, this amounted to an identity-endangering artistic discontinuity for Rudolf Kolisch in particular, regardless of his unconventional attitude toward the concert scene.[41]

The question of a possible remigration, even the question of whether and how to renew former friendships, demonstrates clearly that we would be missing the point if we were to assume a simple spiritual or intellectual, musical-aesthetic continuity in the lives of exiled musicians. In Germany, the generation of the era of reconstruction and the economic miracle (*Wirtschaftswunder*) had its eyes turned toward the future and, consciously or not, refused, in what appeared to be an "inability to mourn,"[42] to engage in a critical reappraisal of the past, at the same time demonstrating considerable indifference, even insensitivity, toward those immigrants who had been forced to flee the country not so long before and were now still searching for their own endangered identity. It is distressing to have to point out that the incomparable experience of being compelled to emigrate from the National Socialist regime to a "normal" situation was quickly forgotten. In many cases emigration was not a question merely of reshaping an existence, or of changing certain factors of identity; rather, it was a question of life and death. To preserve the memory of this is a duty of contemporary musicology.

I would like to conclude this essay by reprinting a letter that speaks directly to the difficulties, the ambivalences, and the effort of self-assertion that was required in the process of finding and shaping a new identity. The author of the letter, Leopold Levis, was a jurist who had fled Germany, and his addressee was the pianist Emma Lübbecke-Job. (In the letter, written about five years after the end of the war, Levis refers to Emma's husband, Fried, as well as to Paul Hindemith.)[43]

Inwood—New York, 20 July 1950

My dear Emma,

Now your birthday has already gone by. Late yesterday evening I was still sitting out in the open, wondering how this day might have passed for you. Last week I had just stuck my letter into the box when—of course—yours arrived! Some things I would have written differently because I had hoped that you were much better. . . . Fried this time wrote several things that irritated me, especially that he would already have died in America long ago!—After all, I did not travel here in a destitute state for the sake of my own pleasure, but because all of us would have died *in Germany. This appears to have been forgotten. If he presented Paul H. with the notion of music "characteristic of the species" [arteigen] and suchlike, then I understand that one or the other door opened up. I can well recall how he, when he met me by chance years ago, told me, enraged, that his mother-in-law had been left to die of starvation. [It is] possible that he will not write another* Mathis; *all right, then he will write something else. After all, Beethoven also composed only one* Fidelio. *Life is immensely difficult here and we all, who have to work so terribly hard, know that only too well; one should not make it even more difficult for us by giving us to understand that life here is unworthy of being lived. Albert Schweizer did not think so; Bruno Walter does not think so; and Thomas Mann, Unruh, Toscanini, Serkin, Busch, and all the rest of them do not think so either. And there is one thing one has to grant the Americans: They rescued the Germans when all life in Germany appeared to have expired, while those* many Germans, *whose present situation is excellent, have nothing left for their own compatriots who were driven out of the country. Only today, a principal of the International Council for Christian leadership gave me an extensive lecture on this. These times are confused and bad, and one has to keep a clear head to avoid being swallowed up by the confusion. Tell Fried this from me, and also tell him that, as a historian, he should become absorbed in the thoughts of Carl Schurz, who was a German and became American home secretary. He was not the worst.*

As always,
your old Lolito

NOTES

1. See, for example, Marc Fischer, "Shaping a New Identity, and Trying to Come to Terms with the Past," *International Herald Tribune*, 21 Apr. 1994, 15.

2. The passage reads in Hegel's original: "Die Bestimmungen des Wesens als *wesentliche* Bestimmungen genommen, werden sie Prädikate eines vorausgesetzten Subjekts, das, weil sie wesentlich [sind], *Alles* ist. Die Sätze, die dadurch entstehen, sind als *die allgemeinen Denkgesetze* ausgesprochen worden. *Der Satz der Identität* lautet demnach: '*Alles ist mit sich identisch*; A = A'; und negativ '*A kann nicht zugleich A und nicht A sein.*'—Dieser Satz, statt ein wahres Denkgesetz zu sein, ist nichts als das Gesetz des *abstrakten Verstandes*" (Georg Wilhelm Friedrich Hegel, *Enzyklopädie der philosophischen Wissenschaften im Grundrisse* [1830]. *Erster Teil. Die Wissenschaft der Logik: Mit den mündlichen Zusätzen*, in *Werke*, vol. 8 [Frankfurt am Main: Suhrkamp, 1970], 237).

3. Georg Wilhelm Friedrich Hegel, preface to *Phänomenologie des Geistes*, 6th ed., ed. Johannes Hoffmeister (Hamburg: Georg Meiner, 1952), 21.

4. Among the many studies, see Rolf Tiedemann, "'Mitdichtende Einfühlung': Adornos Beiträge zum *Doktor Faustus*—noch einmal," in *Frankfurter Adorno Blätter*, ed. Theodor W. Adorno Archiv, vol. 1 (Munich: edition text und kritik, 1992), 9–34.

5. See Theodor W. Adorno, *Negative Dialektik* (Frankfurt am Main: Suhrkamp, 1966), 137–82.

6. Adorno, *Minima Moralia: Reflexionen aus dem beschädigten Leben* (Frankfurt am Main: Suhrkamp, [1951] 1969), 57 (the last sentence of no. 29, "Zwergobst").

7. On the categories of *Identität* (identity), *Nichtidentität* (nonidentity), and *das Nichtidentische* (nonidentical), see Adorno, *Negative Dialektik*, 15ff., which includes

the statement "Dialektik ist das konsequente Bewußtsein von Nichtidentität" (dialectics is the consequent consciousness of nonidentity, 15). See also Adorno, *Philosophische Terminologie: Zur Einleitung*, vol. 2, ed. Rudolf zur Lippe (Frankfurt am Main: Suhrkamp, 1974), 13ff. Among the many studies devoted to this problem and its ramifications, see especially Herbert Schnädelbach, "Dialektik als Vernunftkritik: Zur Konstruktion des Rationalen bei Adorno," in *Adorno-Konferenz 1983*, ed. Ludwig von Friedeburg and Jürgen Habermas (Frankfurt am Main: Suhrkamp, 1983), 66–94; also Albrecht Wellmer, "Adorno, Anwalt des Nicht-Identischen: Eine Einführung," *Zur Dialektik von Moderne und Postmoderne: Vernunftkritik nach Adorno* (Frankfurt am Main: Suhrkamp, 1985), 135–66; and Martin Jay, *Adorno* (Cambridge, Mass.: Harvard University Press, 1984), 20, who states: "The Jew, he now came to understand, was regarded as the most stubborn repository of that otherness, difference and nonidentity which twentieth-century totalitarianism had sought to liquidate. 'Auschwitz,' he grimly concluded, 'confirmed the philosopheme of pure identity as death.'"

8. Martin Heidegger, "Sprache und Heimat," in *Hebbel-Jahrbuch 1960*, ed. Ludwig Koopmann (Heide in Holstein: Westholsteinische Verlagsanstalt Boyens, 1960), 27–50. This essay ends with the following sentences (50): "Die Sprache ist kraft ihres dichtenden Wesens das verborgenste und darum am weitesten auslangende, das inständig schenkende Hervorbringen der Heimat. Damit gewinnt der Titel 'Sprache und Heimat' die ihm gehörige Bestimmtheit. So kann er lauten, wie er lauten muß; nicht obenhin: Sprache und Heimat, sondern: Sprache *als* Heimat" (By virtue of its poeticizing essence, language is the most hidden, and therefore the most expansive, the urgently bestowing creation of *Heimat*. Thus the title "Language and *Heimat*" gains the exactness that belongs to it. So it can read as it must; not superficially: Language and *Heimat*; but: Language *as Heimat*.)

9. Among the rich discussions on canon and culture as musicological and music-historical categories, the following studies are representative: Lydia Goehr, *The Imaginary Museum of Musical Works: An Essay in the Philosophy of Music* (Oxford: Clarendon Press, 1992); Ruth Solie, ed., *Musicology and Difference: Gender and Sexuality in Musical Scholarship* (Berkeley: University of California Press, 1993); and Katherine Bergeron and Philip Bohlman, eds., *Disciplining Music: Musicology and Its Canons* (Chicago: University of Chicago Press, 1992).

10. On the Adlerian approach to style, see Guido Adler, *Der Stil in der Musik* (Leipzig: Breitkopf & Härbel, 1911); and Adler, *Methode der Musikgeschichte* (Leipzig: Breitkopf & Härbel, 1919). Arnold Schoenberg in particular argued against "style"; see his essay "Neue Musik, veraltete Musik: Stil und Gedanke," in *Stil und Gedanke: Aufsätze zur Musik*, ed. Ivan Vojtech, vol. 1 of *Gesammelte Schriften* (Frankfurt am Main: S. Fischer, 1976), 25–34. On the exile status of this group of musicologists, see *Beiträge '90: Österreichische Musik im Exil*, ed. Monica Wildauer, vol. 8 of *Beiträge der Österreichischen Gesellschaft für Musik* (Kassel: Bärenreiter, [1990]), in particular Rudolf Flotzinger, "Österreichische Musikwissenschaft im Exil," 34–38.

11. Hermann Danuser, *Die Musik des 20. Jahrhunderts*, vol. 7 of *Neues Handbuch der Musikwissenschaft* (Laaber: Laaber, 1984), 1–10, 166–90. See also Danuser, "Kulturen der Musik—Strukturen der Zeit: Synchrone und diachrone Paradigmen der Musikgeschichte des 20. Jahrhunderts," in *Musikpädagogik und Musikwissenschaft*, ed. Arnfried Edler, Siegmund Helms, and Helmuth Hopf, vol. 111 of *Taschenbücher zur Musikwissenschaft* (Wilhelmshaven: Noetzel, "Heinrichshofen-Bücher," 1987), 189–209.

12. See in particular Carl Dahlhaus, *Die Idee der absoluten Musik* (Kassel: Bärereiter 1978); and Dahlhaus, *Grundlagen der Musikgeschichte* (Cologne: Arno Volk, 1977).

13. Danuser, "Generationswechsel und Epochenzäsur—Ein Problem der Musikgeschichtsschreibung des 20. Jahrhunderts," in *Komponisten des 20. Jahrhunderts in der Paul Sacher Stiftung*, ed. Hans Jörg Jans (Basel: Kunstmuseum, 1986), 47–56.

14. Danuser, "Die 'mittlere Musik' der zwanziger Jahre," in *La musique et le rite sacré et profane: Actes du XIIIe Congrès de la Société internationale de musicologie—Strasbourg 1982*, vol. 2, ed. Marc Honegger und Paul Prevost (Strasbourg: Association des Publications près les Universités de Strasbourg 1986), 703–21.

15. See Peter Gülke, *Brahms—Bruckner: Zwei Studien* (Kassel: Bärenreiter, 1989), 22–25.

16. *Paul Hindemith: Briefe*, ed. Dieter Rexroth (Frankfurt am Main: S. Fischer, 1982), 245.

17. See, for example, Philipp Jarnach's letter of 24 March 1958 to Heinz Tiessen : "so darf man andererseits nicht übersehen, daß er später noch in sehr jungen Jahren, [in Amerika] sich einer Schaffensart zugewandt hat, bei welcher dieser künstlerische Anspruch nicht mehr anerkannt werden kann. Diese spätere Produktion bedeutet einen völligen Verzicht auf die früheren ernsten Ziele dieses Komponisten, und ich glaube, es geht nicht an, daß man sich heute einreden läßt, sie hätte noch eine stilistische Bedeutung" (one should, on the other hand, not overlook that later [in America], still at a very early age, he turned to a style of composition for which this artistic criterion can no longer be claimed. This later production completely abandons the earlier, serious goals of the composer, and I believe that one should not be persuaded today that it is still of any stylistic importance). See Kim H. Kowalke, "Hin und zurück: Kurt Weill heute," in *Vom Kurfürstendamm zum Broadway: Kurt Weill (1900–1950)*, ed. Bernd Kortländer, Winrich Meiszies, and David Farneth (Düsseldorf: Droste, 1990), 16–27. See also David Drew, ed., *Über Kurt Weill* (Frankfurt am Main: Suhrkamp, 1975), vii–xxxiii, including the following (xxiv): "Somit unterscheiden sich die Broadwaywerke von ihren Vorgängern nicht nur in ihrer äussern Art; sie unterscheiden sich davon im Wesen, im 'Stil' im tiefsten Sinne des Wortes. Es ist daher zwecklos, die den europäischen Werken angemessenen Kriterien auf die Broadwaywerke anzuwenden, und umgekehrt. Weills Versuch, eine konsequente zweite persona zu entwickeln, ist einzigartig in der Geschichte bedeutender Komposition" (Thus the works written for Broadway are distinguished from their predecessors not only in their outer appearance; they are distinguished in their essence, in the deepest sense of the word "style." It is therefore senseless to apply the criteria appropriate to the European works to these works for Broadway, and vice versa. Weill's attempt thoroughly to develop a second persona is unique in the history of meaningful composition).

18. See in particular the studies of Kim Kowalke, including "Kurt Weill, Modernism, and Popular Culture: *Öffentlichkeit als Stil*," *Modernism/Modernity* 2 (Jan. 1995): 27–69.

19. See, among other studies, *A New Orpheus: Essays on Kurt Weill*, ed. Kim Kowalke (New Haven: Yale University Press, 1986); and *A Stranger Here Myself: Kurt Weill Studien*, ed. Kim Kowalke and Horst Edler (Hildesheim: Georg Olms, 1993).

20. See Kowalke's "Reading Whitman/ Responding to America: Hindemith, Weill, and Others" in this volume.

21. Odo Marquard, "Identität: Schwundtelos und Mini-Essenz—Bemerkungen

zur Genealogie einer aktuellen Diskussion," in *Identität,* ed. Odo Marquard und Karlheinz Stierle, vol. 8 of *Poetik und Hermeneutik* (Munich: Fink, 1979), 347–70. On the distinction between immigrant and exile, see Bruno Nettl's "Displaced Musics and Immigrant Musicologists: Ethnomusicological and Biographical Perspectives" in this volume

22. Eric Walter White, *Stravinsky: The Composer and His Works,* 2d ed. (London: Faber & Faber, [1966] 1979), 359–67. On a similar phenomenon in an earlier work by Stravinsky, see Richard Taruskin, "'. . . La belle et saine barbarie': Über den russischen Hintergrund der *Trois pièces,*" in *Igor Strawinsky: Trois pièces pour quatuor à cordes—Skizzen, Fassungen, Dokumente, Essays. Festgabe für Albi Rosenthal zum 80. Geburtstag,* ed. Hermann Danuser, with Felix Meyer und Ulrich Mosch (Winterthur: Amadeus, 1994), 17–28.

23. Gianfranco Vinay, *Stravinsky neoclassico: L'invenzione della memoria nel '900 musicale* (Venice: Marsilio 1987).

24. Rollo Myers, "Igor Stravinsky," in *A Dictionary of Music and Musicians, Edited by Sir George Grove,* 5th ed., ed. Eric Blom (London: MacMillan, 1954), 8:137, 140. Eric Walter White and Jeremy Noble, in *The New Grove Dictionary of Music and Musicians,* ed. Stanley Sadie (London: Macmillan, 1980), 18:254–57, offer a more differentiated view of the period from 1949 to 1952.

25. Michail Druskin, *Igor Strawinsky: Persönlichkeit, Schaffen, Aspekte,* ed. and trans. Christof Rüger (Leipzig: Reclam, 1976), 146.

26. Albrecht Dümling, "Eisler und Schönberg," in *Hanns Eisler,* vol. 5 of *Das Argument,* ed. Wolfgang Fritz Haug (Berlin: Argument, 1975), 57–85, esp. 65–71.

27. Carl Dahlhaus, "Musikalischer Funktionalismus," in *Schönberg und andere: Gesammelte Aufsätze zur neuen Musik* (Mainz: Schott, 1978), 57–71.

28. Alexander L. Ringer, *Arnold Schoenberg: The Composer as Jew* (Oxford: Clarendon Press, 1990). See also Michael Mäckelmann, *Arnold Schönberg und das Judentum* (Hamburg: Karl Dieter Wagner, 1984).

29. This subject is treated in detail in Danuser, "Arnold Schönberg und die Idee einer deutschen Musik," in *Das Deutsche in der Musik: Kolloquium im Rahmen der 5. Dresdner Tage der zeitgenössischen Musik,* ed. Marion Denuth (Leipzig and Dresden, 1997), 26–36. See also Constantin Floros, "Die Wiener Schule und das Problem der 'deutschen Musik,'" in *Die Wiener Schule und das Hakenkreuz: Das Schicksal der Moderne im gesellschaftspolitischen Kontext des 20. Jahrhunderts,* ed. Otto Kolleritsch (Vienna: Universal-Edition, 1990), 35–50.

30. See the analysis of the work by Christoph Keller, "Das Klavierwerk Hanns Eislers," in *Klaviermusik des 20. Jahrhunderts,* ed. Wilhelm Killmayer, Siegfried Mauser, and Wolfgang Rihm, vol. 51 of *Melos: Jahrbuch für zeitgenössische Musik* (Mainz: Schott, 1992), 25–42, esp. 36–40.

31. See Albrecht Dümling, "'Im Zeichen der Erkenntnis der sozialen Verhältnisse': Der junge Schönberg und die Arbeitersängerbewegung," in *Zeitschrift für Musiktheorie* 6 (1975): 11–21.

32. Karol Berger, "The Text and Its Author," in *"Musik als Text": Bericht über den Internationalen Kongreß der Gesellschaft für Musikforschung, Freiburg im Breisgau, 1993,* ed. Hermann Danuser and Tobias Plebuch (Kassel: Bärenreiter, in press), 1:58–60.

33. Anselm Leonard Strauss, *Spiegel und Masken: Die Suche nach Identität,* trans. Heidi Munscheid (Frankfurt am Main: Suhrkamp, 1968), 97 (English ed.: *Mirrors*

and Masks: The Search for Identity [Glencoe, Ill.: Free Press, 1959]); quoted in Helmut Dubiel, "Identität, Ich-Identität," in *Historisches Wörterbuch der Philosophie,* ed. Joachim Ritter und Karlfried Gründer, vol. 4 (Darmstadt: Wissenschaftliche Buchgesellschaft, 1976) 149. A fine survey of the concept of identity and its scholarly history, including a large bibliography, is provided by Bernd Estel in "Identität," in *Handbuch religionswissenschaftlicher Grundbegriffe,* ed. Hubert Cancik, Burkhard Gladigow, and Karl-Heinz Kohl, vol. 3 (Stuttgart: Kohlhammer, 1993), 194–210.

34. Jürgen Habermas, *Erkenntnis und Interesse* (Frankfurt am Main: Suhrkamp, 1969), 178–209; quoted in Dubiel, "Identität, Ich-Identität," 150.

35. Quoted in ibid., 148–49.

36. See Danuser, "Die Kategorie Krise in ihrer Bedeutung für Leben und Kunst," in *Biographische Konstellation und künstlerisches Handeln,* ed. Giselher Schubert, vol. 6 of *Frankfurter Studien* (Mainz: Schott, 1997), 303–318.

37. Arno Borst, "Barbarossas Erwachen—Zur Geschichte der deutschen Identität," in Marquard and Stierle, eds., *Identität,* 20.

38. Hans Ulrich Gumbrecht, "Über die allmähliche Verfertigung von Identitäten in politischen Reden," in ibid., 107–32. The article includes the statement (114): "Identitätstypen sind Interpretationsschemata, die alle unter ihnen zusammgengefaßten Rollen und die auf sie zugeordneten sukzessiven Verhaltensmanifestationen als *stimmig* erscheinen lassen" (Identity types are schemas of interpretation, which make all the roles subsumed under them and all the successive manifestations of behavior appear *stimmig* [in tune]).

39. For the case of exiled members of the musical world in particular, see, for example, *Musik im Exil: Folgen des Nazismus für die internationale Musikkultur,* ed. Hanns-Werner Heister, Claudia Maurer Zenck, and Peter Petersen (Frankfurt am Main: Fischer Taschenbuch Verlag, 1993); *Musiktradition im Exil: Zurück aus dem Vergessen,* ed. Juan Allende-Blin (Cologne: Bund-Verlag, 1993); and *Musik in der Emigration 1933–1945: Verfolgung, Vertreibung, Rückwirkung—Symposium Essen, 10. bis 13. Juni 1992,* ed. Horst Weber (Stuttgart: Metzler, 1994).

40. See Dieter Henrich, "'Identität'—Begriffe, Probleme, Grenzen," in Marquard and Stierle, eds., *Identität,* 133–86.

41. See Walter Levin's "Immigrant Musicians and the American Chamber Music Scene, 1930–1950" in this volume.

42. Alexander Mitscherlich and Margarete Mitscherlich, *Die Unfähigkeit zu trauern: Grundlagen kollektiven Verhaltens* (Munich: Piper, 1994).

43. The letter is preserved in the Lübbecke estate (Nachlaß von Emma Lübbecke-Job), Stadtarchiv Frankfurt am Main. I wish to thank Dr. Giselher Schubert (of the Paul Hindemith Institut, Frankfurt am Main) for bringing this letter to my attention and providing a photocopy. The Frankfurt Stadtarchiv kindly granted permission to publish the letter.

Challenges and Opportunities of Acculturation

Schoenberg, Krenek, and Stravinsky in Exile

Claudia Maurer Zenck

In discussing the experiences of the exiles of the Nazi period, Herbert A. Strauss defined acculturation as "the unstable equilibrium which the fusion of diverse cultural traits brings about when a person or group comes into intimate and prolonged contact with persons or groups of another culture."[1] This process can take many forms, from total identification with the new cultural environment to its complete rejection.[2]

In the remarks that follow, I shall discuss three aspects of acculturation with regard to the experiences of the composers Schoenberg, Krenek, and Stravinsky in the United States through the end of the Second World War. In particular, I shall be asking three questions:

> What conditions (including living conditions) did these composers encounter?
>
> Did they try to transfer their musical culture to the foreign country, and if so, how did they proceed?
>
> How did their acculturation become evident in their daily lives and professional activities?[3]

These questions bring with them difficult issues concerning artistic development. How much adaptation is necessary to survive? Do changes in a person's identity or aesthetic conception neutralize the effects of acculturation or make critical judgment impossible? This is a general problem that one encounters in dealing with music, literature, or art in exile, for it involves a moral dimension relating to the experience of exile itself.[4] An artist's personal integrity or the fact that he is in exile does not itself lend integrity to his creation or make it sacrosanct. Critical evaluation is necessary to distinguish between the reasons for creating a certain work and the value of the artistic result.

Finally, one needs to ask how the émigrés perceived their own situation. To what extent did they expose themselves to their new cultural environment or keep to their own? In what way did artists feel the tension between necessary acculturation and the threatened loss of their artistic identity? Stravinsky, for instance, referred to several compositional details that in his opinion reflected a certain atmosphere or experiences typical for America, while taking pains to explain that conceptual changes did not occur.[5] Schoenberg and Krenek, on the other hand, did not feel it necessary to go into such details. In 1950, with the European horizon back in view, they solved the problem by evading self-inspection and firmly denying any influence that America may have exercised on their works.[6] None of them apparently wanted to think of their artistic identity as being endangered or subject to changes that were not the result of a voluntary response to a challenge. Was it that they did not value America's musical culture as highly as that of Europe? Or were they defending their professional identities as the last bastion against the constraints of exile? This was what Krenek himself supposed when he was able to accept "America's influence on its émigré composers" several years later, after having been reintroduced to and repeatedly confronted with the musical life in the Old World.[7]

THE TRANSFER OF EUROPEAN MUSICAL CULTURE

It so happened that each of these three composers began his life in the United States in Boston. Schoenberg and Krenek, who arrived in 1933 and 1938 respectively, came because they had a contract with the Malkin Conservatory; Stravinsky, who enjoyed the greatest international renown, was invited to be the Charles Eliot Norton Professor of Poetry at Harvard University in 1939.

Schoenberg and Krenek had a similar start. Both had had works, albeit minor ones, performed by the Boston Symphony Orchestra (BSO) once before they arrived: during the BSO's fiftieth-anniversary season beginning in the fall of 1930, Koussevitzky had conducted Schoenberg's orchestral setting of Bach's Prelude and Fugue in E-flat for organ, and the concertmaster and associate conductor Richard Burgin had given the performance of Krenek's *Little Symphony,* op. 58.[8]

Upon Schoenberg's arrival, Koussevitzky invited him to perform *Pelleas und Melisande* with the orchestra on 16 and 17 March 1934. There was no further contact with the orchestra until March 1943, when Carl Engel, Schoenberg's publisher, seems to have interested Koussevitzky in giving Schoenberg an award to write an orchestral work.[9] Nothing came of it at the time, although that May Koussevitzky did commission a work from Stravinsky, the *Ode,* which incorporated an unused film score and was dedicated to the memory of the conductor's late wife, Natalie.[10] One year later the well-paid commission finally came through, and after having overcome his inner conflict between feeling neglected by the conductor and the need for money, Schoenberg offered Koussevitzky the orchestral version of *Theme and Variations,* op. 43b, completed in 1943; the work was premiered in October 1944.[11]

At the end of 1937, during his first stay in the United States (which he undertook to explore professional opportunities were he to emigrate to the United States), Krenek was able to convince Koussevitzky to invite him for a concert in Boston during the following season. On 4 and 5 November 1938, shortly after his arrival in Boston as a refugee, he was given the chance to present himself to an American audience with a recent dodecaphonic work: his second piano concerto, premiered under Bruno Walter in Europe only a few months earlier. Burgin stepped in as conductor when Koussevitzky suddenly developed an "aching arm."[12] Thereafter Krenek's relationship with Koussevitzky and the BSO was as tenuous as Schoenberg's. It was not until December 1944 that another of Krenek's works was performed there. The piece was not one of his best symphonic works, though it was his most recent: the problematic *Symphonic Variations* on a fictive folk tune, op. 94, which had been premiered two years earlier in Minneapolis under Mitropoulos.

Stravinsky enjoyed a far different reception when he arrived in Boston in the fall of 1939. He was invited to conduct the BSO on 6 December 1939 and again at the end of the following March (two weeks earlier he had given a chamber concert with BSO musicians). What is more, Koussevitzky performed more Stravinsky than any other of the important American conductors. The composer himself felt that the BSO considered him as a member of the family.[13]

This pro-Stravinsky atmosphere was due not only to Koussevitzky's Russian background and predilection for Russian music. The conductor was also the owner of the Editions Russes de Musique and as such had published most of Stravinsky's major works written in Europe. Another factor was the presence of Nadia Boulanger, who was living in Cambridge during that time. While teaching at the Ecole Normale de Musique in Paris and at the American Conservatory in Fontainebleau in the 1920s and 1930s, she had encouraged appreciation of Stravinsky's music by introducing the young American composers to his works, especially those of his "neoclassical" period. (Stravinsky himself had been a supervisor there.)[14] Her former students from the United States, among them Walter Piston, teaching at Harvard University, Aaron Copland, and Roy Harris, were thus similarly favored by Serge Koussevitzky and his BSO.[15] In the United States, Boulanger was a no less ardent promoter and advocate for her friend than she had been in Europe. She conducted his works, helped him in practical matters, intervened on his behalf in conflicts, and from 1940 on taught about his work at colleges in Massachusetts.[16] Thus his reception was well prepared in a threefold way: by the presence of his own works in the concert halls; by the music of his younger American colleagues, instructed by his prophet Boulanger; and by Boulanger's own strong personal support. It is not surprising that under these circumstances Stravinsky was invited every season to conduct a group of concerts with the BSO, and that in the spring of 1943 it was not Schoenberg but Stravinsky who was commissioned by the Koussevitzky Music Foundation to write a symphonic piece.

Unlike Stravinsky, Schoenberg and Krenek were not able to start their lives in America as freelance composers, earning their living through commissions and royalties, or by conducting. A comparison of the fees and number of invitations received by Schoenberg and Stravinsky suggests that Schoenberg was considerably less famous than Stravinsky.[17] Commissions, too, were in short supply; for many years, what Schoenberg received from his publisher, Schirmer, was negligible, and his main source of income was derived from his university positions and private teaching.

Krenek, who had lived on his royalties in Vienna (though with increasing difficulty in the last years before his emigration), was in a position similar to Schoenberg's. In the United States he conducted only occasionally, usually without remuneration. Commissions were extremely rare; after the *Symphonic Piece*, op. 86, most of the works he composed in America through the end of the 1940s were written on his own initiative.[18] As a consequence, they either remained in manuscript or were published (often many years later) only in Europe. Those works printed in the United States were published by a variety of sometimes small publishers. Since he received no royalty advances, he had to rely on his teaching salaries from Vassar College, Hamline University, and summer courses at several colleges and universities. His salary levels were distinctly lower than Schoenberg's.

Schoenberg had been an experienced teacher for many years. Krenek considered his new profession as a challenge. Stravinsky did not take his teaching duties seriously, feeling he was neither talented for nor inclined to such a task.[19] When he accepted a private pupil in Hollywood in 1941, it was apparently for purely monetary reasons. Obliged to work with students regularly during the months of his residence at Harvard University, Stravinsky approached the hour-long weekly meetings with the same businesslike detachment as he did his lectures.[20] He did not act as a pedagogue but performed like a celebrity who utters golden words that will be eagerly absorbed by an impressed audience; the same had been the case when he acted as a supervisor in Boulanger's courses in Paris.[21] In keeping with his pedagogical attitude (or lack thereof), Stravinsky later recalled that the meetings with the students had filled him with "the best impressions and interest," whereas he apparently had little concern for the effect he was having on them. It may well be, however, that neither the students nor the university expected anything more from the great man. More than one of them may have been duly impressed by the master's "overwhelming kindness in actually sitting down to the keyboard with me to help me perform the first movement of my string quartet."[22]

Schoenberg was less impressed by his American students, most of whom were beginners and lacked a foundation upon which he could build.[23] He illustrated his frustration by contrasting his American students with the students he had taught in his master classes at the Berlin Academy: "They were graduates . . . many of them talented composers, who's compositorial [*sic*] technique was mature enough to profit from my suggestions; all of them [were] educated to understand the philosophical and aesthetical problems and their solutions which I presented to them."[24]

Schoenberg's experience with American students was similar to that of other colleagues from Europe, including Toch, Krenek, Milhaud, and Hindemith, as well as teachers in other disciplines, all of whom took their profession seriously.[25] The students' deficient background was a direct outgrowth of the American efforts in the 1930s to apply the democratic ideal to education and the arts, a consequence of which was that mass education did not require qualifying skills as a precondition for instruction. Ernst Toch reacted to this shortcoming so strongly that he gave up his position at USC after ten years and later denied that composition could be taught at all.[26] Even Hindemith, who in the preceding decade in Germany had been interested in developing a broad educational basis and wrote *Schulwerke* for school children, became elitist in America. Composers could not be "fabricated by training," the former craftsman declared, for "artistic creation was basically aristocratic and individualistic."[27]

On the whole, the émigré composers acknowledged the talent and intelligence of their American students, despite their frustrations trying to work in the American system. Schoenberg, however, though he did not play the aristocrat, felt that talent and intelligence were not enough. Characteristically, he saw in teaching composition an ethical problem. He wanted to form "men of character" and fortify their morale, their "courage to express what they had to say."[28] This was possible, he believed, only with a sufficient technical knowledge; without that he seemed to fear that they would adapt to new fashions rather than follow their own convictions. Schoenberg's insistence on a moral dimension for composition must have been most unusual against the backdrop of America's prevailing pragmatism.[29] For him, morality was the core of his creativity (hence his devotion, along with that of his disciples, to Karl Kraus). For decades he had been defending his artistic morality, which sprang from a deep commitment as a composer and a teacher to passing tradition on to his potential successors. He continued to do so in the United States, a country that he felt lacked a musical tradition of its own. He therefore analyzed music of the eighteenth and nineteenth centuries to acquaint students with their past and to demonstrate problems and their solutions; short pieces of traditional music also served as points of departure for the students' own compositional attempts.[30] Thus Schoenberg continued his past into the present not only by composing, but also by leading his students to link their American present with the European tradition.

Krenek was younger when he started teaching in America, and he had no solid point of comparison.[31] Thus in some regards he responded differently to the situation in which he found himself. For one thing, he was well aware that just as America served as a refuge against persecution for him and so many others, it was also a shelter for the European musical tradition and for Western culture in general. Krenek, like Schoenberg, therefore aimed at making his students "carriers of the glorious tradition of Western music."[32] He not only confronted them with the immediate past, as Schoenberg did, but he also went back in history as far as the Franco-Flemish epoch. He did so neither because he cared that the students write like Palestrina, for example (as Schoenberg seemed to suspect when Krenek told him about his teaching strategy), nor in order "to justify our own [style]. . . . But to see parallels or to see a certain continuity of basic ideas, that certain basic elements of structure, of form, etc., go through all these styles and find different formulations in different periods."[33]

For him, musical tradition merged in music history, just as music history consisted of continuous musical tradition. At that time he did not, as many a refugee did, feel that history had lost its continuity and broken into parts when the direction, the "tradition," of his own life was interrupted. (Perhaps the turns his life had taken since his move to Berlin in 1920 were of benefit to him now.)[34] He even became aware to his surprise that as a modern composer he was not in a wasteland: when he discovered Charles Ives, he realized that new music existed in the United States too. This was an isolated experience, however, in the "'echolessness' of the vast American expanses," and not enough to give Krenek the feeling of having found a new "home."[35]

His American students generally lacked sufficient knowledge of the music repertory or an awareness of music-historical development and tradition. Moreover, in an atmosphere where the need for "American" music was stressed they found it difficult to see themselves as links in a chain of traditions. Finally, Europe's geographical distance must have caused a temporal gap; music from Europe belonged to history, no matter that it was being created in the students' own time.

Krenek had to awaken in his students a sense of history and tradition, and of their own prospective roles within them.[36] Toward that end, he sought first to build a purposeful curriculum and, second, to influence the musical culture of the community in which he lived. In the former endeavor he had to begin at the beginning; in the latter he followed the lead of his predecessor at Hamline University, John Kuypers, and of John Becker, former director of the Federal Music Project in Minnesota and, together with Ives, Cowell, Ruggles, and Riegger, one of the "American Five."

Olive Jean Bailey has explored in detail the means by which Krenek sought to achieve his goals.[37] It will suffice to summarize her research and emphasize a few unknown aspects concerning the concerts he organized at the International Society for Contemporary Music (ISCM), whose Twin Cities chapter he cofounded with Dimitri Mitropoulos. Louis Krasner, who had toured all over the world, realized with surprise that "such concerts could have taken place in London, or Paris, or in New York,"[38] and it was with immense pride that the participants found in a survey about new music presented in the ISCM chapters of the United States, including New York, San Francisco, and Chicago, that "St. Paul appeared in the extraordinary spot for the number of performances and for the breadth of performances and the number of premieres. At that time, it was incredible to think that Minneapolis and St. Paul was actually a center for contemporary music in the United States and maybe the world during the war."[39]

Disseminating new music in the American hinterlands also served to educate his students; Krenek at the same time showed them "how musical gardens can be made to grow."[40] They never forgot it, and when in 1947 he quit his teaching position in order to concentrate again on composing, they continued his work, feeling strongly that in doing so they also repaid him.[41] Several of the first-generation "true believers," including Robert Erickson, Glenn Glasow, Wilbur Ogdon, and Tom Nee, taught at colleges in the Twin Cities area. It was not by chance that twenty years later, three of the "Krenek dynasty"[42] built up the music department at the newly founded University of California at San Diego.[43] So the pollenization, as Louis Krasner put it,[44] functioned both geographically, between one college and another, between the Midwest and the East (and later the West), and temporally, from one generation to the next down to the present day.

For a composer used to struggling with both audiences and musicians who were reluctant to accept novelty, there were distinct advantages in having students with a poor musical background. A student like Krenek's eventual wife Gladys Nordenstrom seems to have been exemplary. Having grown up in a small town, she played jazz trumpet in a dance band in her early teenage years but did not hear a Schubert symphony until she was seventeen or eighteen. When she encountered Webern's music as a student of Krenek's at Hamline University, she liked it immediately: "my acceptance of new music was no problem; I felt at home with it."[45] Only later did she study Beethoven.

Indeed, these "blank-slate" students proved remarkably receptive to modern music. Krenek had already met such students as early as 1939 during his first experience as a teacher at the Summer School of the University of Michigan, Ann Arbor. After performing his new *Symphonic Piece*, op. 86, with a student orchestra, he recalled: "I felt sorry for the students to whom this 'outlandish stuff' probably seemed stranger than Chinese. . . . The students did not feel at all harassed by the 'awesome' features of atonality and twelve-tone technique. Contrariwise, they are still coming to see me and to speak enthusiastically of the most thrilling experience they had in playing this unusual music."[46]

At Hamline University the students' open-mindedness toward modern music in general and toward his own works in particular had an interesting and heartening consequence, as one of his students related: "When you're singing contemporary music all the time, even if you have only relative pitch, you can sing the notes very easily. You can sing it very accurately; no one even has to give you a pitch, you can just see it and sing it."[47] Bob Holliday, the outstanding director of the Hamline choral groups—which attained national renown during Krenek's years there and also performed early music on Krenek's suggestion—profited from the fact that students were not being preformed by too much tonal music. Krenek the composer also benefited from the resulting high level of students' performance abilities. When asked for an evaluation of Krenek's music three decades after the events, witnesses of his activities in the Twin Cities were of the unanimous opinion that the choral and the chamber works of that time were his best compositions. Whatever the merits of their evaluation, this demonstrates once again that only knowledge and enthusiasm are able to generate the deep understanding necessary for the reception of new music. His students brought an end to the "proverbial loneliness of the Ivory Tower."[48]

ACCULTURATION AND ARTISTIC IDENTITY

The positive aspects of Krenek's experiences teaching students so lacking in historical consciousness may be responsible for a sudden experiment in his *Studies in Counterpoint Based on the Twelve-Tone Technique*. When his courses at the University of Michigan had come to an end in the summer of 1940, he noted in his diary, he "finished the twelve-tone book."[49] It is likely that he was referring to the last two of the book's ten chapters, ones very different in approach from the first eight. Whereas in the earlier chapters Krenek had focused only on contrapuntal subjects derived from the series, examples in the last two chapters are based on a musical phrase put together by several derivations and transpositions of the original row with which the phrase had nothing to do. With such a plainly technical application of the row, in which the thematic material was conceived completely independently, Krenek ignored the historical implications of twelve-tone composition and his own aesthetic position of the 1930s. This remained a side step, however, without any theoretical consequences.

More promising were Krenek's various experiments, begun about the time he wrote his manual, in loosening the strictures of twelve-tone technique. At

Vassar College he soon came into conflict with a rigidly prescribed academic schedule. As a result, he felt isolated both as a composer of avant-garde music and as a teacher of twelve-tone composition. This isolation fostered his concentration on the development of new compositional procedures as well as on an exploration of music history. The results can be understood as different strategies of accommodating his heritage to an atmosphere that did not encourage historical thinking—an outcome more satisfying than the leap into the no-man's-land described above. When he developed his own dodecaphonic procedures, the results were convincing, as in the *Lamentations,* the Third Piano Sonata, the Seventh String Quartet, and the *Symphonic Elegy.*[50] This loosening, which in the *Lamentations* would lead to new strict procedures, also ran the danger of oversimplification. The works in which he tried to streamline the twelve-tone technique by combining heterogeneous elements—such as folk tunes, as in the *Symphonic Variations,* op. 94—were distinctly less convincing and tended to be undermined by their simpler elements.

When looked at in this light, the facets of Krenek's acculturation concerning his profession the following:

The encounter with ahistorical thinking expanded his aesthetic horizon, but at the same time endangered his identity.

Meeting students without a sufficient intellectual background enlarged his pedagogical scope and stimulated his creative thinking and organizational skills.

The community in which he lived while teaching at Hamline University was deeply and permanently influenced through his works and activities.

In his isolation in Poughkeepsie, Krenek could combine creative experimentation with studies in music history, which enabled him to link the present with the past and anchor the future in the present.

The direction of these efforts, including his attempt to free himself from the more rigorous aspects of the twelve-tone technique, may well have been influenced by the pragmatism of his host country. One genuinely convincing masterpiece, the *Lamentations,* grew out of this experience. In his symphonic music, however, he seems to have succumbed to the temptation of making concessions to the general public.

How did a composer like Stravinsky, whose situation was completely different, respond to this cultural encounter? Stravinsky, as we have seen, did not come as a stranger in 1939. The ground was prepared for him, and so he found a warm reception. When he moved to California the following year, however, he did not find anything like the "home" provided him by Koussevitzky and the BSO. Still, he was invited to conduct his works with the most famous orchestras around in the country, and so he must have felt widely appreciated as a composer.

His biographer Stephen Walsh has maintained that in his second exile, Stravinsky was obliged to write according to the laws of the American market.[51] Walsh may, however, have been influenced by Robert Craft's picture of a Stravinsky in precarious straits during his first years in America: "Stravinsky's financial worries were justified. Concert engagements were scarce, his music not being in highest demand in the first place, and, in the second, requiring extra, and expensive, rehearsal time."[52] As always, the justification for such worries is dependent not only on the character of the person in question but also on his or her living standard. To be sure, he was a freelance composer, but did he depend on a market to earn his living? Walsh's assumption would hold true only if Stravinsky earned his living mainly through royalties. This was not so during the first two good years after his arrival in America, when he made more than $39,000 through conducting, playing, recording, and lecturing. As yet no figures are known for the following years up to the fall of 1944. For the 1944–45 season, it is probably true that his main income was derived from royalties.[53]

Be that as it may, the question of adaptation to market conditions must be framed from a slightly different perspective. Did Stravinsky *have* to adapt, or did he adapt because he thought he had to, because he wanted to, or because he was influenced to do so unwillingly?

According to Walsh, Stravinsky was well aware of his concessions to popular taste, as evidenced by the fact that he invented cover stories to conceal that his compositions were only works for money.[54] The means to adaptation lay at hand: parody, a concept long used to justify and elevate Stravinsky's neoclassical works through association with a venerable and pedigreed procedure. The composer himself spoke of "a rare kind of kleptomania," though more recently another psychopathological term has been employed to describe the same phenomenon: necrophilia.[55] One can easily find a critical middle ground to describe Stravinsky's parodies of commercial style. As a procedure adaptable to any new situation, parody can also be construed as a consequence of acculturation.

This technique may not at first have endangered Stravinsky's identity but may simply have added new material to the fund from which he drew. A dash of irony often helped to keep him at a healthy distance from the object of his parody. In the long run, however, this way of acculturation did not pay off but instead served only to disorient him. One result may have been a new inability to complete one piece before beginning the next, as had been his habit before emigrating to the United States.

From 1943 on, his increased use of Russian folk melodies even in his symphonic music flies in the face of the disdain he expressed for the procedure while still a resident of France.[56] Adaptations of folklore are also found in the religious works he wrote in 1944: in the short cantata *Babel,* and in the Kyrie and Gloria of the Mass—the first work he conceived after noting at the end of the last movement, "Apothéose," of *Scènes de ballet,* below the date ("23 août/44 à Hollywood") and in French, "Paris n'est plus aux allemands!"[57] The return to Russian sources as well as the inclination to religion indicate that he longed for deep roots to stabilize his position. He was in need of a more personal and authentic artistic identity than that expressed in his earlier American music. Viewed from this perspective, it is not surprising that Stravinsky was deeply shaken when, in 1951, he became aware that in Italy and Germany his music was regarded as reactionary when compared to Schoenberg's. He burst into tears because he felt he could no longer compose,[58] but then decided to go to school and study the dodecaphonic music of Schoenberg and Webern.[59] Like Krenek, then, he found his way to a more promising compositional approach only several years after the war, through contact with a strict compositional method born in Europe.[60] In fact, it was Krenek who helped him on his way with his twelve-tone manual and influenced him with no other work than his *Lamentations.*[61]

Schoenberg's artistic output in America also reflects his response to the unfamiliar culture. He started composing again in the summer of 1934 when he regained his health and his creative desire and potential. The prospect of finding a wide audience with a work for school orchestra (his tonal *Suite in Olden Style*) was appealing, for he saw it as a chance to use pedagogical means to fight conservatism at its roots. At the same time, he wrote the first movement of a violin concerto. It must have occurred to him that a work for soloist and orchestra offered the best opportunity, since the soloist could promote such a work and he, the notorious inventor of the twelve-tone composition, could present himself in a more popular way.[62] It is characteristic that he set out on this endeavor without first having found a violinist to play such a concerto (negotiations with Jascha Heifetz a year later came to nothing).[63] From then (1935) on, for more than ten years, Schoenberg did not complete any work without a commission or at least strong encouragement.[64]

The two-year gap between the composition of the Violin Concerto's first and its second and third movements, completed in 1936 along with the Fourth String Quartet, marked a pattern for Schoenberg's artistic productivity during his first years in America: *Kol Nidre,* composed in 1938, was followed three years later by the tonal *Variations on a Recitative,* for organ.[65]

In 1942 he received several incentives to write new works: for the League of Composers he composed *Ode to Napoleon Bonaparte;* for his former student Oscar Levant, the Piano Concerto.[66] *Theme and Variations* was conceived in 1943 for reasons similar to those that had produced the *Suite in Olden Style* nine years earlier: the pedagogue in him felt challenged by the idea of writing a piece for high school band, which might be thought to promise a large market—though here again Schoenberg was deceived.[67]

After that there is another two-year gap. Then, in the summer of 1945, his former student Nathaniel Shilkret asked Schoenberg to write a prelude for the project of a Genesis cantata that was to have involved the efforts of seven composers.[68] The resulting prelude was one of but four dodecaphonic pieces Schoenberg wrote through the end of the war. This seems rather strange when one considers that it was the first twelve-tone symphonic music with which he confronted his Los Angeles audience. Schoenberg may have wanted to take this opportunity to present himself from the side for which he was famous as well as to distinguish himself from his coauthors. The other dodecaphonic works (with the exception of the violin concerto) owe their existence to commissions by people capable of understanding and willing to accept a work of that level.

All the nondodecaphonic works (the Suite, *Kol Nidre,* the Organ Variations, and the Band Variations) were written for relatively limited religious or pedagogical use. The *Ode,* which makes a political statement, also belongs in this grouping, even though it was written for the League of Composers.[69] It is likely, however, that with the *Ode* he wanted to address a larger audience, something he in fact realized when the work was broadcast nationwide two days after the first performance in November 1944.

In composing nondodecaphonic works, Schoenberg realized in practice what he tried to do as a professor teaching the tonal idiom: to contribute to "the battle against cowardly and unproductive forces" by giving "a model for the advances that are possible within tonality."[70] For the first time since his atonal period Schoenberg let the purpose for which he wrote music overrule the aesthetic principles that he had, to that point, maintained with conviction—that is, that the only worthwhile idiom was the twelve-tone idiom. Why had he become a Saulus? Was it really because he intended to fill in a lacuna between tonality and dodecaphony that he had not considered relevant before? Or did he want to accommodate himself to American concert life? Did America influence him even against his will?

The works listed above are not all that Schoenberg completed in the first twelve years of his life in America; there are also his arrangements. The Monn and the Handel arrangements, two of the three works written from the end of 1932 through the fall of 1933, thus during a time of upheaval and disorientation, were conceived as free amendments and therefore apparently as compositions of his own. When in 1938 he complained that he had not written anything for two years, he did not count his arrangement of the Brahms quartet op. 25 of 1937 as an original composition. It was Klemperer who had suggested that he try his hand again on some well-known work from the standard repertory.[71] The conductor was so enthusiastic about the result that he held it in higher esteem than the original version.

Klemperer was not the only one with whom Schoenberg discussed arrangements. Conferring with Emanuel Feuermann at the end of 1938, he suggested an arrangement of a "classical" piece (a Bach sonata for viola da gamba) or of a work of his own, and the next March, in discussing with

Fritz Stiedry a new piece for Stiedry's New Friends of Music orchestra, he proposed an arrangement of his Second Chamber Symphony or of op. 26 or 29.[72] Already in 1935 he had written an orchestral version of the First Chamber Symphony and started to make an arrangement for orchestra of *Verklärte Nacht*.[73] When asked repeatedly to write or arrange something for band, he did not think of composing a new work but instead looked for suitable four-hand piano compositions by Schubert.[74] Thus Schoenberg underscored that "accessible" public image of himself he had so bitterly complained about when, arriving on the West Coast, he found that audiences knew nothing of his recent compositions but only the early works like *Verklärte Nacht* (which enjoyed a popularity akin to Tchaikovsky's music), his Bach arrangements, and perhaps the famous recording of the *Gurrelieder* by Stokowski in 1932.[75] Indeed, it seems that he became well known particularly as an arranger. In the summer of 1942 he received a commission for orchestrations, and a year later a publishing house asked him to arrange Beethoven's String Trio op. 8 for string orchestra.[76]

It is significant that in his conversations with Stiedry Schoenberg did not consider writing a new work for chamber orchestra. Perhaps the desire to complete at least one of his three unfinished works, the Second Chamber Symphony, was stronger than his desire to write a new original composition. The arrangements were a relief, an unburdening of his creativity. As he put it, "[The arranger's] first intention to orchestrate a work (as in my case) can be because he loved it and wanted to hear it once, when he conducts it himself, in a better understanding than the usual one. *But he is not responsible for the substance of the work.*"[77]

This approach made it easier to communicate with the conservative audience; "Für wen soll man schreiben?" (For whom should one write?) he had complained in 1938.[78] Thus his arrangements also served as an act of resistance against becoming mute.[79] What on the surface may have seemed like sheer necessity for a composer who wanted to have his music performed (Krenek got into the same situation several years later in the Twin Cities for similar reasons) had a side to it which showed the psychological benefits of the encounter with a culture in which the categories of the practical and the useful played an important role even in art.[80] The composer allowed himself a release—and perhaps not only a release from creativity, as Krenek surmised when, after listening to the Handel arrangement in January 1938, he noted in his diary: "Seems as if he wanted respite from his own music, which only happens if he hides behind someone else. With the string suite this actually didn't work, because that was a real original."[81]

Schoenberg's conviction that he should not teach dodecaphony to his American students and his frequent so-called return to tonality show that he did not want to make a point of blessing the conservative American audience with his "revolution" at all costs. Quite a difference from the old, un-compromising fighter who, probably after only a short time in the United States, had threatened that he would rather destroy America than eat crow![82]

This flexibility reveals an element of moral lassitude or pragmatism in Schoenberg's character that would have been unthinkable in Europe, but which shows up as early as 1934 when in Chautauqua he began writing the *Suite in Olden Style* alongside his dodecaphonic violin concerto. Even his rationalizing this step as necessary to fill the gaping holes in the cultural background of the large American audience reveals a pragmatism more familiar in the New than in the Old World, a pragmatism that seeks to answer pressing needs (including his own need to find an audience) before setting high moral or aesthetic standards. This same lassitude is to be found in his apologia "On revient toujours"; what is more, he seemed to enjoy it.[83] Acculturation has its agreeable side: it may reveal hidden facets of one's personality or develop traits that go untapped under normal circumstances.

Schoenberg's tactic of making arrangements so as to keep his hand in writing without having to invest much creative originality seemed to pay dividends in his dodecaphonic pieces. His Piano Concerto, for example, reveals well his ability to cope aesthetically with his situation as a composer in exile.[84] Nevertheless, in such arrangements as the Brahms and that of his own First Chamber Symphony one cannot help noting a sometimes "thick" quality, the loss of a certain balance, and the occasional proximity to *Kaffeehausmusik*.[85]

Krenek, in his retrospective article about the influences on émigré composers, did not mention the arrangements when he reflected upon Schoenberg. In evaluating compositions written under the conditions of exile, his judgment rested on two aspects: the degree to which changes occurred and were integrated into the conception of the work; and the (subjectively defined) necessity for artistic survival, for which, being an exile himself, he had much understanding. He was inclined to accept Weill's turn to Broadway musicals because this step seemed an absolute need for the colleague of olden days. Had Bartók given evidence of such a necessity or of an artistic reorientation, he would have respected what, in their absence, seemed to him to be concessions. Schoenberg's tonal works did not raise the problem of integrity, however, because Krenek classified—and justified—them as occasional products (in stark contrast to their author's own attempts to justify them aesthetically). At the same time, he understood Schoenberg's (and his own) tendency to incorporate comprehensive forms and writing into his more central creative work as being influenced by the pragmatic atmosphere of the United States. In his own work (though he suspected as much in Schoenberg's) he found evidence of a negative influence that had led him to abandon a line of development that began with his *Lamentations* and was continued only after contact with Europe had been reestablished. The loss of possibility was what he emphasized when he argued about the threat to integrity of acculturation, whether willing or unwilling.

Polarization, it seems, cannot be avoided when judging the inner integrity (*Stimmigkeit*) of a work of art. Nonetheless, one should keep in mind the benefits to be had by maintaining a sense of reality.

NOTES

1. Herbert Arthur Strauss, "The Migration of the Academic Intellectuals," in *International Biographical Dictionary of Central European Émigrés, 1933–1945*, ed. Herbert Arthur Strauss and Werner Röder (Munich: K. G. Saur, 1983), lxvii–lxviii.

2. See Claudia Maurer Zenck, *Ernst Krenek—Ein Komponist im Exil* (Vienna: Lafite, 1980), 181n.93; and Franz L. Neumann, "The Social Sciences," in *The Cultural Migration: The European Scholar in America* (Philadelphia: University of Pennsylvania Press, 1953), 20. Rejection is given as the third of three responses by emigrants in the United States in the study of Gargi R. Sodowsky and Barbara S. Plake, "Psychometric Properties of the American-International Relations Scale," *Educational and Psychological Measurement* 51 (1991): 207–16. Alexander Thomas discusses other possibilities in "Sozialisationsprobleme im Akkulturationsprozeß," in *Sozialisation im Kulturvergleich*, ed. Gisela Trommsdorf (Stuttgart: F. Euke, 1989), 176.

3. The outward forms of adaptation may be as obvious as they are amusing, such as Schoenberg watching a tennis match clad in a T-shirt and cap, Stravinsky wearing swimming trunks in his garden, or Krenek switching to orange-juice-and-whisky cocktails.

4. This problem is discussed at length in my introduction to *Ernst Krenek*, 11–42, esp. 27–28 and 33; and also in my article "Arnold Schönbergs Klavierkonzert: Versuch analytisch Exilforschung zu betreiben," in *Musik im Exil*, ed. Hans Werner Heister, Claudia Maurer Zenck, and Peter Petersen (Frankfurt am Main: Fischer, 1993), 357–58.

5. See Igor Stravinsky, "Programme Notes: Symphony in C, Danses Concertantes," in *Themes and Conclusions* (London: Faber & Faber, 1972), 49–51.

6. Arnold Schoenberg and Ernst Krenek, contributions responding to a letter of Albert Goldberg in "The Transplanted Composer," *Los Angeles Times*, 14 May 1950, 4:5; 21 May 1950, 4:6. For Krenek's changing position, see *Ernst Krenek*, 181–82.

7. Ernst Krenek, "America's Influence on Its Émigré Composers," *Perspectives of New Music* 8 (spring–summer 1970): 112–17; German version in *Musica* 13 (Dec. 1959): 757–61 and in Krenek, *Im Zweifelsfalle* (Vienna: Europeverlag, 1984), 136–43.

8. Burgin had also conducted the Boston premiere of *Pierrot lunaire* with a chamber ensemble of BSO players in 1928. See Hugo Leichtentritt, *Serge Koussevitzky, the Boston Symphony Orchestra, and the New American Music* (Cambridge, Mass.: Harvard University Press, 1947), 154, 73.

9. See Carl Engel to Schoenberg, telegram, 27 Apr. 1944, which refers to Engel's letter of 15 March 1943; in H. H. Stuckenschmidt, *Schönberg: Leben, Umwelt, Werk*

(Zurich: Atlantis, 1974), 422 (telegram), 416 (letter). Although Engel does not mention the Koussevitzky Music Foundation or the conductor by name, he alluded to a member of "that committee, which spends money to composers" (as Schoenberg repeated in his reply of 6 April 1943). I am grateful to Wayne Shoaf of the Arnold Schoenberg Institute, Los Angeles (hereafter cited as ASI), for providing access to Schoenberg's letters to Engel.

10. See Koussitzky to Stravinsky, 10 May 1943, Paul Sacher Stiftung, Basel (hereafter cited as PSS). The middle movement was said to have been originally composed to accompany a hunting scene in the movie *Jane Eyre;* see *Stravinsky in Pictures and Documents,* ed. Vera Stravinsky and Robert Craft (New York: Simon & Schuster, 1978), 357. For more details about Stravinsky's film scores as well as about his first years in the United States, see my article "Leben und Überleben als Komponist im Exil: Die ersten Jahre Strawinskys in den USA," in *Exilkomposition während der NS-Zeit,* ed. Friedrich Geiger and Thomas Schäfer (Hamburg: von Bockel, in press).

11. Schoenberg had alternatively offered a part of the *Jakobsleiter.* See his letter to Engel dated 22 April 1944, ASI.

12. Diary entry of 27 October 1938, in Ernst Krenek, *Die amerikanischen Tagebücher, 1937–1942: Dokumente aus dem Exil,* ed. Claudia Maurer Zenck (Vienna: Böhlau, 1992), 88.

13. Stravinsky to Nadia Boulanger, 4 Dec. 1940, in Stravinsky, *Selected Correspondence,* ed. Robert Craft (London: Faber & Faber, 1982), 1:238.

14. Stravinsky to Samuel Dushkin, 4 July 1940, PSS.

15. Not so Roger Sessions, who was the exception. He had lived in Europe (France, Italy, Austria, and Germany) from 1925 through 1933 but had not studied with Boulanger.

16. Boulanger proofread some of Stravinsky's new works, serving as a mediator between the composer and the publishing house. It was also through her urgent intervention that *The Poetics of Music* was not published in August 1940, because she supported Stravinsky's (or her own?) wish that Harvard University Press publish a bilingual (French-English) edition. See Edward Forbes to Stravinsky, 20 May 1941, PSS. Nothing came of the plan, and the following year Harvard University Press published a French edition first.

17. For this reason, Schoenberg was not in the position to promote his works by conducting. But he did link up with Klemperer, who was mainly interested in performing arrangements, and Stokovsky, who premiered several of the more demanding works.

18. The commissions Krenek received again in 1950 and during the following years indicate the same fixed rates as before (see below, note 40). For a large composition (for example, a concerto) he got $1,000; for a smaller work (for example, lieder), $500.

19. Stravinsky, *Gespräche mit Robert Craft* (Zurich: Atlantis, 1961), 191.

20. Excerpts printed ibid., 351–52.

21. See Maurice Perrin's report "Stravinsky dans une classe de composition," in *Feuilles musicales* (Lausanne) 4 (Dec. 1951): 207–12.

22. Stravinsky and his student are both quoted in *Stravinsky in Pictures and Documents,* 352.

23. Schoenberg to Krenek, 1–12 Dec. 1939, in Schoenberg, *Briefe*, ed. Erwin Stein (Mainz: Schott, 1958), 225–26.

24. In Alan P. Lessem, "Teaching Americans Music: Some Émigré Composer Viewpoints," *Journal of the Arnold Schoenberg Institute* 11, no. 1 (June 1988): 19–20.

25. "Auszug des Geistes: Bericht über eine Sendereihe [von Radio Bremen]" (Bremen, 1962), 210.

26. Lessem, "Teaching Americans Music," 11; and in an interview Toch gave in 1959, "Auszug des Geistes," 180.

27. Paul Hindemith, *A Composer's World*, quoted in Lessem, "Teaching Americans Music," 11.

28. Broadcast interview, 1 Nov. 1933, quoted ibid., 14.

29. This is not to say that music and morality were never juxtaposed. One of Krenek's former students related that after the first new music concerts at Hamline University, someone or other from the audience would inevitably come up and complain about the "immoral" music to which they had been exposed. Interview with V. Cooper Artis, in Olive J. Bailey, "The Influence of Ernst Krenek on the Musical Culture of the Twin Cities" (Ph.D. diss., University of Minnesota, 1980), 292.

30. Dika Newlin, for example, wrote "Mozart Variations" (i.e., variations on a Mozart theme) for string quartet; see her *Schoenberg Remembered: Diaries and Recollections 1938–1976* (New York: Pendragon Press, 1980), 20.

31. Schoenberg only once seems to have tried out a new method, though only on summer school students who had no professional ambitions. Against his principles he gave them "hard and fast rules" (Lessem, "Teaching Americans Music," 16) with his *Models for Beginners in Composition,* published in 1942: "I made this syllabus, because I was at first desperate to teach students, who have no special talent for composition, in *six* weeks matters which only the best could master (?) in a regular semester of 16 weeks. The success surprised me very much" (Schoenberg to Engel, 8 Aug. 1942, ASI).

32. Ernst Krenek, "The Composer Speaks," in *The Book of Modern Composers,* ed. David Ewen (New York: Knopf, 1942), 355.

33. Interview with Ernst Krenek, 27 Feb. 1976, in Bailey, "Influence of Krenek," 458.

34. In later years he sought to establish a certain pattern in his life by speaking of his years in Kassel, Wiesbaden, etc., as "years of exile"; see Maurer Zenck, *Ernst Krenek,* 181.

35. Krenek, "America's Influence on Its Émigré Composers," 117.

36. In his lectures and especially in the concert series he arranged in 1934–35, he aimed at making his audience aware of the roots new music had in history.

37. Bailey, "Influence of Krenek."

38. Interview with Krasner, ibid., 426.

39. Interview with G. Glasow, 31 Aug. 1975, ibid., 37. The survey Glasow mentioned has not been tracked down, but it is confirmed by Krenek's report on the activities of the Twin Cities chapter of the ISCM, 1943–45, quoted ibid., 126.

40. Robert Erickson, "Krenek 1938–1948," ms. of 22 February 1974; quoted in Maurer Zenck, *Ernst Krenek,* 253. Krenek accomplished all this with extremely limited funds. The musicians played without a fee; Mitropoulos, whose model was St.

Francis, paid, when necessary, the travel expenses (in the case of Eric Simon, for example); and the Coolidge Foundation sponsored at least one concert (the seventh ISCM concert, in February 1947).

41. Interview with S. Hammergren Kartarik, 27 May 1975, in Bailey, "Influence of Krenek," 425.

42. Interview with Sister M. D. Wood, 6 July 1977; in Bailey, 567.

43. The provost of John Muir College at UCSD, Professor John L. Stewart, shared Krenek's approach to teaching and asked the composer to help him find like-minded personalities. Ogdon and Erickson were appointed on Krenek's recommendation, and Ogdon, who became department chair, recruited Nee. Personal communication, Stewart to author, 8 Dec. 1993.

44. Interview with Krasner, in Bailey, "Influence of Krenek," 441. Krasner followed Krenek's lead and founded chamber music groups first at Macalester College, in Syracuse, N.Y., and later in Boston (Friends of Chamber Music).

45. Interview with Nordenstrom, ibid., 505. The émigré pianist Konrad Wolff reported the same experience with his students; see his "Klavierpädagogik in Amerika unter dem Einfluß der Hitler-Emigration," in *Musiktradition im Exil: Zurück aus dem Vergessen,* ed. Juan Allende-Blin (Cologne: Bund-Verlag, 1993), 99.

46. Krenek, "Students in America," *New York Times,* 17 Sept. 1939, 10:5.

47. Interview with C. Dower, 2 June 1977, in Bailey, "Influence of Krenek," 337.

48. Krenek, "The Ivory Tower and the Common Man," *Music* 1 (Nov. 1944): 34.

49. Krenek, *Amerikanische Tagebücher,* 121 (entries of 18 Aug.–4 Sept. 1939).

50. Diane P. Jezic's puzzling evaluation of this work as a "concession to Americanism" (*The Musical Migration and Ernst Toch* [Ames: Iowa State University Press, 1989], 143) is perhaps in keeping with other errors in her passage about Krenek.

51. Stephen Walsh, *The Music of Stravinsky* (London: Roubledge, 1988), 181. Most recently, Albrecht Dümling came to a similar conclusion in his article "Zwischen Außenseiterstatus und Integration: Musiker-Exil an der amerikanischen Westküste," in Heister, Maurer Zenck, and Petersen, eds., *Musik im Exil,* 326.

52. *Stravinsky in Pictures and Documents,* 359.

53. This conclusion comes from letters concerning engagements and receipts from the fall of 1939 through the end of 1941 and from 1944–45 (PSS).

54. For sources concerning *Circus Polka, Scènes de ballet,* and *Four Norwegian Moods,* see Walsh, *Music of Stravinsky,* 181. The case of *Danses concertantes* is also remarkable because Stravinsky did not want the commission by Werner Janssen to become public knowledge; see Janssen to Stravinsky, 17 Jan. 1942 (PSS).

55. Heinz-Klaus Metzger, "Strawinsky und die Nekrophilie," *Musik-Konzepte,* nos. 34–35 (Jan. 1984): 99–106 (special issue on Igor Stravinsky); Stravinsky, *Gespräche,* 191.

56. Already in 1942 in his *Four Norwegian Moods* he had used folk music, in this case from Norway. Maurice Perrin, one of Boulanger's students in Paris, related Stravinsky's advice: "Il ne faut jamais utiliser le folklore dans une œuvre symphonique. . . . Le folklore empêche de construire une forme" (Perrin, "Stravinsky dans une classe de composition," 212).

57. Score in PSS. The temporal relation to a most important event of the war

may indicate another reason for the conception of the Mass besides the more general "deeply felt spiritual need" (Walsh, *Music of Stravinsky*, 192).

58. Robert Craft, "Assisting Stravinsky," *Atlantic Monthly*, Dec. 1982, 70–71.

59. D. L. Crawford, "Peter Yates and the Performance of Schoenberg Chamber Music at Evenings on the Roof," *Journal of the Arnold Schoenberg* Foundation 12, no. 2 (Nov. 1989): 197–98.

60. The end of the war also broke the spell that lay on Ernst Toch's artistic production. Occupied with teaching and writing film scores during the war, he had composed only one additional work, *Poems to Martha*, significantly a commission (see Jezic, *Musical Migration*, 87).

61. See Stravinsky, *Selected Correspondence*, 2:325n.2; and Igor Stravinsky and Robert Craft, *Dialogues and a Diary* (London: Faber & Faber, 1968), 103.

62. When Peter Yates wrote in retrospect that Schoenberg with his two concertos was trying to compose popular works, if in vain (quoted in Crawford, "Peter Yates," 199), it is not clear whether he was alluding to an utterance of Schoenberg's or it was his own interpretation. Dieter Schnebel may have had the same in mind when in a broadcast in 1955–56 he designated the two concertos (and even the Fourth String Quartet) as "tonally oriented" (*tonal orientiert*); see Schnebel, "Schönbergs späte tonale Musik als disponierte Geschichte," in *Denkbare Musik: Schriften, 1952–1972* (Cologne: M. DuMont Schonberg, 1972), 195.

63. Stuckenschmidt, *Schönberg*, 370. Apparently this work was conceived without any commission or suggestion.

64. It was not until a year after the war, when contact with Europe had been reestablished, that Schoenberg once again wrote a work, the String Trio, op. 45, without an outside impulse.

65. Before he followed the suggestion of Rabbi Sonderling in the summer of 1938, he complained that he had not composed anything for two years; Schoenberg to Jakob Klatzkin, 19 July 1938, in *Briefe*, 221. Schoenberg began a twelve-tone organ sonata when he was addressed by an organist and a publishing house putting together a series of modern organ works, but he gave up this plan; see Paul S. Hesselink, "Variations on a Recitative for Organ, Op. 40: Correspondence from the Schoenberg Legacy," *Journal of the Arnold Schoenberg Institute* 7, no. 2 (Nov. 1983): 143–44.

66. Arnold Schoenberg, "Wie ich dazu kam, *Ode to Napoleon* zu komponieren," *Journal of the Arnold Schoenberg Institute* 2, no. 1 (Oct. 1977): 55–57; Walter B. Bailey, "Oscar Levant and the Program for Schoenberg's Piano Concerto," *Journal of the Arnold Schoenberg Institute* 6, no. 1 (June 1982): 56–79.

67. It was Carl Engel who had suggested that Schoenberg write a piece for symphonic band. The piece had its first performance under Koussevitzky in October 1944, in an arrangement for symphonic orchestra that Schoenberg had furnished a few months after the completion of the original score. It remains for further research to determine whether the band version was performed with any frequency thereafter.

68. Shilkret had apparently embarked on this project one year earlier, since Stravinsky was approached in March 1944. Shilkret probably contacted the other composers at about the same time, and in April 1945 the first performance of *Gene-*

sis by the Werner Janssen Symphony Orchestra was announced in a program book, though Hindemith was listed as the composer of the Prelude instead of Schoenberg. See the correspondence between Associated Music Publishers (AMP) and Stravinsky (complete in PSS); Stravinsky's and Shilkret's letters to Hugo Winter of AMP, 5 and 9 Mar. 1944; and Winter's letters to Stravinsky, 14 Mar. 1944; 12 Apr., 8 May 1945. It may be that Hindemith did not finish his contribution, as John Russell Taylor suggests without giving a source for this explanation; see Taylor, *Strangers in Paradise: The Hollywood Emigrés, 1933–1950* (New York: Holt, Rinehart & Winston, 1983), 207. (Taylor also mentions Bartók, though his name does not appear in the *Genesis* program book.) It is possible that Schoenberg was Shilkret's second choice after Hindemith. Stuckenschmidt's statement (*Schönberg*, 430) that each composer was offered $300 is not correct. Shilkret offered Stravinsky and Schoenberg each $1,000, but Schoenberg refused because the sum excluded the payment of royalties; Schoenberg to Shilkret, n.d., ASI. It is not known on what grounds they finally came to an agreement.

69. Without any honorarium; see his letter to Gertrud Greissle, 17 May 1942, in Nuria Nono-Schoenberg, ed., *Arnold Schönberg 1874–1951: Lebensgeschichte in Begegnungen* (Klagenfurt: Ritter Klagenfurt, 1992), 384.

70. Schoenberg to Berg, [25] Nov. 1934, in *The Berg-Schoenberg Correspondence: Selected Letters,* ed. Juliane Brand, Christopher Hailey, and Donald Harris (New York: W. W. Norton, 1987), 458. Christian Martin Schmidt made the hypothesis that Schoenberg returned to tonality because he had become aware that advancing the dimension of counterpoint by his dodecaphonic procedure resulted in a "allenthalben apostrophierte Vernachlässigung der Harmonik" ("Über Schönbergs Geschichtsbewußtsein," *Zwischen Tradition und Fortschritt: Über das musikalische Geschichtsbewußtsein. Veröffentlichungen des Instituts für neue Musik und Musikerziehung Darmstadt* 13 [Mainz: Schott, 1973]: 88). Schoenberg himself, however, stressed his pedagogical motivation.

71. Peter Heyworth, ed., *Gespräche mit Klemperer* (Frankfurt am Main: S. Fischer, 1974), 130. So Mathias Hansen is wrong in assuming that there was no direct motivation for this arrangement ("'Ich wollte einmal alles hören': Arnold Schönbergs Orchesterfassung des Klavierquartetts op. 25 von Johannes Brahms," in *Verteidigung des musikalischen Fortschritts: Brahms und Schönberg,* ed. Albrecht Dümling [Hamburg: Argument, 1990], 23–48). Klemperer's interest may also have encouraged the arrangement (op. 9b) of the First Chamber Symphony, which Schoenberg worked on when the first performance of the suite was prepared. But Klemperer was not interested in conducting only Schoenberg's arrangements; he planned to perform the Violin Concerto in several cities in the United States and in Europe during the 1937–38 season. See Schoenberg to Engel, 3 Feb. 1937, ASI.

72. Stuckenschmidt, *Schönberg*, 393.

73. Schoenberg to Engel, 22 July and 2 Oct. 1935, ASI.

74. Schoenberg to Engel, 8 Aug. 1942 (ASI).

75. See Schoenberg to Webern, 15 Jan. 1936, in Ernst Hilmar, "Arnold Schönberg an Anton Webern: Eine Auswahl unbekannter Briefe," in *Arnold Schönberg: Gedenkausstellung 1974* (Vienna: Universal Edition, 1974), 63; and "Brief an die Freunde" (Nov. 1934), in Nono-Schoenberg, ed., *Arnold Schönberg*, 306.

76. See Schoenberg to Stiedry, 25 August 1942, in Stuckenschmidt, *Schönberg*, 412; also ibid., 417. The Beethoven arrangement was meant for high school orchestras; see Schoenberg to Engel, 15 May 1943, ASI. Neither project was realized.

77. Schoenberg to Engel, 25 February 1939, ASI. The italics are mine. Although he claimed to be joking, he came back to the financial argument in a postscript (written at the top of the first page): "I did certainly not orchestrate the Brahms because I wanted to increase my income: it was not my first reason, but it was my second. This is why I wanted to sell you the whole work including all the rights for a lump sum." Schirmer bought the rights for this arrangement only in 1939; in the meantime, Schoenberg had earned a considerable sum by renting the parts and through royalties; see Schoenberg to Engel, 17 or 19 May 1939, ASI.

78. Schoenberg to Jakob Klatzkin, 19 July 1938, in *Briefe*, 221.

79. Krenek had sensed this pragmatic reason when at about the same time he renewed his acquaintance with Schoenberg in Los Angeles and heard Klemperer perform the Handel arrangement: "Für Schönberg selbst mag der Beweggrund zu solchen Arbeiten darin liegen, daß er gern etwas von seiner Musik hören möchte, und daß er Musik, in der er seine eigene Persönlichkeit rückhaltlos ausspricht, nicht zu hören bekommt, während ihn Versuche, 'spielbare' Musik aus Eigenem zu schöpfen, wie er sie in der Suite für Streichorchester unternommen hat, vielleicht nicht recht befriedigt haben. Kennzeichnend für die Situation ist, daß trotz der persönlichen Beliebtheit und Verehrung, derer sich Schönberg in Californien erfreut, weder dort noch sonst in Amerika jemand wagt, etwas von seinen späteren Orchesterwerken aufzuführen" (For Schoenberg himself the motivation for such works may lie in the fact that he likes to hear something of his music and that he does not get to hear music in which he expresses his personality without reserve, while attempts to create his own "playable" music may not have satisfied him. It is significant for the situation that, in spite of his enjoying personal popularity and veneration in California, nobody there or elsewhere in America dares to perform any of his later orchestral works); Krenek, *Amerikanische Tagebücher*, 38n.146. The article for which these notes were taken remained unpublished.

80. Schoenberg himself hinted at these connections when he wrote to Carl Engel on 3 May 1935 (ASI) that in his opinion the orchestral version of the *First Chamber Symphony* guaranteed a success in America comparable to that of *Verklärte Nacht*, *Gurrelieder*, and *Pelleas und Melisande*.

81. "Makes the impression as if he wanted to recover from his own music, which is possible only when he hides behind someone else. Did just not work with the suite for strings because it was original"; diary entry of 7 January 1938, in Krenek, *Amerikanische Tagebücher*, 38. Hansen's suggestion ("'Ich wollte einmal alles hören,'" 74) that with his arrangements of German music Schoenberg wanted to point out who were the legitimate heirs of this tradition does not appear well founded.

82. Stuckenschmidt, *Schönberg*, 365. Also, Hindemith seems to have lost the uncompromising attitude shown in the rigid system underlying his *Craft of Musical Composition;* see Howard Boatwright's recollections, quoted in Geoffrey Skelton, *Paul Hindemith: The Man behind the Music—A Biography* (New York: Crescendo, 1975), 104. Its first volume was published while he was still in Germany, and connections with the political system under which it was conceived can be easily discerned; see my study

"Zwischen Boykott und Anpassung an den Charakter der Zeit: Über die Schwierig-keiten eines deutschen Komponisten mit dem Dritten Reich," *Hindemith-Jahrbuch 1980* (Mainz: Schott, 1982), 127–29.

83. " . . . Sie [die tonalen Werke] gefallen mir" (Schoenberg, "On revient tou-jours," in *Stil und Gedanke: Aufsätze zur Musik,* vol. 1 of *Gesammelte Schriften,* ed. Ivan Vojtech [Frankfurt am Main: S. Fischer, 1976], 147).

84. See above, note 4.

85. For example, the high strings in mm. 92–100 of the Brahms arrangement, which are not counterbalanced by any other group of instruments.

Reading Whitman/
Responding to America
Hindemith, Weill, and Others

Kim H. Kowalke

Not songs of loyalty alone are these,
But songs of insurrection also;
For I am the sworn poet of every dauntless rebel, the world over,

Revolt! and the downfall of tyrants!
The battle rages with many a loud alarm, and frequent advance and retreat,
The infidel triumphs—or supposes he triumphs,

The named and unnamed heroes pass to other spheres,
The great speakers and writers are exiled.

WALT WHITMAN, FROM
"TO A FOIL'D EUROPEAN REVOLUTIONAIRE"

Walt Whitman stands undisputed at the center of American poetic history. As Ezra Pound quipped, "His crudity is an exceeding great stench, but it is America."[1] Whitman thought of himself above all as an American poet, and as such he helped to forge an identity both of and for Americans. Yet well within his lifetime his work crossed the Atlantic, allowing even those who knew no English to claim him as their own. By 1921, Carl Sandburg could declare that no other American poet had achieved rank abroad comparable to Whitman's, whose gift for human affirmation transcended national boundaries.[2] William Rosetti's selection of poems from *Leaves of Grass* had been published in England in 1868, and the first German translations of individual Whitman poems by Ferdinand Freiligrath appeared in that year as well and soon influenced many naturalist authors. By the turn of the century his impact on German literature warranted a monograph, *Walt Whitman and the Germans*.[3] In his *Literaturgeschichte* of the late 1920s, Klabund asserted that many young German poets still tended to imitate Whitman, who, "like a buffalo in heat, wildly pounds across the North American plains, runs the race with wild horses, and sleeps at night in the high grass under the stars."[4] Speaking for the generation to follow Sandburg, the Harlem Renaissance poet Langston Hughes summarized Whitman's pervasive influence: the "Lincoln of our Letters was able to project a voice, ventriloquistically, outside his own socially constructed role within American culture, a voice that resonated in the sensibilities of a tremendous range of writers throughout the world."[5] Even today, Whitman's shirtsleeve discourse remains politically engaged, agitating for change in diverse cultural contexts. "I too," Whitman wrote, "am not a bit tamed. . . . I sound my barbaric yawp over the roofs of the world."

He had titled that poem "Song of Myself." In fact, much of his poetry aspired to universal song, a rhapsody of brotherhood: "nothing more spiritual, nothing more sensuous, a god, yet completely human," he extolled in "Democratic Vistas." Music had been as essential to Whitman as his poetry would become to American music: "But for opera," he claimed, "I could never have written *Leaves of Grass.*"[6] Music, he suggested, "has so many good words of such rich and juicy character that they ought to be taken for common use in writing and speaking." He did just that, infusing his poetry with musical titles, idioms, structures, motifs, gestures, instruments, sounds, cadences, and especially rhythms. He considered his poetic technique to be symphonic or leitmotivic. His principal constructive mechanism was recapitulation and transformation; more than 40 percent of the 10,500 lines of *Leaves of Grass,* for example, repeat key words or phrases to structure Whitman's free verse and create a textual melody. Although its idiosyncratic musical poetics—tension-filled negotiation between the conventional and the free, the stable and the destabilizing—have made Whitman's poetry a challenge to set to music, it has proven irresistible to hundreds of composers. A far-from-complete catalog of musical settings of American poetry lists 539 musical compositions based on Whitman (as of 1985), more than for any other English-language poet except Shakespeare.[7]

British musical interest in Whitman adumbrated comparable attention from American composers, with Coleridge-Taylor, Stanford, Holst, and Delius leading the way. The long and plentiful Whitman tradition in England climaxed in 1936 with *Dona nobis pacem,* Ralph Vaughan Williams's antiwar cantata, which framed three Whitman settings ("Beat! Beat! Drums!" "Reconciliation," and a reworking of the composer's much earlier "Dirge for Two Veterans") with an Agnus Dei and a finale incorporating passages from a speech by John Bright (1855) and excerpts from the Bible pleading that "nation shall not lift up a sword against nation" again. During the same year in Italy, Mario Castelnuovo-Tedesco composed twelve Whitman songs in their original language, all but one of which remained unpublished during his lifetime ("Louisiana" was printed in the United States after his emigration).[8]

Although such diverse expressionist figures as Ernst Ludwig Kirchner, Johannes Becher, Ernst Toller, and Gustav Landauer acknowledged their debt to Whitman's poetry, few German-speaking musicians seem to have been drawn to it. In 1915 the Swiss composer Othmar Schoeck had set Johannes Schlaf's 1907 translation of "Beat! Beat! Drums!" for chorus and orchestra. After the war he sent it to Ferruccio Busoni in Berlin, but Busoni found the "uncivilized, fanatic tone" of these "Trommelschläge" incompatible with his own aristocratic pacifism—though he did admit that Whitman had "a certain power to agitate the masses."[9] Perhaps it was precisely this quality, rather than merely the centenary of Whitman's birth, that made 1919 such a banner year for the poet in Germany. The Weimar Republic celebrated its own birth with the publication of a new translation of *Leaves of Grass* by Hans Reisiger, as well as dozens of critical essays reinterpreting Whitman as an archetypal utopian socialist. The Spartacists even transformed "To a Foil'd European Revolutionaire" (1856) into a tribute to the fallen Karl Liebknecht.

Among Whitman's most ardent young admirers were Franz Werfel and Paul Hindemith, who later claimed to have taught himself English at that time by reading *Leaves of Grass*. Hindemith considered his three Whitman settings of 1919—"Der ich, in Zwischenräumen," "O, nun heb du an, dort in deinem Moor," and "Schlagt! Schlagt! Trommeln!"—to be key transitional works toward his so-called expressionist idiom: "In the Whitman Hymns I have almost succeeded in pinning down the things that have been going around in my head from the start. But they still cling in many places to all sorts of old-fashionedness."[10] Schott declined to publish these "hard nuts," ostensibly because of their "difficult" musical style, but more likely because of the blatant autoeroticism of the first song, a setting of "Ages and Ages, Returning at Intervals": "Und mich selbst bade und meine Lieder im Zeugenden,/Meine Lieder, die Sprößlinge meiner Lenden" (Bathing myself, bathing my songs in Sex,/Offspring of my loins). Nevertheless, these settings were apparently the composer's first lieder to be performed publicly, and Hindemith based the second movement of his Cello Sonata, op. 11, no. 3, on material from the second song (a setting of Schlaf's translation of the ninth section of "When Lilacs Last in the Dooryard Bloom'd").[11] A decade later Hindemith composed "Dies ist deine Stunde, o Seele" for male chorus as a companion piece to his setting of Brecht's "Über das Frühjahr." In 1923 Franz Schreker confronted the transcendentalist side of Whitman in two songs for voice and piano, which he orchestrated in 1927 as *Vom ewigen Leben*.[12] For the most part, however, Whitman remained on the periphery of musical *Amerikanismus* during the 1920s. He also seems to have been absent from the many American sources that provided material for the collaboration of Weill and Brecht, except as he was mediated through the poetry of his "Canadian cousin" Robert W. Service, whose Whitmanesque *Songs of a Sourdough* provided inspiration for *Mahagonny*.

As war again loomed on the European horizon in the mid-1930s, Whitman was reconfigured once more for a changing cultural context. That Whitman was anything but politically correct under the new German regime did not prevent Karl Amadeus Hartmann from adapting four of his poems as the libretto of a "Lamento" he began in December 1935. Having been harassed by the Reichsmusikkammer for failing to affirm adequately his Aryan origins and deeply depressed by the Nazi dictatorship as well as by the death of his mother, Hartmann confided to a friend: "I am working now on a cantata (for alto voice and large orchestra) with texts freely adapted from Walt Whitman, in which I outline our life. The poems, which I have radically changed, underscore our generally difficult, hopeless existence."[13] The second of five movements, entitled "Spring," utilized the first stanza of Reisiger's translation of "When Lilacs Last in the Dooryard Bloom'd." To express his own situation, however, Hartmann removed any specific references to Lincoln or more general allusions to America. "What merely embittered other liberal-minded among us," observed Hartmann's friend Max See, "compelled him to express his anger and deep-seated sorrow in music."[14] Before the resulting lament was finally performed in 1948 as a "Symphonic Fragment" and then revised in 1954 as Symphony no. 1 ("Versuch eines Requiem"), its composer had spent a decade in "inner exile," and one of its texts had acquired an even more tragic subtext: "I sit and look out upon all the sorrows of the world, and upon all oppression and shame / I see the workings of battle, pestilence, tyranny, I see martyrs and prisoners."

Meanwhile, composers in the United States had conscripted Whitman into their aesthetic battles over a distinctive identity for American art music. In his witty memoir from 1947, *Menagerie in F Sharp,* Hans Heinsheimer, himself a refugee from Universal Edition in Vienna to Boosey & Hawkes in New York, observed that every composer whom the émigré conductor Max Reiter encountered in the United States was writing either the great American symphony or a monumental Whitman cantata. Even Mr. Jenkins, "the organist of the First Congregationalist Church in Norfolk, who was also quite a composer," Heinsheimer reported, had managed to haul out a symphony in C-sharp minor and an "Ode to Walt Whitman for mixed voices, four soloists, orchestra, and organ."[15] While there was nearly unanimous agreement among the various ideological camps of nationalist composers with Randall Thompson's Whitmanesque dictum, "The European Yardstick is no measure for the things we do," Whitman-based compositions of the period demonstrate little further consensus.

On one flank, the Composer's Collective laid strategies, its spokesman Aaron Copland said, "to develop a school of composers who can speak directly to the American public in a musical language which expresses fully the deepest reactions of the American consciousness to the American scene."[16] He included on the first of the Copland-Sessions Concerts in 1928 "Songs of a Coon Shouter," four of nine Whitman settings by Marc Blitzstein, all of which were jazz-influenced, most of which were unambiguously homoerotic, and one of which had been composed while attending Arnold Schoenberg's master class in Berlin. In title, idiom, and content, Blitzstein's Whitman songs almost seem to have been designed to taunt those trying to guard American art music against the alien alliance they perceived in the "primitive sensuality" of African American jazz, the "hedonistic charm of Jewish art," and the open political agenda of homosexual and left-wing populists. The triple threat that such readings of Whitman posed to mainstream American modernism can be perceived in Arthur Mendel's review of the concert in *Modern Music*, which prolonged the metaphorical smirk of its title, "First Fruits of the Season," by suggesting that "Marc Blitzstein hid his talent behind his collection of *Coon Shouts*. I suppose that is one form of modesty."[17]

On another front, composers in quest of a more "wholesome," middle-of-the-road voice for American music appropriated Whitman to very different ends. Roy Harris (*Whitman Triptych* and *Song Symphony*), Howard Hanson (*Songs from "Drum Taps"*), Ernst Bacon (*Songs of Parting*), and Harl McDonald (*Pioneers, O Pioneers*) aligned themselves with the prairie nationalism of Sandburg and Sherwood Anderson in celebrating Whitman for successfully throwing off foreign domination to establish his own independent artistic domain in the wide-open metaphorical space of America.[18] Such composers followed in the footsteps of Edward MacDowell and Henry F. Gilbert, who described his own Nocturne (1928) as a "symphonic mood after Walt Whitman." "As many of us delight in Walt Whitman's 'barbaric yawp' . . . so we exult in this hilarious, screaming, exciting outburst of Mr. Gilbert's rugged muse," one critic wrote of his *Symphonic Piece* (1926). "No one but an American, regardless of traditions, free from European influence and academic conventionalism, could have written this music."[19] And although Charles Ives composed a memorable song entitled "Walt Whitman," he never fulfilled his plan to write a Whitman Overture. Nevertheless, in 1932 Bernard Herrmann dubbed Ives the Walt Whitman of American music. The analogy stuck; two decades later *Newsweek* captioned its obituary of Ives "Musical Whitman."

As America mobilized for war following the attack on Pearl Harbor in December 1941—eighty years after the first shots were fired at Fort Sumter—new editions of *Leaves of Grass* flooded the market and biographies of Whitman competed for readers under such overtly nationalistic titles as *Walt Whitman: Poet of Democracy* and *American Giant: Walt Whitman and His Times*.[20] What is perhaps the greatest collection of war lyrics by a single author—inspired by Whitman's first-hand experiences in the field hospitals of the Civil War and first published in 1865 under the title *Drum Taps*—and its sequel (which included Whitman's famous poems in memory of Abraham Lincoln) had by now been subsumed into the ever-expanding *Leaves of Grass*. As its so-called reveille and wound-dresser poems reverberated louder and with greater urgency than ever before, Elliott Carter, William Schuman, Otto Luening, and William Grant Still joined the ranks of Whitman composers. Recruiting poems written at the outset of the Civil War rallied prospective soldiers to the cause, and "Beat! Beat! Drums!" launched American troops into battle around the world. As casualties mounted, Whitman's "wound-dresser" dirges and elegies comforted the maimed and the mourners while reminding all of war's costs for the individual. And when Franklin Delano Roosevelt died in office, fourscore years almost to the day after Lincoln, "O Captain! My Captain!" and "When Lilacs Last in the Dooryard Bloom'd" paid tribute to the only president a generation of young Americans and grateful European émigrés had ever known.[21]

Just ten days after the United States had officially entered World War II, the conductor André Kostelanetz commissioned Jerome Kern, Virgil Thomson, and Aaron Copland to compose musical portraits of great Americans. Copland recalled: "My first choice was Whitman, but when Kern chose Mark Twain, Kostelanetz requested that I pick a statesman rather than another literary figure. [But] I was skeptical about expressing patriotism in music."[22] Nevertheless, as the nation's morale waned that spring, Copland, who needed the $1,000 fee, went on to finish his thirteen-minute *Lincoln Portrait*. On the Fourth of July Sandburg narrated it from a barge on the Potomac in front of the Lincoln Memorial. Copland wrote to Benjamin Britten, who had just returned to England after three years of exile in America: "Reports say that audiences get all excited by it. Moral: you can't go wrong with the Gettysburg Address to end a piece (Why not try Magna Carta?)."[23]

Someone already had. But Kurt Weill was neither British nor yet an American. He was an enemy alien, fingerprinted and registered as such, forced to request travel permits and to observe an 8 P.M. curfew when in California. Yet before Copland decided against Whitman, Weill had followed up his radio cantata, *The Ballad of Magna Carta*, with several Whitman songs. (More surprising, perhaps, are eyewitness reports from the mid-1940s of Bertolt Brecht coaching Charles Laughton on his public Whitman readings.) Such propagandistic appropriation of Whitman during World War II was anything but remarkable. Yet composing a Whitman text must have been more of a political or moral act than an aesthetic one for a refugee from an enemy country. By embracing Whitman, such artists were metaphorically also embracing America and thereby turning their backs on the culture left behind. Therefore, those few foreign figures who took a stand on Whitman's platform in the United States offer a provocative perspective from which to examine the émigré experience, to reinterpret images of *Heimat* and "ewige Kunst," and to question some of the fundamental assumptions of postwar European modernism in general and Eurocentric *Exilforschung* in particular. Could an émigré composer identify fully with Whitman without suffering what Adorno termed the "mutilation of self" caused by adjustment or assimilation, "an extinction of the spontaneity and autonomy of the individual"?[24] Which Central European composers were fluent enough in the American idioms of both language and music to tackle Whitman? Were the technical problems that Whitman's poetry posed for even the most talented of American composers soluble by outsiders? Could a composer surmount the cultural barriers that Whitman himself had transcended?

In the case of Stefan Wolpe, on the evidence of his setting of "O Captain! My Captain!" the answer would seem to be no. Wolpe's sole Whitman setting was published in 1946, the third in a group of three songs also containing two strophic workers' songs with lyrics by Elizabeth Papernow, "Unto the New Day" and "People's March."[25] Although Austin Clarkson's Wolpe catalog dates the Whitman setting as 1936, no surviving evidence confirms this conjecture. It is more likely that all three songs originated at war's end, because the second song celebrates the "magnificent workers'" victory over "the tyrants on land and on sea" while cautioning them to "stay alert until all men are free." Wolpe's awkward attempt at a strophic setting of "O Captain! My Captain!" is such a peculiar, not to say inept, combination of agit-prop, cabaret, and folk idioms that one might suspect, if it had been published in a different context, that it was intended as a parody. Unidiomatic text-setting indicates that its composer knew little or no English; one of the best-known and most often recited poems of the day (especially after the death of FDR in 1945) is mangled, with the music adhering to neither sense nor structure. All except two bars are built over an irregularly descending bass line, and the bland vocal part, though doubled throughout by the piano, spans nearly two octaves. There is no record of a public performance, and, understandably, it has never been reprinted. If the motivation behind Wolpe's Whitman setting was genuine rather than commercial, the musical result turned out to be neither.

In contrast, it was probably inevitable that cultural forces in America would draw both Hindemith and Weill to Whitman. Their respective Weimar experiences, aesthetic postures, and assimilative aptitudes had predisposed them to respond to Whitman more substantively in emigration than any of their European colleagues, albeit very differently. Having played artistic leapfrog with one another in the theatrical and concert arenas during much of the 1920s, the rivals' careers had conjoined only briefly in 1929 when they composed alternate movements of Brecht's radio cantata *Der Lindberghflug*, with Hindemith setting those sections with an American milieu.[26] After its premiere in Baden-Baden, Hindemith quietly withdrew his portion of the score and made no protest when Weill decided to compose the whole. Weill published a diplomatic explanation, "Keine Differenz Weill-Hindemith": the great divergence that had become evident in their work on the cantata, he stated, had merely demonstrated how varied were their artistic natures.[27] Privately, however, he railed against Hindemith with such vehemence that their never making an effort to meet during the decade they shared in the United States comes as no surprise.[28] It also indicates how few were the points of contact between their environments and experiences in "exile." In effect, they divided up the professional opportunities open to an émigré composer, each taking two: Hindemith a primary academic appointment, augmented by freelance performing and conducting; Weill the commercial musical theater, augmented by periodic and largely unhappy forays into the mass media of radio and film.

If Hindemith and Weill had each been compelled to answer the question put to Ernst Krenek in 1943—"What do you think is the composer's wartime function?"—their responses would have been as disparate as their careers in the United States were. Krenek's own reply could have been Hindemith's: "Compose music."[29] During his thirteen years in America, despite a heavy teaching load and more than forty professional appearances as a conductor and performer, Hindemith gathered fourteen commissions, more than any other composer, native or émigré.[30] He took no active role in the American war effort or political causes; Whitman would serve him only commemoratively.

In contrast, Weill confided to Ira Gershwin in May 1941: "I've written some orchester [*sic*] music but I threw it away. It seems so silly just to write music in a time like this."[31] Weill's engagement with Whitman, therefore, can be understood only in light of his determination to participate actively in the struggle of his new nation against his former homeland. During no period of Weill's life was he as politically mobilized. In the Whitman-related chronology I've assembled for Hindemith and Weill (table 1) I had to include virtually everything Weill wrote in America during the decade 1937–1946, with the exception of *Lady in the Dark, One Touch of Venus, The Firebrand of Florence,* and his three original Hollywood film scores—although even the last of those, *Where Do We Go from Here?,* was intended to rally the nation against Germany. His activism engaged four arenas: direct contributions to the military effort, such as composition for films, broadcasts, and recordings by the Office of War Information and the War Department as well as plane spotting for the local Civil Defense in Rockland County, New York; mass propaganda, war bond campaigns, and morale enhancers produced by such organizations as Fight for Freedom, We Fight Back! and Lunchtime Follies; more generalized musical and dramatic celebrations of the democratic ideal and American way of life, such as *The Ballad of Magna Carta, The Common Glory,* and *Fun to Be Free;* and pageants and projects alerting America to the Holocaust and, later, supporting a Jewish state in Palestine, including *We Will Never Die* and *A Flag Is Born.*

In February 1941, less than a month after *Lady in the Dark* had triumphed on Broadway, Weill told Ira Gershwin that he was thinking of composing "a book of songs (not popular songs but 'Lieder') for concert singers."[32] There is no further mention of the project, but shortly after the bombing of Pearl Harbor in December Weill turned to the edition of *Leaves of Grass* which Paul Green had given him in 1937 and jotted the titles of five poems on a scrap of paper: "To a Foil'd European Revolutionary"; "Beat! Beat! Drums!"; the third section of the first poem in *Drum Taps,* "First, O Songs, for a Prelude"; "O Captain! My Captain!"; and "O Star of France."[33] On Christmas Day he presented his neighbors Maxwell and Mab Anderson with the holograph score of "O Captain! My Captain!" As if his recent experience with Whitman had been a turning point, in mid-January Weill told an interviewer from *Aufbau,* the major German-language newspaper in New York: "I've been completely drawn into the American cultural orbit. . . . I totally feel like an American and no longer look back at all."[34] On 28 January he reported to Lenya (who was on tour in Maxwell Anderson's *Candle in the Wind* with Helen Hayes): "I'm finishing another Whitman song (Dirge for Two Veterans), which I think will be the best."[35] He wrote to his parents the following week: "Everybody tries to help the enormous war effort in his own way. Among other things, I've written some songs to poems by Walt Whitman, the great American poet."[36] That same day he told Lenya: "The three Whitman songs will be printed and I'll try to get Paul Robson [*sic*] to sing them first."[37] When Weill visited Lenya in Detroit in March, he performed "O Captain! My Captain!" "Beat! Beat! Drums!" and "Dirge for Two Veterans" for her and Hayes. Lenya reported that "Helen loved the songs (so did I—I think they are the best songs you have ever written. They are the most effortless (at least that how they sound) songs, you ever wrote. I'll sing 'My Captain' all day, the other ones are too difficult to remember after one hearing."[38]

In fact, Hayes was so impressed that within days she asked Weill to compose underscoring for patriotic recitations she was going to record for RCA Victor as a benefit for the American Theatre Wing War Service. On only a few days' notice, Weill arranged the "Star-Spangled Banner," "Battle Hymn of the Republic," and "America," as well as his own "Beat! Beat! Drums!," as "spoken songs" and supervised Hayes's recording in Chicago.[39] In his notes for the record jacket, Weill confessed that he had been inspired "by the extraordinary timeliness of Whitman's poem, which is a passionate 'call to arms' to everybody in the nation." Hayes recalled that Weill had asked for a reading that highlighted the poem's disruptive, uncivilized subtext: "I took my directions from Kurt. He had taken it into his soul, and I tried to get a sort of a throb in my reading, to give the feeling of the ominous beat of the drum. . . . But I got nervous and strained too hard. My reading was too pressed."[40] Lenya didn't think so. After hearing Hayes's spoken version of "Beat! Beat! Drums!" she exclaimed in her newly acquired English: "It just lifts you right out of your sit. . . . I am sure [RCA Victor] will do it over gain with [Lawrence] Tibbett or [John Charles] Thomas."[41] Although Chappell

published the songs almost immediately, there is no record of a public performance during the composer's lifetime. In May 1942, however, he confirmed to Gershwin that the songs would be recorded by the Metropolitan
opera baritone John Charles Thomas. It's likely, therefore, that Weill's mas-
terful but hastily copied orchestrations were intended for this recording,
which then apparently never occurred (or was never released).[42]

What Weill's mentor Busoni had described as a "fanatical tone" of the
strophic poem permeates every dimension of "Beat! Beat! Drums!" Whitman's narrator demands that nothing, no individual's protest or entreaty,
be allowed to interfere with the mass summons to a just war. In fact, Whitman had written the poem in 1861 shortly after the Battle of Bull Run, when
he was as caught up in the emotional moment of mobilization as the narrator within his poem seems to be. The first published version's antepenul-
timate line was "Recruit! Recruit!"[43] The poetic imagery is almost entirely
aural, as the loud, shrill, fierce drums and bugles are exhorted through in-
cessantly repeated phrases and obsessive iambic-anapestic meter to beat,
burst, rumble, rattle, whir, pound, and thump quicker, wilder, heavier, cli-
maxing in a crescendo that leaves the reader breathless. The force of Whitman's language overwhelms the poem's critical subtext, which warns of war's
barbaric threat to individual autonomy. Few composers who have set the
text have been able to argue with the narrator. This, and the poem's own in-
trinsic music, surely accounts for some of the striking similarities of Weill's
setting to Vaughan-Williams's, Hanson's, and especially Hindemith's of 1919.

Weill's assertion that "every text I've composed looks entirely different
once it's been swept through my music" does not seem to apply to his Whitman songs.[44] His autobiographical identification with the poems, so obvious
from the five initial selections he made, seems to have prevented him from
distancing himself from the text. In his so-called Brechtian mode, he would
have underlined the subtext to undermine Whitman's ruthless force. Instead,
Weill's strophic variations fully obey Whitman's command to "rattle quicker,
heavier drums, you bugles wilder blow." The composer deflected the threat
that Whitman's reveille poems pose to the maternal values of family, home,
and civilization into his setting of "Dirge for Two Veterans," a wound-dresser
poem in which the aural imagery of drums and bugles is transformed into a
funeral march for "father and son, fallen together in battle." In the ethereal
coda of its orchestral version—one of the most exquisite passages in Weill's
oeuvre—harp and woodwinds assume the composer's voice: "The moon
gives you light,/And the bugles and the drums give you music;/And my
heart, O my soldiers, my veterans,/My heart gives you love."

In 1947, shortly after he had returned from his only trip back to Europe,
Weill added a fourth song to the set. His postwar rereading of Whitman
was again prompted by personal experience, as he wrote to the Andersons:
"Coming home to this country had some of the same emotion as arriving

here 12 years ago. . . . Strangely enough, wherever I found decency and humanity in the world, it reminded me of America. . . . I'll write a few more Whitman songs (which will be recorded) and a symphonic suite from *Street Scene.*"[45] Again, annotations in Weill's copy of *Leaves of Grass* document the poems he considered. Now, after the war, not surprisingly all of the candidates depicted the tragedy and dehumanization of the individual soldier: "By the Bivouac's Fitful Flame" (which Hanson had set), "In Midnight Sleep," and "Come Up from the Fields, Father." Only "Come Up from the Fields, Father" is known to have been completed. (Weill seems instinctively to have selected the poem that had immediately followed "Beat! Beat! Drums!" as its antidote in the first edition of *Drum Taps,* even though his volume of *Leaves of Grass* did not preserve that ordering.) All four songs were then recorded by William Horne and Adam Garner for Concert Hall Records with Weill's participation, including, I assume, the new sequencing, which converts the group into a genuine cycle: linked by Whitman's musical imagery, "Beat! Beat! Drums!" and "Dirge for Two Veterans" frame the individual tragedies of the two veterans portrayed in "O Captain! My Captain!" and "Come Up from the Fields, Father." The four songs constitute a compelling minidrama, inflected with vernacular Americanisms but resonating with Schumann, Puccini, and Mahler—a mediation, if not a resolution, of the conflict between the Old World and the New.[46]

Hindemith had taken his next turn in the game of leapfrog as he picked up Whitman again in November 1943, the day after the premiere of his Fifth String Quartet by the Budapest Quartet. Having completed the *Symphonic Metamorphosis* during the preceding summer, Hindemith now set anew the original English-language text of the second of the 1919 *Hymnen,* "Sing On, There, in the Swamp," the fragmentary and enigmatic ninth section of "When Lilacs Last in the Dooryard Bloom'd." (It was one of twenty-six songs he composed in 1942–43.) Half the length of the German-language song, "Sing On" is vastly different in idiom and tone from "O, nun heb du an, dort in deinem Moor," sharing little beyond the pervasive melodic gesture of a descending minor third, the call of the "gray-brown bird." Comparison of the two settings evinces aesthetic shifts that had already prompted Hindemith to revise or recompose such works as *Das Marienleben* and "Frau Musica." "Sing On" was not published until 1945, when it appeared in a volume entitled *Nine English Songs.* In May 1946 Hindemith presented, as a "musical token of gratitude," his holograph score of the song to the judge who had administered the oath of American citizenship to him on 11 January. (Fearing that the gift might be construed as a bribe, Judge Hincks immediately passed it on to a Yale faculty member.)[47]

Meanwhile, Hindemith was being pressured to return to Germany. On the day after Christmas 1945 he wrote to his publisher, Willy Strecker, at Schott:

The calls for my return came in daily for a while and with increasing urgency. . . . But whoever is given the power to try to clean out the pigsty will simply be and always remain the pigsty-cleaner, and the really reconstructive work can be done only by his successor. I can't imagine anything that would interest me less! I feel that the best thing I can do, during the few years in which I shall still be in possession of my full faculties, is to write as much and as well as I possibly can.[48]

Two days after Hindemith had officially become an American citizen, Gertrude reported that Paul had decided to write a "Requiem on texts of Whitman" to fulfill a $1,000 commission for a major choral/orchestral work from Robert Shaw and the Collegiate Chorale.[49] Hindemith suggested, post facto, that his choice of "When Lilacs Last in the Dooryard Bloom'd" had been inspired by the parallels between the deaths of Lincoln and Roosevelt and the tragic toll of their respective wars. (When Gertrude presented the autograph to Yale in 1964, she further personalized its genesis: "It really belongs to New Haven and to our life in Alden Avenue with its fence of lilacs.")[50] Hindemith had, of course, long been attracted to the poem, with its three recurring images of death, loss, and mourning: the sprigs of lilac, the singing of the hermit thrush, and the fallen western star. It is one of the most musical of all poems, as the act of singing structures the text itself, with the hermit thrush's song recurring at key points. But as Howard Taubman suggested, setting the whole poem posed daunting problems for any composer, but especially one foreign born: "Paul Hindemith is a brave man. He has had the temerity to set Walt Whitman to music . . . [and] Whitman is not easy to set."[51] However, the poem's sheer length, awesomely complicated imagery and symbolism, intertwining structural patterns, and modulating motivic repetition seem not to have intimidated Hindemith.

According to his diary, he began composition on 17 January by transposing his 1943 setting of "Sing On, There, in the Swamp" down a whole tone for the mezzo-soprano soloist as section 5 of the new work, then varying that material for the other occurrences of the thrush song, and generating much of the remainder of the work from its motivic and harmonic cells.[52] Four days later Hindemith told his American publisher that the work would be subtitled "An American Requiem." After two months the vocal score was finished; Hindemith had altered very little of the text in compressing Whitman's sixteen sections into eleven, which he then grouped into four large movements, with soprano and baritone soloists augmenting the chorus and orchestra. The final page of the full score was dated 20 April, almost a month in advance of the premiere on 14 May. During rehearsals, Shaw extolled the composer's sensitive text setting, his mastery of prosody and musical form, by which he was able to articulate musically in about an hour what an orator would take twenty minutes to declaim.[53] But reviews were decidedly mixed. In a nine-page, handwritten, strategic letter to his publisher, Hindemith gave a rosy account of the reception of the *Whitman-Requiem,* while at the same time taking the opportunity to vent his resentment of and disappointment with his former countrymen:

> The oratorio was presented in New York in mid-May in a really splendid performance. The Collegiate Chorale, which performed it, is by far the best choir in the world, and the success was analogous. Last week it was broadcast on all the Columbia stations throughout the country. You certainly know the Whitman poem. . . . Everybody seems to know exactly what I ought to do now. The musical needs of Germany at the moment are all that matters and they must be tended to at once! It never seems to occur to any of them that perspectives change, that people who have been thrown out are neither willing nor capable of building up a new life for themselves every few years, that there might be things to do other than trying to rebuild a ruined musical culture. . . . And all that in the name of artistic ideals! *I* am supposed to be idealistic enough to give up everything that I've painstakingly achieved here [in the United States], simply to assist the machinations of *others.* . . . Now you will surely understand how I loathe the idea of throwing a piece like the *Marienleben,* which has grown particularly close to my heart, into this cesspool. It will undoubtedly flourish much better in the healthier, even if not ideal, climate here.[54]

Meanwhile, in January 1946, Weill had also begun composition of his next "Whitman-piece," the opera *Street Scene.* After the war he had finally convinced Elmer Rice that the time was right for a musical adaptation of his Pulitzer Prize–winning play of 1929, which Weill had seen in Berlin as *Die Straße.* Rice described *Street Scene* as his "most experimental" play, a "patterned mosaic" whose construction depended upon "concealed architectonics." He characterized its constructive technique in Whitmanesque terms, as "symphonic," "the statement, restatement and development of themes."[55] Act 1 of the 1929 script had climaxed with Sam, with whom Rice closely identified, reciting to Rose half of the first and all of the third stanzas of "When Lilacs Last in the Dooryard Bloom'd." Although Rice insisted that he adapt the book himself, he agreed to bring in a lyricist, someone, Weill recommended, who could "lift the everyday language of the people into simple, unsophisticated poetry." That they offered the task to the African American poet Langston Hughes, who had no previous experience writing song lyrics, has been portrayed as a bold choice: two "outsiders" of German-Jewish descent commission a representative of the quintessential American "Other" to give voice to the play's underlying Whitmanesque vision of the urban American melting pot. Langston Hughes may have been a Broadway novice, but he was widely recognized as the foremost Whitman disciple of his generation. Hughes claimed that at a crucial point in his life he had thrown away every book he owned except *Leaves of Grass.* He celebrated its centenary by writing "Old Walt" and concluded his first poetry collection, *The Weary Blues,* with an epilogue: "I, too, sing America. / I am the darker brother. / They send me to eat in the kitchen/When company comes."[56] During the two years he worked on *Street Scene,* Hughes edited and introduced two collections of Whitman's poetry and proposed to Doubleday an anthology of recent Negro and Indian poetry entitled "Walt Whitman's Darker Brothers."[57] Thus, Whitman had helped to shape all three collaborators' impressions of the American scene, and by the time the opera opened, a web of Whitman-esque imagery linked dialogue, lyrics, and music.

To make sure that the Broadway audience for *Street Scene* understood its most important intertextual reference, the inside front and back covers of the souvenir program book featured photographs of lilac sprigs to illustrate two stanzas of "When Lilacs Last in the Dooryard Bloom'd." In both play and opera the scene containing the Whitman recitation serves a pastoral function within *verismo* surroundings, a ritual of innocence preceding a ritual of violence. In the opera, a single stanza stands in for the entire elegy, because Weill omitted the first strophe, the "false start" of the poem in the play. "The great star early droop'd in the western sky" has been deleted and thus is available only to those in the audience already familiar with the entire poem. The remaining fragment seems entirely self-contained in its imagery: Sam and Rose, first-generation children of immigrants, yearn for a small parcel of utopian America, symbolized by lilac sprigs (now symbols of hope rather than mourning) and denied those trapped in urban "prisons for the human spirit." Weill's reading makes Whitman's text seem both more and less than it was originally. As soon as Sam begins to recite the poem, to luxuriant, *cantabile* orchestral sonorities, intratextual musical references that had structured the scene up to that point give way to an intertextual allusion to the last vocal utterance in act 2 of Puccini's *Madama Butterfly,* "Dammi sul viso un tocco di carmino," with Weill's melody nearly identical to Puccini's for three measures. The moment in Puccini's opera follows immediately upon Butterfly and Suzuki's famous "flower duet," which had been prompted by the appearance of an American warship in port, the *Abraham Lincoln.* No mere musical pun, the allusion allows Weill to turn Whitman's text inside out; Sam and Rose's relationship is doomed before it has a chance to blossom. The cultural chasm separating Russian Jewish and Irish Catholic immigrant families living within the same apartment building is as forbidding as the one separating Puccini's couple. Such a filtered reading conveys a vision of Whitman's "Mighty Manhattan" very different from Hindemith's straightforward characterization in the requiem.[58]

Weill had special regard for his Whitman opera: "Seventy five years from now, *Street Scene* will be remembered as my major work."[59] Hindemith was equally fond of his Whitman requiem: "In due time and after the waning of musical ignorance it may well become one of the few musical treasures of the nation."[60] Subsequently critics have identified these works as their respective composer's most "American" compositions. David Drew writes, for example, that "no Broadway score of Weill's seems so remote from his European experience [as *Street Scene*]."[61] David Neumeyer suggests that the *Whitman-Requiem* is "Hindemith's only profoundly American work."[62] Luther Noss concurs that the form and substance of Hindemith's works "were in no way affected by the fact that he was living here, with one notable exception: the *Lilacs-Requiem* is a distinctly 'American' work in its concept and construction."[63]

Noss's use of prophylactic quotation marks indicates that he at least is aware of the problem of using the adjective "American" as if it were a stylistic label connoting a set of generally accepted musical characteristics. Yet the opera and requiem composed by these two newly naturalized Americans share little in style, aesthetic, or audience beyond what is derived directly from their intersecting Whitman texts. The one delights in vernaculars, the other avoids indigenous inflections; one wears its commonplace Americanisms on its shirtsleeve, the other hides them beneath a cosmopolitan modernist veneer; one curtails the text to heighten a personal drama, the other attempts to convey the entire poem in all its spacious grandeur. Thus Hindemith and Weill joined the ongoing debate about an appropriate identity for American art music, a debate that had intensified and grown more complex as the foremost European modernists migrated to the United States, bringing their yardsticks with them and quickly making their marks on "high" musical culture, especially within academia. In these changed circumstances of postwar culture, Virgil Thomson, in an essay entitled "On Being American," abandoned his erstwhile support for the cultivation of a self-consciously national idiom: "Citizens of the United States write music in every known style. . . . All this music is American nevertheless, because it is made by Americans."[64]

Even before the premiere of his *Whitman-Requiem*, however, Hindemith had deemphasized the specifically "American" dimension of the piece by changing the subtitle, with its unmistakable allusion to *Ein deutsches Requiem*, to the more universal "A Requiem 'For Those We Love,'" a cryptic reference to the Episcopal hymn of commemoration "For Those We Love Beyond the Veil" in movement 8.[65] Subsequently, in October 1947, he completed his own German translation of the text, thus bringing his reading of Whitman full circle. In the remaining fifteen years of his life, Hindemith would conduct the work throughout Europe to greater acclaim than it received in the United States. Meanwhile, in the published piano vocal score of *Street Scene*, Weill had changed that work's generic subtitle from "A Dramatic Musical" (which had been deemed more effective for the Broadway box office) to "An American Opera" and added operatic set-piece labels to the musical numbers. Hoping to prolong the life of *Street Scene* beyond its run of 148 performances on Broadway, Weill also planned to enlarge its orchestration and reduce its spoken dialogue in order to make the work seem more suitable to European opera houses and publishers. Although he himself promoted it to Covent Garden, La Scala, and even the Berlin Staatsoper, Weill would not live to see the stage work that he deemed his most significant performed in the Old World.[66] At that time, none of Weill's other works for the American commercial theater could possibly have survived the trip across the Atlantic. Nor could his European works be performed there, either. In May 1947 he informed Georg Kaiser's widow: "I've just had a letter from Universal Edition with the offhand notice that all my full scores had been confiscated by the Gestapo. . . . I don't have a single partitur of my European works and therefore at the moment I can't say if one can procure them anywhere."[67]

In contrast, after Hindemith had overcome his initial reluctance to release some of his most recent works in postwar Germany, most of his music commissioned and composed in America transferred rapidly and successfully. His publisher, unlike Universal Edition, was in a position to gloat, since Schott had "made a sport" of publishing Hindemith's new works, even under the Nazi ban: "It is a stroke of good fortune that all your works are available and performance materials remain intact. . . . Hardly any other publisher can respond to requests, and consequently Krenek, Schoenberg, Bartók, Weill, Berg, etc. have virtually fallen into oblivion. You and Stravinsky are the only ones of the whole former group to have survived."[68]

This postwar publishing situation allowed Wilhelm Furtwängler to write Hindemith from Switzerland in 1947 that he had been able to follow all of his work with great attention and sympathy: "Recently I had the opportunity of making the acquaintance of your latest compositions and formed the impression that the encounter with America has done the composer no harm (a theory that is frequently advanced here), but that, on the contrary, the works are more accomplished and mature than ever before."[69] European knowledge of Weill's work in America, in contrast, was based on far less reliable and comprehensive sources. Furtwängler's colleague in Los Angeles, Otto Klemperer, for example, reported that "Weill got too involved in American show business and all the terrible people in it. Weill's last pieces I find awful."[70] With even Marlene Dietrich chiding Weill about "the different quality" of his music in America, no wonder Hans Curjel, before visiting Weill in New City in 1950, had feared he would find truth in persistent rumors in Germany that "Weill now acted like a super-American, that he wanted to hear nothing of Europeans, that money alone interested him."[71]

It came as no surprise to Weill, therefore, but no less a disappointment, that the only bit of his music he heard on his trip to London, Paris, Zurich, and Palestine in the summer of 1947 was Lenya's recording of "Seeräuberjenny" over a loudspeaker on the beach in Palestine. Declining Brecht's invitation to join the Berliner Ensemble, Weill never set foot in Germany again. Hindemith, too, avoided Germany during his first visit, also in summer 1947, a five-month stay that included a heavy schedule of conducting engagements in Italy, Austria, Switzerland, Holland, Belgium, and England and a six-week Swiss holiday. He turned down dozens of offers inviting him to return to Europe permanently—to head the Berlin Hochschule für Musik, to found a new music school in Frankfurt, and to conduct the Berlin Philharmonic: "The Rhine is not any more important than the Mississippi, Connecticut Valley, or the Gobi Desert," he remarked in a letter; "it depends on what you know, not where you are."[72] Hindemith's second trip, in 1948–49, however, did include Germany, as well as the Italian, Austrian, and German first performances of the *Whitman-Requiem.* Thereafter, the composer's center of gravity gradually shifted back toward Europe, his ties to America grew less binding, and his identity as an American citizen weakened, as if under siege: "I was 14 years in America and did my best to collaborate in the development of American music. Nobody ever bothered to call me an American musician; I always remained for them a foreigner."[73]

That, of course, wasn't true, for in 1947 the exclusive National Institute of the American Academy of Arts and Letters, whose membership was limited to 250 U.S. citizens "qualified by notable achievements in art, music, or literature," elected him as a regular member, shortly after his American citizenship had disqualified him from the status of "honorary foreign member" he had enjoyed since 1943. That same year, the institute awarded Arnold Schoenberg its "Distinguished Achievement Award," including a stipend of $1,000, and Elmer Rice nominated Kurt Weill to membership, asking Aaron Copland to second the nomination. Copland agreed, but warned, "I expect strong opposition." The composer Douglas Moore, president of the academy and institute, explained his own negative response: "Weill has marvelous technique and impressive facility but heart and conscience I can't find anywhere."[74] As had been the outcome in Berlin when nominated to the academy by Schoenberg, Weill was not elected. But his theatrical colleagues honored him with a Tony, in the inaugural year of the awards, for the outstanding score of a musical (*Street Scene*). Precisely ten years later, in response to a poll of the membership of Berlin's Academy of Arts concerning a proposal to commission from David Drew a catalog of Weill's works, his erstwhile mentor and champion Philipp Jarnach voted negatively: "Weill's American works represent the utter denial of the serious goals that he had formerly pursued, and one cannot be persuaded that they are of any stylistic significance." Weill had, in this view, indeed "danced himself too far into the land of the foxtrot," Weill's own characterization of Hindemith to Busoni in 1923.[75]

When the newly arrived Alfred Einstein suggested in 1939 that "the hospitality which America has offered so many musicians from old Europe has its complications, the invasion must be 'digested,'" he could not have predicted that more than fifty years later that process would not yet be complete.[76] From today's postmodern perspectives, the postwar European reception of Weill's and Hindemith's American works in general, and their Whitman pieces in particular, may tell us as much about technical, aesthetic, and sociological issues of music at midcentury on both sides of the Atlantic as about the nature and consequences of emigration for either composer. Their very different responses to Whitman evince equally divergent attitudes toward the meaning and purpose of art, especially musical expression. Their Whitman settings reify the modernist dilemma and challenge us to reframe central issues of *Exilforschung*. Again Whitman now seems prophetic:

To Foreign Lands

I hear that you ask'd for something to prove this puzzle the New World,
And to define America, her athletic Democracy,
Therefore I send you my poems that you behold in them what you wanted.

Walt Whitman, *Inscriptions*

TABLE 1   A Chronology of Weill and Hindemith in America

Weill	*Hindemith*
10 Sept. 1935: arrives in America	1935–36: "leave of absence" from Hochschule; 6-week stints in Turkey
Nov. 1936: *Johnny Johnson* (Paul Green)	Mar.–Apr. 1937: first U.S. concert tour
4 Jan. 1937: *The Eternal Road* (Franz Werfel)	
27 Aug. 1937: first citizenship application after reentry	
31 Aug. 1937: Paul Green gives Weill *Leaves of Grass*	
Aug.–Dec. 1937: work with Green on "The Common Glory," a musical pageant about the U.S. Constitution	
Jan.–Apr. 1938: work with H. R. Hays on "Davy Crockett"	Feb.–Apr. 1938: second U.S. tour; proposes International Music Festival for 1939 World's Fair
May 1938: Germany annexes Austria	
	Sept. 1938: leaves Berlin; residence in Switzerland
	Feb.–Apr. 1939: third U.S. tour

TABLE 1   A Chronology of Weill and Hindemith in America *(continued)*

Weill	Hindemith
3 Sept. 1939: Britain and France declare war on Germany	
19 Oct. 1939: *Knickerbocker Holiday* (Maxwell Anderson)	
4 Feb. 1940: CBS broadcast of *Ballad of Magna Carta* (Anderson)	15 Feb. 1940: emigrates to U.S.; teaches at Cornell, Buffalo, Wells
17 June 1940: proposes "Alliance of Loyal Alien Americans"	
June 1940: France falls; blitz on London begins	
15 July 1940: welcomes the Milhauds to New York	15 Sept. 1940: Gertrude arrives; Yale visiting professorship
20 Feb. 1941: plans "book of songs for concert singers"	25 Jan. 1941: Yale offers permanent appointment
	9 Mar. 1941: NBC Dept. of Justice's "I'm An American!"
June 1941: Moves into Brook House, New City	
5 Oct. 1941: *Fight for Freedom* calls for end to America's isolationism	
7 Dec. 1941: attack on Pearl Harbor	
25 Dec. 1941: gives "O Captain! My Captain!" to Max and Mab Anderson	
Jan. 1942: composes "Beat! Beat! Drums!"; "Dirge for 2 Veterans"	1942–Jan. 1943: composes 26 new songs (10 German, 9 English, 5 French, 2 Latin); AMP does not publish
28 Feb. 1942: *Your Navy* (Maxwell Anderson), NBC	
12 Mar. 1942: Brecht sends "Und was bekam des Soldatenweib?"; Weill offers setting for shortwave broadcast to Germany	
30 Mar. 1942: recording with Helen Hayes of "Four Patriotic Recitations," including orchestration of "Beat! Beat! Drums!" spring 1942: chairman of Production Committee, "Lunchtime Follies"; works as air spotter and for Civil Defense	

TABLE 1   A Chronology of Weill and Hindemith in America *(continued)*

Weill	Hindemith
4 June 1942: "Song of the Free" (Archibald MacLeish), Roxy Theater	
summer 1942: Chappell publishes *Walt Whitman Songs* (edition of 3 songs)	
1942: "Final Solution" implemented; in U.S. 100,000 Japanese-Americans interned	
Jan. 1943: attempts to expedite final citizenship papers in order to enter factories for "Lunchtime Follies"	
9 Mar. 1943: *We Will Never Die* (Ben Hecht); mass memorial at Madison Square Garden for 2 million Jewish dead	
27 Aug. 1943: U.S. citizenship	8 Nov. 1943: composes "Sing On, There, in the Swamp" for voice and piano
spring 1944: "Wie lange noch?" (Mehring) for Office of War Information (OWI)	
May 1944: *Salute to France* for OWI	
12 Apr. 1945: FDR dies 8 May 1945: victory in Europe	
Aug. 1945: Elmer Rice agrees to Weill's proposal for a musical version of *Street Scene*	1945: "Sing On" published in *Nine English Songs*
14 Aug. 1945: World War II ends; casualties estimated at 30 million, not including Holocaust victims	
Nov. 1945: *Down in the Valley,* pilot folk opera for radio series	Nov. 1945: negotiations with Robert Shaw for commission for choral-orch. work
1945–46: collaboration on *Street Scene* with Rice and Langston Hughes	11 Jan. 1946: U.S. citizenship
	17 Jan. 1946: begins composing "When Lilacs Last in the Dooryard Bloom'd: An American Requiem"

TABLE 1   A Chronology of Weill and Hindemith in America *(continued)*

Weill	Hindemith
	20 Mar. 1946: piano score finished
	20 Apr. 1946: partitur finished
	14 May 1946: world premiere by Collegiate Chorale
	May 1946: presents Judge Hincks with manuscript of "Sing On"
9 Jan. 1947: *Street Scene;* program reprints 2 sections of "Lilacs"	Mar. 1947: elected to National Institute of Art and Letters
6 May 1947: Weill's first return to Europe, en route to Palestine	23 Apr. 1947: first European tour
July 1947: "Come Up from the Fields, Father"; plans a symphonic suite from *Street Scene*	
	17 Oct. 1947: translates "Lilacs" into German; AMP publishes vocal score
1947: recording of *Walt Whitman Songs*	26 Sept. 1948: European premiere of *Requiem* in Perugia
3 April 1950: dies after coronary	
19 Mar. 1955: first known performance of orchestral versions of *Walt Whitman Songs* by Utah Symphony, Maurice Abravanel, conductor; Arthur Kent, baritone	
1956: Carlos Surinach orchestrates "Come Up from the Fields"	
	28 Dec. 1963: dies of acute pancreatitis
1981: Lenya bequeaths all American holographs to Yale	8 Oct. 1964: Gertrude gives partitur of *Requiem* to Yale

NOTES

Unpublished material cited in this essay is found in the Paul-Hindemith-Institut, Frankfurt am Main (PHI); the Paul Hindemith Collection of the Music Library of Yale University, housed in the Beinecke Rare Book Library (PHC); and the Weill-Lenya Research Center, New York (WLRC). I am grateful to the respective archivists and their staff members for assistance, and for permission to quote from the documents. Translations are my own unless otherwise noted. Topics introduced here have been explored in greater depth in two articles that preceded this essay into print:

"Kurt Weill, Modernism, and Popular Culture: *Öffentlichkeit als Stil,*" *Modernism/Modernity* 2 (Jan. 1995): 27–69; and "For Those We Love: Hindemith, Whitman, and 'An American Requiem,'" *Journal of the American Musicological Society* 50 (spring 1997): 133–74.

1. Ezra Pound, "What I Feel about Walt Whitman," in *Walt Whitman: A Critical Anthology*, ed. Francis Murphy (Harmondsworth, Eng.: Penguin Books, 1969); cited by Alicia Ostriker in "Loving Walt Whitman and the Problem of America," in *The Continuing Presence of Walt Whitman: The Life after the Life*, ed. Robert K. Martin (Iowa City: University of Iowa Press, 1992), 219. Pound called himself "a Walt Whitman who has learned to wear a collar and dress shirt."

2. Carl Sandburg, introduction to the Modern Library Edition of *Leaves of Grass* (New York: Random House, 1921), vi: "He is the single American figure that both American and European artists and critics most often put in a class with Shakespeare, Dante, Homer."

3. Richard H. Riethmüller, *Walt Whitman and the Germans* (Philadelphia: Americana Germanica Press, 1906). See also Karl Knortz, *Walt Whitman, der Dichter der Demokratie*, 2d ed. (Leipzig: Fleischer, 1899). For a comprehensive discussion of Whitman publication and reception in Germany, see Walter Grünzweig, *Walt Whitmann: Die deutschsprachige Rezeption als interkulturelles Phänomen* (Munich: Wilhelm Fink, 1991).

4. Klabund, *Literaturgeschichte: Die deutsche und die fremde Dichtung von den Anfängen bis zur Gegenwart*, ed. Ludwig Goldscheider (Vienna: Phaidon, 1929), 251.

5. Cited by George B. Hutchinson, "Langston Hughes and the 'Other' Whitman," in Martin, ed., *Continuing Presence*, 19.

6. John Townsend Trowbridge, "Reminiscences of Walt Whitman," *Atlantic Monthly*, Feb. 1902, 163–75; quoted in John Dizikes, *Opera in America: A Cultural History* (New Haven: Yale University Press, 1993), 184.

7. Michael A. Hovland, comp., *Musical Settings of American Poetry* (Westport, Conn.: Greenwood Press, 1986).

8. "I Saw in Louisiana a Live Oak Growing" was published under the title "Louisiana" by Galaxy Music in 1940.

9. Busoni to Othmar Schoeck, 30 Aug. 1920, quoted in *Othmar Schoeck: Leben und Schaffen im Spiegel von Selbstzeugnissen und Zeitgenossenberichten*, ed. Werner Vogel (Zurich: Atlantis, 1976), 98. See also Werner Grünzweig, "Music in the Rhythm of War: Othmar Schoeck and the Beginning of Whitman-Music in the German-Speaking Countries," *Walt Whitman Quarterly Review* 8 (summer 1990): 29–40.

10. Hindemith to B. Schott Verlag, 11 Apr. 1920, PHI. See Kurt von Fischer, "Hindemith's Early Songs for Voice and Piano," *Proceedings of the Royal Musical Association* 109 (1982–83): 147–59. Although they were unpublished, Hindemith did not lose interest in the songs, and as late as 1953 he recopied the second song and provided the others with some corrections and expression marks.

11. The "Drei Hymnen" were performed in Frankfurt on 20 February 1920 by Helge Lindberg, a friend of the expressionist painter Oskar Schlemmer. The original version of the second movement of the sonata carried a title, later suppressed, "Im Schilf, Trauerzug und Bacchanale." The final movement derives motivic material from the third of the hymns.

12. The songs were "Wurzeln und Halme" and "Ein Kind sagte"; see Christopher Hailey, *Franz Schreker: A Cultural Biography* (Cambridge: Cambridge University Press, 1993), 355.

13. Hartmann to Alexander Jemnitz, 7 May 1936, quoted in Andrew D. McCredie, *Karl Amadeus Hartmann: Thematic Catalogue of His Works* (New York: C. F. Peters, 1982), 17.

14. Quoted ibid., 16.

15. Hans Heinsheimer, "Bus Stop in Waco," in *Menagerie in F Sharp* (Garden City, N.Y.: Doubleday, 1947), 30. I am grateful to Carl S. Leafstedt for pointing out this passage to me.

16. Aaron Copland, "The Composer in America," *Modern Music* 10 (1932–33): 91.

17. Arthur Mendel, "First Fruits of the Season," *Modern Music* 6 (Jan.–Feb. 1929): 30–32. For a provocative and problematic reading of Blitzstein's settings of Whitman, see David Metzer, "Reclaiming Walt: Marc Blitzstein's Whitman Settings," *Journal of the American Musicological Society* 48 (summer 1995): 240–71.

18. That's just what Hanson himself had been trying to do as director of the Eastman School of Music, particularly in his annual Festivals of American Music in Rochester. When he recorded his "Songs from *Drum Taps*" with the Eastman-Rochester Orchestra, the companion work was Randall Thompson's *The Testament of Freedom*. Both works raise a Whitmanesque democratic ideal to the realm of secular religion.

19. Philip Hale, quoted in Claire McGlinchee, "American Literature in American Music," *Musical Quarterly* 31 (Jan. 1945): 108.

20. Hugh Fausset, *Walt Whitman: Poet of Democracy* (London: J. Cape; New Haven: Yale University Press, 1942); Frances Winwar, *American Giant: Walt Whitman and His Times* (New York: Harper, 1941); and Henry Seidel Canby, *Walt Whitman, an American* (Boston: Houghton Mifflin, 1943).

21. Hovland lists, for example, twenty-four settings of "O Captain! My Captain!" At the time, the poem was included in virtually every student anthology and thus was one of the ten best-known English-language poems in America.

22. André Kostelanetz to Copland, 18 Dec. 1941: "Next summer I am conducting a number of concerts with major symphony orchestras. The first part of each program will consist of standard symphonic repertoire, and the second part of the program will be devoted entirely to three new works by American composers. These three works have a correlated idea in that they are to represent a musical portrait gallery of great Americans. . . . Some of the personalities which occur to me are George Washington, Paul Revere, Walt Whitman, Robert Fulton, Henry Ford, Babe Ruth" (quoted in Aaron Copland and Vivian Perlis, *Copland: 1900 through 1942* [New York: St. Martin's, 1984], 342).

23. The premiere performance occurred on 14 May in Cincinnati with Kostelanetz conducting and William Adams as speaker. The letter from Copland to Britten of 16 June 1942 is quoted in Copland and Perlis, *1900 through 1942*, 344. In August, Harold Clurman, Clifford Odets, and Hanns Eisler heard Edward G. Robinson narrate it at the Hollywood Bowl; Clurman reported to Copland: "Odets said he was proud of you, Eisler said, 'a good job'" (ibid.).

24. Theodor W. Adorno, "Scientific Experiences of a European Scholar in America," in *The Intellectual Migration: Europe and America, 1930–1960*, ed. Donald Fleming and Bernard Bailyn (Cambridge, Mass.: Harvard University Press, Belknap Press, 1969), 338–39.

25. Stefan Wolpe, *Three Songs for Medium Voice and Piano* (New York: Transcontinental Music, 1946). I am grateful to Austin Clarkson for information concerning this set.

26. For an account of their artistic rivalry, see David Drew, "Musical Theater in the Weimar ˀⲻpublic," *Proceedings of the Royal Musical Association* 88 (1961–62): 89–108. See also Stephen Hinton's essay in this volume.

27. Kurt Weill, "Keine Differenz Weill-Hindemith," *Filmkurier* (Berlin), 8 Aug. 1929, reprinted in Kurt Weill, *Musik und Theater: Gesammelte Schriften*, ed. Stephen Hinton and Jürgen Schebera (Berlin: Henschelverlag, 1990), 303–4.

28. In a letter to Hans Curjel, the dramaturg of the Kroll Opera in Berlin, Weill reported on 2 August 1929: "Things were really shitty in Baden-Baden. Hindemith's work on *Der Lindberghflug* and the *Lehrstück* were of a scarcely to be surpassed superficiality. It has very clearly demonstrated that his music for Brechtian texts is too harmless. It's astonishing that even the press has noted it and put me forward as the brilliant example of how Brecht must be composed" (original in the Deutsches Literaturarchiv, Marbach; photocopy in WLRC, series 40).

29. Krenek to Ross Lee Finney, 2 Nov. 1943, quoted in John L. Stewart, *Ernst Krenek: The Man and His Music* (Berkeley: University of California Press, 1991), 248. Krenek himself composed a *Cantata for Wartime*, op. 95, using texts by Melville.

30. See Luther Noss, *Paul Hindemith in the United States* (Urbana: University of Illinois Press, 1989), 154–155.

31. Weill to Ira Gershwin, 28 May 1941; original in the Music Division of the Library of Congress; photocopy in WLRC, series 40.

32. Weill to Ira Gershwin, 20 Feb. 1941; original in the Music Division of the Library of Congress; photocopy in WLRC, series 40.

33. The Universal Library edition of *Leaves of Grass* was published by Grosset & Dunlap in New York. Green inscribed the volume, "For Kurt Weill, May his trouble increase on account of me being so troubled! Hail Columbia!" P.G. 8/31/37 (WLRC, series 90, 219). In the same volume from Weill's library, the present author found a second list with the titles of five other poems written on a nearly identical scrap of paper; their content and tone suggest that this list represents a second pass through the collection in 1941–42, but Weill set none of the poems: "France: The 18th Year of These States," "Europe: The 72d and 73d Years of These States," "Drum Taps: First, O Sons," "Rise, O Days, from Your Fathomless Deeps," and "Long, Too Long, O Land." In August 1937 Weill had visited Green in Chapel Hill to discuss plans for *The Common Glory*, a musical pageant about the origins of American democracy, with production by the Federal Theatre Project in mind. At the end of the month, Weill had taken the first steps toward American citizenship: having entered the United States on a temporary visa, which had been extended, he and Lenya reentered the country from Canada in order to establish status as immigrants. He allowed the lease on his apartment outside Paris to lapse and asked Madeleine Milhaud to arrange for his belongings to be shipped to New York.

34. A. H. [?], "Gespräch mit Kurt Weill," *Aufbau*, 16 Jan. 1942.

35. Weill to Lenya, 28 Jan. 1942, WLRC, series 44.

36. Weill to Albert and Emma Weill, 5 Feb. 1942, WLRC, series 45.

37. Weill to Lenya, 5 Feb. 1942; in *Speak Low (When You Speak Love): The Letters of Kurt Weill and Lotte Lenya,* ed. Lys Symonette and Kim H. Kowalke (Berkeley: University of California Press, 1996), 287–88 (letter no. 227). On 11 June 1942 Weill wrote to Mrs. Robeson: "I have tried many times, through Mr. Rockmore, to get hold of Paul because I wanted to show him those three Walt Whitman songs and also the 'Song of the Free' which I wrote with Archibald MacLeish, but he never seemed to have time for me and I am afraid he is not interested. The songs are printed now and will be sent out by the publisher. I will send him copies" (carbon copy in WLRC, series 40).

38. Lenya to Weill, 6 Mar. 1942; in *Speak Low,* 304 (letter no. 246).

39. RCA Victor released the 78s as a two-disc set, *Mine Eyes Have Seen the Glory: Four Patriotic Melodramas for Speaker, Chorus, and Orchestra.*

40. Helen Hayes, oral history interview with Margaret Sherry, 25 July 1991 WLRC, series 60. Hayes also recalled: "I remember when we were in Tennessee, I think it was Memphis, and we stayed in an old-fashioned hotel with pipes in the bathroom that ran up, from floor to floor, along the corner of the bathroom. And I got into the tub where I could be relaxed, and I had begun reciting 'Columbia, the Gem of the Ocean, the pride of the red, white, and blue,' or whatever it was, and I was saying it all with such passion, lying there, trying to hear it and feel it. I was making my selection of what I wanted to do when we got to that point. So I got through 'Three cheers for the red, white, and blue, three cheers for the red, white, and blue, the army and the navy forever, three cheers for the red, white, and blue' and a voice through the pipes said, 'Atta girl,' (laughter) from the bathroom above me. Oh boy, I've never been so embarrassed. I had a strong desire to sink down into the tub and drown quietly."

41. Lenya to Weill, 3 Apr. 1942; in *Speak Low,* 316–17 (letter no. 257).

42. The first known performance of the orchestrated version of the songs by the Utah Symphony was conducted by Maurice Abravanel, with baritone Arthur Kent, in a concert on 19 March 1955 in celebration of the three hundredth anniversary of Jewish settlement in the United States. Weill's musical assistant Irving Schlein completed the orchestration of the "Dirge for Two Veterans" after the first seven pages in the holograph full score.

43. The poem was first published in the *Boston Daily Evening Transcript* on 24 September 1961. This version is reprinted in William White, "'Beat! Beat! Drums!': The First Version," *Walt Whitman Review* 21 (Mar. 1975): 43–44.

44. Weill to Erika Neher, n.d. [April 1933]; photocopy in WLRC, series 40.

45. Weill to Maxwell and Mab Anderson, 22 June 1947; photocopy in WLRC, series 40.

46. In both "Dirge" and "Come Up from the Fields, Father" Weill omits a stanza of Whitman's poem, probably because they would have interfered with the musical arch and dramatic pace of his setting. Recently, another holograph of "Come Up from the Fields, Father" has come to light among William Horne's papers at the Jerusalem Rubin Academy of Music and Dance. For more detailed consideration of aspects

of Weill's Whitman Songs, see Jürgen Thym, "The Enigma of Kurt Weill's *Whitman Songs*," and Werner Grünzweig, "Propaganda der Trauer: Kurt Weills *Whitman-Songs*," in *A Stranger Here Myself: Kurt Weill Studien*, ed. Kim H. Kowalke and Horst Edler (Hildesheim: Georg Olms, 1993).

47. The score, now in the Hindemith Collection of the Yale Music Library, bears the inscription: "Dear Judge Hincks, we would be glad if you would accept this musical token of gratitude for your kindness/Gertrude and Paul Hindemith/May 1946."

48. Hindemith to Willy Strecker, 26 Dec. 1945; photocopy in PHI; also quoted and translated in Geoffrey Skelton, *Paul Hindemith* (London: Victor Gollancz, 1975), 219.

49. Gertrude Hindemith to Jean Moran Myer, 13 Jan. 1946, PHC.

50. Gertrude Hindemith to Luther Noss, 6 Oct. 1964, PHC.

51. Howard Taubman, review of the premiere performance, *New York Times*, 15 May 1946.

52. For an introduction to the musical structure of the work, see David Neumeyer, *The Music of Paul Hindemith* (New Haven: Yale University Press, 1986), 215–23.

53. Robert Shaw, *Newsletter* to Friends of the Atlanta Symphony (1971), 2–3; PHC, Box 6, Folder 185/1946.

54. Letter from Hindemith in Mexico to Willy Strecker in Mainz, 15 July 1946; photocopy in PHI. In 1959, however, Hindemith recalled some of the shortcomings of the premiere performance: "The man who sang the premiere in New York years ago [George London] sang well, but nothing came out from him to move the people. They were bored to death" (letter to Oscar Cox, 28 Sept. 1959, PHI).

55. Elmer Rice, *Minority Report: An Autobiography* (New York: Simon & Schuster, 1963), 237.

56. Hutchinson, "Hughes and the 'Other' Whitman," 22.

57. The two collections were published by Young World Books and International Publishers. Both Doubleday and Oxford University Press rejected the anthology of black poetry. See Arnold Rampersad, *The Life of Langston Hughes*, vol. 2: *1941–1967* (New York: Oxford University Press, 1988), 109ff.

58. For a detailed analysis of this scene, see Kim H. Kowalke, "Kurt Weill, Modernism, and Popular Culture: *Öffentlichkeit als Stil*," *Modernism/Modernity* 2 (Jan. 1995): 27–69, an essay that postdates the present essay.

59. Arnold Sundgaard, "Portrait of the Librettist as Silenced Composer," *Dramatists Guild Quarterly* 16 (winter 1980): 26.

60. Hindemith to Oscar Cox, 14 Dec. 1956, PHC.

61. David Drew, *Kurt Weill: A Handbook* (London: Faber & Faber, 1987), 354.

62. Neumeyer, *Music of Paul Hindemith*, 216.

63. Noss, *Hindemith in the United States*, 123–24.

64. Virgil Thomson, "On Being American," *New York Herald Tribune*, 25 Jan. 1948.

65. For an in-depth analysis of the requiem, including the autobiographical resonances of the Episcopal hymn, itself based on a traditional Jewish *Yigdal*, see my "For Those We Love: Hindemith, Whitman, and 'An American Requiem,' " *Journal of the American Musicological Society* 50 (spring 1997): 133–74, which postdates the present essay.

66. When it received its European premiere in 1955 in Düsseldorf, Caspar Neher designed the sets, and Adorno wrote a program note that sabotaged its critical reception and estranged the piece from German opera houses for the next thirty years.

67. Weill to Margarethe Kaiser, 1 May 1947; photocopy in WLRC. In 1949 Weill discouraged the notion of a German production of *One Touch of Venus,* his Broadway piece most closely resembling conventional musical comedy: "From all I know about the present status of the German theatres my impression is that they are in no way equipped to do justice to a piece like *Venus,* and a bad production would do a lot of harm to me. My European reputation is worth more to me than the very negligible amount of money I can make with this production." (Weill to agent Leah Salisbury, 7 Jan. 1950; original in Columbia University Rare Book and Manuscript Library, Leah Salisbury Collection, catalogued correspondence; photocopy in WLRC, series 40.)

68. Willy Strecker to Hindemith, 16 Aug. 1946; photocopy in PHI.

69. The letter from Furtwängler to Hindemith (quoted by Skelton, *Hindemith,* 231) was not sent, however. Instead Furtwängler mailed only a short note dated 15 April (PHI).

70. Peter Heyworth, comp. and ed., *Conversations with Klemperer,* rev. ed. (London: Faber & Faber, 1985), 78.

71. Hans Curjel, "Erinnerungen an Kurt Weill," *Melos* 37 (Mar. 1970): 84.

72. Hindemith to Willy Strecker, 20 Jan. 1947, PHI.

73. Hindemith to Oscar Cox, 14 Dec. 1956, PHI.

74. Douglas Moore to Elmer Rice, 24 Mar. 1947, and Copland to Rice, 25 Mar. 1947; Harvard Theatre Collection, Elmer Rice Papers, bMS thr 380 (172), (45).

75. Weill to Busoni, June 21, 1923; photocopy in WLRC. The Hindemith-Amar Quartet was performing Weill's String Quartet, op. 8, in the Frankfurt Kammermusikwoche, and Weill was disappointed by the group's reaction to the piece: "I'm going to hear my quartet for the first time today, because the Hindemith people are terribly overburdened. Strangely enough, the last movement—which for me, as well as for you, is the most mature one—seems to meet with the least approval from those four gentlemen. I'm afraid that Hindemith has already danced himself a bit too far into the land of the foxtrot."

76. Alfred Einstein, "War, Nationalism, Tolerance," *Modern Music* 17 (Oct.–Nov. 1939): 9.

PART FOUR

Case Studies
Individuals, Places, and Institutions

A Viennese Opera Composer in Hollywood

Korngold's Double Exile in America

Bryan Gilliam

When one thinks of Hollywood film composers, images emerge of talented, overworked musicians enduring unreasonable deadlines, often under the scrutiny of meddling, musically illiterate producers. Such was, indeed, often the case for the likes of Max Steiner, Franz Waxman, Frederick Hollander, and others; but it was not the case for Erich Wolfgang Korngold, a celebrity Austrian composer, admired by Mahler, a student of Zemlinsky, and a Jewish Hollywood émigré. Curiously, this same biographical description also applied to Arnold Schoenberg, Korngold's putative aesthetic opposite. Both enjoyed fame in the early 1920s, both were declared degenerate by the Nazis in the 1930s, and both ended up in Southern California, although they took entirely different paths. One—Schoenberg—found a home of sorts in the musical academy; the other—Korngold—found one at Warner Brothers.

And for that Korngold would pay a price. The composer who had filled Richard Strauss with awe and fear, the child prodigy championed by Artur Nikisch, the wunderkind who had achieved such early fame that his biography had already been written by the time he was twenty-five,[1] would receive only a perfunctory obituary, at age sixty, in the *New York Times*,[2] and he still remains unmentioned in most music-history surveys.[3] Part of the reason, no doubt, lay in the fact that in the 1920s Korngold was still composing lush orchestral music when the chamber symphony had become the new prototype: he retained a tonal vocabulary when atonality was the progressive force. But far worse was his migration into mass culture—from stage to screen—when Schoenberg's high-modernist dogma dictated that "if it is art, it is not for all, and if it is for all it is not art."[4] For these sins Korngold would be excluded from the modernist historical narrative, which in the 1960s and 1970s adhered to the Schoenbergian paradigm, a worldview that placed fundamental emphasis on "value" in a twentieth-century work, principally on the notion of technical progressivity, whereby musical style was viewed as an obligatory, linear, evolutionary process.[5]

It is perhaps more revealing to compare Korngold to Kurt Weill than to Schoenberg, for, despite their artistic differences, both Korngold and Weill were accused of "selling out" in their new American environments. For Weill the new venue was Broadway; for Korngold it was Hollywood, a place where the tension between high and low art was thrown into high relief by California modernism, where Schoenberg and others would survive even as they lamented the cultural wasteland that surrounded them.[6] Disgruntled émigrés spoke of feeling uprooted. The use of the time-honored, Germanic botanical metaphor of "rootlessness" for this negative state of being was, ironically, an image also used by National Socialists to criticize so-called eclectic, nonorganic Bolshevistic music composed by Jews.[7]

Ernst Krenek, whose *Jonny spielt auf* was deemed degenerate and rootless by Nazi commentators, himself described America as a vast "echoless" expanse. He spoke of European composers in the "shock of uprooting" who denied, as a defense mechanism, that this rootless state had encroached upon their art, their "innermost life substance." Such a state of denial, according to Krenek, made them neglect their "sense of responsibility"; instead they wanted to become more intelligible, more appealing, more useful and practical.[8] In short, these composers, trapped in a rootless, delusional state and pressured by the "public mentality of pragmatism," wanted to write more functional music. Boris Schwarz likewise commented on this émigré phenomenon of rootlessness; creative artists, especially musicians, he said, were apt to "dry up when . . . removed from their native land."[9] Schwarz's essay, "The Music World in Migration," leaves no doubt as to the identity of this musical world: it was Europe, and more specifically, Germany. The United States could be little more than an alien realm, providing a culturally barren soil that could not properly nourish these newly replanted diasporan roots.

The prevailing historical narrative has tended to focus on the inevitable losses and hypothetical missed opportunities of émigrés, rather than on the benefits and achievements of those who fled Nazi persecution, finding a safe haven in the United States. In Europe, where social strata were discrete and clearly marked, artists and intellectuals enjoyed greater respect than in the United States, where class boundaries were less distinct and intellectuals commanded neither comparable prestige nor significant social distance. In the New World the émigré was directly confronted by mass culture.[10] Those who forfeited a cultivated European way of life had to cope in a virtual vacuum, especially those who moved west to a landscape vastly different, both physically and culturally, from that which they had left behind. Although this generalized picture has a certain truth value, its reductive paradigm ignores émigrés for whom the United States indeed represented a realm of potential.

Neither Korngold nor Weill felt comfortable in the role of dislocated "cultural hero" among the unenlightened,[11] nor did they, in their removal from "the music world," believe themselves to be lost in an "irreconcilable breach" between mass culture and "responsible work," as did Adorno (who returned to Europe).[12] They, like many of their colleagues, declined to join the ranks of the American musical academy, feeling no strong compulsion to compose messages to be floated in Adorno's bottles for future generations. For them the United States was not an *Ausflugsort,* but rather a new *Heimat,* and, in contrast to many other émigrés, neither Weill nor Korngold wished to isolate himself from his newly adopted soil. Disillusioned with the European theater scene of the late 1920s, they saw real potential within the realm of American commercial musical culture.[13]

Korngold's situation was somewhat different from Weill's however, in that film composers have generally been marginalized in the academic discourse, both by musicologists (despite forays into music beyond the "canon") and by film theorists (who have traditionally been more visually and textually oriented).[14] Even "classical music" audiences seem ill informed on the subject, as is suggested by a recent compact disk anthology of Mahler selections that claims: "Most 'movie music' sounds like Mahler because many of the early Hollywood composers—Korngold, Steiner, Rózsa, Tiomkin—knew Mahler's music in Vienna before emigrating, and they merrily stole from it."[15] Such blatant inaccuracies (Tiomkin, for example, came to the United States from St. Petersburg via Berlin and Paris) betray an ignorance both of Austro-German music of the early twentieth century and of Hollywood film music itself (Korngold, Alexander von Zemlinsky, and Franz Schreker have all been described as having a "Hollywood sound" before such a phenomenon even existed). The liner notes to the aforementioned recording presume no stylistic differences between Dmitri Tiomkin's *Lost Horizon* and Miklós Rózsa's *Lost Weekend,* or Max Steiner's *King Kong* and Korngold's *King's Row.*

FROM VIENNA TO HOLLYWOOD

Korngold's musical migration involved both the transition from Austrian to American citizenship and the journey from stage to screen. It was an experience of initial ambivalence and vacillation, a phenomenon that cannot be fully appreciated outside the context of biographical events in the 1920s and 1930s.[16] With the composition of his two one-act operas *Der Ring des Polykrates* (1915) and *Violanta* (1915) the eighteen-year-old Korngold achieved significant international fame. No longer a mere child prodigy, he had become an opera composer of stature. The culmination was the twenty-three-year-old composer's immensely successful *Die tote Stadt,* first performed on 4 December 1920.

The young Korngold would never match that early stage success, nor would he complete another opera for seven years. During that time he focused on lieder and chamber music and even contributed a left-handed piano concerto to Paul Wittgenstein's repertoire. But this hiatus also saw the period of Weimar hyperinflation, a difficult time for Korngold to marry and try to raise a family. Worse yet, the Vienna Opera was no longer a friendly venue for Korngold the composer and frequent guest conductor—this thanks to his father Julius Korngold's vehement campaign in the press against codirectors Franz Schalk and Richard Strauss.[17] Young Korngold, who lived entirely off his own composing and conducting, therefore found it necessary to undertake operetta arrangements for the Theater an der Wien and other musical stages. The chore was not only lucrative but one that he performed with great delight. It also brought him into artistic contact with stage director Max Reinhardt, with whom he collaborated on an arrangement of *Die Fledermaus,* which later toured throughout Europe.[18]

The Reinhardt connection would be critical to Korngold's survival after Hitler assumed power in 1933, for despite the fact that Austria was not yet under the Nazi flag, all German opera houses were closed to his music; now even arrangements of Offenbach and Johann Strauss could not offer him significant material support.[19] On the strength of their earlier mutual work, Reinhardt, already in the States, asked that Korngold score the film version of his successful American production of *A Midsummer Night's Dream.*[20] This was 1934, ironically the same year in which the Nazis were calling for the liberation of Shakespeare's play from the Jew Felix Mendelssohn. Newly arrived in the United States, Korngold was asked about Hitler at nearly every stop along the way from New York to Hollywood. "Ich glaube, daß Mendelssohn Hitler überleben wird" soon became his stock reply.[21] For the film Korngold arranged Mendelssohn's incidental music as well as fragments from others of his works. He was also given unprecedented artistic reign, even to the point of being allowed to coach the actors in the reading of their lines, which were to be integrated with his score.

The *Midsummer Night's Dream* project, a film-play with music, brought immense prestige to Warner Brothers. In 1934 sound film was relatively young. The first major full-length film score (Steiner's *King Kong*) had been composed only a year earlier. Questions about the relationship between sound film, theater, and opera during this time recalled those posed over a decade earlier in Germany, when, in the wake of the November revolution of 1919, composers, critics, and directors worried whether film might render opera obsolete.[22] With the advent of "talkies" the debate resurfaced with new aesthetic concerns. In the United States Copland and Thomson, as well as Toch, Weill, Milhaud, and Eisler, believed there might be genuine potential to this burgeoning art. Even the skeptical Julius Korngold in 1940 wrote a letter to Jack and Harry Warner outlining his plan for film-opera. Predicting a Europe reduced to rubble, he said that the task of rescuing culture would fall "to the United States [which] will have to save art [and] music . . . for an impoverished, hungry Europe which will be bereft of its art centers and of its opera houses."23

Many who held great hope for film-opera would, in one way or another, be disappointed. Reinhardt's noble Shakespearean project represented more the exception than the rule. The closest thing to film-opera that Hollywood produced was film-operetta, a genre that had a relatively short life span during the 1930s.24 After *A Midsummer Night's Dream* Korngold, in fact, was asked by Paramount to collaborate with Oscar Hammerstein on the film-operetta *Give Us This Night,* featuring Gladys Swarthout and Jan Kiepura. Korngold's verdict summed the situation up beautifully: "This thing gets worse from week to week—by the time they film it, it will be useless."25

During these years Korngold was working on his final opera, *Die Kathrin,* and he and his family divided their time between Hollywood and Vienna. Korngold still naively hoped for a continued career in Vienna, where he planned on premiering *Die Kathrin* early in 1938, and therefore would not emigrate, although he probably knew deep down that ultimately emigration would be his only path. Thus, while Austria remained his home from the mid-1930s through the Anschluß, he spent his winters in Hollywood, which offered both income and a climate that was ideal for the health of his younger son, Georg, who suffered from tuberculosis.

After it became clear that *Die Kathrin* would be postponed until the spring of 1938, Korngold accepted Warner's request that he score the film *The Adventures of Robin Hood.* He left for California with his wife and Georg in January, while the older son, Ernst, remained with his grandparents in Vienna. What follows is fairly well known: after seeing *Robin Hood* Korngold declined the offer to score it; the film contained too much action for his style of music. He was preparing to return to Vienna when he got news of Hitler's meeting with Austrian chancellor Kurt von Schuschnigg in Berchtesgaden. This event changed his mind about composing *Robin Hood,* although he refused a formal contract. One day after the Anschluß Korngold's parents, who wisely had gotten visas months in advance, escaped through France with Ernst; Korngold's in-laws fled through Switzerland. It was a time of personal despair and professional disappointment for the composer, whose *Kathrin* was canceled in Vienna (it finally received a lukewarm premiere in Stockholm a year later). From that moment on Korngold also had to support members of his immediate and extended family, his in-laws, and close friends—some five households in all, according to his son Ernst. Letters at the Library of Congress also suggest his activity in sponsoring refugees living in England, France, Sweden, and Switzerland for American visas through affidavits.

According to his family, after the Anschluß Korngold vowed not to compose what he called "his own music" until Hitler was dead or overthrown. But then, what alternatives did he have in America? His former venues, the Austrian and German opera stages, were closed to him, and the Metropolitan Opera was not interested in German operatic premieres during the war years (it had already rejected *Die Kathrin*). To earn income, therefore, he operated on a year-by-year contract with Warner Brothers, an agreement unprecedented in Hollywood. The music was to be his and not the property of the studio, and his scores would remain untampered with. He could, moreover, score as few films as he desired. Thus, while Max Steiner, despite his own hard-earned prestige, averaged over a dozen films a year during the 1930s and 1940s, Korngold averaged but one or two annually. Korngold enjoyed composing music for films, relishing the challenge of coordinating music with image, word, and gesture. He also took great delight in the fact that, through film, his music could engage a far wider audience than ever before.

With the fall of Hitler and the death of his father, both in the same year, Korngold retired from film scoring and began composing, among other things, his Third String Quartet (1945), Violin Concerto (1946), Symphony in F-sharp Major (1952), and several lieder (1947). His son Ernst has suggested that he may have felt that he owed something to his father, who was never entirely happy with his son's Hollywood career.[26] By then, however, Korngold was outdated in a progressive postwar world of concert music. The paradigm had shifted long before. He was thus doubly an exile, with no strong base of support in the concert world after 1945. This was as true in the United States as it was in Europe, where in 1950 he experienced a disastrous concert tour. Korngold, in short, left Austria a "degenerate" and returned an anachronism.[27]

FROM OPERA TO FILM

What, indeed, was degenerate about Korngold's music according to Nazi cultural views as defined, for example, by the 1938 exhibit "Entartete Musik"? Korngold's lack of enthusiasm for jazz and atonality hardly challenged the Nazis' reactionary stance. His only error lay in being Jewish, a fact that lends support to Richard Taruskin's assertion that the Nazi concept of degeneracy was "incoherent and opportunistic" and that from their list of banned works no lessons are to be learned.[28] True, the National Socialists were not concerned with aesthetics as such; rather, their goal was an opportunistic spinning of historical threads into an ideological web that could as easily ensnare Schoenberg as Korngold, or Offenbach as Krenek. When one makes political ideology the central ingredient of a cultural discourse, glaring hypocrisies are unavoidable. One important thread in the Nazi criticism of Korngold was derived straight from the anti-Mendelssohn campaign launched nearly a century earlier by Wagner, Wilhelm Heinrich Riehl, and Hans von Wolzogen, and it bears important lessons.

Leon Botstein has observed that what made Mendelssohn, an assimilated Jew and the father of the Bach revival, so reprehensible to these critics was that he passed as a good German in his music—music that, as mere entertainment, "sullied art and rendered it socially and morally irrelevant."[29] From the Nazi standpoint, Korngold's post-Wagnerian music likewise did not conjure up real emotion; lacking any real cultural roots, he could only imitate and thus exploit that culture. Hitler himself argued that, for the Jew, the soil could be nothing more than an object for Jewish exploitation.[30] Returning again to the old botanical metaphor, we see that for a musical work to be "authentic," it not only had to be a unified organism but it should be rooted with its tradition in its own culture. This notion was part of a broader view that linked the German soul with its natural landscape, with its indigenous soil.[31] Paradoxically, though not incoherently, this view emanated at once from the right and the left, for both sides firmly believed musical style to be a critical moral issue.[32]

One Nazi commentator took Wagner's strategy, as expressed in *Das Judentum in der Musik* (1850),[33] a step further when he asserted that Jewish musicians made ideal film composers. In "Der Jude als Musik-Fabrikant" Julius Friedrich recognized a Jewish music boom in conjunction with the silent film industry. The Jew as *Musikdekorateur*, he said, manufactured "musical wallpaper on the assembly line for every cinematic possibility." Friedrich saw capital-driven Jewish composers raiding and debasing the symphonic and operatic literature for music capable of mere illustration, where with stopwatch precision they could create "one and a half minutes of rebellion" or "three minutes of gossip." More important, he noted, with the advent of talking pictures "the Jew is once again at hand with fresh speculation"; only time and "cleansing" could restore the current German film industry to health.[34]

If we probe beneath the anti-Semitic surface of Friedrich's essay we find a certain accord among members of the German right and left. One cannot help detecting Frankfurt School thinking in the Nazi criticism of authentic musical gestures being debased, stripped of any real content, separated from the musically genuine, and ultimately commodified. These are essentially Adorno's own words, though he used them against Rachmaninoff, who, he said, "emptied [the musical gesture] of all content, freed it of every genuine musical event and threw it on to the market as a commodity."[35] Indeed, Adorno would later describe Broadway composers such as Weill not as *Komponisten* but as *Musikregisseure,* a term recalling Friedrich's label *Musikdekorateur* for Jewish composers engaging in popular or commercial ventures.[36] These words bring to mind the clever, well-known gibe: "Korngold has always composed for Warner Brothers, only he was at first unaware of the fact." This remark traveled far and wide, originating with Ernst Toch in a conversation with Otto Klemperer, who savored the remark and retold it many times.[37] But Korngold was not the first to be accused of writing movie music. Adorno had already declared that Tchaikovsky's symphonies "satisfied the demands of the cinema before the cinema was invented. . . . [They were] part of the culture industry before the real consumers of [that] industry had come into existence."[38]

Curiously, Adorno rarely singled out Korngold, who would seem a logical companion to Richard Strauss and Wagner, the latter of whom Adorno explicitly charged with creating an illusion of form by sheer repetition of the reified leitmotiv, as if Wagner were unconcerned with vertical structures.[39] Generally speaking, in fact, there is little in his collaborative work with Eisler on the Hollywood film industry, *Composing for the Films,* that is not also in the two essays he wrote about Strauss or in *Versuch über Wagner,* where he lays out this criticism.[40] And indeed, despite Adorno's naiveté about form in Wagner or Strauss, he is quite right with respect to film, for film music does tend to lack structural autonomy. In a film score musical details adhere not to an overarching structure but to images on celluloid; unable to generate its own musical meaning, the score thus subordinates itself to the textual system. Eisler further criticized the suturing effect of film music, which masks the fragmentary nature of the music and its technical apparatus. Eisler's dream score would deconstruct the very film it is supposed to accompany by exposing rather than concealing its contradictions. Although he had had success in Germany with such film scores as *Kuhle Wampe,* it was difficult for him to apply these principles as a film composer in Hollywood.[41]

Ernst Toch's comment on Korngold's "lifelong" career as a composer for Warner Brothers was compellingly inverted by Taruskin, who suggested that it is not so much that Korngold was the perennial film composer even while in Vienna but rather that he remained the opera composer even while in Hollywood.[42] It is an appealing hypothesis and, in certain ways, plausible. When asked about his musical activity in America, Korngold would inevitably reply, "I've been composing operas," and his characterization of film as "opera without singing" has been quoted time and again. Although he used the word "opera" in a nostalgic, metaphorical sense, Korngold—if in a superficial, limited way—was right, for he surely scored films like no other Hollywood composer. He refused to use a stopwatch and never employed the click-track method as he conducted in the Hollywood recording studio.

Indeed, his early sketches reveal certain intriguing compositional similarities between opera and film.

At work, Korngold's first step was to get in the proper frame of mind by sitting at the piano improvising themes while he watched the film. His compositional approach in fact recalls a statement made by his teacher Zemlinsky with respect to composing opera: he said that in order to set a scene to music one must be clear, early on, about which basic motives should rule that scene. The composer should probe beneath the surface of the dialogue and discover the primary motivations and mood that the librettist (one could also say screenwriter) envisioned for the scene. Equating mood with basic leitmotiv, Zemlinsky continued: "Undisturbed by the back and forth of the dialogue, the mood can then govern the entire scene with only minor modifications. . . . At this level this means a purely musical translation of the text [without thought of singing]."[43]

Intriguing though this argument is, any equation between opera and film has inherent complications. In cinema the action exists in the film footage, and although the music may accompany that action, it does not generate it. The cinematic narrative is created by a series of edited fragments; it offers shifting perspectives and angles, often in rapid juxtapositions. In classic Hollywood cinema, music is used to connect those fragments—leading to that very suturing effect criticized by Eisler. Opera, in contrast, is live and nondiegetically continuous. Unlike in cinema, moreover, where the composer is usually brought in at the end of the process, the opera composer is an active participant from its inception. With the help of the librettist (and sometimes without), the composer can shape musical moments and create autonomous forms in his score. Indeed, it was the film composer's very lack of artistic and structural autonomy that so annoyed Eisler and Adorno.[44]

The sweeping critique of Hollywood music by Eisler and Adorno ignores form on a more localized level, however, and, more important, it lumps most film composers into a monolithic group, as did the liner notes quoted earlier. Indeed, during his time at Warner Brothers, Korngold created scores unlike those of most of his contemporaries, both in overall quality, style, and sound and in terms of his unorthodox compositional techniques—which, as we have seen, were informed by his experience as an opera composer and conductor.[45] Korngold's scores brought the musical component of film closer to the cinematic surface. Audiences now focused their attention on an element of film that in the past had been largely ignored. The film composer had achieved celebrity status: Korngold's name was usually as large as the director's in the opening credits, a first in Hollywood history.

More than any predecessor or contemporary in his field, Korngold saturated the cinematic space with his music, which contained both an unprecedented multiplicity of themes for a Hollywood score and enough musical space to accommodate motivic development. Indeed, whereas the typical

Hollywood score might be heard for a third or, at best, half of the total film, Korngold's scores easily accounted for half to, more usually, three-quarters of the footage. His predilection for long musical passages, moreover, could be quite effective for long stretches of wordless action, such as nautical battles in *The Sea Hawk* or sword fights in *Robin Hood*.

Korngold, though, was equally keen on providing lengthy musical sections to accompany dialogue; in this technique, called "underscoring," music is subdued just beneath the decibel level of the dialogue, with inaudibility serving as the guiding principle. Classic Hollywood underscoring of the 1930s and 1940s—of which Max Steiner was the most venerable practitioner—usually involved one or two short, open-ended sequential progressions played by muted strings, generally violins.[46] Korngold's score to *King's Row* (Sam Wood, 1942), however, demonstrates a significant departure from the Hollywood norm. In Parris and Cassy's seduction scene, which, framed by a thunderstorm, is just under four minutes in duration, Korngold, employing and juxtaposing not one but several different themes or thematic fragments ("Parris/King's Row," "Sexual Attraction," "Cassy/Psychosis," "Conversation," "Growing Passion," "Love Theme," etc.), breaks with the tradition of inaudibility and treats the scene more like one in an opera (see table 2 and examples 1a–e).

Korngold makes good use of this material, and by opposing static, harmonically unstable moments (representing Cassy's mental instability) with lyrical, stable stretches (representing the pair's physical attraction), he creates convincing sexual tension in which moments of expectation or fulfillment are constantly thwarted. Oppositions of motion and stasis at first move at a leisurely pace, but as that pace quickens and the juxtapositions become more jarring, Korngold invokes an effective *Steigerung*, which culminates in a new climactic theme (actually a reworking of the opening four-note "Cassy/Psychosis" idea, example 1c) as the couple finally embrace (see example 1e, "Love Theme"). Korngold savors these sharply contrasting timbres and thematic gestures, which in turn coordinate with sudden clashes of mood, the entire effect being accentuated by the flashes of lightning from the thunderstorm outside. Despite the trite dialogue (indeed, pantomime would be equally, if not more, effective), this scene works splendidly thanks to the camera work of James Wong Howe and the music of Korngold.

At face value the statements by Toch and Taruskin appear to be contradictory, for they posit two different Korngolds: the covert film composer on the one hand and the covert opera composer on the other. Moreover, the contradiction is hardly clarified by the impression that, consciously or subconsciously, Korngold himself seems to have wanted it both ways. There is,

TABLE 2   Seduction Scene from *Kings Row*

Time elapsed	Action	Music
0:00	Parris approaches Dr. Tower's house during storm.	"Storm," "Kings Row" (minor mode)
0:18	Looks through window, seeing only Cassy's legs.	"Attraction"
0:24	Taps on window, Cassy looks up.	"Psychosis/Cassy" (a & b)
0:33	Cassy gets up to greet Parris at door.	"Psychosis/Cassy" (a)
0:40	He enters, explaining that he left his medical notebooks.	"Kings Row" (minor mode)
1:10	After retrieving them, Cassy asks: "Would you like to sit down?"	"Psychosis/Cassy" (a & b)
1:20	Parris sits opposite her, then gets up to leave after learning that her father is not at home.	"Psychosis/Cassy" (a & b)
1:36	Cassy asks him to stay and sit next to her.	"Psychosis/Cassy" (a & b)
1:51	Cassy laments that she can't see anyone. Parris asks why; she becomes defensive.	"Psychosis/Cassy" (a & b)
2:23	Cassy: "Let's just talk." Conversation ranges from matters past and present to Parris asking Cassy why her father took her out of school.	"Psychosis" (variant), "Conversation"
3:46	Cassy: "You were always the nicest."	"Attraction," "Psychosis/Cassy" (a & b)
3:56	He kisses her hand; they stand, embrace, and kiss.	"Escalating Passion," "Love Theme"
4:06	Cassy breaks off the embrace, turns out the lights. They embrace and kiss again, illuminated by flashes of lightning.	"Psychosis/Cassy" (a), "Escalating Passion," "Love Theme"

of course, the nostalgic composer who in his imagination seemed, with his boast that Hollywood was his opera house, to be still composing for the Wiener Staatsoper.[47] But there is also the Korngold who stated that he felt compelled to compose what he termed "his own music" after World War II, as if the film music had been written by someone other than himself.[48]

Ultimately these apparently contradictory views of Korngold are in fact

Example 1: Themes for *Kings Row* seduction scene
Example 1a: "Storm"

Example 1b: "Parris/ Kings Row" (minor version)

Example 1c: "Sexual Attraction" and "Psychosis/Cassy"

two sides of the same modernist coin; neither one, that is, fully defines this composer whose musical career spanned two opposing spheres—the elevated realm of the Vienna State Opera and the popular world of Warner Brothers. Instead they offer an "either/or" picture of Korngold, as a composer of either high or low culture (not unlike the "two" Kurt Weills), kept separate as contradictions coexisting in what Ernst Bloch called the "unbearable Now."[49] As the musicological discourse has changed over recent years, however, that boundary of separation has eroded, and such binary oppositions as progressive/regressive, high art/ low art have been called into

Example 1d: "Psychosis" (variant), "Conversation"

"Psychosis" (variant)

"Conversation"

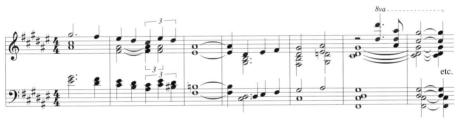

Example 1e: "Escalating Passion"

"Love Theme"

question, allowing us to view composers such as Weill or Korngold through a wider lens.

Although the notion "postmodern" had not yet been coined, Korngold surely savored the application of techniques he had learned as an opera composer and conductor to the world of cinematic scoring, despite the stigma attached to the label "Hollywood film composer" in the 1930s and 1940s, a stigma that he surely felt. Admittedly, he may have sacrificed creative autonomy in a medium where, unlike in opera, music is subordinated to a larger textual system, but Korngold was fascinated by the challenges of this relatively new medium and approached each project with enthusiasm.[50] Although he composed no more than twenty scores (a modest number compared to the more than two hundred of Steiner), his influence in Hollywood was enormous during a time when the genre of synchronized film music was in its infancy. As Hugo Friedhofer, a leading film composer of the next generation, once observed, "We were all influenced by him."[51]

But Korngold's influence would take on greater significance with the rebirth of the full-orchestral romantic film score in the 1970s. The greatest benefactor was no doubt John Williams, whose *Star Wars* fanfare owes so much to the opening of *King's Row*. It is therefore hardly coincidental that, along with *Star Wars, Close Encounters of the Third Kind,* and the like, the 1970s saw the release of several Korngold film-score recordings. Twenty years later, the number of Korngold recordings has increased dramatically. And it is revealing that these newer recordings are not primarily film scores, as was the case during the "either/or" 1970s, but rather feature his chamber music, orchestral music, lieder, and the ambitious 1927 opera *Das Wunder der Heliane.* Although ignored by musicologists for years and only narrowly understood by film specialists, Korngold may be emerging at long last from his most recent exile.

NOTES

I gratefully acknowledge Thomas Hansen, Stephen Hinton, Kim Kowalke, Neil Lerner, and Pamela Potter for their assistance and advice.

1. Rudolf Hoffmann, *Erich Wolfgang Korngold* (Vienna: Carl Stephenson, 1922).

2. "Erich Korngold, Composer, Dead," *New York Times,* 30 Nov. 1957.

3. As a tonal Hollywood composer and a supposed "sellout," Korngold's very character becomes suspect. A paper read at the May 1994 Harvard conference on the German musical emigration, for example, Horst Weber, "Emigrant Musicians in California," questioned the extent of his activity on behalf of other Jews, particularly with regard to affidavits for visas. The charge, which may or may not have been meant to reflect on his moral character as a composer, is at best gratuitous, at worst historically inaccurate, being refuted by documents in the Korngold Collection, Library of Congress, Washington, D.C. (hereafter cited as Korngold Collection). These docu-

ments also show Korngold's activity (organizational and financial) in various cultural-political organizations: the United Jewish Welfare Fund, Mailamm (American-Palestine Music Association), the Free Austria Movement, the Associated Refugee Artists Guild of America, the American Guild for German Cultural Freedom, among others. I am grateful to James Pruett, director of the Music Division of the Library of Congress, for allowing me to examine the yet uncataloged Korngold Collection, of which a significant portion has been lost.

4. Arnold Schoenberg, "New Music, Old Music: Style and Idea," in *Style and Idea: Selected Writings of Arnold Schoenberg*, ed. Leonard Stein (Berkeley: University of California Press, 1984), 124. Although the original text was written in German (*Neue und veraltete Musik, oder Stil und Gedanke*) in 1933, this text was given in English probably within that year and was further revised for a lecture at the University of Chicago in May 1946. Schoenberg's notion is in consonance with Adorno's criticism of writers and intellectuals whose "irresponsible formulations" are readily understood by a mass audience. These "advocates of communicability," who seek to engage a wider audience, are ultimately "traitors to what they communicate." See Adorno, "Morality and Style," in *Minima Moralia: Reflections from Damaged Life*, trans. E. F. N. Jephcott (London: New Left Books, 1974), 101. Although Adorno refers to the written word, the analogy with music is clear. Indeed, Martin Jay has referred to Adorno's deliberately complicated prose as "atonal," as a style of writing "like the music of Arnold Schoenberg . . . designed to thwart an effortless reception by passive readers." See Jay, *Adorno* (Cambridge, Mass.: Harvard University Press, 1984), 11.

5. In an unpublished letter (16 Dec. 1961) to Leonard Bernstein, Glenn Gould once described this master narrative for twentieth-century music as the "time-style equation" (National Library of Canada, Glenn Gould Collection).

6. "Here I die of disgust," confided Schoenberg in a letter to Oskar Kokoschka, then in New York. See Jarrell C. Jackman, "German Émigrés in Southern California," in *The Muses Flee Hitler: Cultural Transfer and Adaptation*, ed. Jarrell C. Jackman and Carla M. Borden (Washington, D.C.: Smithsonian Institution Press, 1983), 97.

7. Although the biological concept of "organicism" pervades Western thought back to the ancient Greeks, Ruth Solie reminds us that "organic unity" became a central theoretical criterion for German philosophers during the late eighteenth century, "an era in which biology was gradually replacing mechanics as the central intellectual paradigm" (Solie, "The Living Work: Organicism and Musical Analysis," *Nineteenth-Century Music* [fall 1980]: 148). This Teutonic preoccupation with organic unity, with an "ideal substance" explainable only by its parts, permeates German thought from the writings of Goethe to the philosophy of Hegel, from Guido Adler's theories of *Musikwissenschaft* to the analytical thought of Heinrich Schenker, who forges an implicit link between background, middleground, and foreground with that of nation, clan, and individual. See his *Free Composition* (*Der freie Satz*, 1935), trans. Ernst Oster (New York: Longman, 1979), 3. Schenker, moreover, takes the biological model to a metaphysical level: "The whole of foreground, which men call chaos, God derives from His cosmos, the background. The eternal harmony of His eternal Being is grounded in this relationship" (xxiii). The fixation on organic unity in German aesthetic discourse acquires even greater meaning when one considers how relatively late Germany came together as a unified nation.

8. Ernst Krenek, "America's Influence on its Émigré Composers," *Perspectives* 8

(spring–summer 1970): 117, 112. David Drew recognized such behavior in the Americanized Kurt Weill, arguing that Broadway box office pressures "exacted from [Weill] a degree of self-sacrifice greater than any that would have been demanded by a totalitarian minister of culture" (Drew, "Weill, Kurt," in *The New Grove Dictionary of Music and Musicians,* ed. Stanley Sadie [London: Macmillan, 1980], 20:307).

9. Boris Schwarz, "The Music World in Migration," in *The Muses Flee Hitler: Cultural Transfer and Adaptation, 1930–1945* (Washington, D.C.: Smithsonian Institution Press, 1983), 137. Schwarz, himself an émigré, was a violinist and a scholar whose musicological training at the University of Berlin was interrupted with the rise of Nazism.

10. H. Stuart Hughes suggests that European intellectuals, "shielded by the ramparts of traditional status and respect . . . had been able to keep at a safe distance the grosser and more offensive manifestations of mass taste. With the move to America, these walls collapsed: a flood of vulgarity struck the new arrivals in the face" (Hughes, *Between Commitment and Disillusionment: The Obstructed Path and the Sea Change* [Middletown, Conn.: Wesleyan University Press, 1987], 138).

11. Not without sarcasm, Kurt Weill described such discomfort at a party at Alma Mahler Werfel's home one Sunday afternoon in a letter to Lotte Lenya (30 Aug. 1944): "It was the most luxurious gathering I've ever seen, all poor refugees, drinking French champagne (in the afternoon) and eating the best cold buffet imaginable, with caviar of course. The language was entirely a mixture of Viennese and Hungarian which I liked so much. Well, I talked to Bemmelman for half an hour and left, leaving behind me a storm of indignation which I still could hear 10 blocks away" (quoted in Kim Kowalke, "Formerly German: Kurt Weill in America," in *A Stranger Here Myself: Kurt Weill Studien,* ed. Kim Kowalke and Horst Edler [Hildesheim: Georg Olms, 1993], 45–46).

12. Adorno, "Protection, Help, and Counsel," in *Minima Moralia,* 33.

13. John Rockwell points out that Weill's ultimate disappointment with the Weimar government's administrative role in German music-theatrical life "helped to convince him that his best hope for operatic reform lay in just the commercial theater . . . eventually on Broadway" (Rockwell, "Weill's Operatic Reform and Its Context," in *A New Orpheus: Essays on Kurt Weill,* ed. Kim Kowalke [New Haven: Yale University Press, 1986], 55–56). One sees strong parallels with Korngold, who had a successful career not only in Hollywood but on Broadway as well. Notably, recent scholarship has challenged the notion of the "Two Weills"; two essays, both by Kim Kowalke, are exemplary in this regard: "Formerly German: Kurt Weill in America"; and "Kurt Weill, Modernism, and Popular Culture: *Öffentlichkeit als Stil,*" *Modernism/Modernity* 2 (1995): 27–69. The case for Korngold, however, has not yet been made.

14. In the four years since this essay was written, however, studies in film music have increased significantly.

15. Angel Records "Key to Classics" series, *Mahler* (EMI 65142).

16. Since Hoffmann's 1922 biography no major study of Korngold's life appeared until Brendan G. Carroll's *The Last Prodigy: A Biography of Erich Wolfgang Korngold* (Portland, Ore.: Amadeus, 1997), which appeared while this essay was in press.

17. Julius Korngold (1860–1945) succeeded Eduard Hanslick as head music critic for Vienna's *Neue freie Presse.* The elder Korngold had been highly critical of

Strauss's music well before the composer's arrival in Vienna as codirector of the Vienna State Opera. Strauss ultimately succumbed to vehement criticism in the press, resigning his post in 1924, though he continued as a regular guest conductor in Vienna throughout the 1920s.

18. In 1942 the arrangement would enjoy a successful revival at the New York City Opera, again with Reinhardt, under the title *Rosalinda*. Reinhardt died within a year, and Korngold, whose friendship with Reinhardt had become increasingly strong during the 1930s and early 1940s, was given power of attorney by Reinhardt's widow over her husband's estate. See Korngold Collection.

19. Although Jacques Offenbach was a highly profiled target of Nazi anti-Semitism, Johann Strauss, the popular "waltz king," presented a more difficult problem, and his Jewish ancestry was erased from official records. Indeed, Strauss's *Kaiser-Walzer* was performed on the second day of the 1938 Reichsmusiktage in Düsseldorf.

20. Reinhardt directed *A Midsummer Night's Dream* for the Hollywood Bowl in 1933. In the wake of its great success, Warner Brothers asked Reinhardt whether he would consider undertaking a film version of his production. Reinhardt readily agreed.

21. Luzi Korngold, *Erich Wolfgang Korngold* (Vienna: Elisabeth Lafite, 1967), 64.

22. See Bryan Gilliam, "Stage and Screen: Kurt Weill and Operatic Reform in the 1920s," in *Music and Performance in the Weimar Republic* (Cambridge: Cambridge University Press, 1994), 1–12, 154–59.

23. Korngold to Jack and Harry Warner, 1940, Korngold Collection.

24. Film versions of operettas were popular as early as the silent film era, often with an orchestra playing from an adapted score. One of the most notable was Erich von Stroheim's *The Merry Widow* of 1925. By the mid-1930s operetta was revived in sound film with such productions as MGM's *Naughty Marietta* by Victor Herbert, which served as vehicles for the popular team of Jeanette MacDonald and Nelson Eddy. The Paramount operetta project was in turn partly a response to a string of successes by MGM.

25. Tony Thomas, *Music for the Movies* (Cranbury, N.J.: A. S. Barnes, 1973), 131.

26. Personal conversation with Ernst Korngold, May 1994.

27. Korngold and his family considered their home to be the United States; thus, while on tour in Vienna, Korngold sold all real estate that had been confiscated by the Nazis.

28. Richard Taruskin, "The Golden Age of Kitsch," *New Republic*, 21 Mar. 1994, 28.

29. Leon Botstein, "The Aesthetics of Assimilation and Affirmation: Reconstructing the Career of Felix Mendelssohn," in *Mendelssohn and His World* (Princeton, N.J.: Princeton University Press, 1991), 20.

30. George L. Mosse, *The Crisis of German Ideology* (New York: Grosset & Dunlap, 1964), 295.

31. By extension, Jews were the shallow, arid, nomadic people of the desert. Mosse (ibid., 4–5) summarizes this dichotomy between Jewishness and Germanness: "Because of the barrenness of the desert landscape, the Jews are [viewed as] a spiritually barren people. They thus contrast markedly with the Germans, who, living in the dark, mist-shrouded forests, are deep, mysterious, profound."

32. See above, note 4. According to National Socialist ideology, morality and

style were closely linked. Degenerate, atonal music allegedly threatened to undermine the health of the German nation; by the same token, "healthy" tonal language could not be entrusted to Jewish composers, who would only exploit it. In progressive musical circles, in contrast, the composition of music in an affirmative tonal idiom was perceived as a sort of "aesthetic immorality" (see above, note 3), and until recent years, composers who favored the aesthetically moral "high ground" were forgiven various political sins, or—as with Webern and Stravinsky, among others—their political views were misrepresented.

33. Richard Wagner, *Gesammelte Schriften und Dichtungen* (Leipzig: E. W. Fritzsch, 1873), vol. 3.

34. Julius Friedrich, "Der Jude als Musik-Fabrikant," *Die Musik* 28 (Mar. 1936): 428–30.

35. Theodor W. Adorno, "Commodity Music Analysed," in *Quasi una Fantasia: Essays on Modern Music,* trans. Rodney Livingstone (London: Verso Books, 1992), 39. In this essay Adorno criticizes Rachmaninoff for using an outmoded, reified post-Romantic gesture in a modern age.

36. See Adorno's "Vortupp und Avantgarde: Replik an Horst Koegler," in Adorno, *Gesammelte Schriften,* ed. Rolf Tiedemann (Frankfurt am Main: Suhrkamp, 1984), 18:800–804.

37. Peter Heyworth, *Otto Klemperer: His Life and Times, 1885–1933* (Cambridge: Cambridge University Press, 1983), 153. Toch composed two film scores for Warner's rival, Paramount Pictures (*Peter Ibbetson* in 1935 and *Ghost Breakers* in 1941). Korngold, moreover, bore Toch no grudge for the remark; in fact, he found some work for him at Warner, whereToch orchestrated several scenes for *Devotion* (1943).

38. Adorno, "Commodity Music Analysed," 42.

39. In the essay "Gesture" in *In Search of Wagner,* trans. Rodney Livingstone (London: New Left Books, 1981), Adorno calls Wagnerian form an illusion, "a cloud of hot air" (38) where thematic "repetition poses as development, transposition as thematic work" (41).

40. For the essays, see "Strauss at Sixty" (1924), trans. Susan Gillespie, in *Richard Strauss and His World,* ed. Bryan Gilliam (Princeton, N.J.: Princeton University Press, 1992), 406–15; and "Richard Strauss, Born June 11, 1864," trans. Samuel and Shierry Weber, *Perspectives of New Music* 4 (1965): 14–32, 113–29. The original English version of the film-music collaborative work is [Theodor Adorno and] Hanns Eisler, *Composing for the Films* (London: Oxford University Press, 1947). The complicated genesis of this book has been discussed at some length by various scholars over the past couple of decades; see, for example, Martin Marks, "Film Music: The Material, Literature, and Present State of Research," *Notes* 36, no. 2 (Dec. 1979): 321; Eberhardt Klemm, preface to *Komposition für den Film,* vol. 4 of *Hanns Eisler: Gesammelte Werke,* ser. 3 (Leipzig: VEB Deutscher Verlag für Musik, 1977), 5–24; Claudia Gorbman, "Hanns Eisler in Hollywood," *Screen* 32 (Aug. 1991), 272–85; and James Buhler's and David Neumeyer's review of Caryl Flinn's *Strains of Utopia* and Kathryn Kalinak's *Settling the Score, JAMS* 47 (summer 1994): 369–70n.27. The most recent discussion by Graham McCann seems the most straightforward and convincing; see his introduction to Adorno and Eisler, *Composing for the Films* (London: Athlone Press, 1994). Although the work was coauthored by Eisler and Adorno in 1944, the latter

allegedly asked that his name be removed from the 1947 English-language edition for political reasons. When Eisler published a revised edition (Berlin: Bruno Henschel, 1949) in German, Adorno's name was still omitted; it was not reinstated until the original version was translated and reprinted in 1969 by Rogner & Bernhard. A curious mixture of practical Brechtian aesthetics and abstract Frankfurtian critical theory, the precise breakdown of the Eisler-Adorno collaboration has not been fully determined.

41. Gorbman points out that, for his book, Eisler drew examples mostly from non-Hollywood films ("Eisler in Hollywood," 281). Moreover, she observes that in such films as RKO's *The Spanish Main*, Eisler applied his characteristic sound "to serve the most orthodox purposes"—an observation that Eisler would probably not have denied: "[The score to the *Spanish Main*] is pure nonsense, garbage—I had to do it for the money" (ibid., 282).

42. "He [Korngold] was writing opera all along" (Taruskin, "Golden Age of Kitsch," 32).

43. Horst Weber, *Alexander von Zemlinsky* (Vienna: Elisabeth Lafite, 1967), 49.

44. In his recent article "Melodrama as a Compositional Resource in Early Hollywood Sound Cinema," *Current Musicology* 57 (1995), David Neumeyer also describes Korngold's film scores as being "operatic" (93) without explaining what he means by the term. Instead he refers the reader to Robbert van der Lek's monograph *Diegetic Music in Opera and Film* (Amsterdam: Rudopi, 1991). But van der Lek himself points to the problems in comparing these two genres, admitting that in no film by Korngold is the action generated by the singing; "it can be concluded that the degree of optimal similarity between Korngold's films and operas is zero" (13). In this sense, the term "operatic" to describe Korngold's film scores is no more useful than the word "symphonic," used by some contemporary critics to describe Korngold's operas, which relied heavily on a colorful, expressive orchestra.

45. The complete list of films scored by Korngold is as follows: *A Midsummer Night's Dream*, arr. Mendelssohn, 1934; *Captain Blood*, 1935; *Another Dawn*, 1936; *Anthony Adverse*, 1936; *Give Us This Night*, 1936; *The Green Pastures*, 1936; *Rose of the Ranch*, 1936; *The Prince and the Pauper*, 1937; *The Adventures of Robin Hood*, 1938; *Juarez*, 1939; *The Private Lives of Elizabeth and Essex*, 1939; *The Sea Hawk*, 1940; *Kings Row*, 1941; *The Sea Wolf*, 1941; *The Constant Nymph*, 1942; *Devotion*, 1943; *Between Two Worlds*, 1944; *Of Human Bondage*, 1945; *Deception*, 1946; *Escape Me Never*, 1946; and *Magic Fire* (after Wagner), 1954.

46. Gorbman discusses the principle of "inaudibility" in her chapter titled "Classic Hollywood Practice: The Model of Max Steiner," in *Unheard Melodies: Narrative Film Music* (Bloomington: Indiana University Press, 1987), 76–79.

47. Unpublished script for CBS radio program on Korngold, 11 Nov. 1942: "[Korngold] considers all Hollywood his opera house. To anyone who inquires what he's done during his ten [*sic*] years in America, he says, 'I've written 18 operas' " (Korngold Collection).

48. This situation is further complicated by the fact that some of "his own" postwar instrumental works, such as the Symphony in F-sharp, draw on material from his film scores.

49. See Ernst Bloch, "Nonsynchronism and the Obligation to Its Dialectics"

(1932), trans. Mark Ritter, *New German Critique* 11 (spring 1977): 22–38. He offers such modern-age "nonsynchronisms" as primitive farms and high-tech factories, remote villages and bustling urban centers. Certainly, in modern music, one of the greatest nonsynchronisms would have been that of tonality and atonality, where, in the "unbearable Now" of, say, 1912, two works fragmenting the tradition of *commedia dell'arte*—Schoenberg's *Pierrot lunaire* and Strauss's *Ariadne auf Naxos*—could coexist, the former as a part of history, the latter as an ahistorical anomaly.

50. Korngold once remarked: "[When] I am watching the picture unroll, when I am sitting at the piano improvising or inventing themes and tunes, when I am facing the orchestra conducting my music, I have the feeling that I am giving my own and my best" (quoted in Fred Karlin, *Listening to Movies* [New York: Schirmer Books, 1994], 284).

51. Thomas, *Music for the Movies*, 125. Friedhofer began his Hollywood career as an orchestrator for Max Steiner and Korngold, among others. He went on to compose film scores of his own, including *The Best Years of Our Lives* (1946), which won him an Oscar.

Strangers in Strangers' Land
Werfel, Weill, and *The Eternal Road*

Alexander L. Ringer

"Ein Fremder ward ich im fremden Land" (A stranger am I in a strange country), allows Moses, the Egyptian prince descended from Pharaoh's Hebrew slaves, in response to his sister Miriam's bitterly ironic appraisal of his exalted role at the oppressor's court. With that belated recognition of his true condition still on his lips he approaches a gang of emaciated laborers pleading in muffled cries for their "brother's" help. And as he confronts, perhaps for the first time, the human misery to which he had long closed his eyes and ears, resignation and self-pity quickly yield to outrage. Witnessing the vicious beating of a prisoner and hearing the victim in his final moments invoke the name of the "God of Abraham and Isaac and Jacob," he can no longer contain himself and slays the brutal Kapo with his princely golden staff.

This is how it happens in Franz Werfel's "biblical play" *Der Weg der Verheißung*, written at a time when such scenes were almost a daily occurrence in Nazi Germany. The Hebrew Bible gives a somewhat different account of these events—the prelude, as it were, to the contest of wit and wills won by Moses, the trusted servant of the Lord of heaven and earth, who led the children of Israel out of Egypt toward ultimate freedom under the sacred law promulgated at Mount Sinai. According to the book of Exodus, Egypt's golden boy, fearing for his life after his impulsive act of murder, found shelter with Yethro, the high priest of neighboring Midian, whose large herds he managed so successfully that he was given Yethro's daughter Tsipporah in marriage, presumably to make him a permanent member of the tribe. It is only with the naming of their first son, Gershom—a combination of the Hebrew *ger* (stranger) and *shom* (there)—that the refugee Moses fully acknowledges the illusory nature of his ostensibly enviable life in the Egyptian diaspora: "For he said, I have been a stranger in a strange land" (Exodus 2:22).

243

No biblical statement was likely to reflect more accurately the feelings of rapidly growing numbers of Central European Jews in 1933 when the American Zionist producer Meyer Weisgal first visited Franz Werfel, the celebrated Austrian writer, with an idea for a large-scale dramatic representation of some of the most poignant moments in the long, often agonizing history of ancient Israel. Given the ominous situation across the border in Germany, where a fanatic modern Pharaoh was now using his unlimited powers to restore his country's "honor" by cleansing it of all "alien" elements, Werfel readily acceded to Weisgal's entreaties. By the end of the year he was hard at work on his *Bibelspiel,* a personal yet respectful rendering of biblical scenes carefully selected and arranged to convey an inescapable sense of immediate relevance.

Like many another Jewish intellectual on the road to worldly success, Franz Werfel had long since left much of his forebears' formal religious baggage behind. But religious experience as such continued to fascinate him all his life, albeit more often than not from a primarily christological point of view. Still, even his Roman Catholic wife, the former Alma Mahler, proved unable to pry him away from the Jewish fold. It was the Jewish Kabbalah to which this mystically inclined twentieth-century Jew turned for fundamental questions, if not necessarily answers, regarding the perennial vagaries of human existence.

In 1933, of course, one's religious affiliation no longer mattered. What counted officially in the "new" Germany, as well as unofficially in still nominally independent Austria, was "race," as defined by the self-appointed guardians of "Aryan" purity and supremacy. Werfel's numerous poems, plays, and novels, at any rate, soon joined most of Germany's best modern literature on Propaganda Minister Joseph Goebbels's burning book piles, which heralded the Third Reich's triumphant defeat of the "Jewish-Bolshevist" conspiracy against Teutonic culture. If anything, this grotesque, pagan *Feuerzauber* drove home the long-ignored message that the assimilationist stance of the majority of Jewish writers, artists, and musicians rested on a painful illusion. As a result, not a few began to reassess their modernistic attitudes and goals, an often confusing process that for some was bound to end in tragedy.

Rather typically, Franz Werfel had not waited for disaster to strike before visiting Palestine to see for himself to what extent the unsparing efforts of the Zionist pioneers had actually managed to turn that sorely neglected, largely barren land into a modern Jewish national home "flowing with milk and honey." The Jewish question, so called, was indeed never far from his mind, if only because his heart was with all the persecuted of an ever-restless world. Thus, just about the time the aged German president, Field Marshall Paul von Hindenburg, yielded to rightist pressure and appointed Adolf Hitler Reichschancellor, Werfel published one of his finest novels, a moving account of the Armenian people's plight at the hands of Germany's World War I ally Turkey. But by implication at least, *Die vierzig Tage des Musa Dagh* (The forty days of Musa Dagh) also offered a timely warning of the Führer's own genocidal plans. For all we know, Werfel remembered Adolf Hitler's terrifying threats inserted in a speech he had delivered a decade earlier—not long, in fact, after the Turks had perpetrated their wholesale slaughter of innocent men, women, and children. The novel's title, at any rate, with its unmistakable Old Testament allusions, speaks for itself. Not only did the deluge last forty days, but Moses (Musa) also descended from Mount Sinai after forty days, the tablets of the divine law in his hands, only to find an unruly crowd that had forgotten nothing and learned nothing from four hundred years in Egypt. And those sinful "children" of Israel, in turn, had to spend forty difficult years in the wilderness before maturing to the point where they could finally take possession of their promised land.[1]

It may well have been on the strength of reports praising this little-short-of-sensational novel that Meyer Weisgal approached Werfel in the first place, foreseeing few problems under these circumstances in getting him onto "the road of promise." In any event, the committed pacifist deftly came to terms with the unabashed realism of the Hebrew Bible, a historical as well as a purely religious document, which in contrast to most ancient chronicles details the miseries of defeat no less meticulously than the joys of victory. Acts of violence were, as he well knew, inescapable facts of life even, if not in particular, at the dawn of an epoch that gave birth to what has since come to be known, rightly or wrongly, as Judeo-Christian civilization. And with a "new" pagan Germany increasingly recalling the children of Israel's hereditary foe Amalek, those biblical tales of woe surely deserved retelling in all their stark detail. Werfel did give ancient Israel's bloody saga of armed struggle its proper due but stressed above all the historic pursuit of the ethical ideals proclaimed at Mount Sinai and chosen, after considerable initial hesitation, by a "stiff-necked" people ready to ensure their survival down the ages, if need be at the price of martyrdom. Writing for a New World unswervingly dedicated to "the pursuit of happiness," Werfel also realized, of course, that this, his American *Lehrstück,* had to convey a palpable sense of the seemingly endless suffering that ensued for those whose chosenness was predicated on their choosing *af al pi hen*—despite everything—their forebears' sacred covenant with the one, unitary, indivisible Lord in defiance of a barbaric world forever at odds with itself. And since his congenial partners Kurt Weill and Max Reinhardt were in full agreement, what ensued was a dramatic venture exceeding all expectations, not in the least, perhaps, because it offered each and every one of the principals a long-overdue, welcome opportunity for personal redemption. In Kurt Weill's case the biblical "road" kept its "promise" in more than one way. By leading him permanently back to his ancestral heritage, it also kept him firmly out of the Gestapo's reach and before long pointed him in the right direction for ultimate success in the admittedly quite secular theatrical world of New York's Broadway.

Meanwhile, the seemingly endless preparatory road to the opening of *The Eternal Road*, Ludwig Lewisohn's American version, turned into a veritable obstacle course, so unwieldy, in fact, that an amended German title began to make the rounds at rehearsals in the Manhattan Opera House: *Weg der Verzweiflung* (Road to despair) The published recollections of two prominent participant-observers, Gottfried Reinhardt, the director's son and assistant, and Meyer Weisgal, the enterprise's ubiquitous *spiritus rector*, suggest that many a problem was rooted in the foolhardy determination to present a multi-dimensional musico-dramatic spectacle of outdoor proportions on an admittedly large yet by no means sufficiently large indoor stage.[2] Others have more recently dealt with numerous specific details.[3] But the entire complex story still remains to be told, if only because even the late Meyer Weisgal's often rollicking remarks deserve additional scrutiny. None who knew this remarkable man, in later years president of Israel's Weizmann Institute of Science, would question his basic veracity any more than his unswerving dedication to the welfare of his people. But as an unequaled fund-raiser and after-dinner speaker he did not mind embellishing a good story occasionally for the sake—and to the obvious delight—of an audience he hoped to rally to some cause close to his heart. By and large, though, the historical record does tend to support his at times distinctly anecdotal retelling of what was for all intents and purposes an extraordinary public relations effort, even for him.

Weisgal's first large-scale production in response to the slanderous lies emanating from Hitler's Germany had been an outdoor pageant, *The Romance of a People*, that toured a number of American cities successfully for the benefit of needy German-Jewish refugees. *The Eternal Road*, by contrast, was conceived from the outset as anything but "a means of raising funds for the victims of Nazi persecution."[4] Had such a possibility ever crossed Weisgal's mind, his Salzburg meeting with Max Reinhardt in the late fall of 1933 would have disabused him of any notion that this, his latest brainchild, was likely to make money, provided it actually managed to break even. In light of what was happening in Germany, needless to say, material considerations hardly mattered. The hour called for immediate action, and no sacrifice appeared excessive if *The Eternal Road* succeeded in moving the hearts and minds of ordinary American citizens, not to mention the politicians on whose understanding and empathy the fate of thousands of Jewish refugees was apt to depend. Even when threatened with personal bankruptcy at the height of the financial crisis facing his beloved project, he refused to yield. By then, to be sure, his and his artistic collaborators' tireless efforts had produced far more than a mere token of spiritual resistance to the Nazi horrors overseas. Night after night thousands upon thousands witnessed the brilliant fulfillment of Weisgal's original challenge to Max Reinhardt: "Dieses Schauspiel muß Hitler unsere Antwort geben" (The play must be our answer to Hitler).[5]

Reinhardt deserved extra credit not merely as the show's peerless director but also because it was he who recommended Kurt Weill for the all-important musical score at a time when Weill was little known in the United States beyond some well-received *Threepenny Opera* songs. Weisgal, for one, wondered what special professional and, for that matter, emotional qualifications this reputed socialist fellow traveler could possibly bring to an assignment that called for high aesthetic standards and practical experience in composing for the theater, to be sure, but a thorough background in Hebrew cantillation and liturgy as well, not to speak of Jewish culture at large. Once he got to know him, though, the shrewd producer quickly agreed that Cantor Albert Weill's son was indeed the best possible choice. And Kurt Weill seized the opportunity with alacrity, even though he had his head and hands full with French commissions, in particular the Second Symphony, to be premiered by Bruno Walter in Amsterdam the following year. The American challenge simply proved irresistible, and as soon as Werfel's text reached him he went to work, feeling once again like the proverbial fish in familiar deep waters after his narrow escape from the land where, all his remarkable achievements notwithstanding, he, too, had in the end become a "stranger in strangers' land."

Franz Werfel, the lifelong student of the Bible and knowledgeable opera lover with a penchant for that peculiar literary genre the libretto, lost no time in completing his astute dramatization of four carefully chosen biblical scenes, beginning with father Abraham's trek from Ur to the land of Canaan and ending with the Babylonian conquest of Jerusalem and the destruction of the First Temple. In an attempt to involve American audiences more closely in so much "ancient history," the action was to take place on several stage levels, a relatively new dramatic procedure gratefully exploited by Max Reinhardt and his designer Norman Bel Geddes for all it was worth. The show's contemporary ramifications emanated primarily from the lowest level, which depicted the interior of a small synagogue where Jews from all walks of life, rich and poor, young and old, firm believers and agnostics alike, were gathered in mortal fear of an expected pogrom. Hoping to help this haphazard flock through the long, presumably sleepless night in a historically and religiously meaningful way, the synagogue's Rabbi decides to draw their attention to particularly instructive stories of *Tenach,* the Hebrew Bible. Chanting in the traditional manner, he brings to life scene after scene, and with every new beginning the stage lights shift to one or more of the upper levels, where the events in question are colorfully acted out. The Rabbi's function is not unlike that of the *testo* in a seventeenth-century oratorio. More specifically, though, the Evangelist of Johann Sebastian Bach's *Saint Matthew Passion* comes to mind, except that the Rabbi's extensive reliance on Hebrew cantillation variants inevitably limits his purely musical expressiveness. In more general terms, Weill's conception betrays a remarkable affinity with George Frideric Handel's notion of "sacred drama," so splendidly realized especially in *Solomon*.

But whatever inspiration Kurt Weill may have drawn from the past, Franz Werfel did his best to bypass some of the less appealing language of German Bible translations without losing any of Martin Luther's often overpowering verbal strength in particular. While striving above all for ready semantic accessibility, Werfel, who during the immediately preceding years had completed new German libretto versions for no less than three Verdi operas, also looked for sonorous-rhythmic qualities apt to stimulate a composer's musical imagination. Conceived in a spirit of genuine humility, his text followed the biblical story lines as closely as possible. Only in a rare instance like the death of Moses, where the Bible remains purposefully silent, did he turn to rabbinical sources. His single goal, he confided to a preface left unpublished during his lifetime, was to "to serve, to praise God in his own words, and to show the world the everlasting plan that is Israel's trust."[6] The net result was a text virtually unprecedented in musical history, given the fact that biblical oratorios were typically based on the often labored products of christologically safe writers of the second or third rank, who in some instances barely disguised their evident discomfort with the Old Testament's unadorned realism. Julius Schubring's "theologically correct" suggestions for Felix Mendelssohn's *Elijah* offer a relatively recent case in point. Mendelssohn himself once tried his hand at an oratorio text for his friend Adolph Bernhard Marx, who promptly rejected it and—long before Arnold Schoenberg—decided instead to assume full responsibility also for the literary aspects of his *Moses*. Kurt Weill, on the other hand, attending Werfel's first reading of what was at that time still called *Das Volk der Verheißung*, realized then and there at Reinhardt's Schloß Leopoldskron how privileged he was have this latter-day Boito by his side.

And so he went to work without even awaiting Werfel's finishing touches. By October 1934 he was in a position to inform Max Reinhardt that his score had passed the halfway mark.[7] And less than a year later, on 10 September 1935, he landed in New York with the completed piano-vocal score ready for rehearsals. Werfel, meanwhile, decided to return to Vienna, where his play was promptly published without any mention whatsoever of its origins or true purpose, even though on the other side of the Atlantic feverish preparations continued for an early premiere of Ludwig Lewisohn's English version. But Weisgal's hopes for the 1935–36 season proved futile, and Lewisohn's by-and-large faithful adaptation, too, appeared prematurely in print, with a title, moreover, that gave no inkling of the original's unmistakable messianic overtones. Far from alluding to the Jewish people's historic mission, *The Eternal Road* invited, if anything, painful associations with the notorious myth of "the eternal Jew" condemned to roam the earth forever for denying the Christian Savior—paradoxically, a Jew who is said to have died for all of mankind's sins. Theology aside, however, national socialism was making the most of that age-old vilification for its own nefarious reasons. And for that reason alone, Lewisohn's title represented a most regrettable, albeit no doubt unintentional, faux pas. Adding insult to injury, Werfel's humble *Bibelspiel* was now billed as a "biblical mystery play," which made it sound more like a belated American response to the annual anti-Semitic Passion play at Oberammergau than a determined "Jewish answer to Hitler."

Lewisohn did attach a brief note to the effect that his English translation would see the footlights first. But the target period, January 1936, remained unchanged, anticipating the actual opening by a full year.[8] The merciless perfectionism of the autocratic director and his stage designer Norman Bel Geddes had necessitated a tremendously time-consuming and costly modification of the Manhattan Opera House's interior to accommodate several massed groups of actors, dancers, and choruses moving at times simultaneously across the huge set. By 7 January 1937, when the curtain finally rose, the resulting debt load had already reached threatening proportions. And after eighteen weeks of consistently well attended performances, the widely acclaimed show was forced to lower the iron curtain for the last time, a powerless victim of economically indifferent artistic intransigence.

Having claimed even the orchestra pit for his synagogue interior, Bel Geddes suggested that Leopold Stokowski be commissioned to record Weill's music for nightly playbacks. In that way, he averred, Weill's richly orchestrated score would certainly receive "an incomparably finer rendition" than from some twenty-odd "live" musicians under a much lesser conductor. Weill, at any rate, had little choice but to agree, and Stokowski reportedly used the same "Photophone" technique, RCA's experimental sound-on-film process, with which he produced such astonishing results in Walt Disney's *Fantasia*. Nobody, it seems, reckoned with James Petrillo, the uncompromising head of the American Federation of Musicians, who insisted that twenty-eight union members be hired anyway. "And since a second complication—secretly anticipated by Weill—arose and no one was able to solve the problem of coordinating the singing on the various levels of the gigantic stage with a mechanical equipment, Stokowski's discs [*sic*] were abandoned. They had cost sixty-eight thousand dollars."[9]

RCA's subsequent decision to forgo any further "Photophone" development may well have sealed the fate of that unique sound document, which to date has eluded all efforts to locate it. For all we know, it was quickly canned and eventually, in accordance with the industry's practice, destroyed. Then again, time may simply have taken its inescapable toll. Adding to the mystery, the orchestral parts, too, appear to have vanished without a trace. Fortunately, Weill's original piano-vocal score of *Der Weg der Verheißung* has been preserved, together with the mostly untexted full score used by the conductor of *The Eternal Road,* Isaac Van Grove, Meyer Weisgal's earlier collaborator on *The Romance of a People.* Beyond these two invaluable sources in the possession of the Kurt Weill Foundation in New York, the Weill-Lenya Collection at Yale University owns a small manuscript of "United States additions composed in 1934–1935." Exactly what was recorded or performed at the Manhattan Opera House in January 1937 is, however, bound to remain an open question, if only because of the many deletions, substitutions, and additions reportedly made throughout the eighteen-week run. Any such ubiquitous facts of musico-theatrical life, needless to say, may tend to complicate but in no way preclude the much-hoped-for preparation of a proper critical edition of Franz Werfel and Kurt Weill's unique joint effort, a by no means flawless yet in its day highly effective paean to Jewish pride and hopes in the face of events already pregnant with unmitigated horror and destruction.[10]

Considering what they contributed individually to the performing arts throughout a goodly portion of the twentieth century, any combined achievement of Franz Werfel, Kurt Weill, Max Reinhardt, and Norman Bel Geddes would invite close scholarly scrutiny as well as public attention for its own sake alone. But the prolonged obstacle course that was *The Eternal Road* also exemplifies some of the difficulties as well as possibilities of characteristic fruits of the Central European humanistic tradition upon their transplantation to the distinctly more arid American cultural soil. In the wake of the First World War the American public tended to identify Europe rather with France. And by the 1930s even cosmopolitan New York, in the throes of a deep economic depression, cared little about what was happening elsewhere. The popular press either dismissed Hitler as some kind of political clown or viewed him as the "godfather" of a mafia about to turn the Valentine's Day massacre into a daily German routine. Political refugees, meanwhile, tended to neutralize the potential effects of the most compelling eyewitness accounts with their psychologically understandable but politically disastrous campaigns on behalf of the "true" Germany, the Germany of "Goethe and Schiller," which, they trusted, would reemerge before long in all its past glory. Nor did Charles Lindbergh and his ilk help matters with their gospel of the "new Germany" as the world's last bastion against "international communism."

Boycott or no boycott, visiting German musicians, singers in particular, continued to enchant the same socially inbred circles that looked upon Jews generally with a good deal of suspicion, if not outright contempt, causing even some of the most gifted of newcomers to suffer at least initially the indignities of an expatriate ghetto existence. *The Eternal Road* enjoyed one distinct advantage over most theatrical or musical works trying to breathe

Example 2a–b: from Weill, *Der Kuhhandel*, no. 7 (left) and Weill, *Der Weg der Verheißung*, act 2 (right)

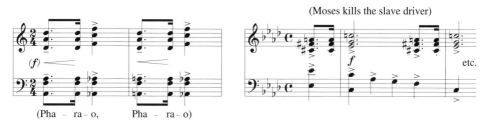

"air from other planets" in the United States: an almost guaranteed public of sympathetic European immigrants and their first-generation American offspring. This enviable edge certainly facilitated the transition from *Der Weg der Verheißung* to *The Eternal Road*—as compared, say, with the stormy Channel crossing from which Weill's unfinished operetta *Der Kuhhandel* emerged at London's Savoy Theatre of Gilbert and Sullivan fame quite changed as *A Kingdom for a Cow*.[11] Incidentally, these two chronologically overlapping twin sets betray their contemporaneousness in several admittedly minor yet not uninteresting substantive ways. To mention only the most obvious: the initial motif of the operetta's "Ballade vom Pharao" resurfaced in *Der Weg der Verheißung* hardly by accident in connection with Moses, Pharaoh's nemesis (ex. 2a–b).

Linguistic, dramatic, and strictly musical adaptations to satisfy national or local tastes and practices have, needless to say, always been part and parcel of operatic history. Earlier, however, a basic acquaintance with the principal events and figures of the Bible as well as classical history and mythology, the primary textual sources of opera, could be expected of any halfway educated person anywhere, and more so than ever once a liberal bourgeoisie committed to *Bildung* and humanistic values supplanted the traditional clerical and aristocratic European patronage. Nor was nineteenth-century genteel America, in its pervasive thirst for "improvement," as yet ready to let strictly material considerations dictate its educational aims and substance. Depression-era New York, on the other hand, teeming with lower-class immigrants, its once all-powerful social elite financially battered, would rather spend its last nickels on "democratic" forms of entertainment like the highly polished productions of Hollywood and, indeed, Broadway. Ludwig Lewisohn, moreover, knew only too well that even the orthodox parents of first-generation American Jews, anxious to "fit in," were apt to abandon the religious world for a "reform" movement that substituted English for Hebrew and took its ceremonial cues from American Protestantism.

Whatever the ultimate ramifications of the public's cultural diversity and

Example 3: from Weill, *Der Weg der Verheißung,* act 1

predilections, Lewisohn's American version of *Der Weg der Verheißung* had
to satisfy before everything else the sophisticated European author's sensi-
tivities as well as a first-rate composer's legitimate musical requirements. In
the end, the former fared on the whole remarkably well, the latter less so.
There was clearly no way a literal translation like "In the beginning God
made earth and heaven" was going to suit the rhythmic, accentual, and phonetic characteristics of a melody tailor-made for "Gott schuf im Anfang
Himmel und Erde" (ex. 3). But beyond specific problems of this nature,
Lewisohn did have a keen ear for Franz Werfel's more general musico-
poetic concerns, especially "a metre which Werfel has invented. This is a
descending rhythm, that is, dactylic-trochaic: long-short-short, long short. He
frequently uses anacrusis. . . . " And Lewisohn was confident that "the translation reproduces the precise pattern of the line. The effect aimed at is one
of *chant.*"[12] And by taking advantage of the inherent rhythmic flexibility of
Masoretic cantillation, Kurt Weill, for his part, managed to preserve this particular quality, at least throughout the Rabbi's intermittent Bible readings.

   In the last instance, though, the potential success or failure of *The Eternal Road* was not a matter of phonetics or prosody but of environment and
mentality beyond any translator's control. What had been conceived originally as a kind of Jewish *Jedermann* play, in the sense of Max Reinhardt's
world-famous annual Salzburg production, faced in its American guise theatrical as well as economic conditions endemic to Broadway that bore little
resemblance to anything Werfel, Reinhardt, or Weill had ever experienced.
Weisgal's popular fund-raiser of 1933, *The Romance of a People,* had attracted
large numbers of people to cavernous armories and sports arenas. *The Eternal Road,* by contrast, was an intellectually and aesthetically demanding event
destined from the outset for a regular season in a midtown theater lacking
any state support whatsoever. Yet its prologue alone called for more than
thirty singing and speaking parts supplemented by a substantial "synagogue
choir." The "Golden Calf" orgy of the second act went even farther with its
multitudes of elaborately choreographed dancers and some twenty vocal
soloists as well as one large and one smaller choir. And all this and much
more occupied "five stages, which rise in ascending order like the steps of a
stairway," allowing "the Angel of the End of Days" in the final apotheosis to
lead "the eternal procession of Israel in such a manner that the *Heavenly
Stair* is never empty." As the final curtain slowly descended, the entire huge

company was seen trekking up the mountain to the massed sounds of Psalm 126: "When the Lord brings back the redeemed to Zion. . . . "

That extraordinary scene represents not, as one might expect, the trance-like vision of some venerable sage, a lifelong student of the Kabbalah perhaps, but the messianic dream of a thirteen-year-old boy deprived by his father, a dyed-in-the-wool agnostic, of the very minimum of religious instruction that would have permitted him to assume the sacred duties of a bar mitzvah, a full-fledged member of the Jewish community. Untutored in matters of religion though he may be, it is this youngster and he alone who prophetically grasps the true meaning of this long, fearful night. And his confirmation as a faithful son of Israel rests on an act of pure creative inspiration that transcends the limitations of any communal puberty rite, however religiously sincere or intellectually respectable. So overwhelming is the force of his conviction, it causes even his apostate father to embrace the long-rejected heritage once more "with his whole heart and his whole soul." The message is clear: Jewish youth is the guarantor of Jewish survival and renewal. And with that lesson of hope firmly rooted in the teachings of yore, the engrossing journey on the "road of promise" in the footsteps of the patriarchs—of Moses, who alone knew the Lord face-to-face; of the great kings Saul, David, and Solomon; and last but not least of the troubled and troubling prophets Isaiah and Jeremiah—has reached its goal. Fulfilling the Rabbi's fondest hopes, the erstwhile disparate and desperate gathering of individuals sharing little more than the fearful consequences of their Jewish descent now exudes the collective sense of peace and serenity of a community ready to face the future with confidence in the consoling certainty that the divine promise is yet to be fulfilled.

For Cantor Albert Weill's son, *Der Weg der Verheißung* marked an irreversible personal return, the recovery of a spiritual wealth he had been ready to renounce at least temporarily in favor of a sincere yet ultimately futile secular quest for universal peace and justice. Characteristically, his extensive progress report of October 1934 ended with a reaffirmation of his deeply personal commitment to the common task: "In concluding I would like to tell you once again how infinitely happy this work has made me and how firmly convinced I am that we can create something uniquely beautiful, if we manage to achieve all that we envisage."[13]

In this spirit of undivided devotion Weill completed his score in record time. Werfel's text had been meticulously set word for word, with the exception of an occasional, musically mandated repetition. But by the same token, the composer wondered to what extent Lewisohn's translation would meet his legitimate musical expectations.[14] It turned out, of course, that all the hurry had been in vain, since Meyer Weisgal was still looking for ways and above all means to meet the far larger than life demands of Max Reinhardt and Norman Bel Geddes. Werfel, who reached New York before Weill, chose not to wait and soon returned to Europe. Weill stuck it out, working on his first Broadway score for Paul Green's *Johnny Johnson* and responding repeatedly to calls for orchestral interpolations needed to cover the constant displacements not only of massed actors and singers but also of loads of hardware and carpenter's work onto, across, and off the huge stage expanse of *The Eternal Road.*

The premiere, when it finally took place on 7 January 1937, lasted till three o'clock in the morning, if one is to believe Brooks Atkinson, the *New York Times* critic who admittedly left the Manhattan Opera House sometime before midnight in order to meet his paper's deadline.[15] But whether that memorable first night's extraordinary teething pains actually dragged things out that long or an hour less, as Gottfried Reinhardt seemed to remember, something clearly had to give. The ensuing radical amputation of much of the final act certainly confirmed Franz Werfel's worst fears. For all we know, though, it was not merely a question of length but also the perceived need of a considerably happier ending than the dire consequences of the rejection of Jeremiah's desperate plea for a "peace settlement" held in store, an ending rather like that which the colorful dedication of King Solomon's Temple readily provided. A less sophisticated public than that of the gala opening might well have taken umbrage at the apparent victory of evil over good. In that regard, however, the final apotheosis extolling the as yet unfulfilled messianic hopes of the "timeless community of Israel" in the "equally timeless night of Israel's persecution" may have appeared even more problematic, since it risked offending Christian believers in a Savior long since risen. Franz Werfel's Roman Catholic wife answered that question quite unequivocally with her later retort that the alpha and omega of biblical history was and always would be Jesus Christ.[16] That this widely shared Christian view is by definition irreconcilable with the Jewish conception of the one and only, unitary, and indivisible God of Abraham, Isaac, and Jacob did not seem to occur to Alma Mahler-Werfel, even though, if anything, it was this fundamental conflict that paved the Jewish people's "eternal road" with untold numbers of martyrs.

Whatever the reason or reasons for the drastic cut, the elimination of the particularly strong Jeremiah music must have been more disappointing than anything else for a composer who in 1923, nominally still under Ferruccio Busoni's tutelage, had started on his own "road of promise" with a remarkable setting of texts from the biblical Book of Lamentations, the unaccountably long-neglected *Recordare* for mixed and children's voices a cappella. A decade later, the chastened refugee from Hitler's Germany expressed himself in a distinctly milder musical idiom, deeply touched though he was by the most timely message of the great yet humble Prophet whose tireless warnings of impending disaster went so tragically unheeded. As it happened, Franz Werfel, too, had long drawn strength from the Bible's arguably most powerful champion of truth and justice in an idolatrous world contemptuous of the weak and helpless. In light of the precipitous events in Austria as well as Germany, it was hardly an accident that Jeremiah became the central character of Werfel's novel *Höret die Stimme* barely a year after the truncated *Eternal Road* closed down. Weill, in turn, resuscitated appropriate elements of the abandoned fourth act in his music for Ben Hecht's *We Will Never Die*, their joint "answer to Hitler" after news of the "final solution" to "the Jewish question" had finally begun to find stunned credence in an America long inclined to discount as mere propaganda Hitler's commitment to the destruction of the Jewish people as a sacred mission entrusted to him by the Almighty.

Hitler was not yet formally in power, of course, when Weill's opera *Die Bürgschaft* created an uproar among his henchmen, not in the least, perhaps, because of its unmistakable Old Testament overtones. It took a series of coups and "special measures," undermining what was left of a Weimar Republic already in ruins, before he turned, however briefly, to a biblical story proper, that of Naboth, who refused to cede his vineyard to King Ahab and, as a result, fell victim to his Phoenician wife Jezebel's "final solution." Falsely accused of blasphemy, the recalcitrant neighbor was condemned to death and promptly executed. Urgent preparations for the impending premiere of *Der Silbersee* and Weill's subsequent flight to France intervened, and this particular project never came to fruition. But its underlying theme resurfaced in the original Jeremiah portion of *Der Weg der Verheißung*, where an equally gullible king's ready ear for even more dangerous demagoguery speeds his own ruin as well as that of his subjects.

"Naboth's Vineyard" might have become the kind of *Lehrstück* that *Die Bürgschaft*, to the manifest disappointment of the political left, quite evidently was not.[17] The opera's moral lessons should have been obvious, nevertheless, so shortly before Germany's Social Democrats, in a desperate final attempt to save the republic, jettisoned their long-cherished convictions and threw their still considerable numerical weight behind the aging President von Hindenburg, the very symbol of German militarism. By the time "Naboth's Vineyard" came into Weill's purview, Franz von Papen, Hindenburg's chosen head of government, was busily making secret deals with the National Socialists that ensured their triumph in the next round of elections. With its thinly disguised references to acquisitive militarists, cleverly manipulated mobs, and, for that matter, David Orth's betrayal of an old benefactor, once "die Verhältnisse" changed in his disfavor, *Die Bürgschaft* was bound to prove a painful thorn in the political eyes of the radical right. Yet neither the rowdies in and around Berlin's Städtische Oper nor Hermann Goering's iron grip on the Reichstag discouraged Weill from declaring openly that he and his librettist, Caspar Neher, had indeed wished to depict in theatrically appropriate ways "human events against the background of an idea that knows no time."[18] *Überzeitlich* was the German word he used; *zeitlos* would be Werfel's for the "timeless community of Israel" and "the equally timeless night of its persecution." And Weill himself was obviously aware of the deeper connections between *Die Bürgschaft* and *Der Weg der Verheißung.* For on 16 September 1934 he wrote to Lotte Lenya: "Musically, this Bible-thing is becoming very beautiful and very rich. I actually note in it how far I've developed since *Die Bürgschaft.* It's just as serious, but in expression much stronger, richer, more varied."[19]

Der Weg der Verheißung and *Die Bürgschaft* do share some general as well as specific features. While the opera involves far fewer vocal soloists, both reserve important functions for two choruses of distinctly different sizes. Motivic similarities pertain as a rule to corresponding moods, attitudes, or thoughts, except that some musical ideas expressive of purely personal sentiments in the opera acquired broader spiritual meanings. Pooling his melodic resources in this way and combining, where necessary, the new with the preexisting, Weill managed to stress in strictly musical terms, perhaps subconsciously but also quite logically, the universal human concerns at the core of each of these, his most extensive theatrical compositions: freedom of choice under divine guidance, spiritual as opposed to material wealth, minority status as a privilege, justice versus power, love and devotion against overwhelming odds, survival for the sake of a just cause.

The beginning of act 4 of *Der Weg der Verheißung* offers an instructive example of a simple, indeed minimal musical device put to effective metaphoric use, since the stepwise descending minor seventh of Isaiah's opening questions—"Watchman, how far is the night gone? Watchman when endeth the darkness?"—is identical with Anna's early on in *Die Bürgschaft* for her no less weary "Mir liegt die Angst so schwer in meinen Gliedern." In the second act of *Der Weg der Verheißung* Moses uses the same motif, though a third lower, in his plea with the Lord to free him of any further attempts to transform the "stiff-necked" children of Israel into a cohesive, law-abiding people worthy of its sacred destiny. Moses, however, relies on it only for his anxious opening words, "Oh Lord of the World" (ex. 4a–c). His ensuing compromise proposal ("if that be [asking] too much") actually anticipates the "golden calf" motif of the forthcoming idolatrous frenzy at the foot of Mount Sinai in a brief musical vision, as it were, of the trials and tribulations fate still holds in store for him. Curiously, that later orgiastic scene led the composer himself into temptation. There the maddened crowd, seduced by Aaron's "familiar" and "beautiful" creature, a sensual idol far more attractive than the intangible spiritual force Moses alone knew "face-to-face," actually quotes the very first notes of the most "familiar" and "beautiful" musical idol of the time, Tchaikovsky's B minor piano concerto (ex. 5).

At the beginning of the third act Naomi addresses Ruth, her faithful daughter-in-law, with a reminiscence of Anna's "So war es immer" early on

Example 4a: from Weill, *Weg der Verheißung,* act 4

(Largo)
Isaiah

Wäch - ter wie weit ist die Nacht schon

Example 4b: from Weill, *Die Bürgschaft,* act 1

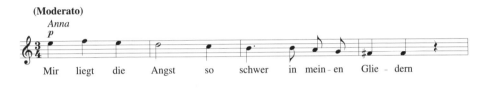

(Moderato)
Anna
p

Mir liegt die Angst so schwer in mein-en Glie - dern

Example 4c: from Weill, *Weg der Verheißung,* act 2

(Allegro agitato)
Moses

Oh Kö - nig der Welt, tu den Mo - se von mir und

lass mich hi - nü - ber als nie - dri - gen Mann

Example 5: from Weill, *Weg der Verheißung,* act 2

(Vivace assai)

Das ist ein Gott, _____ der uns sieg - reich ge - führt hat...

in *Die Bürgschaft*—appropriately so, since loyalty, a universal human affection in no way limited to any specific era or social milieu, is the central issue in both instances (ex. 6a–b). Naomi, however, takes recourse to a specific musical procedure much favored by Weill in a reflective or melancholy mood: starting every second measure a tone lower, she ultimately comes to rest on F-sharp, a diminished seventh below her initial pitch. As for her

Example 6a: from Weill, *Weg der Verheißung,* act 3

Example 6b: from Weill, *Die Bürgschaft,* act 3

motif's multiple upbeat pattern, that particular Weill trademark is easily traced to any number of antecedents in late-nineteenth-century Jewish liturgical music.

One hardly has to be an expert in Hebrew cantillation to admire Weill's judicious use of traditional *ta'ame hamikra* in the Rabbi's scriptural recitations with their characteristic melodic cadence, the descending skip of a fourth, the *sof passuk,* marking important textual intersections. But the Rabbi also breaks repeatedly into more florid song, adding his voice to the virtually seamless musical connections between different eras and personages. At the onset of the third act, for example, he joins the biblical figures in a succession of individually sung phrases strung together by ties across the bar line from the last beat of each of the three-measure phrases to the first beat of the next, quite independently of the orchestra's recurring first-beat pedal chords. What ensues is a model of flawless melodic continuity counterbalanced by a strong sense of metrical irregularity, which permits the Rabbi to render his Bible passage in conjunction with the orchestra's respective second phrases but without in the least affecting the flow of Naomi's melodic line. Indeed, expert that he was in providing instrumental support to singing actors, Weill also managed time and again with the simplest of means to turn sheer technical necessity into unqualified artistic virtue.

Weill's early exposure to cantorial music, reinforced in 1934 by pertinent research at the Bibliothèque Nationale in Paris, proved its value in several significant instances. Thus, about to reveal itself as the God of Abraham, Isaac, and Jacob, "the voice out of the burning bush" warns Moses not to draw closer with the very melody reserved in many German synagogues for Exodus 34:6 and 7, where the Lord, yielding to Moses' entreaties, reveals his thirteen spiritual attributes.[20] Weill must have realized that the metaphorical implications of this and similar musical allusions might be lost on audiences unfamiliar with the German Jewish tradition; but such practical considerations were obviously quite beside the point for one who had personally much more at stake than merely another musico-dramatic success.

The widely known and revered *Kol Nidre* melody was another matter altogether. Weill resorted to it freely in a number of more or less appropriate connections. In a striking coincidence, King David in dire straits actually intones its principal motif accompanied by the same quivering string tremoli that Arnold Schoenberg later employed to such inspiring effect in his *Kol Nidre*, op. 38. Since Schoenberg could hardly have seen, let alone heard, Weill's score, it appears that both quite independently relied on that long-established orchestral device specifically with reference to the act of divine creation, though in different, if equally incongruous, biblical and liturgical contexts. Schoenberg typically resorted to melodrama, whereas the Busoni pupil Weill, motivated no doubt by Werfel's brief mention of the abortive sacrifice of Isaac, celebrated that happy turn of events with a quasi-Bachian a cappella motet as poignantly concise as it is joyful.

In the end, *The Eternal Road* led to Kurt Weill's permanent residence and eventual full citizenship in the United States. Considering how little time elapsed before the German armies crushed France, driving countless refugees into the bloodied hands of Pierre Laval's fascist henchmen, it may actually have saved his life. Less dramatically, but with equally lasting consequences, the extensive production delays allowed him to get the feel of an altogether different culture replete with ever new challenges to his artistic imagination and, indeed, integrity. Above all, it kept its true promise by moving him once and for all away from the ubiquitous lures of mindless assimilation, the tragic mark of the "estranged one" in Werfel's play, and restored a precious sense of continuity nearly lost during the heady days of *Mahagonny* and *Die Dreigroschenoper.* If in 1923 both *Frauentanz* and *Recordare* could still lay claims to the budding composer's multiple talents, by 1947 it was again not only *Street Scene* that represented the new American and humble Jew but also the blues-inspired *Kiddush,* with which he surprised his aging cantor-father, now living in relative safety, if not peace, in Palestine, like thousands of others who had finally come to realize that in the European diaspora, as in that of ancient Egypt, they and their kind had in fact always been "strangers in strangers' land."

NOTES

1. See Peter Jungk, *Franz Werfel* (Frankfurt am Main: S. Fischer, 1987), 204, for a brief reference to the biblical connection.

2. Gottfried Reinhardt, *The Genius* (New York: Alfred A. Knopf, 1979); Meyer Weisgal, *So Far . . .* (London: Weidenfeld & Nicolson, 1971).

3. Guy Stern, "The Road to the Eternal Road," in *A New Orpheus: Essays on Kurt*

Weill, ed. Kim H. Kowalke (New Haven: Yale University Press, 1986), 268–84; David Drew, *Kurt Weill: A Handbook* (London: Faber & Faber, 1987), 262–68, 280–82; David Farneth, "Retracing 'The Eternal Road,'" *Kurt Weill Newsletter* 6 (spring 1988): 10–13. The author gratefully acknowledges the important, though mostly unpublished, contributions of Lys Simonette, whose expert translations of pertinent correspondence also benefited some of the quotations in this essay.

4. Drew, *Kurt Weill,* 267.

5. Weisgal, *So Far . . . ,* 117.

6. Franz Werfel, *Die Dramen,* vol. 2, ed. Adolf D. Klarmann (Frankfurt am Main: S. Fischer, 1959), 509.

7. Letter addressed to Max Reinhardt from Louveciennes, 6 Oct. 1934.

8. Franz Werfel, *The Eternal Road: A Drama in Four Parts,* trans. Ludwig Lewisohn (New York: Viking Press, 1936), vi.

9. Reinhardt, *Genius,* 258. *Variety* reported on 18 January 1937 that the music had indeed been "heard through the RCA Photophone Ultra-Violet System" and that "there were times at the opening when the amplification was too loud."

10. A number of excerpts based on the piano-vocal score of *Der Weg der Verheißung* performed at the Kurt Weill Festival concert of the Musica Sacra Chorus, Richard Westenberg cond., in New York's Merkin Hall, 20 September 1987, merely whetted appetites for more of the same.

11. David Drew, "Reflections on the Last Years: 'Der Kuhhandel' as a Key Work," in Kowalke, ed., *New Orpheus,* 217–67.

12. Werfel, *Eternal Road,* vii.

13. Cf. Weill's letter of 6 October 1934 to Max Reinhardt.

14. Ibid.

15. Brooks Atkinson in the *New York Times,* 8 Jan. 1937. See also Reinhardt, *Genius,* 261. Whatever the precise hour, apparently everything possible did go wrong with the final act. Luckily, by that time the critics had all left.

16. Alma Mahler-Werfel, *Mein Leben* (Frankfurt am Main: Fischer Taschenbuch Verlag, 1960), 216.

17. Herbert Trantow, "Fragen an Kurt Weill, seine 'Bürgschaft' betreffend," *Melos* 11, nos. 8–9 (Aug.–Sept. 1932): 276–77.

18. "Kurt Weill antwortet," *Melos* 11, no. 10 (Oct. 1932): 337.

19. This letter, like others quoted here, is part of the collection of the Kurt Weill Foundation, New York.

20. For additional identifications, see Alexander L. Ringer, "Recordare—Never to Forget," *Canadian University Music Review* 13 (1993): 47.

Hindemith and Weill
Cases of "Inner" and "Other" Direction

Stephen Hinton

The thinking person in emigration should not pretend to begin a new life, but should proceed from the past life, from his entire experience, including the European catastrophe and the difficulties in his new country.

THEODOR W. ADORNO,
"FRAGEN AN DIE INTELLEKTUELLE EMIGRATION"

In postwar Germany no two composers' reputations were more adversely affected by the critical strictures of New Music guru Theodor W. Adorno, himself recently returned from emigration in the United States, than those of his fellow émigrés Kurt Weill and Paul Hindemith. Some of Adorno's rigid dismissals of Hindemith's work came to be anthologized in 1968 in the essay collection *Impromptus,* in which five polemical pieces spanning forty-six years, from 1922 through 1968, are sandwiched between a prelude and a postlude and given the pretentious Latin title "Ad vocem Hindemith," with the sober subtitle "Eine Dokumentation."[1] Adorno justifies the subtitle in terms of providing documentation of his own views, which changed. Yet since they did not change *that* much, the effect is rather to raise his own judgments to the level of recordability and hence historical significance. Apart from the first piece, written when the author was an extremely precocious nineteen-year-old, the essays are negatively critical. They document a gradual progression or development rather than any kind of apostasy or flip-flopping.

It is remarkable how much Adorno's philosophy of music was in place so early in his career.[2] Details and interpretations changed, rather than fundamentals. All but one of the essays present what he calls his "position against neoclassicism," moving inexorably to the damning diagnosis of the postlude: "[Hindemith] was the compositional prototype of a now widespread social phenomenon: that of impotent pseudo-activity."[3] In fact, as Rudolf Stephan has shown in his account of the Adorno-Hindemith relationship, although Adorno continued to write about Hindemith well into the

1960s, he seems to have eschewed any active interest in Hindemith's actual compositions as early as 1933.[4] Later remarks about Hindemith are of the kind suggested as a "compositional prototype."

In the immediate postwar period Adorno considered Hindemith "immeasurably overrated" (to use Stephan's description)—a critical situation that he set about reversing, evidently with some success.[5] It hardly needs mentioning that many of Adorno's opinions became critical orthodoxy among prominent and influential figures of musical life in postwar Germany. The arguments he advances "against neoclassicism" in "Ad vocem Hindemith," although not Adorno's sole intellectual property, are historically significant to the extent that they resonate in many other writings on Hindemith.[6]

Adorno's relationship to Weill is no less problematic, and no less influential. Although no "documentation" exists such as that presented in the *Impromptus,* there are many documents, covering the early period of Weill's career in the 1920s to well after his death in 1950; isolated but telling comments can also be found in publications from the 1960s such as the *Einleitung in die Musiksoziologie.*[7] Adorno's period of approval lasted longer for Weill than for Hindemith, and he seems to have had considerable affection both for the man and for some of his music, but only for some of it. This is not the place to discuss Adorno's interpretations and justifications of works such as *Die Dreigroschenoper* in the spirit of Frankfurt school critical theory or to analyze the role Weill plays in Adorno's 1932 tract "Zur gesellschaftlichen Lage der Musik." That has been done elsewhere.[8] Immediately relevant here is a remark from Adorno's obituary of Weill, published in the *Frankfurter Rundschau* on 15 April 1950. The six-paragraph piece opens with a provocatively paradoxical, question-begging statement: "The profile of this composer, who died in America, is hardly commensurate with the concept of 'composer.'"[9] If Adorno was to go on to describe Hindemith as the musical embodiment of "impotent pseudo-activity," here he invents another "type": "the *Musikregisseur.*" The *Musikregisseur* (literally, music director) submits himself to artistic and, to a certain degree, political ends. Weill managed to make a virtue of such a submission—a compensation, according to Adorno, for his limited powers of invention—and he did so "to the point of self-renunciation." The penultimate paragraph turns to Weill's Broadway career. "Concessions to the commercial enterprise" obviously weigh heavily, given Adorno's abhorrence of the culture industry. Weill further succumbed, he says, to "the constraints and temptations of exile," which presumably prevented him from remaining a "German" composer. The self-renunciation was complete: in America the *Musikregisseur*'s willingness to make the music meet theatrical demands turned into "nothing but conformity, obedience." The compositional "self" was annihilated.[10] Such is Adorno's concept of the composer, at least negatively defined.

The theme of "self-renunciation" echoes loudly in the 1980 *New Grove* article on Weill by David Drew. Drew goes so far as to state that Weill "[did] away with his old creative self." He speaks of "self-sacrifice greater than any that would have been demanded by a totalitarian ministry of culture," and concludes that Weill's development "is not attributable to any development which could be understood as normal."[11] What, one may ask, is "normal"? Whose yardstick is being applied? Beethoven's? Schoenberg's? And what about the humanities subdiscipline "Exile Studies," known in German as *Exilforschung?* What provides the norm there? Drew's normative statement of course begs a question similar to the one posed by the opening gambit of Adorno's obituary.

The present discussion aims to scrutinize the expectations and prejudice that attach themselves to such question begging. It will conclude by proposing an alternative model of interpretation, according to which Weill as a composer can be seen to find fulfillment in the United States. The assertion seems to state the obvious, given the biographical facts, but it also has its absurd side. Typecasting appears to preclude change and development, and Weill clearly did change and develop. On the other hand, the typologies to be invoked describe the very mechanisms that govern development, dealing as they do with questions of conformity and nonconformity, or in Freudian terms, superego controls. What was it that changed and developed in Weill? And how did he and Hindemith each cope with the upheavals of exile? However extreme the upheaval may have been in cultural and artistic terms, in what way can their response to it be described as characteristic?

Addressing these questions involves continuing a line of investigation initiated by Drew, the doyen of Weill studies, in his seminal article "Musical Theatre in the Weimar Republic." In that essay Drew compared Weill's and Hindemith's early careers in terms of "an unusual but friendly game of artistic rivalry."[12] The story begins, of course, in the early Weimar Republic, but I will continue the comparison into the American years, where the two composers' paths clearly diverged.

They were born within five years of each other, Hindemith in 1895 and Weill in 1900. Their early successes in Germany swiftly established them as that country's foremost young composers, as leaders of the New Music's second generation. Hence they were also in competition with each other. At one point the rivalry was such—that is, sufficiently strong but also sufficiently kept in check—that they collaborated on a single work, a radio cantata entitled *Der Lindberghflug,* performed with considerable success in 1929.[13] But the fortune of the two composers was soon swept along by the tide of political events. Both were forced out of Germany by Hitler's regime—Weill in 1933, Hindemith in 1938—and their work was officially denounced as "degenerate." Eventually they both settled on the East Coast of the United States and acquired American citizenship, with each in his own quite distinctive way becoming a respected figure of 1940s American cultural life.

For all the parallels in their careers—particularly evident in their Berlin years, and inevitable perhaps because of enforced exile—their music and personalities could scarcely be more different, as their respective contributions to *Der Lindberghflug* demonstrated. Each composer made his separate way to America: Weill in September 1935 (after living in Paris and London), Hindemith in February 1940 (after a stay in Switzerland and discounting the handful of short U.S. tours he made prior to emigration). But in a sense they and their generation had already made a spiritual journey to what they took for the New World a decade or so earlier. To borrow a phrase from the 1990 Grosz exhibition at Harvard, they had already "envisioned" America in the 1920s, being influenced by that era's *Neue Sachlichkeit* or New Objectivity, a salient ingredient of which was "Amerikanismus."[14] American values—or what was taken for American values—provided the younger generation of Germans with an alternative to the discredited nationalistic ones of their parents. Germany's dependence on America became not only economic, thanks to the Dawes Plan, but also cultural and spiritual.

In music, the influence began with an infusion of dance music (or jazz, as it was then called) into so-called serious music.[15] The resulting mix, often intended to shock, is no better illustrated than by Hindemith's *Suite 1922*, composed in that year. The enterprise is impertinent and antimetaphysical in the extreme, as reflected by the notorious note, described in the score in French and English as "Mode d'Emploi—Direction for Use!," with which Hindemith supplies the suite's final movement, the Ragtime. Other such works include his first *Kammermusik*, with its notorious fox-trot finale, and the triptych of one-act operas, with which Hindemith temporarily acquired a reputation as an iconoclastic *enfant terrible*.

Weill's musico-dramatic "Americanisms" may have been exaggerated. In his preface to the production book of the opera *Aufstieg und Fall der Stadt Mahagonny*, for example, he warned against looking "for psychological or contemporary relevance." The name Mahagonny, he stated, "was chosen for timbral (phonetic) reasons. The city's geographical location does not play any role."[16] Nonetheless, Americanisms in his European works, from *Royal Palace* (1925–26) through *Die sieben Todsünden* (1933), are pervasive.

The "game of artistic rivalry" between Hindemith and Weill concerns the type of works they composed. On the surface there is perhaps nothing remarkable in this. Hindemith matched Weill's ballet-pantomime for children, *Die Zaubernacht*, composed in 1922, with his own "Christmas fairy tale" *Tuttifäntchen*. Both made settings of Rilke: Weill in *Das Stundenbuch* for baritone and orchestra; Hindemith in his song cycle *Das Marienleben*, completed in 1923. The parallels become more substantial, and the contrasts more obviously striking, in their works for the stage. Weill's opera about artistic vocation, *Der Protagonist* (produced in 1925). was followed in 1926 by Hindemith's *Cardillac*. Both operas deal with the artist's fatal identification with his work, an identification so intense that he ends by committing murder.

Both composers were indeed concerned as a matter of principle with the artist's responsibility to society, replacing what they saw as the isolationism of the Schoenberg school with social usefulness. In the spirit of radical artistic experimentation, but with a view to creating new platforms for art, they both wrote short operas for the Baden-Baden festival of 1927: Weill his *Songspiel Mahagonny;* Hindemith his "Sketch" *Hin und Zurück.* It is also worth noting that Hindemith passed up the opportunity to write music for John Gay's *The Beggar's Opera* after his publishers had suggested it to him in 1925.[17] It was left to Weill to make his immortal setting, *Die Dreigroschenoper,* in 1928. And, as mentioned, 1929 brought their collective effort, *Der Lindberghflug,* also for Baden-Baden.

By this time, however, Hindemith had all but abandoned the use of popular dance music, whereas Weill had assimilated it into his easily recognizable but inimitable Berlin idiom. Whenever Hindemith had employed jazz, it always felt like quotations from a foreign language. Weill's approach was more, if not wholly, integrative. Some of the best examples are to be found in the otherwise ill-fated show *Happy End,* which attempted to repeat the stir *Die Dreigroschenoper* had caused a year earlier. A less well known example from the same year, 1929, is his *Berliner Requiem,* also to texts by Brecht. Writing about the work in the radio journal *Der deutsche Rundfunk,* Weill stated that the *Requiem*'s content "undoubtedly corresponds with the feelings and views of the broadest strata of the population. An attempt has been made to express what the contemporary city dweller has to say about the phenomenon of death."[18]

By this time in their careers, one basic difference had become evident. Weill was a man of the theater; Hindemith was not. Hindemith was a versatile and prolific all-rounder: an established soloist, someone who had turned his hand to all kinds of music-making, including amateur music. This latter pursuit had revealed his affinity for the aims of the Youth Movement.[19] If Weill sought to capture the sentiments of the city dweller, Hindemith's *Musikantentum,* his instinctive musicality, lauded as much as it was criticized, made him a community (as opposed to a society) person. True, his early operas had earned him renown as a rowdy upstart. Moreover, his opera *Cardillac* had established him as a composer seriously to be reckoned with.[20] But his approach to composition was not innately theatrical, as Weill's patently was. An analogous distinction can be drawn between Bach and Handel. The difference is not absolute but one of tendency, of general type. Much of Bach's music tends toward the cerebral, much of Handel's toward public effect—particularly in his operas and oratorios, of course. Similarly, Hindemith's guiding interests lie with music as a craft, both composition and performance, whereas Weill's is with music's expressive and theatrical potential.

Hindemith's move to Berlin in 1927 thus brought to light a quite substantial discrepancy between the two composers. The reason for the move was his appointment to the chair of composition and theory at Berlin's Hochschule für Musik. The former prankster of the *épatant* one-act operas and the 1922 Suite became a respectable professor. Weill, in contrast, was no pedagogue. He had never taught anything but theory and composition for money. Nor, moreover, would he ever try writing music theory, as Hindemith was soon to do. One of Weill's few written utterances on the subject is preserved in a letter from 1949 in which he is responding to the question "What are the most essential factors in composition?" He begins his response with a general observation: "It is one of the hardest things for a composer to talk about his own work and even harder to develop a theory about the process of composition, since, in my opinion, it is one of the main factors of creative art to keep a certain innocence about this process of creation, to follow that stream of imagination (or, to use a much abused word, of inspiration) without looking around for the source of the stream." He then suggests an analogy: "It is a bit like the process of falling asleep. If you try to watch how you fall asleep you'll have a hard time to pass into Morpheus' arms. By the same token, you cannot write music if you are watching yourself [to see] how you do it. That is, of course, the only comparison between falling asleep and writing music." The remarks that follow offer a potted summary of Weill's approach to musical composition, stressing in particular his vocation as a composer for the theater: "I have learned to make my music speak directly to the audience, to find the most immediate, the most direct way to say what I want to say, and to say it as simply as possible. That's why I think that, in the theater at least, melody is such an important element because it speaks directly to the heart—and what good is music if it cannot move people?"[21] That was Weill in 1949, a year before his death, but the sentiments surely hold good for many of his European works as well.

The relationship between Hindemith's theory and practice is much more complex. While the theory, which he began writing in the 1930s, largely serves to rationalize his own musical practice, the practice is also affected by the theory.[22] The development of the theory, in particular the invocation of nature and universal harmony as a legitimizing authority, guides the composer through the turbulence of Nazi Germany. In general, then, Hindemith's *Unterweisung im Tonsatz,* first published in 1937, both reflected the composer's pedagogical methods and defined the parameters of his own musical language.[23] In its specific appeals to universal values, however, it also documented a craving for continuity and identity at a time of increasing alienation from active musical life. That alienation was a direct result of National Socialism; but Hindemith's sense of it also continued after his return to Europe in the 1950s, despite widespread recognition and celebrity.[24]

Weill's departure from Germany was short and swift, and he was never permanently to return to Europe. Before coming to the United States in September 1935 he had two distinct periods of exile: one in Paris, from March 1933 through December 1934, followed by one in London. Two critical flops—a BBC broadcast of *The Threepenny Opera* and the premiere of his operetta *A Kingdom for a Cow* at London's Savoy Theatre—were enough to suggest that England was not the place for him.[25] In a letter to his former wife Lotte Lenya (whom he was soon to remarry), he parodied the famous poem *Nachtgedanken* by Heinrich Heine: "Wenn ich an London denke in der Nacht, dann bin ich um den Schlaf gebracht" (When at night I think of London, then I am robbed of sleep). The difference from the Heine original is notable: Heine lost his sleep over thinking of his homeland, Germany; Weill lost his over a city, London, that could have become his adopted home. "This London flop," he continued after the Heine parody, "was a severe blow for me." And then he parodied himself, with a line from *Happy End:* "Aber nur nicht weich werden!" (Just don't get softhearted!).[26] The strategy is typically Weillian. In order to express emotion, Weill uses a well-worn phrase, which he then immediately undermines in some way—in this case with a piece of his own Berlin theater.

Hindemith's extrication from his native country was more protracted and painful; it involved the whole "Hindemith Case" (*der Fall Hindemith*), the political tug-of-war between various parties over Hindemith's acceptability as a composer living in Nazi Germany. It was not just a matter of interpreting his oeuvre but of deciding what the criteria for that assessment should be in the first place.[27] Just how wide of the mark some of the assessments were is illustrated by the nature of Hindemith's presence at the exhibition "Degenerate Music," staged in Düsseldorf in May 1938, where he was lumped together with Schoenberg as a "theorist of atonality." The charge is absurd in both cases and indicative of the ideological opprobrium practiced by the Nazis. In Schoenberg's case the tribute referred to his harmony textbook of 1922, which deals only briefly, in an appendix, with the dissolution of tonality. And Hindemith's *Unterweisung im Tonsatz* (Craft of musical composition) is anything but an apology for atonality. In the war of racist and ideological slander, technical details evidently mattered little.

Despite his evident professional successes in America, Hindemith eventually returned to pursue his academic vocation at the University of Zurich and also his career as a conductor. His ties to Germany and to Europe were patently stronger than Weill's. If he reveled in Americanisms in Germany, in America he seemed to crave attachments to Europe and its traditions.

Hindemith's invocation of universal laws of nature can be read as a response to his growing sense of isolation, an attempt to absolve himself from the pressures of history. The theoretical thought also so affected his practice that he began to question the validity of earlier compositions in the light of new ideas. The theory was not value free, in other words, but had distinct aesthetic implications. In the first edition of the *Unterweisung* he even appended a list of his own works that he considered consistent with his theory, works in which "the realization of the views put forward in this book concerning compositional technique can best be followed."[28] The works he omitted were branded, by implication, as aesthetically inferior. In a handful of instances he set about revising earlier compositions and hence justifying their inclusion in the newly defined canon of his oeuvre. One such, and the best known, is *Das Marienleben,* originally composed in 1922–23.[29] Although not published until 1948, the revised version was apparently contemplated shortly after completion of the first. His diaries and work catalogs show, however, that Hindemith did most of the work on it over a decade later and in two stages: in 1936–37 before his departure from Berlin while drafting the *Unterweisung,* and in the first half of 1941 shortly after joining the Yale School of Music full time.[30]

The foreword, in which Hindemith describes the motives, aims, and achievements of his revision, is a remarkable document of his aesthetic credo in matters general and particular. It was completed at New Haven in June 1948. He sees *Das Marienleben,* he says, as having met an "interest in Western music."[31] The historical context in which he places himself is wide, stretching back to the Middle Ages. The contemporaries from which he distances himself are all those modernists who in their "new art" overstress "new" and forget "art."[32] For his part, he stresses the "ethical necessities of music and the moral duties of the musician"—qualities, he says, of which he had been aware since the performance of the first version of *Das Marienleben.* His revisions are undertaken in the spirit of approaching an ideal. He calls them "attempts at a solution which run parallel to the great issues of the general compositional development of our age."[33] He criticizes the vocal lines of his first version as unamenable to the voice, as having been conceived in abstract musical terms. Guidelines for revision were the principles laid down in his own theory. He was also concerned in the new version with the coherence of the cycle as a whole. Its unity should be guaranteed not only by the text but also by musical means, by the repetition of motives, by piano postludes, and by tonal relations. The purpose behind the revision can be summed up in his concept of "the total vision of the work" to which all its elements are subordinate.[34] Of the original fifteen songs, Hindemith retained only one unaltered. Two were completely recomposed, and the remainder revised, most of them thoroughly.

The idea of returning to an earlier work with a view to revising it, particularly one from 1923, would have been anathema to Weill, except in the event of an actual production. (He did entertain a revival of *Die Dreigroschenoper* during his American years, but to no avail.)[35] But there are numerous examples of his reusing earlier material in a way comparable to Handel's self-borrowings.[36] He was more pragmatic than Hindemith, less concerned about continuity and consistency within his oeuvre as a whole.

Hindemith's revising his own work may initially suggest discontinuity. But the consistency of his style, the similarity between his earlier and later works, was sufficient for him to consider the revision in the first place.[37] And the

effort expended, including the self-justifying apology of the revision's foreword, speaks for itself.

When Hindemith was writing that foreword, Weill would have had anything but his own earlier Rilke settings on his mind. He was at work with
Alan J. Lerner on their "vaudeville" *Love Life,* having completed the year before his "American opera" *Street Scene.* A manuscript version of an article by
Weill that eventually found its way into the liner notes for the cast recording of *Street Scene* bears the title "Two Dreams Come True."[38] The first dream
involved what Weill saw as the fulfillment of his life's ambition as a composer of music for the theater. The second was the dream of an American
opera. His description of the first dream begins as follows: "Ever since I made
up my mind, at the age of 19, that my special field of activity would be the
theater, I have tried continuously to solve, in my own way, the form-problems
of the musical theater, and through the years I have approached these problems from all different angles." The continuity of Weill's oeuvre, a continuity that has often eluded critics, is to be found precisely in its plurality: in
answers to the general question, inherited from his teacher Busoni, about
the viability of musical theater.[39] "Every new work," as Virgil Thomson observed in his obituary for Weill, "was a new model, a new shape, a new solution of dramatic problems."[40]

When Weill died in 1950, a book came onto the market that was soon to
capture the imagination of the thinking American public. It eventually sold
over half a million copies in paperback, and a picture of its author, David
Riesman, appeared on the cover of *Time* magazine. The book was called *The
Lonely Crowd.*[41] In it, Riesman drew up character typologies—those alluded
to in the title of this paper—which he intended as ideal types to describe
shifts in socioeconomic attitudes in the modern age. The two principal types
of modern character structure he posits are "inner-direction" and "other-
direction," primarily intended to illuminate overall social and historical tendencies rather than individuals. The two types are outlined in the following
excerpts:

> The source of direction for the individual is "inner" in the sense that it is im-
> planted early in life by the elders and directed toward generalized but nonethe-
> less inescapably destined goals. . . . The problem of personal choice . . . is
> solved by channeling choice through a rigid, highly individualized character.[42]

> Aims are ideologically interrelated, and the selection made by any one in-
> dividual remains relatively unalterable throughout his life. . . . The inner-
> directed character . . . is very considerably bound by traditions; they limit his
> ends and inhibit his choice of means. . . . He cannot help becoming aware of
> competing traditions—hence of tradition as such. . . . The inner-directed per-
> son becomes capable of maintaining a delicate balance between the demands
> upon him of his life goal and the buffetings of his external environment. . . .

> The diary keeping that is so significant a symptom . . . [of the inner-directed type] may be viewed as a kind of inner time-and-motion study by which the individual records and judges his output day by day. It is evidence of the separation between the behaving and the scrutinizing self.[43]

> The inner-directed man becomes vulnerable to himself when he fails to achieve his internalized goals. Able to forget the invisible hand as long as he is successful, he seeks in his baffled failure to make it visible so that he can smite it.[44]

> He becomes a "moralizer-in-retreat."[45]

And now for the other-directed type:

> What is common to all other-directeds is that their contemporaries are the source of direction for the individual—either those known to him or those with whom he is indirectly acquainted, through friends and through the mass media. The source is of course "internalized" in the sense that dependence on it for guidance in life is implanted early. The goals toward which the other-directed person strives shift with that guidance: it is only the process of striving itself and the process of paying close attention to the signals from others that remain unaltered throughout life.[46]

I am inclined to think that the other-directed type does find itself most at home in America.

> The other-directed person wants to be loved rather than esteemed; he wants not to gull or impress, let alone oppress, others but, in the current phrase, to relate them; he seeks less a snobbish status in the eyes of others than assurance of being emotionally in tune with them.[47]

It is scarcely necessary to quote David Drew's closing description of the composer in the foreword to his *Weill Handbook*—"a man who was much loved"—to guess which type best fits which composer.[48] It should be abundantly obvious, in particular, which character model best explains the two composers' quite different reactions to emigration. In some ways such typologies can be no more and no less relevant or useful than astrology charts or I Ching readings. Not only can they be applied in a statically essentialist way, despite their having been intended to capture a historical process; but the positing of just two types can also seem too limited, like any binary opposition.[49] These and other objections have already been voiced in the substantial secondary literature on *The Lonely Crowd*.[50]

In the 1961 collection of essays *Culture and Social Character,* Quentin Bell addressed the question of conformity and nonconformity in the fine arts. His perspective, like Riesman's, is both culturally and historically specific. With the help of Riesman's categories, Bell identifies artistic types as they change throughout history. He writes, for example, of "the social situation of the artist in the state of inner-direction"—by which he is referring to the nineteenth- and early-twentieth-century, principally European conception of the artist as autonomous, even nonconformist, creator whose activity follows patterns related to Riesman's "inner direction."[51] Applying the typology in this way seems adequate for the comparison of Hindemith and Weill to the extent that we are interested less in their individual character traits than in how they plotted their artistic careers. It can also result in our finding unity and continuity where before we may have expected and registered disruption and discontinuity.

In inner-directed terms, the purported differences between early and late Hindemith may seem less marked than is often suggested. Adorno perhaps sensed that inner continuity when he remarked apropos the *Suite 1922* and the fox-trot finale of the first *Kammermusik,* "'It can't go on like this' is, as it were, part of the composition."[52] Hindemith's gyroscopic sense of European tradition, in short, is pronounced, whether he is apparently opposing or affirming it.[53]

As for Weill, diagnosing his American works in terms of "doing away with his old creative self" or describing his development as abnormal seems informed by expectations that closely resemble Riesman's inner-directed type.[54] In other-directed terms, the transition from Weill's European to his American career seems utterly "normal."

However limiting typologies as such may initially seem, their possibility alone serves to challenge preconceptions about composers, such as Adorno's. An alternative model may invite us to consider differently how creative energies can be channeled, in spite or because of adversities. In that sense, the type holds a possible key to the individual, a framework for interpretation or, as Young-Bruehl describes it, a "map for further inquiry."[55] Descriptions of émigré artists and intellectuals based on the inner-directed model seem to be the norm, with Adorno's own writings, informed as they are by German musical expressionism, supplying an especially drastic example.[56] This is understandable. In many ways, as the stereotype of the European artist, it is a model that has defined the very image of the exile experience.[57] The other-directed type suggests another, quite different experience, which ultimately subverts the very notion of "exile."[58]

In his recent book *Culture and Imperialism,* Edward Said offers a definition of exile that is as true for Hindemith as for Weill, but relevant for each in differing degrees. "Exile," he says, "is predicated on the existence of, love for, and a real bond with one's native place." Said precedes this truism with what he calls a "hauntingly beautiful passage" by the twelfth-century monk Hugo of Saint Victor:

> It is a . . . source of great virtue for the practiced mind to learn, bit by bit, first
> to change about in visible and transitory things, so that afterwards it may be
> possible to leave them behind altogether. The person who finds his home-
> land sweet is still a tender beginner; he to whom every soil is as his native one
> is already strong; but he is perfect to whom the entire world is as a foreign

place. The tender soul has fixed his life on one spot in the world; the strong person has extended his love to all places; the perfect man has extinguished his.[59]

Seymour Martin Lipset has argued that "other-directedness may permit, or even demand, inner autonomy."[60] That would appear to accord with Hugo's "strong person." Meanwhile, papers like this, or indeed studies of musical émigrés generally, thrive on the fact that nobody is perfect.

NOTES

1. Adorno, "Ad vocem Hindemith: Eine Dokumentation," in *Impromptus* (Frankfurt am Main: Suhrkamp, 1970), 51–87.

2. Lucia Sziborsky has convincingly shown how much of Adorno's philosophy of music was already evident in the 1928 essay on Schubert. She has demonstrated, moreover, the close connection between the musical writings and the later antisystematic philosophical ones. See her essay "Dialektik aus dem Geist der Musik: Verborgene werkgeschichtliche Voraussetzungen der Negativen Dialektik," in Jürgen Naeher, *Die negative Dialektik Adornos* (Opladen: Leske, 1984), 90–129.

3. *Impromptus*, 87. Compare this disparaging characterization of Hindemith with Adorno's idealization of Beethoven as the "musical prototype of the revolutionary bourgeoisie" (Prototyp des revolutionären Bürgertums) in *Einleitung in die Musiksoziologie*, 2d ed. (Frankfurt am Main: Suhrkamp, [1962] 1975), 247.

4. Rudolf Stephan, "Adorno und Hindemith: Zum Verständnis einer schwierigen Beziehung," in *Adorno und die Musik*, ed. Otto Kolleritsch (Graz: Universal Edition, 1979), 180–201.

5. Ibid., 180.

6. A level-headed account of Adorno's representative role in postwar West Germany can be found in Claudia Abert, "Adorno und Eisler: Repräsentanten des Musiklebens in den beiden deutschen Staaten der Nachkriegszeit," in *Exil und Remigration*, ed. Claus-Dieter Krohn (Munich: edition text und kritik, 1991), 69–80. Abert discusses in detail how the postwar generation of academics and intellectuals emphatically identified with Adorno in their reading of his work ("emphatisch-identifikatorische Adorno-Lektüre"). She quotes Joachim Kaiser, the doyen of postwar music critics, who, like so many others, identified in particular with Adorno's *Philosophie der neuen Musik*. In this seminal book were to be found, in Kaiser's words, "the analytical utensils [*Besteck*]" for diagnosing "that which was inadequate or neoclassical or . . . no longer permitted by the world spirit" (74).

7. Adorno's first substantial publication on Weill was his 1928 review of the two one-act operas *Der Protagonist* and *Der Zar läßt sich photographieren*, in *Die Musik* 20 (1927–28); reprinted in Theodor W. Adorno, *Gesammelte Schriften*, 20 vols. (Frankfurt am Main: Suhrkamp, 1979–86), 19:133–36. He was especially impressed by *Der Zar*: "It legitimates itself fully, here and today. Put it together with Stravinsky's *Soldier* [*L'histoire du soldat*] or with *Renard*, and it will reveal its true face: a fact than can have a disturbing effect."

8. For a discussion of Weill in Adorno's "Zur gesellschaftlichen Lage der Mu-

sik," see my essay "Neue Sachlichkeit, Surrealism, and Gebrauchsmusik," in *A New Orpheus: Essays on Kurt Weill,* ed. Kim H. Kowalke (New Haven: Yale University Press, 1986), 61–82. I have dealt with Adorno's reading of *Die Dreigroschenoper* in "Misunderstanding *The Threepenny Opera,*" in *The Threepenny Opera,* ed. Stephen Hinton (Cambridge: Cambridge University Press, 1990), 181–92. Extensive reference to Adorno's attitudes toward Weill is also made in the following publications: David Drew, "Kurt Weill and His Critics," *Times Literary Supplement,* 3 and 10 Oct. 1975, 1142–44 and 1198–1200; Drew, "Reflections on the Last Years: *Der Kuhhandel* as a Key Work," in Kowalke, ed., *New Orpheus,* 217–67; Kim Kowalke, "Kurt Weill, Modernism, and Popular Culture: *Öffentlichkeit als Stil,*" *Modernism/Modernity* 2 (1995): 27–69; and Hinton, "Fragwürdiges in der deutschen Rezeption," in *A Stranger Here Myself: Kurt Weill Studien,* ed. Horst Edler and Kim Kowalke (Hildesheim: Georg Olms, 1993), 23–33.

9. Adorno, "Kurt Weill: Musiker des epischen Theaters," reprinted in *Gesammelte Schriften,* 18:544–47.

10. Adorno reiterates his critique of the *Musikregisseur* in the penultimate chapter of his *Einleitung in die Musiksoziologie* (228–29). In addition, he coins here the synonym "Manager-Komponist," of which Weill again serves as his "prototype" (289).

11. David Drew, "Weill, Kurt," in *New Grove Dictionary of Music and Musicians,* ed. Stanley Sadie, vol. 20 (New York: Grove, 1980), 300–310.

12. David Drew, "Musical Theatre in the Weimar Republic," *Proceedings of the Royal Musical Association* 88 (1961–1962): 89–108.

13. Apart from the work itself, one of the few documents pertaining directly to the process of collaboration is an interview with Weill published as "Keine Differenz Weill-Hindemith" in the Berlin journal *Filmkurier* (8 Aug. 1929); reprinted in Kurt Weill, *Musik und Theater: Gesammelte Schriften,* ed. Stephen Hinton and Jürgen Schebera (Berlin: Henschel, 1990), 303–4. An unsubstantiated rumor had been circulating that Hindemith had forbidden any further performances after the successful 1929 premiere in Baden-Baden. Weill responded as follows: "There is no conflict whatsoever between Hindemith and me. Together Brecht and I wrote *Der Lindberghflug* in the autumn of last year, with my having already sketched the music when the work was first published in a journal [*Uhu* 5 (1929)]. . . . Hindemith took over the composition of the elements and the words about America, and I the part in which Germany speaks. We both viewed this Baden-Baden version merely as an interesting, one-off experiment created for a particular purpose. We were quite aware that no artistic unity could emerge, given our different natures. The work indeed revealed a great divergence, which—and that was part of the purpose—was interesting to observe."

14. Beeke Sell Tower, *Envisioning America: Prints, Drawings, and Photographs by George Grosz and His Contemporaries, 1915–1933* (Cambridge, Mass.: Busch-Reisinger Museum, Harvard University, 1990).

15. Two recent studies by J. Bradford Robinson have shed considerable light on the German conception of jazz peculiar to the Weimar Republic: "Jazz Reception in Weimar Germany: In Search of a Shimmy Figure," in *Music and Performance in the Weimar Republic,* ed. Bryan Gilliam (Cambridge: Cambridge University Press, 1994), 107–34; and "The Jazz Essays of Theodor Adorno: Some Thoughts on Jazz Reception in Weimar Germany," *Popular Music* 13 (1994): 1–25.

16. Weill, "Vorwort zum Regiebuch der Oper *Aufstieg und Fall der Stadt Maha-gonny*," *Gesammelte Schriften*, 77–79.

17. Hindemith's publisher Schott wrote to him proposing a new version of *The Beggar's Opera* on 28 January 1925: "The way you drew the fox-trot of your Kammer-musik No. 1 into the sphere of serious music would be the right thing in this case: refined popular music or a caricature thereof, at the same time a satire of the sort of modern opera music composed by d'Albert" (see Hinton, ed., *Threepenny Opera*, 16). Hindemith, it would appear, never responded.

18. Weill, "Notiz zum Berliner Requiem," *Der Deutsche Rundfunk* 7 (1929); reprinted in *Gesammelte Schriften*, 289–91.

19. Writing in 1927, Weill singled out Hindemith (along with Ludwig Weber) as one of a number of musicians within the youth movement (*Jugendbewegung*) who were attempting "directly to attract a public for understanding and cultivating new music." Approving in principle, Weill nonetheless wondered "whether this youth movement is not too restricted to certain circles of the population really to create the basis of a rejuvenation of musical culture or even of forming a people's art [*Volks-kunst*]" (Weill, "Verschiebungen in der musikalischen Produktion," *Berliner Tageblatt*, 1 Oct. 1927; reprinted in *Gesammelte Schriften*, 45–58).

20. In the introduction to his edition of the opera, Christoph Wolff has described *Cardillac* as Hindemith's "first really large-scale [*großformatige*] composition"; the reception, in Wolff's informed description, was a *succès d'estime* (*Achtungserfolg*). See Paul Hindemith, *Cardillac*, vol. 4 of *Sämtliche Werke*, ser. 1 (Mainz: B. Schott, 1979), ix–xxiii.

21. Kurt Weill to G. F. Stegmann, 14 Feb. 1949; quoted by permission of the Kurt Weill Foundation, New York.

22. See my article "Hindemith: Pedagogy and Personal Style," in *Hindemith-Jahrbuch 1988* (Mainz: B. Schott, 1989), 54–67.

23. See Giselher Schubert, "Vorgeschichte und Entstehung der *Unterweisung im Tonsatz*," in *Hindemith-Jahrbuch 1980* (Mainz: B. Schott, 1982), 16–64.

24. Reinhold Brinkmann has expounded on the late Hindemith's "sense of isolation and artistic uncertainty," even "melancholy"; see Brinkmann's article "Über Paul Hindemiths Rede *Sterbende Gewässer*," in *Hindemith-Jahrbuch 1984* (Mainz: B. Schott, 1985), 71–90.

25. See my article "Großbritannien als Exilland: Der Fall Weill," in *Musik in der Emigration, 1933–1945: Verfolgung, Vertreibung, Rückwirkung*, ed. Horst Weber (Stuttgart: J. B. Metzler, 1994), 213–27.

26. Letter dated 17 July 1935 from Kurt Weill to Lotte Lenya; quoted by permission of the Kurt Weill Foundation. The opening of the original poem by Heine reads: "Denk ich an Deutschland in der Nacht,/Dann bin ich um den Schlaf gebracht."

27. For an account of the "Fall Hindemith," with particular reference to the symphony *Mathis der Maler*, see my introduction to Paul Hindemith, *Orchesterwerke 1932–34: Philharmonisches Konzert; Symphonie "Mathis der Maler*," vol. 2 of *Sämtliche Werke*, ser. 2 (Mainz: B. Schott, 1991).

28. Paul Hindemith, *Unterweisung im Tonsatz: Theoretischer Teil* (Mainz: B. Schott, 1937), 251.

29. Other revised works are *Cardillac* (1926; 2/1952), *Frau Musica* (1928; 2/1943), and *Neues vom Tage* (1929; 2/1953; 3/1960).

30. David Neumeyer, *The Music of Paul Hindemith* (New Haven: Yale University Press, 1986), esp. 137–67.

31. Paul Hindemith, *Das Marienleben* (London: B. Schott, 1948), iv.

32. Ibid., x: "Bei aller Wertschätzung, die man billig den technischen Neuerungen entgegenbringen kann, da sie uns ja die Arbeit erleichtern sollen, ist es doch angezeigt, in der Bezeichnung 'Neue Kunst' die Betonung des Wortes 'neu' zu vermindern und dafür die 'Kunst' um so mehr hervorzuheben."

33. Ibid., iv.

34. Ibid., x.

35. See Kim Kowalke, "*The Threepenny Opera* in America," in Hinton, ed., *Threepenny Opera*, 78–119. In June 1939 Weill wrote to Brecht: "It wouldn't be impossible to mount *Die Dreigroschenoper* again in America at some point. . . . One could risk it, of course, only with a completely new adaptation . . . and with one of the best Broadway producers" (quoted ibid., 90).

36. A comprehensive study of Weill's self-borrowings remains a desideratum of Weill scholarship. The borrowings, linking works otherwise quite dissimilar in style and type, are too numerous to list here. In *Kurt Weill: A Handbook* (London: Faber & Faber, 1987), David Drew has detailed thirteen borrowings from *Kingdom for a Cow* alone. *Der Silbersee* (1933) borrows from *Die Bürgschaft* (1932), and *Die sieben Todsünden* (1933) from *Der Silbersee*. But early and late works also share common material: the orchestral introduction to act 2 of *Street Scene* (1946) borrows from Weill's own theater music to Erwin Piscator's 1928 production of *Konjunktur*.

37. See Hinton, "Pedagogy and Personal Style," for a discussion of this issue.

38. Weill, "Two Dreams Come True," undated manuscript, Weill-Lenya Archive, Yale University, New Haven; reproduced, without title, on the cover to the gramophone recording of *Street Scene* (Columbia OL 4139).

39. Weill's concept of the operatic "prototype" or "Urform," with which he described his stage works of the 1920s, can be seen to hold good as a consistent model for his entire oeuvre. See my article "Zur Urform der Oper," in *Vom Kurfürstendamm zum Broadway: Kurt Weill (1900–1950)*, ed. Bernd Kortländer et al. (Düsseldorf: Droste, 1990), 40–46.

40. Virgil Thomson, "Kurt Weill," *New York Herald Tribune*, 7 Apr. 1950; reprinted in *A Virgil Thomson Reader* (Boston: Houghton Mifflin, 1981), 342–44.

41. David Riesman (in collaboration with Reuel Denney and Nathan Glazer), *The Lonely Crowd: A Study of the Changing American Character* (New Haven: Yale University Press, 1950).

42. Ibid., 15.

43. Ibid., 16.

44. Ibid., 196.

45. Ibid., 195.

46. Ibid., 22.

47. Riesman, preface to the 1961 revised edition of *The Lonely Crowd,* xxxii.

48. Drew, *Kurt Weill: A Handbook,* 3.

49. Riesman in fact posits a third type: "tradition-directed." It is redundant here,

however, insofar as he tends to restrict its applicability to less developed countries: "in India, Egypt, and China . . . for most preliterate peoples in Central Africa, parts of Central and South America, in fact most of the world relatively untouched by industrialization" (10). But it also applies to earlier historical periods in the West: "In western history the Middle Ages can be considered a period in which the majority were tradition-directed" (13). In any event, certain aspects of "tradition direction," as defined by Riesman, are clearly pertinent to Hindemith's case, especially the emphasis he placed on the *Gemeinschaft* (community) as against the *Gesellschaft* (society), a distinction also drawn by Riesman in his book (13).

50. See esp. Elisabeth Young-Bruehl, *Creative Characters* (New York: Routledge, 1991); and Seymour Martin Lipset and Leo Lowenthal, eds., *Culture and Social Character: The Work of David Riesman Reviewed* (New York: Free Press of Glencoe, 1961).

51. Quentin Bell, "Conformity and Nonconformity in the Fine Arts," in Lipset and Lowenthal, eds., *Culture and Social Character,* 399.

52. Adorno, "Das 'So kann es nicht weiter gehen' [ist] gleichsam mitkomponiert," in *Impromptus,* 82.

53. There may be, as Hindemith experienced, particularly in the 1930s, a clash between tradition and character. In defining the "inner-directed type," Riesman writes of a "psychological gyroscope": "This instrument, once it is set by the parents and other authorities, keeps the inner-directed person . . . 'on course' even when tradition, as responded to by his character, no longer dictates his moves" (*Lonely Crowd,* 16). Riesman's contrasting metaphor for the "other-directed" type is that of radar: "As against guilt-and-shame controls, though of course these survive, one prime psychological lever of the other-directed person is diffuse anxiety. This control equipment, instead of being like a gyroscope, is like radar" (ibid., 26). Another attempt to apply Riesman's model of "other direction" to the arts can be found in Helmut Lethen's book *Verhaltenslehren der Kälte: Lebensversuche zwischen den Kriegen* (Frankfurt am Main: Suhrkamp, 1994), a study of interbellum cultural shifts in Germany as reflected in literature. Lethen quotes from Helmut Schelsky's introduction to the German edition of *The Lonely Crowd* (*Die einsame Masse: Eine Untersuchung des amerikanishen Charakters* [Reinbek: Rowohlt, 1958]), in which the author shows how difficult it is for German sociologists to detach the "other-directed" type from associations with Nazi collectivisim on the one hand and bourgeois ideals on the other (297). Especially relevant to the cases of Hindemith and Weill against the background of recent *Exilforschung* is the following remark: "Thus [because of the Nazi regime] possibilities once accorded the Neue Sachlichkeit were obscured" (243).

54. Drew, "Weill, Kurt," 307.

55. Young-Bruehl, *Creative Characters,* 251.

56. Adorno's views on his status as an emigrant in particular and on the problems of intellectuals exiled from Germany in general are summarized in the lecture entitled "Fragen an die intellektuelle Emigration," which he gave to the Jewish Club of Los Angeles on 27 May 1945; published in *Gesammelte Schriften,* 20(1):352–59. The lecture concludes with four theses: "1. The thinking person in emigration should not pretend to begin a new life, but should proceed from the past life, from his entire experience, including the European catastrophe and the difficulties in his new country. . . . 2. The power of the immeasurable industrial apparatus over the indi-

vidual should not seduce us into idolizing the world in which we live and which controls us. . . . 3. We should remain unswerving in our objective work. That is to say, we should seek to express things for their own sake, without regard to ends and communication. . . . 4. We should not succumb to stupidity. We should not assume for ourselves a suspension of thought because of the pressure to translate everything that can cure us of the manic aspect of German thought, we should not rob ourselves of imagination, speculation, unrestrained insight." The theses both characterize his attitude to his own work during his American period and serve as a reminder of why he failed to appreciate Weill's position.

57. Helmut Lethen has pertinently suggested that the inner-directed prototype may ultimately serve a compensatory purpose: "Inner direction, which shines forth in such an exemplary fashion in cultural criticism, is empirically difficult to prove. That is why the nineteenth-century public devoured it so readily in novels so as to assimilate it as a compensatory yardstick. The numerous documents of the bourgeoisie stylizing itself as inner-directed subjects in bourgeois novels do not permit the automatic conclusion that inner direction ever existed. . . . We should probably assume the norm of other direction, which appears in epoch-specific variations as if human beings were guided 'from within'" (*Verhaltenslehren der Kälte*, 267).

58. The issue of terminology is a sensitive one. Hanns-Werner Heister et al., editors of the book *Musik im Exil: Folgen des Nazismus für die internationale Musikkultur* (Frankfurt am Main: Fischer Taschenbuch Verlag, 1993), argue strongly against replacing the term "exile" with that of "emigration." The latter, they contend, represents a "neutralization [*Entschärfung*] . . . a dispossession of the history and identity of those who fled abroad from the Nazis." While their objection is justified in one sense, it necessarily involves difficulties in another. The problem has to do with "exile" being an equivocal concept. "Exile" can signify both the process of enforced emigration on the one hand and, on the other, a sense of alienation and loss in the foreign culture to which the emigrant has fled. While the former sense—the historical process—is a historically undeniable fact, the latter sense—the matter of cultural identity—is hard to ascertain in individual cases. Both Weill and Brecht were exiled from Germany, but only Brecht continued to insist on his status as an exile in America (cf. Brecht's poem "Über die Bezeichnung Emigranten," from the *Svendborger Gedichte,* with the lines "Und kein Heim, ein Exil soll das Land sein" and "Aber keiner von uns / Wird hier bleiben"; originally published London: Malik-Verlag, 1939; quoted here from *Gedichte 2,* Große kommentierte Berliner und Frankfurter Ausgabe [Berlin: Aufbau, 1988], 81). In other words, applying the term "exile" with respect to cultural identity requires interpretation. As such, it has both political and aesthetic implications, which are clearly expressed in an editorial statement from the inside cover of *Musik im Exil:* "As a whole, the volume accomplishes a further act of coming to terms with a past whose consequences are still with us, and at the same time, an act of spiritual atonement, coupled with the attempt to uncover progressive traditions." The question remains to what extent national history, collective guilt, political significance, and aesthetic judgment are separate and separable. In the above volume they tend to be treated as all of a piece. Thus Heister "rescues" Weill as a "progressive" by claiming his alienation from the "ideologically dominant 'mainstream,'" and appropriates him from German history by positing a

link with the emphatic sense of "in foreign parts [*in der Fremde*]" (435). "Exile" may be the unfortunate badge of prestige in German political history. Whether it should be in music history is another matter.

59. Edward W. Said, *Culture and Imperialism* (New York: Knopf, 1993), 336, 335.

60. Seymour Martin Lipset, "A Changing American Character?" in Lipset and Lowenthal, eds., *Culture and Social Character,* 171. See also the preface to the 1961 edition of *The Lonely Crowd,* where Riesman comments on "the tendency among readers . . . to equate inner-direction with autonomy" (xxiv).

Wolpe and Black Mountain College

Anne C. Shreffler

Going into exile, an act usually undertaken out of desperate necessity, forces a person to make equally desperate adaptations. For a creative artist it can be devastating, as it was with Bartók and Zemlinsky, if age, ill health, or an inflexible personality hinder one's adaptation to the new environment. Some, on the other hand, such as Weill, Korngold, and Krenek, managed to turn massive psychic and physical disruption to creative advantage. Stefan Wolpe (1902–72) is another who played the role of exile with profound virtuosity, possibly because he had played it all his life. He was always an outsider: first a Jewish Communist in Berlin, then a German-Jewish refugee in Palestine, then one of a long stream of musically gifted immigrants to the United States. His music, although always stamped by a strong personal style, changed to reflect each environment. Wolpe was wide-ranging and omnivorous in his search for stimulation, turning not just to the art music tradition, but also to Jewish folk music, American jazz, abstract expressionist painting, and modern American literature, which influenced his music and thought alike. Unlike many other German emigrants to the United States, who saw only the conservative cultural mainstream, Wolpe profited from and contributed to an existing American avant-garde.

Born in Berlin in 1902, Wolpe was impelled by his Jewish heritage and his involvement with left-wing politics to flee Germany in 1933.[1] In Vienna during the summer of 1933 he undertook a brief but formative course of study with Anton Webern. Then Wolpe moved on to Palestine, where he taught at the Palestine Conservatory and explored Jewish folk music. Anxieties about the approaching war in Europe as well as the cool reception given his more avant-garde compositions in Palestine drove Wolpe to emigrate to the United States in 1938. Settling in New York, he taught while keeping up a steady stream of composition. His pupils from the jazz world, who included George Russell, Eddie Sauter, and Tony Scott, brought him closer to an idiom that he had admired in Berlin. At this time he became closely involved with the "New York school" painters; his friends among the abstract expressionists included Philip Guston, Franz Kline, Willem de Kooning, and Mark Rothko. Wolpe's compositional style evolved over a similarly wide spectrum: his output includes agit-prop ballads, children's pieces, music for theater, works for amateur chorus, expressionistic chamber music, as well as some of the most complex serial music of the century. But always resisting the serialist aesthetic of unity, Wolpe refused to reduce his disparate ideas into an internally consistent style.

An important but neglected chapter of Wolpe's emigration experience centers on the experimental Black Mountain College in North Carolina, where he taught from 1952 to 1956. During his time there, which resulted in a substantial reformulation of his approaches to composition and aesthetic theory, he began to develop an uncompromising late style based on volatile oppositions of extremes rather than more traditional organic development. These crucial years at Black Mountain have been virtually missing from the story of Wolpe's several exiles, which up to now has focused on New York.[2] Central to his Black Mountain experience was his interaction with his colleagues, including the leading figures of a budding postwar American avant-garde: John Cage, Merce Cunningham, David Tudor, Robert Creeley, Robert Rauschenberg, and, of greatest significance, the poet Charles Olson. Wolpe forged a strong friendship with Olson, whose ideas left indelible traces on his work and thought. I shall focus here on this interaction, drawing upon unpublished letters from Wolpe to Olson and communications from Mrs. Hilda Morley Wolpe. My goal is not to make a documentary study of Wolpe's years at Black Mountain but rather to present a kind of aesthetic history, as refracted though the works and writings of those involved. In doing so, I would like to suggest another, more positive side of Wolpe's experience in America, which has elsewhere been described as an uneasy and problematic exile.[3]

BLACK MOUNTAIN COLLEGE

A job at Black Mountain College was not like most academic appointments. Founded in 1933 by the pedagogical visionary John A. Rice, the college was conceived from the beginning as an alternative to the traditional university. Rice based his new college in rural North Carolina on the then radical idea that students should play an active role in their educations. For the twenty-three years of its existence, the college maintained its precepts of communal living, small informal classes, and focus on the individual student. There were no required courses, no grades, and no administration. All important decisions were made collectively, among students and faculty, who also collaborated in working on the farm, maintaining the buildings, and performing the day-to-day chores. Although the Black Mountain experiment was never duplicated in its entirety, many of the "radical" pedagogical policies introduced by Rice, including the teaching of methods rather than facts, the encouragement of dissent and discussion, and active participation by students in the learning process, have become widely accepted since the late 1960s.

Central to Rice's philosophy of teaching was the notion that practicing the arts is crucial to learning to think. He believed that an active confrontation with the materials and processes of art can teach students to cope with a changing world better than simply learning to absorb information. Accordingly, everyone was encouraged to participate in some artistic activity. Concerts, plays, art shows, and poetry readings took place regularly. The German-(American) artist Josef Albers, who had helped to open the college in 1933 and remained for sixteen years, played an especially influential role in developing the arts program.

From the beginning of its existence Black Mountain College became a place of refuge for emigrant artists, musicians, and intellectuals who, after fleeing Europe, often had difficulty finding positions comparable to the ones they had left. The college, which cared little about degrees, previous university experience, or proficiency in English, took on men and women they believed could contribute to the intellectual and artistic environment. Emigrants from Germany and Austria played a prominent role; during the 1940s the faculty included (in addition to Josef and Anni Albers), Max Dehn, Walter Gropius, Edward and Gretel Lowinsky, Heinrich and Johanna Jalowetz, Alfred Einstein, Frederic Cohen, Ernst Krenek, Rudolf Kolisch, Erwin Bodky, and Edward Steuermann.

In keeping with the college's goal of general arts education, the music curriculum focused more on practical music making—chorus and study of an instrument or voice—and on basic music courses than on academic subjects. The content of the offerings centered on music of the Western canon, reinforced by performances of major works by students and faculty. Topics were determined by the interests of the faculty; with the arrival of Lowinsky in 1942, study and performance of Renaissance music became frequent subjects.[4] Although Heinrich Jalowetz, who had been closely associated with the Schoenberg circle, was on the faculty, music of the twentieth century was evidently not a priority in the curriculum.[5] This is not surprising, given that the school aimed to provide a broad general education in the arts rather than specialized training.

The Black Mountain College that Wolpe and his third wife, the poet Hilda Morley, entered in the summer of 1952 was quite a different place from the better-known one of the 1940s. First, the college had just undergone a substantial shift away from a European orientation to a more American one.

After Albers's resignation in 1949 the influence of the "immigrant faction" had waned. By the spring of 1951 most of the faculty were new, and Black Mountain College became, in the words of the historian Martin Duberman, "for the first time since the days of its inception . . . a decidedly American, and a decidedly radical environment."[6] With the increasing influence of Charles Olson (who was later appointed rector to reflect his de facto leadership), the faculty became more and more dominated by practitioners— writers, composers, and artists—whom he hired as the more traditional scholars on the faculty began to leave.

When Charles Olson arrived at Black Mountain he had just begun what would become his magnum opus, the epic-length *Maximus Poems.* He had also written a critical study on Melville, entitled *Call Me Ishmael,* and a slim brochure on his poetics, *Projective Verse.*[7] This established him as a protagonist for a new kind of poetry in reaction to the dominant poetic establishment represented by Robert Lowell and T. S. Eliot and given academic respectability by the New Criticism.[8] Olson synthesized the proselike minimalism of William Carlos Williams and the radical modernism of Ezra Pound into what he called "open verse" and "composition by field." Around the magazine that Olson directed from the college, the *Black Mountain Review,* a circle of poets sympathetic to his ideas began to gather: Robert Creeley, Robert Duncan, Denise Levertov, and Cid Corman, among others, became known as "Black Mountain poets." Olson made Black Mountain College in its declining last years into a center for experimental literature in America. Although Olson's poetry is more uneven in quality than that of his two main predecessors, Williams and Pound, as the acknowledged heir of the Poundian tradition he was a central figure in postwar American poetry.[9]

Olson viewed his role as more than just that of poet and teacher. His mission encompassed a complete rewriting of history, in order to enable modern man to connect with the elemental life force that he believed had been circumscribed by rational thinking since the ancient Greeks. History is not, he wrote, "events of the past," "fate or destiny," or even what the media mindlessly records day-to-day. Rather, "history is the intensity of the life process—its *life value.*"[10] Olson believed that music could provide a key to this ur-irrational state. After hearing David Tudor perform Boulez's Second Sonata in 1951, Olson became fascinated with new music and serial structures. Boulez he saw as a kindred spirit, an iconoclast who exploded existing conventions. In characteristically colorful (and highly gendered) language, Olson expressed his enthusiasm to the poet Robert Creeley: "Christ, does he come straight from himself, compose as a man, with none of the shit of 'music,' or experiment."[11] He urged Creeley to find Boulez in Paris and invite him to Black Mountain to replace the current composer-in-residence, Lou Harrison, who had received a Guggenheim grant for the following year. Apparently unable to get Boulez, Olson then wrote to Wolpe, probably also on Tudor's recommendation.

Wolpe first joined the college as a guest artist during the summer session of 1952, an "arts session" which featured a large invited faculty. Tudor gave several recitals that summer, presenting music of Boulez, Cage, Feldman, and Wolpe (the difficult, serial Passacaglia from the *Four Studies on Basic Rows*). Cage and Cunningham were also there, and raised eyebrows with their staging of what later became known as the first "happening." Many of the people commonly associated with Black Mountain during these years, most notably Cage, Cunningham, and Tudor, were in residence *only* during the summer. An idea of the energies that steered the school can be gained from the program of the next and final summer session in 1953:[12]

Artists in this series:

IRMA WOLPE, Pianist
RUDOLPH BENETSKY, Pianist
Assistant Director of Music at Drexel University, Philadelphia
DAVID TUDOR, Pianist
ALICE BURNETT, Soprano
JOSEF MARX, Oboist
ABRAHAM MISHKIND, Violinist
member of the Pittsburgh Symphony
STEFAN WOLPE, Composer
Director of Music at Black Mountain College
CHARLES OLSON, Writer in Residence, Black Mountain College
MERCE CUNNINGHAM AND COMPANY
HANS RADEMACHER, Professor of Mathematics, at the University of Pennsylvania

JULY 25: *Piano Concert* Irma Wolpe

Bagatellen Op. 126	Beethoven
Sonata Op. 31 No. 3	Beethoven
5 Pieces for Piano Op. 23	Schoenberg
Toccata	Wolpe
Gaspard be [*sic*] la Nuit	Ravel

AUGUST 2: *Lecture* Stefan Wolpe
   A Lesson on Elements of Composition

AUGUST 9: *Reading* Charles Olson
   The Maximus Poems 1–10 read by their author

AUGUST 14: *Lecture* Stefan Wolpe
   Report on my Composing

AUGUST 21: *Program of Dances* by Merce Cunningham
   and Company; also student dances

AUGUST 26: *Lecture and performance*
   "7 Pieces for 3 Pianos" by Stefan Wolpe
   Distances, Proportions, and Space in Music

AUGUST 29: *Oboe Concert* Josef Marx, Irma Wolpe

Trio Sonata from the Musical Offering for Oboe, Violin, and Piano	Bach
Trio Sonata for Oboe, Violin, and Piano	Handel
Sonata for Oboe and Piano	Wolpe
Sonata for Oboe and Piano	Vivaldi

When Wolpe became director of music in the fall, he was one of the (literally) handful of faculty in residence year around. As the only music teacher he was responsible for basic courses like harmony, ear training, counterpoint, and analysis and composition.[13] Virtually all the musical activities at the college fell under his supervision. For a production of Brecht's *The Good Woman of Setzuan*, Wolpe not only wrote new music for the play (as the theater director had decided not to use Kurt Weill's), he also performed it and coached the singers.[14] Other theater music that Wolpe produced at Black Mountain included music for Robert Duncan's *Faust Foutu*, Ibsen's *Peer Gynt*, and Pound's translation of *Women of Trachis*.

When the summer sessions were over and the high-profile visitors had dispersed, Wolpe and the half-dozen other faculty settled down to a job in a place that by that time resembled a commune more than an institution of higher learning. By the early 1950s the college's financial situation was quite precarious. Buildings were being sold off one by one; faculty salaries were reduced, then stopped altogether. Student enrollment dropped into the low double digits; by 1954 there were only nine students.[15] During the winter of 1954–55, the community experienced real poverty; since there was not enough money to buy coal for the furnaces, they decided to suspend classes until spring.[16] Only about eight people, including Olson, Wolpe, and their families, stayed on.[17] Morale was often very low. According to Robert Creeley, Wolpe once remarked in disgust that "in Switzerland we used to have parties and everybody used to sit around on lovely iron chairs and people came to serve us beautiful things to eat, and look at us now, we're on the garbage heap of the world."[18]

It is difficult to imagine working under such conditions. Yet work they did, very productively, and often happily. Duberman suggests that the very lack of structure facilitated intellectual exchange: "'Any place you went, day or night,' as one resident put it, 'there were always people arguing and talking. . . . All kinds of people with completely different, associated interests and fields.'"[19] Moreover, the same hardships that had restricted teaching had provided that rarest of commodities: time, in abundance. Friendships forged in this environment of isolation and interdependence were all the more intense. Wolpe would have had daily contact with Olson in particular. When they met, the two had apparently "hit it off immediately";[20] one observer described the summer of 1953 as "a marathon of 'esoteric incomprehensible conversations' with Wolpe and Olson each trying to out-talk the other."[21] Wolpe's letters to Olson from the late 1950s show the strength of this friendship.[22] In one letter Wolpe reminisces about their nonstop conversations; like many of his letters, this one is written in the form of a poem:

> Of course I [miss] our rest (tangential)
> often, often frontal
> depth of speaking to each other
> especially when both of us felt
> lonely in the wilderniss of so much
> unforgotten
> unredeemable B.M.C. Bliss[.][23]

These letters also document another side of Wolpe's Black Mountain experience, for in spite of the hardship, he was finally able to devote himself fully to his work. He wrote to Olson in 1957: "Alltogether—I feel I have come to an end of a circle of works of which most of them were written in Black Mountain and I wished BMC stood there forever ever and my longing for it sits deep and I hold with a smiling eye the place in my hand."[24] One could dismiss these remarks as sentimental nostalgia (claiming, for example, that he just didn't remember the cold and the hunger), but that would overlook the real contribution that his Black Mountain experience had given him: space and time to produce a series of major works, and the constant intellectual stimulation of people who were responsive to his ideas.

WOLPE'S VOLATILE OPPOSITIONS AND OLSON'S PROJECTIVE VERSE

During four years at the college, Wolpe achieved what he considered to be a compositional breakthrough. In addition to the two major works composed in recent years—the Violin Sonata (1949) and the Quartet for Trumpet, Tenor Saxophone, Percussion, and Piano (1950)—before coming to Black Mountain he had also produced a series of studies (table 3). In these works he sought nothing less than a rethinking of his entire musical technique. After his studies with Webern, Wolpe had adopted the principles of serialism, but with typical Wolpean maximalism had expanded these principles immediately into a multilayered, essentially three-dimensional conception (best exemplified by his Passacaglia of 1936). During the 1940s he aimed to achieve the greatest possible variety by exploring the properties of interval complexes, different registral dispositions of chords, and "the creation of a non-motivic continuum of highly contrasted . . . basic shapes."[25]

While at Black Mountain, Wolpe produced four large-scale pieces and a thorough revision of his quartet, in which he was able to bring together the compositional and theoretical insights he had achieved in the studies. In

TABLE 3   Stefan Wolpe's Compositions:
The Black Mountain Works and Related Studies

Studies, 1944–51

Music for Any Instruments (1944–48) [11 pieces]
Piano Studies (1946–49)
Two Studies for Piano, Part II (1948)
Set of Three Movements for Two Pianos and Six Hands (1949)
Twelve Pieces for String Quartet (1950)
Seven Pieces for Three Pianos (1951)

Major works begun, composed, or revised at Black Mountain College, 1952–56

Enactments for Three Pianos *(1953; based on Seven Pieces for Three Pianos)*

1. Chant
2. In a state of flight
3. Held in
4. Inception
5. Fugal motions

Quartet for Trumpet, Tenor Saxophone, Percussion and Piano (1950, rev. 1954)
Piece for Oboe, Cello, Percussion, and Piano (1954–55)

1. Early morning music
2. Calm
3. Intense and spirited
4. Taut; to oneself

Symphony (1955–56)

1. Not too slow
2. Charged
3. Alive

Quintet with Voice (1956–57)

1. Of festive grace
2. Here the sun violet (text by Hilda Morley)
3.   Variations

Incidental music and smaller pieces composed at Black Mountain College

Incidental music for *The Good Woman of Setzuan* (Brecht), *Faust Foutu* (Robert Duncan), *Peer Gynt* (Ibsen), *Women of Trachis* (trans. Ezra Pound)
Three Pieces for Mixed Chorus
"To Hilda, a Little Song of Confidence"
"David's Lament over Jonathan" (published in *Six Songs from the Hebrew*)

Enactments for Three Pianos, his Oboe Quartet, his Symphony, and the Quintet with Voice, there is a perceptible change in technique and aesthetic orientation. Between the Violin Sonata of 1949 and *Enactments,* Wolpe moved away from a linear, progressive mode of presentation to a multilayered, simultaneous one. What in the Violin Sonata are heard as successive, continuously developing events, in *Enactments* become fractured, explosively juxtaposed sonorities. The primary feature of the latter piece, suggested by its title, is its sense of motion. "Enactments," Wolpe wrote, "doesn't mean anything else but acting out, being in an act of, being the act itself."[26] In *Enactments,* contrasting music is juxtaposed and layered; the opposites—stasis and motion, singleness and multiplicity, expectedness and surprise—are combined.

Wolpe developed the musical techniques in the five-movement, thirty-minute-long *Enactments* from the shorter Seven Pieces for Three Pianos, composed as examples for a lecture he gave in 1951. He wrote in 1952: "I am busy till my neck [aches] with writing—writing the music which I started to write in 'Seven Pieces for Three Pianos' . . . only doing it on a much vaster and bolder scale. What intrigues me so thoroughly is to integrate a vast number of *different organic modes,* existing simultaneously under different conditions of age, time, function, and substance."[27] Wolpe's "organic mode" is a musical event that evokes its own space, properties of motion, and relation to the outside or psychological world. In a lecture from 1959, "Thinking Twice," he describes the fourth mode: "(4) A certain organic mode may exist . . . in ever-expanding trajectory curves, or in double, triple, or multiple curves that are clearly regulated. For example, two may move up a small distance, while one moves down a large distance and another moves forward and backward."[28]

So far Wolpe uses terms that can be easily applied to music: lines that ascend or descend by intervals of varying sizes, which can be deployed in retrograde or inversion. A page from the first movement of *Enactments* exemplifies the organic mode just described (example 7). The "ever-expanding trajectory curves" are heard in the continuous line in eighth notes that runs through the movement (here Wolpe has literally drawn the "curves" with his wide-ranging slur marks, as seen especially in the second system). In a piece of music, as opposed to a study, of course, different modes are combined. Here the melodic line is punctuated by widely spaced chords and faster thirty-second-note figures.

For each organic mode, Wolpe describes the musical phenomena also in terms of the "extramusical" features they embody (this continues the previous quotation): "As an organic, structural phenomenon it [the organic mode] signifies an interplay of curves, a simultaneous release of impulses. As a pictorial sensation it is birds' flight, movement of waves. As an expressive sensation it is extension on all sides, giving and being given."[29]

Example 7: Wolpe, *Enactments for 3 Pianos,* 4 (Peermusic New York-Hamburg. Used by permission.)

In discussing each of the six organic modes, Wolpe provides description in four different metaphor systems: he describes first a musical aspect, followed in turn by an organic (or structural) aspect, a pictorial sensation, and an expressive sensation. This is a broad, ambitious vision of musical technique. Each musical gesture evokes not only a particular sonic realization, but also certain properties of motion, visual images, and psychological, even bodily effects. The titles of the five movements in *Enactments*—"Chant," "In a State of Flight," "Held In," "Inception," and "Fugal Motions"—are therefore not to be seen as programmatic in any loose illustrative sense, but rather as evocations of specific musical and physical characteristics. Rejecting the obsession with musical raw materials that dominated composition of the 1950s and 1960s, Wolpe sought instead to work with metaphors of music's motion, energy, and direction.

Many of Wolpe's ideas resonated with, and were quite possibly inspired by, Olson's theories of "projective verse." Olson's primary aim in writing the polemic *Projective Verse* in 1950 was to revive poetry's ancient role as public, spoken, and active. Consider the first page:[30]

PROJECTIVE   VERSE

(projectile   (percussive   (prospective

vs.

The NON-Projective

(or what a French critic calls "closed" verse, that verse which print bred and which is pretty much what we have had, in English & American, and have still got, despite the work of Pound & Williams:

it led Keats, already a hundred years ago, to see it [Wordsworth's, Milton's] in the light of "the Egotistical Sublime"; and it persists, at this latter day, as what you might call the private-soul-at-any-public-wall)

Verse now, 1950, if it is to go ahead, if it is to be of essential use, must, I take it, catch up and put into itself certain laws and possibilities of the breath, of the breathing of the man who writes as well as of his listenings. (The revolution of the ear, 1910, the trochee's heave, asks it of the younger poets.)

I want to do two things: first, try to show what projective or OPEN verse is, what it involves, in its act of composition, how, in distinction from the non-projective, it is accomplished; and II, suggest a few ideas about what stance toward reality brings such verse into being, what that stance does, both to poet and to his reader. (The stance involves, for example, a change beyond, and larger than, the technical, and may, the way things look, lead to new poetics and to new concepts from which some sort of drama, say, or of epic, perhaps, may emerge.)

The immediacy of projective verse is in opposition to the "non-projective," in Olson's words, "that verse which print bred . . . and it persists, at this latter day, as what you might call the private-soul-at-any-public-wall." To Olson,

poetry was born of the breath, not the printed word; the basic units of poetry then become the syllable and the line. Conventional forms of poetry are
therefore irrelevant; his model of projective, or open, verse rejected larger
units such as the stanza, quatrain, metrical pattern, or refrain. To replace previous print-oriented forms, Olson proposed a concept called "composition
by field." This is poetry made up of syllables, and by extension, lines, which
are combined according to three principles:

(1) Energy, or what Olson called "the *kinetics* of the thing." "A poem is
energy," Olson wrote, "transferred from where the poet got it . . . by way of
the poem itself to, all the way over to, the reader." He also called this kinetic energy in a poem the "push."

(2) In the absence of conventional poetic forms, form is determined by
content, or as Olson puts it, "FORM IS NEVER MORE THAN AN EXTENSION
OF CONTENT." This notion, rather commonplace in itself, has to be seen
in the context of what Olson called "objectism" (derived from the "objec-
tivist" poets of the 1930s): "Objectism is the getting rid of the lyrical interference of the individual as ego, of the 'subject' and his soul, that peculiar presumption by which western man has interposed himself between
what he is as a creature of nature . . . and those other creations of nature
which we may, with no derogation, call objects." The poet therefore creates
shapes out of words, and through their energy these "shapes will make their
own way."

(3) The third feature of "composition by field," related to the first two,
is process. As Olson puts it, "ONE PERCEPTION MUST IMMEDIATELY AND DI-
RECTLY LEAD TO A FURTHER PERCEPTION." He explains (and his wording il-
lustrates the point as well): "It means exactly what it says, is a matter of, at
all points . . . get on with it, keep moving, keep in, speed, the nerves, their
speed, the perceptions, theirs, the acts, the split second acts, the whole business, keep it moving as fast as you can, citizen."

Olson's concept of projective verse and its three concomitants—verse as
a transference and release of energy, form as an extension of content, and
verse as process—intersect in many ways with Wolpe's notions about musical composition. Fundamental to Wolpe's aesthetic is the idea of kinetic musical shapes. Each of his "organic modes," for example, describes a state of
energy, either moving in a single direction, in multiple directions, in a con-
stricted and narrow area, or completely immobile. As we saw earlier, these
notions are not limited to musical technique, but also describe pictorial,
expressive, and physical sensations.[31] Like Olson's "composition by field,"
Wolpe's "organic modes" cannot be reduced to a single set of attributes;
rather, they describe a locus of possibilities.

Wolpe's concern with music as kinetic shapes is also reflected in his titles: "In a State of Flight"; "Held In"; "Charged"; "Taut; to oneself." The
most Olsonian title of all, though, is *Enactments*. In *Projective Verse,* Olson de-

scribed poetry in just these terms, referring to "the act of the poem" and "the acting-on-you of the poem."[32] Wolpe seemed to have associated this piece particularly with Olson. In a letter from 1959, Wolpe wrote to him:

> I missed most intensely your presence at a last concert of mine where my Oboe quartet (the one for Oboe Cello Percussion and Piano) and 3 movements of my "Enactments" for 3 Pianos were played. . . . You would have understood it[:] its vast torsos, its rumblings[,] its simultaneous extensions of opposites, of approaches, of meddlings, of interfering opposites, you would have liked it (as there is nothing like it among the stuff I have written). If you come to New York I will play the records for you![33]

In this piece, Wolpe inscribed a universe as encompassing as Olson's; *Enactments* describes, he wrote, "Grand Chant, Stones Sing, flowers, throats, the chlorophyll, the dead leaves, the traces, the history with chemical reactions, the pulses of cells, of what is in the making and in the changing phase."[34]

Projective verse echoes in Wolpe's typically poetic language as well, as the above quotation shows. In its energy ("push"), rhythm, and most of all its aural immediacy, his speech about music goes far beyond conventional musical analogies and weaves an Olsonian tangle of vocabularies and metaphor systems. This was not simply a case of a composer adopting a congenial poetic model to describe his compositions, however. For Wolpe, who was as gifted verbally as he was musically (and this was as true in his adopted languages as in his native German), words and music come from the same creative impulse.[35] Writing, speech, song, and composition merge into a seamless continuum, each sharing aspects of the others. In introducing his Quartet for trumpet, saxophone, percussion, and piano to an audience at Darmstadt, he drew upon the metaphor of composition as speech:

> Manchesmal wird man selber unter seine eigene Sprache greifen[;] man fängt an zu singen und fängt an, sich durch seine eigenen Konsonanten und Vokale hindurchzubeißen, man hat das Gefühl, man faltet die Zungen aller Völker in seiner eigenen Zunge zusammen.[36]

As Wolpe read this passage aloud, he enacted the musical events he spoke of in his lively rhythmic speech that verged on chanting. His words themselves illustrate the "biting into" consonants and vowels, the concrete speech act whose motion and energy reflects that of his music.[37] Wolpe's lecturing style always made a big impression on his audiences; Cage once presented Wolpe with a volume of Ezra Pound, inscribed with a dedication to Wolpe's mastery of speech.[38]

The impact of Olson's theories on Wolpe's thinking should not be reduced to a simple transfer of ideas. In describing connections between mutually sympathetic and creative people, one must speak of interactions rather than influences, since much of what Olson and Wolpe had in common they probably shared before they ever met; moreover, both were formidably strong personalities who were known to be less than malleable. For Wolpe, the idea of art as enactment or motion is also fundamental to the abstract expressionist painters, as it was to the jazz musicians he knew. Edgard Varèse's notion of colliding sound masses comes to mind as well (and Wolpe acknowledges Varèse with the dedication to the Seven Pieces for Three Pianos). In this context, Olson's ideas would have been all the more welcome to Wolpe: *Projective Verse* provided him, in succinct form, with a theoretical distillation of ideas to which he had long been sympathetic.

WOLPE'S LETTERS TO OLSON: DOCUMENTS OF AN EXILE

After his four years at Black Mountain College, Wolpe returned to Europe in 1956 for the first time in over twenty years, traveling on a Fulbright fellowship to Israel and Germany, where he presented "On New (and Not-So-New) Music in America," the first of a series of lectures at the Internationale Ferienkurse für neue Musik in Darmstadt. During the next few years Wolpe, who had taken U.S. citizenship in 1945, seriously considered returning to Germany, but he was unable to find a position there.[39] As Martin Zenck has described, Wolpe hoped remigration would allow him to resolve a split, or doubleness, in his psyche, expressed in a 1959 letter to the director of the Darmstadt summer courses: "Ach, ich halte es manchmal einfach nicht länger aus, sprachberaubt zu leben, in einer dauernden Doppelheit der Zunge und des physischen Sitzes der Sprache."[40]

In his letters to Olson we get a rather different picture. For eight years Wolpe kept in touch with Olson, writing long and detailed letters that document his impressions of his travels, his job, and his composition.[41] The opening of his first letter to "Charles, there on lovely, nonforgotten grounds," in a gesture toward the recipient, is pure projective verse: "Slowly I come back to my self, having stopped for a while traveling, galloping around, sight-, Picture-, friends-seeing sighing consuming wondering languageing French Italian Dutch Hebrew."

Writing from Berlin in 1956 to Olson at Black Mountain, Wolpe expressed a sense of acute displacement at being in Germany again. First and most palpable was the shock of seeing Berlin again after the war:

> So much is destroyed here and there are wide stretches where I don't recognize anything. My friends are exiled, dead, shot, [gone]. . . . I visited all the houses I spent my childhood in and the years til I was 18. These houses stood there, battered and s[m]ashed. What to do with those years with all those years?! Some of my surviving friends (those is the West Sector) got ashen, old and closer to death.

Coupled with the distress of reencountering his battered homeland is a sense of estrangement: "And now between the Germans! I feel katapulted from most intimate zones to strange shores! . . . Here (among those suspected strangers) history is felt concretely and inside the flesh."[42] In another letter he concludes, "The Germans are a strange people."[43]

He describes his love for Rome and Spain; "Of all Places *really* only Rome corresponds to my (organic) Self ";[44] and "How deeply I love Spain. Its the second time we return to this Island which is like Islands in Greece and with a light and a weather of eye-depth, touch-depth and a sea which needs to be described in new terms of expectancies and analysis and a people of a marvellous fierce gracefulness and a language of firm vowels and teethy consonants and the steps of downwardly strong and stressed endings."[45]

Wolpe writes repeatedly of his fond memories of Black Mountain and asks about its future. In a dream, he even imagined that it would be revitalized: "How is B.M.C.? Today I dreamed you sent me a telegram to rejoin the place. It has 160 pupils and 30 music students."[46]

Much of Wolpe's nostalgia for Black Mountain College stemmed from his current precarious professional and financial position. His desperation and his reluctance to return to his job at the undistinguished C. W. Post College run through the letters to Olson like a leitmotiv: "I loathe to be at Post College. But what to do? With money gone and a nervous state of mind ahead of me. I hate that sort of reality and the mediocre temperaments and the dayly decisions. I hate to toughen my mind and deprive myself of a *state of improvisation* (or poetry) in which I exist best to do what I plan."[47] After three years of a grinding and unsatisfying teaching schedule, Wolpe's frustration grew unbearable:

> That part (with the third year starting in September) is as senseless and foul as only those can imagine who are coupled up with the keepers of cultural joints so dull and treacherous and self arrogating as human things like being are this side of empty exists . . .
> It cuts my lifetime
> I don't get enough paid
> I have to have private pupils
> It slices me it slices the slice of me.
> I want to stay here [Spain]: say is there some money coming from BMC this year, perhaps enough I can live on 1 or 2 years and do nothing but composing. Let me know.[48]

These are poignant documents of an exile. Although their themes of displacement, financial hardship, and ill health are consistent with the experiences of many other emigrants, they show Wolpe's unusual openness to his environment and his extraordinary powers of perception. His poetic use of the English language shows that he could not have meant "sprachberaubt zu leben," not in a literal sense at least. In these letters to Olson, Wolpe articulates the massive changes that had taken place both in the land he fled and in himself. They show how the complex reactions of someone in exile are inevitably colored by circumstances, interlocutor, and physical location. His sympathy for his adopted country perhaps awakened by travel and by the act of writing to his American friend, Wolpe reveals at the same time the permanent sense of displacement that the exile experiences, regardless of where he is.

Wolpe's years at Black Mountain were a crucial part of his immigration experience. They provided him with something almost totally absent from American society during the 1950s: a place where artistic experimentation was encouraged. Far from the McCarthyite spotlight, which would have singled out a person with Wolpe's political views unmercifully, he was able to devote himself to work that would bring him to a new stage of development. But Black Mountain College was not just a rustic refuge; gathered there were the central figures of a vital American avant-garde, who saw the interaction of poetry, music, art, dance, and media as the key to a future postmodern art.

Although Wolpe—ever the individualist—did not "join" either the Cage or the Olson circles, he perceived and grappled with the challenges they posed. Out of this encounter came the complex post-serial late style that was so influential for the next generations of American musicians, particularly on the East Coast. This influence was both personal and musical. Wolpe's New York apartment, Cage related, was "the true center of New York," a meeting place for composers, performers, and artists.[49] Through regular performances of his music by New Music ensembles primarily in New York, Wolpe's reputation there became greater than it had been (or still is) in Europe.[50] His unorthodox yet uncompromising music offered an alternative to the prevailing academic serial style.[51] But it was in teaching that Wolpe made his most direct contribution to American culture. Although his resistance to an official serialism probably contributed to his inability to find a good university position, he attracted many students anyway, perhaps because of his outsider status. The legacy of these students, who included Morton Feldman, Leonard Meyer, Herbert Brün, Ralph Shapey, and George Russell—reflecting a diversity that shows how little Wolpe was interested in founding a "school" in his own image—transformed Wolpe from an exile to a force in contemporary music in America that continues today.

NOTES

1. Biographical information from Austin Clarkson, "Wolpe, Stefan," in *The New Grove Dictionary of American Music*, ed. H. Wiley Hitchcock and Stanley Sadie (New York: Grove, 1986), 4:548–49.

2. See part 6: "New York—Landschaft des Exils," in *Stefan Wolpe: Von Berlin nach New York, 14., 15., und 16. September 1988. Sechs Konzerte in der Musikhochschule Köln,* ed. Harry Vogt, Renate Liesmann-Gümmer, and Rainer Peters (Cologne: Westdeutscher Rundfunk, 1988), 118–47.

3. Martin Zenck, "' . . . In einer dauernden Doppelheit der Zunge': Zum Exilwerk des Komponisten Stefan Wolpe," in Vogt, Liesmann-Gümmer, and Peters, eds., *Stefan Wolpe,* 21–36.

4. Anna Margaret Hines, "Music at Black Mountain College: A Study of Experimental Ideas in Music" (D.M.A. thesis, University of Missouri–Kansas City, 1974), 115.

5. Programs reproduced in Hines, "Music at Black Mountain College," show a preponderance of canonical classical music. Jalowetz did apparently teach a course called "Viennese School in Music" (Hines, "Music," 124), but it is not clear whether this concerned the first or the second "Viennese School."

6. Martin B. Duberman, *Black Mountain: An Exploration in Community* (New York: W. W. Norton, 1993), 341.

7. Charles Olson, *The Maximus Poems* (New York: Jargon/Corinth Books, 1960); Olson, *Call Me Ishmael* (New York: Reynal & Hitchcock, 1947); Olson, *Projective Verse* (New York: Tubern Press, 1959).

8. Mary Emma Harris, *The Arts at Black Mountain College* (Cambridge, Mass.: MIT Press, 1987), 196.

9. For evaluations of Olson's life and work, see Robert von Hallberg, *Charles Olson: The Scholar's Art* (Cambridge, Mass.: Harvard University Press, 1978); and Tom Clark, *Charles Olson: The Allegory of a Poet's Life* (New York: W. W. Norton, 1991).

10. Charles Olson, "A Special View of History," in *Human Universe and Other Essays,* ed. Donald Allen (San Francisco: Auerhahn Society, 1965).

11. George F. Butterick, ed., *Charles Olson and Robert Creeley: The Complete Correspondence,* vol. 7 (Santa Barbara, Calif.: Black Sparrow Press, 1987), 111.

12. Charles Olson Papers, Thomas J. Dodd Research Center, University of Connecticut Libraries.

13. Based on student report cards in the Black Mountain Archives, Thomas J. Dodd Research Center, University of Connecticut Libraries, Storrs.

14. See Fielding Dawson's account, "How Stefan Got Me to Sing," in *The Black Mountain Book* (Rocky Mount: North Carolina Wesleyan College Press), 34–36.

15. Duberman, *Black Mountain,* 430.

16. Ibid., 426.

17. These difficult conditions took their toll on Wolpe, who in the winter of 1955 wrote to Steinecke at Darmstadt inquiring about the possibility of giving lectures there (cited in Zenck, "Zum Exilwerk des Komponisten Stefan Wolpe," 26).

18. Introduction to Olson, "Special View of History," 2.

19. Duberman, *Black Mountain,* 432.

20. Ibid., 366.

21. Harris, *Arts at Black Mountain College,* 238.

22. There are nine letters, dated between 1956 and 1964, from Wolpe to Olson in the Charles Olson Papers, Thomas J. Dodd Research Center, University of Connecticut Libraries, Storrs. I have preserved Wolpe's idiosyncratic spelling, punctuation, and capitalization. Cited with permission.

23. Wolpe to Olson, 1 Nov. 1958.

24. Wolpe to Olson, 2 May 1957.

25. Austin Clarkson, *Stefan Wolpe: A Brief Catalogue of Published Works* (Islington, Ont: Sound Way Press, 1981), 9.

26. Letter cited in Clarkson, liner notes accompanying 1984 recording of *Enactments* (Nonesuch 78024).

27. Letter cited in Clarkson, preface to score to Seven Pieces for Three Pianos (New York: Southern Music, 1981).

28. Wolpe, "Thinking Twice," in *Contemporary Composers on Contemporary Music,* ed. Elliott Schwartz and Barney Childs (New York: Da Capo Press, 1978), 304–5.

29. Ibid.

30. The following quotations from *Projective Verse* are from Charles Olson, *Selected Writings,* ed. Robert Creeley (New York: New Directions, 1966), 15–26. Used with permission.

31. In Wolpe's words, "certain modes disintegrate and fragment; certain modes are polymorphic; certain others alternate with noises and jump off their pitch rails. . . . While one part of the mode . . . is speaking the language of its contemporary tongue, the other part resets the material for quotational language; one mode is strict, ceremoniously strict, the other set has no order, is willful, anarchic and ill" ("Thinking Twice," 305–6).

32. That the word "enactment" itself was associated with Olson is suggested by the chapter title for the section on Olson, "Art as Enactment," in Harris, *Arts at Black Mountain College.*

33. Wolpe to Olson, 22 July 1959.

34. Quoted in Harris, *Arts at Black Mountain College,* 206.

35. As Austin Clarkson points out with respect to Wolpe, "The composer's music and his theory of music have joint custody of his creativity. . . . They must be taken together in order to formulate the composer's paradigm of musical meaning" ("'The Fantasy Can Be Critically Examined': Composition and Theory in the Thought of Stefan Wolpe," in *Music Theory and the Exploration of the Past,* ed. Christopher Hatch and David W. Bernstein (Chicago: University of Chicago Press, 1993), 505–6.

36. "Sometimes one reaches below one's own language; one begins to sing and to bite into one's own consonants and vowels; one has the feeling of folding up together the tongues of all peoples in one's own tongue"; Stefan Wolpe, "On New (and Not-So-New) Music in America," trans. Austin Clarkson, *Journal of Music Theory* 28 (1984): 32.

37. The archives of the Internationale Ferienkurse für Neue Musik in Darmstadt contain a tape of Wolpe giving this lecture.

38. Hilda Morley Wolpe, personal communication with the author, 15 March 1994.

39. Clarkson, *Brief Catalogue.*

40. "Oh, sometimes I just can't stand it anymore, to live robbed of speech, in a constant doubleness of tongue and of the physical center of language!" (my translation); Zenck, "Zum Exilwerk des Komponisten Stefan Wolpe," 25.

41. According to Hilda Morley Wolpe, Olson never wrote back more than a

short note or to send a check; Wolpe was extremely disappointed at Olson's failure to respond (personal communication).

42. Wolpe to Olson, 30 Oct. 1956.

43. Wolpe to Olson, 2 May 1957.

44. Wolpe to Olson, 2 May 1957.

45. Wolpe to Olson, 22 July 1959.

46. Wolpe to Olson, 30 Oct. 1956.

47. Wolpe to Olson, 2 May 1957. Wolpe had taken on the chairmanship of the music department at C. W. Post College upon his return from Europe in the fall of 1957.

48. Wolpe to Olson, 22 July 1959.

49. Walter Levin, the first violinist of the LaSalle Quartet, relates how the quartet's first concert took place before a small audience at Wolpe's apartment (personal communication with the author).

50. There were performances during the 1950s and 1960s under Ralph Shapey. Later, the Group for Contemporary Music (under the leadership of Charles Wuorinen and Harvey Sollberger), Continuum, and Parnassus were prime advocates of Wolpe's music.

51. Wolpe's music, along with Carter's, was seen as a way to "combine serial pitch organization with gestural and dramatic formal conceptions" (Charles Wuorinen, "The Outlook for Young Composers," *Perspectives of New Music* 1 [1963]: 59).

From Jewish Exile in Germany to German Scholar in America

Alfred Einstein's Emigration

Pamela M. Potter

THE BRAIN GAIN/BRAIN DRAIN PHENOMENON
IN MUSICOLOGY

In the 1930s and 1940s many arts and sciences in the United States profited unexpectedly from the influx of Jewish refugees from Germany, from German-occupied lands, and from countries threatened by German invasion. The impact of these refugees on American intellectual growth was ultimately so significant that in retrospect we may tend to romanticize their sagas, conjuring up images of bedraggled scholars disembarking from ocean liners, greeted on the shores with open arms by their magnanimous American colleagues who usher them off to the laboratories and other workspaces set up in anticipation of their arrival. This all may have been true in some fields, such as physics, but in the case of musicology we are more likely to find that even though German scholars had a tremendous impact on American musicology after their arrival, the experience of immigration for the majority was not as smooth as we might imagine.

When we look back at the development of American musicology, almost every other name that comes to mind is that of a German refugee. A recent bio-bibliography of the formative years of American musicology names thirty-five individuals who had an impact on the discipline in the first half of this century, fifteen of whom were refugees from Hitler.[1] Figuring prominently in this pantheon is Alfred Einstein, one of those individuals who should have been welcomed with open arms in his new homeland. An examination of his accomplishments before his emigration, the details surrounding his ostracization in Germany, his rocky road to the United States, and his appointment to the faculty of Smith College at the age of fifty-nine gives us not only a glimpse into the experiences of one man and his family, but also provides insights into the conditions from which Jewish scholars were fleeing and the effects of their migration on scholarship on both sides of the Atlantic.

While a transformation of American cultural and intellectual life is undeniable, a corollary misconception that emerges from considering this "brain gain" phenomenon in American musicology is the notion that Germany immediately felt the effects of its losses and that scholarly activity in Germany came to a screeching halt. The "brain drain" side of the equation cannot be taken for granted without some refinements, however, for although the departure of musicologists, most of them Jewish, may have had a qualitative effect on German scholarship, their absence did not necessarily disrupt the operation of musicology as much as one would assume, simply because most of those Jewish refugees had never been allowed to play a significant role in German academic life.

The Germany that Einstein left in 1933 had been well prepared for a complete eradication of Jews from scholarly professions, especially within the universities. Under the Kaiser, university teaching had been one of the most favorable professions for Jews to enter, presumably less vulnerable to nepotism and prejudice than other professions, and for a brief period in the late nineteenth century a number of Jews flourished at German universities. These opportunities would soon diminish, however, when the number of Jewish full professors in German universities dropped from twenty-five in 1909 to thirteen in 1917 and, despite the expansion of university faculties, from 2.8 percent of the total academic staff in 1889 to 1.2 percent in 1917.[2] A downward trend continued after the First World War, despite stronger measures in the Weimar constitution to ensure equal opportunities for members of all religions.[3]

The university in the Weimar Republic distinguished itself as a bastion of conservatism and a fertile environment for anti-Semitic practices. Students were gravitating toward the political right, professors openly defied all measures proposed by the republic, and Jews were assumed to have liberal leanings and were therefore held responsible for the current ills of society. Jewish instructors could lose their teaching privileges on the mere suspicion of their harboring antinational leanings,[4] and since professorial appointments were usually political, it was extremely difficult for Jews to rise beyond a certain rank.[5] Anti-Jewish sentiment gradually gained public acceptance and even showed signs of becoming institutionalized. In 1925 the German Academic Convocation issued a proclamation that "the alienation of German colleges performed at the hands of Jewish instructors and students must be barred. No more teachers of Jewish extraction are to be hired. Jewish students will be limited to a quota."[6]

It is not hard to imagine that eight years later, in 1933, universities were all too ready and willing to implement the official exclusion of Jews from higher education. The removal of Jews from academic posts in 1933 was, in effect, little more than a legalization of long-standing practices and deep-seated prejudices. The Nazi Students League boycott of Jewish professors and the immediate imposition of the civil service law in April 1933 that sanctioned the removal of Jews from university posts faced little protest or resistance, undoubtedly because in practice Jews had already been kept from the upper ranks of the universities for many years.

Even in times when it was easier for Jews to attain positions in German universities, there was a clear differentiation among academic disciplines in their receptivity to Jewish colleagues. It was much easier, for example, for Jews to excel in natural sciences, mathematics, medicine, and other disciplines considered "value free" than in disciplines more readily associated with German national ideology and *Kultur.*[7] Musicology, like the study of German literature, bore the responsibility of studying and preserving a cultural product that was closely associated with German identity and was too subjective to be entrusted to those who were not considered "true Germans" (as Alfred Einstein's experiences discussed below will show, the Jew had long been regarded as not truly German and incapable of contributing to German culture).

Thus when anti-Jewish legislation forced the emigration of numerous musicologists who were to become the most prominent figures in the field outside Germany, in fact only two out of this large group were vacating positions as professors in German institutions. These two, Curt Sachs and Erich von Hornbostel, were both on the Berlin faculty, and both had unique qualifications for developing new areas of musicology—in fact, the more "scientific" and "value-free" branches of systematic musicology. Without the help of Carl Stumpf, who recognized their indispensability for building up Berlin's reputation as a center for comparative musicology, neither of these scholars would have come as far as they did. Even then, neither one ever became a full professor. Sachs recounted bitterly after the war that "in a 'Fatherland' where anyone exhibiting the slightest mediocrity could achieve full professor," he was unable to earn that ranking in all of his fourteen years on the faculty.[8]

Both Sachs and Hornbostel received letters in September 1933 stating the withdrawal of their teaching privileges, citing paragraph 3 of the new civil service law that allowed for the removal of non-Aryans.[9] Hornbostel died in England shortly after leaving Germany, while Sachs arrived in the United States, via Paris, in 1937, where he went on to build a musicology department at New York University, served as a consultant at the New York Public Library, became an adjunct faculty member at Columbia University, and received honorary degrees and memberships from a long list of institutions. Sachs, however, was in a unique position when he emigrated: the majority of Jewish musicologists who arrived in the United States came without hands-on experience in a university setting, and the skills they could offer to a new potential homeland were not easily demonstrable. Younger scholars (recent Ph.D.'s such as Edward Lowinsky, Manfred Bukofzer, and Willi Apel) tended on the average to fare better in adjusting to American academic life and ultimately in having an impact on the growth of the discipline. An older generation—the generation that includes Alfred Einstein—faced considerably more challenges as émigrés, not merely because of their maturity and their difficulties in uprooting themselves, but to a large extent because anti-Semitism before 1933 had done irreversible damage to their careers by excluding them from academic positions.[10]

If the older émigrés had managed to make names for themselves as scholars while in Germany, their scholarship was usually a side activity conducted in the off hours of full-time occupations in journalism, publishing houses, and other nonacademic jobs. Some of this group had been better situated than others, able to move in the outer circles of academe by working in libraries and archives and succeeding in building up a research portfolio that eased their transition to full-time academic life outside Germany. Those who had to devote most of their time to journalistic and editorial activities, however, were in an especially precarious position. By making their living through the written word, they were ill equipped to continue their careers as journalists in a country where they could no longer write quickly and voluminously in their mother tongue. They were also poorly prepared to enter academic life, since they had generally spent many years laboring in a milieu foreign to their musicological training and had had little time left over to pursue their scholarly interests.[11]

Alfred Einstein was perhaps more successful than most in making the transition, since his achievements before 1933 elevated him to a position of respect in the international musicological community, even though he had conducted most of his serious research and writing in his spare time. For the most part, though, the large group of scholars who were to constitute American musicology's "brain gain" did not represent the driving force behind German musicology at the time of their departure. Rather, they comprised a handful of younger colleagues, an assortment of journalists, archivists, librarians, and freelance authors, hardly significant enough for their absence to have immediate deleterious effects on German musicology as a whole.

ALFRED EINSTEIN'S "EXILE" IN GERMAN ACADEMIC LIFE (1903–33)

The term "exile" and its implications of displacement and cultural estrangement have been addressed in other essays in this volume in considering the experiences of German and Austrian refugees in their new American surroundings. But given the tenuous status of the Jewish intellectual in Germany at the turn of the century, it may be just as appropriate, if not more appropriate, to describe the life of the Jewish musicologist in the German academic world as a form of professional exile. Einstein provides a stunning example of the displaced intellectual groomed in a strict scholarly environment who was then summarily cast out of his intellectual "home," the university, upon earning his doctorate, forced thereafter to fend for himself in "foreign" (his own description) working environments. Just as the exiled will long for the cultural trappings of their homeland, Einstein could indulge in his "home" activities of musicological scholarship only in his spare time; and just as the exiled are barred from returning to their homeland, Einstein was essentially barred from the university and occasionally from participating in other scholarly enterprises. A Jewish musicologist, regardless of his accomplishments, could never be fully accepted as a member of the German scholarly community.

Einstein was denied the chances he deserved to pursue the career of a full-time scholar from the time he completed his doctorate to the moment of his forced emigration, and the reasons for his exclusion always came back to the fact that he was a Jew. The first obstacle in his career came in 1903, when his own doctoral adviser, Adolf Sandberger, refused to allow him to complete his *Habilitation,* thereby ruining his chances of ever holding a university position. It was fairly well known throughout the musicological community that Sandberger's discrimination against Einstein early in his career was motivated by anti-Semitic feelings.[12] Even though Einstein continued to collaborate and correspond with Sandberger at least up to 1938, he was thoroughly convinced that Sandberger's anti-Semitism was the cause for his misfortune and expressed this openly in letters to friends.[13] Einstein further speculated that Sandberger realized that a lack of a *Habilitation* would be a permanent impediment and, to ease his guilt, endorsed Einstein as general editor of the *Zeitschrift für Musikwissenschaft (ZfMw),* the organ of the newly formed German Musicological Society (Deutsche Musikgesellschaft, DMG), in 1918, but this act of contrition did little to alleviate Einstein's financial hardships and his exclusion from university posts.[14]

Einstein never gave up trying to better his situation, and whenever a suitable opening came along, he always made a valiant attempt. Upon hearing that Hans Joachim Moser was leaving his position in Heidelberg, Einstein saw an opportunity to enter academe and wrote to Theodor Kroyer for advice, since Kroyer had recently been director of the department there. Kroyer had been a mentor and confidante since Einstein's student days, and this personal plea to Kroyer of 12 May 1927 describes Einstein's existence in very poignant terms:

I'm not sure how much you know about my present conditions. I used to be a private instructor who could not live off scholarly inclinations alone, but who nevertheless got by, but due to our great losses at the hands of the inflation I am now employed at a publishing house. This job at the Drei Masken Verlag is thoroughly unglamorous but provides the broadest base of my economic existence. Since this is only a half-time job, that base is rather narrow, but at least it allows me to maintain some link to my scholarship. I'm now in my sixth year of this slavery. In my most productive hours of the day, I waste my time with publishing matters that don't interest me in the least and take me away from what's really important to me; it is simply an unworthy preoccupation. Still, I won't complain. Without this slavery, I and my family would have gone hungry long ago, because no one could live on the salary I receive as a critic for a Social Democratic newspaper and the 600 mark annual honorarium from the *ZfMw.*

You know very well there are no prospects for me in Munich, as I have just realized: [first of all,] I'm not a member of the Bavarian People's Party, [second, I'm] an independent thinker, and people are afraid that I can see through them, and [finally,] I'm a Jew! Nothing can be done. I have to escape from these conditions, I have to get out of Munich. And now there seems to be a way: Moser is leaving Heidelberg—it's not clear where he's going, but he is leaving. So please tell me if you think I would have any prospects there, and since you know the situation there all too well, please give me some indication of what steps I should take in approaching the department and the education ministry. I would be thrilled to know at least that they are considering me. . . . In a way, this opportunity may be a sign: my mother is from Heidelberg, so I would, in a manner of speaking, be going home![15]

Kroyer was willing to help Einstein, but the latter learned directly from Moser that his chances were slim, and Moser confessed to Kroyer that one of the key reasons for Einstein's disfavor was his religious affiliation.[16] Moser thought that Einstein's chances should have been good, since he had earned respect from the entire field with his impressive publication record, but scholarly achievements alone would not suffice; as he wrote to Kroyer: "First of all, he doesn't have his *Habilitation,* and then his Judaism—this isn't a problem at the university level, on the contrary we're all very liberal here. But the fact is that there are already so many Jews here that the ministry would hesitate to increase the number."[17]

Thus Einstein was condemned to live the life of a professional exile while in Germany, an accomplished scholar kept from returning to his true calling by virtue of political and religious discrimination, and as such he fell victim to feelings of isolation, envy, and insecurity. He confessed to Guido Adler, the pioneer Viennese musicologist and fellow Jew, that he could not repress his resentment toward those who enjoyed what he so desired: "It is

becoming more and more urgent to save my scholarly soul, to return *completely* to my field, not to have to devote the best hours of the day to activities that are totally fruitless and inherently foreign to me. With bitterness I
think of those who are allowed to do this and who—forgive my arrogance—
stand well below me in ability and seriousness."[18]

Einstein managed to "escape" from Munich when he was offered a position as music critic at the *Berliner Tageblatt* in the same year he applied for
Moser's position. Einstein's daughter, currently residing near Berkeley, California, remembers the years in Berlin as some of the happiest, filled with
concert, opera, and theater attendance, and writing criticisms was an activity that Einstein truly enjoyed. He was happy to leave Munich not only for
the conditions described in his plea to Kroyer but also for personal reasons,
since he and his family had been living with his in-laws, and he was eager
for the opportunity to support his family on his own.[19] Munich was also a
constant reminder of his strained relationship with Sandberger, and in contrast to the drudgery of spending valuable hours on tedious editorial tasks,
the Berlin duties offered him more productive time for his scholarship. He
wrote to Adler: "Every day I feel more secure, every day happier that I left
Munich. It was high time . . . Sandberger wrote me that he regretted my departure—but he had watched my slavery at Drei Masken Verlag for many
years and never lifted a finger on my behalf. Now I have mornings to do my
own work, which I consider a gift from heaven; since I no longer have any
editorial obligations, I can finally, finally return to scholarly work."[20]

In the last years before Hitler's seizure of power, Einstein continued to
grow as a scholar and earn respect from colleagues in his uninterrupted
tenure as editor of the *Zeitschrift für Musikwissenschaft.* But he was never allowed to forget that his Jewishness would be an impediment to realizing his
full potential, not only by closing university doors to him but also by keeping him from participating in other activities. In 1929, for example, he was
excluded from contributing a chapter on Protestant church music to a projected volume entitled *Die Musikhochschule,* edited by Hermann von Waltershausen. Waltershausen offered the reasons for his rejection not as anti-
Semitism per se, even though he had never made a secret of his feelings
regarding the "dangers and limitations" of Jews in German culture. Rather,
he explained that this particular work was directed toward a general public,
and that J. S. Bach in particular bore a special significance for devout Protestants. A Jew contributing to studies on Bach would be just as inappropri-
ate as a Protestant trying to deal with central questions in Catholic church
music or non-Jews presenting scholarly findings on essential elements of
Jewish ritual.[21] Waltershausen drew this questionable analogy even after Einstein had pointed out the absurdity of reserving Protestant music scholarship for Protestants and limiting his own work to "Jewish music history, to
Mendelssohn and Meyerbeer."[22]

Waltershausen's rationales for rejecting Einstein's work, as well as Moser's reasons for casting doubt on Einstein's chances in Heidelberg, are typical of the varieties of "benign" anti-Semitism among German intellectuals before 1933. They may seem blatantly discriminatory today, but given the sentiments of the time, these two authors believed to be offering perfectly acceptable explanations for Einstein's exclusion. It was not much more than a century earlier that European Jews had not even enjoyed rights of citizens, and only half a century earlier they had been excluded from the civil service throughout Germany. When Moser stated that Heidelberg was liberal but already had its lion's share of Jews, he was speaking from the vantage point of someone who knew of times when Jews had virtually no chance of holding university positions: Heidelberg was liberal, according to Moser, but there was only so much change a community could tolerate at once.

Waltershausen's statements are also very revealing. First, like many Germans at the time, he felt strongly that Jews were limited in their ability to contribute to German culture, a sentiment that was born with the earliest movements of German nationalism and gained momentum in the course of the following century.[23] Second, in trying to explain Einstein's inappropriateness for the tasks at hand, he admitted his own reluctance to delve into issues of Catholic music and ritual, hinting at the persistence of the Catholic-Protestant division that had existed since the Reformation. Even though Germany had been unified for over fifty years, the borders between Catholic and Protestant regions were still clearly drawn. This issue came up often in questions of university appointments, as Protestants had much better chances of advancing in Protestant areas and Catholics in Catholic areas. The problem for the Jew in this situation, however, was the complete absence of Jewish regions in Germany where Jews could thrive at the expense of Protestants and Catholics.

These statements are manifestations of a cultural anti-Semitism prevalent among intellectuals, but this would quickly be superseded by a different brand of anti-Semitism—racial anti-Semitism—that could not be remedied by religious conversion. As Einstein learned within a few years of receiving the last letter quoted, the designation "Jewish" not only came to imply "non-Christian" and "non-German," but also implied the possession of inborn character traits that no amount of assimilation and acculturation could obliterate. In 1932, Alfred Heuss felt compelled to end his long-standing friendship with Einstein after an altercation with Einstein's wife that revealed to him "the crudest side of Jewish character."[24] This Swiss-German was not a citizen of the German Reich, yet he compared himself to the Austrian Hitler, feeling more German than any Jew living in Germany and resenting being treated like a stranger when in Germany, especially by Jews such as Einstein and another Jewish musicologist and critic, Adolf Aber.[25]

EXPULSION AND MIGRATION, 1933–39

After Hitler's accession, the signs pointing to emigration were becoming clearer every day, but it was only after a dramatic and irreversible change of circumstances that Einstein realized that he must leave. When he departed Germany in 1933, it was not because of the civil service law, since he was not, after all, a university professor, but rather because he was a highly visible Jew in a discipline whose future in the new state was uncertain. In fact, there is reason to believe that if Einstein had not been so visible he may have been allowed to continue working in Germany, at least for a few more years.[26]

As editor of the *Zeitschrift für Musikwissenschaft* (after 1926 the only scholarly musicological journal in Germany), Einstein was under the close scrutiny of skeptical colleagues who questioned whether a Jew could really produce an accurate representation of German scholarship. Even as early as 1931, when Einstein showed reluctance to accept an article by Bartók, Edwin von der Nüll consoled Bartók with the explanation that in the current atmosphere of growing nationalism, Einstein was under pressure from both the publisher and the current German-conscious leadership of the Deutsche Musikgesellschaft to promote the work of German rather than foreign scholars, and the fact that Einstein was a Jew made his position that much more precarious.[27]

In 1933, the overhaul of the German government caused tensions to run high in the Deutsche Musikgesellschaft. Already facing financial difficulties and conflicts with Breitkopf & Härtel, the publisher of the journal, the society suddenly had to deal with a new regime that appeared to be even more anti-intellectual than the preceding one and displayed unprecedented designs on controlling all of cultural life. The leaders of the DMG started searching for a way to demonstrate that musicology had something to offer to the state, and having a Jewish editor supervising their central organ was more than a minor embarrassment.

One of the first major gestures of sympathy with the Nazi regime was a complete voluntary overhaul of the society. Under the supervision of President Arnold Schering, and without any external order from above, the Deutsche Musikgesellschaft changed its name to the Deutsche Gesellschaft für Musikwissenschaft (DGMW) and formally adopted the National Socialist leadership principle, or *Führerprinzip*. Its new charter stated that the society was built on the "leader and management principle," that the directives of the president were to be "binding for all work of the society," and that complaints against the decisions of the president were not permitted.[28] Having taken the initiative to conform to National Socialist guidelines, the society was then in a position to express its willingness to work together with the state. Schering addressed a letter to Nazi Propaganda Minister Joseph Goebbels in November 1933 announcing the restructuring of the society, its "joyful will to work together to build a new German culture with all of its strength," and its consciousness of the "high responsibility placed upon it for its part in the administration and proliferation of the immortal musical culture of our people."[29]

This *Gleichschaltung* was believed to have been initiated by Einstein's allegedly voluntary resignation as editor of the society's journal four months earlier.[30] The actual circumstances of Einstein's departure were far more complex, however, and reveal that it was far from voluntary.[31] Einstein in fact "received his farewell" on 24 June with the explanation that "conditions are stronger than we are and force us, in the interest of the DMG, to execute a change in the editorship of our journal by the end of the fiscal year (September 1933)."[32] Johannes Wolf, who had penned this letter, clarified in a personal note that "what you already feared, and what I naively thought impossible, has come to pass: they have demanded your termination as editor of the journal. The board had to deal with the question a few days ago and came to the conclusion that it is impossible to run against the current, especially since the enterprise must request a subvention from the state."[33] Einstein wrote to Kroyer that his "amputation" resulted from the "all too plausible reason that the DMG will have to approach the new regime with a request for support, rendering the retention of a non-Aryan editor impossible."[34]

At the end of this dramatic turn of events, and after several visits from the Gestapo and the revocation of contracts by German publishers, Einstein resigned from several musicological organizations and from his post at the *Berliner Tageblatt*, packed up his household, set off to attend Bayreuth and a conference in Cambridge, and resolved never to return to Germany.[35] The Einstein family spent the next six years in England and Italy before settling in the United States in 1939, confronting an assortment of troubles along the way.

Shortly after arriving in London in 1933, Einstein described his status as tenuous and could not help noticing the huge difference between the experiences of the prominent and of the not-so-prominent refugees. He observed the ease with which some German scholars had settled into life in England, but these were mostly physicists, chemists, and psychologists whose English colleagues gave up part of their salaries to support them. Einstein did not expect similar behavior from musicologists.[36] Einstein and his family then would have liked to settle down in Florence, but felt compelled to leave in 1938, explaining that "our Führer's visit to the other clown drove us out of Italy."[37]

Despite his low expectations, help did in fact come forth from influential colleagues and friends on more than one occasion, and this aided considerably in the navigation of complex immigration policies. In 1938, Ernst

Kurth helped Einstein and his family enter Switzerland,[38] Percy Scholes endorsed his visa to the United Kingdom,[39] and the physicist Albert Einstein sent a letter addressing him as "Dear Cousin," which he would then be able to present to the consulate as proof of sponsorship to gain entry into the United States.[40] Then in 1939, Werner Josten of Smith College arranged for Einstein to receive a guest professorship for the fall semester, which was renewed for a second semester and indefinitely thereafter.[41] This position required him to teach three graduate seminars per year and allowed him to devote most of his time to his scholarly work.[42]

THE IDENTITY OF THE ÉMIGRÉ

Einstein the émigré obviously had to make several adjustments when he settled in America: entering a new profession, dealing with a new language, and assuming a new identity as an American citizen, which he became in 1945. The first adjustment seems to have been the easiest, since this was the profession for which he had been trained and which he longed to practice. His light teaching load at Smith allowed him to indulge in essentially full-time research and writing, and in his first eight years there he completed the books *Greatness in Music, Mozart, Music in the Romantic Era,* and the three-volume history of the Italian madrigal, along with several music editions and an expanded Köchel catalog of Mozart's works.[43] Language, although a continuous problem in the classroom, was less so than if he had continued to work as a journalist, since it was possible for him to continue writing in German and to have his works translated.[44]

Furthermore, in at least one very practical sense, Einstein remained a German musicologist even after the Nazi government had revoked his citizenship. He was still regarded as indispensable to the functioning of German musicology, and his collaboration remained the mainstay of vital projects and research areas, particularly in his capacity as a Mozart expert. The most telling proof of his crucial role was the continuation of a technically illegal collaboration with Breitkopf & Härtel on the completion of the revised Köchel catalog of Mozart's works, which appeared in 1937 with Einstein's name on the title page. According to postwar accounts, Hellmuth von Hase of Breitkopf & Härtel went directly to Peter Raabe, president of the Reichsmusikkammer in the Propaganda Ministry, and secured permission to release the Köchel edition and to give Einstein full recognition.[45] Raabe, heading the powerful professional organization that encompassed all musicians and music-related industries, was himself a musicologist and undoubtedly respected Einstein, having turned to him several years earlier for advice on publishing his own work on Liszt.[46] Einstein also continued to receive royalties from the music publisher Bärenreiter until as late as 1935, and in 1937 Peters expressed interest in publishing some unpublished Mozart works naming Einstein as editor and considered carrying out the project through an English affiliate.[47] Friedrich Blume continued to rely on Einstein's expertise, corresponding with him throughout 1934 while working on editions of Mozart piano concertos, and, as promised, thanked him in the acknowledgments to the editions he prepared.[48]

Other relationships were not so harmonious, as when Schott purchased the rights to the Riemann lexicon from Max-Hesse-Verlag, the last three editions of which had been Einstein's work, and announced the preparation of a new edition by Joseph Müller-Blattau in 1938. Einstein protested that Riemann had designated him as the sole editor of subsequent editions, but Schott responded that the purchase of the rights gave them free rein to do what they wanted with the work.[49] Nevertheless, Einstein had the last laugh when, after the war, Schott tried to get him back to take over the lexicon, and he triumphantly mused in a letter to Nicolas Slonimsky that Riemann had been "ent-müller-blattlaust."[50]

Despite his painful experiences, Einstein remained a German scholar, and his respect for the German musicological tradition could not be completely lost, thus he could not help viewing some of the postwar products of German musicology with reserved admiration. His first reaction to the new reference work *Die Musik in Geschichte und Gegenwart* was basically positive, even though he found it to be overrun with Nazi language,[51] and even though he had refused to have an entry on him included in the work while he was still alive.[52] His opinion of American musicology appeared to be more positive, and he even cited Grout's history of opera as "better than anything European," but most of his praise for "American" musicology was reserved for the recent products of fellow émigrés. In a 1948 assessment of American scholarship, he singled out the works of Bukofzer, Plamenac, and Hewitt (a Besseler student) alongside that of Grout as recent outstanding accomplishments in American musicology.[53]

In an ironic sense, it was Einstein's emigration that allowed him to flourish as a German musicologist, enabling him to put his German training in practice as never before. His identity as a German on a more personal level was less straightforward, however. It seems that as Einstein grew more comfortable with his living circumstances outside Germany, especially after arriving in the United States, he became increasingly intent on breaking all associations with Germans, German enterprises, and anyone remotely linked to Germany.[54] Upon leaving in 1933, he still considered himself a German, but not in the sense of what Germanness had become. He bade farewell to his estranged friend Alfred Heuss with the words "From this Germany of bestiality there can never be a Germany of humanity; whoever identifies himself with it has lost the right to utter the names of Mozart, Beethoven, Goethe, and Schiller."[55] Months later, even when his status in England was still hanging in the balance, he nevertheless was glad to be there. Yet he held

on to the hope that the Germany of old would be restored, and he characterized the current Nazi state in some of the most negative terms imaginable for the time: "No one can ever take away my Germanness, my love for
everything that is truly German, as opposed to that theatrical Germanness
of a state that stands morally, intellectually, and culturally far below the Negro state of Liberia."[56]

As the years passed, he gradually distanced himself from his former homeland even more and ultimately concluded that he would find no successor
to that "Germany of humanity" in the two German states that emerged after the war. In 1949 he received an invitation to speak at the Free University
in West Berlin but expressed no desire to visit "the Fourth Reich."[57] One
could even detect something of an obsession with the notion of Germany's
decline (a reaction not unique among émigrés, but also not universal), keeping close tabs on the behavior of his former compatriots and anyone associated with them and withdrawing from numerous organizations and projects on grounds of perceived Nazi sympathies.[58] In 1938 he refused to write
a monograph on Mozart for an Italian publisher because of rising anti-
Semitism there.[59] By 1948 he had withdrawn from the International Society
for Contemporary Music (ISCM) and the International Musicological Society (IMS) because of the growing influence of Germans in those organizations;[60] in the same year he announced the end of any active involvement
in British musical life because of the favorable treatment of former Nazis;[61]
and in 1949 he declined to accept the Golden Mozart Medal from the Austrian government.[62]

Einstein also assumed a moral responsibility for sending out warning signals whenever he saw the slightest indications of Nazi or Nazi-like sentiments
outside Germany. This ranged from his harsh criticism of Leo Kestenberg,
another Jewish refugee, when the latter invited Germans to a conference on
music education in Prague in 1936, to outspoken condemnations of poten-
tially harmful statements about Jews.[63] Having lived through the transition
from an atmosphere of seemingly benign anti-Semitism to that of an outright witch-hunt, he had become extremely sensitized to any linguistic sub-
tleties reminiscent of Nazi or pre-Nazi rhetoric. The main catalyst for his
leaving Italy was Mussolini's "In Defense of the Race" of 1938. Italian colleagues such as Fernando Liuzzi tried to reassure Einstein that, alarming
as Mussolini's statements might be, one could count on the good sense of
the Italian people,[64] but Einstein could only conclude: "The author of 'difesa della razza' claims the document to be original, but to us it sounds very
familiar."[65]

Einstein also reacted very strongly to an article by Cecil Gray that appeared in the *Music Review* in 1945 and was sprinkled with less than complimentary remarks about Jews. Einstein decided to withdraw contributions
he had promised to the journal and wrote to the editor: "You are wrong

if you think I am offended by the passage about 'musical gangsters . . . largely of Jewish extraction' in Mr. Cecil Gray's 'Contingencies.' I am simply sad. Trust my experience: Hitlerism in Germany began exactly with remarks like that; and if they are possible in a democratic country even before V-E day was achieved, the five and more years of 'blood, sweat and tears' are, in my opinion, wasted."[66]

Einstein closely followed the denazification of leading musical figures and saw no reason to hold back his disgust. He noted that Pfitzner was exonerated in spite of friendships with influential Nazis, he characterized the denazification of Furtwängler as "Nazis denazifying Nazis,"[67] and he agonized over the fact that a "Schwein" such as Heinz Tietjen could go on with his career.[68] His judgments of his former colleagues were equally negative, and he became adamant in his refusal to renew ties with German musicologists. Einstein was particularly vexed by a lack of insight on the part of the non-German world in their reconciliations with German scholars after the war. He reviled Blume for passing himself off as an opponent to Nazism and for enjoying praise in *Music and Letters* and warned Slonimsky not to fall for Blume's overtures to establish good relations with Americans.[69] He agonized over Robert Haas's good fortune when Haas, after having been forced to give up his position in Austria by virtue of his political record, was rehabilitated in that country, apparently because an article of his appeared in the *Musical Quarterly* under Paul Henry Lang's editorship. Einstein stressed the irony of the situation, since he believed that Haas's article was accepted only after fellow émigré Paul Nettl reassured Lang that Haas was "pure and white as a lily." He was also sadly amused by the news that individuals such as Hans Engel and Joseph Müller-Blattau could continue to hold academic positions and could proceed to influence the next generation of musicologists.[70]

CONCLUSION

The existence of a brain gain in American musicology is undeniable. Although this was not the case in all fields, where established methodologies sometimes conflicted with those of the new arrivals, musicology in the United States was particularly receptive to the contributions of émigrés, because American musicology was already strongly influenced by German thought.[71] German musicologists had long stood at the forefront of the discipline, enjoying an international reputation as leaders in research and methodology, as organizers of societies and conferences, and as founders of scholarly journals and large-scale editorial projects. While musicology departments certainly existed in the United States before 1933, most American musicologists had either received their training in Germany or were at least steeped in the German tradition.[72] The arrival of a significant number of refugee musicologists led to a surge of musicological activity in the United States, and programs at several major universities were either founded or substantially enhanced by German émigrés, resulting in an essentially German approach to music history that still forms the basis of our discipline.

The other side of the story, the impact of the brain drain in Germany, is considerably less dramatic. Many disciplines clearly suffered, some more than others, but the fabric of German academic life remained essentially intact throughout the duration of the Third Reich. German academe was not going to be paralyzed by the departure of Jewish scholars, simply because most of them were not occupying influential positions at the time of their dismissal. In view of their impact on American academic life, we tend to assume that they were giants in Germany as well and that their departure would have to result in the collapse of the German university system. We cannot glibly overgeneralize that Germany's "loss" was our gain; rather, we must conclude that we benefited from Germany's failure to recognize the value of what it possessed.

In the case of musicology, exaggerations of the brain drain phenomenon are understandable owing to the high brain gain factor in the United States, but musicological activity in Germany similarly did not cease and desist in 1933. Many important publications and editorial projects came out of the Third Reich, university departments continued to flourish, and new research institutes and research funding sources were established. Although Germany lost some of its greatest musicologists, the majority of those who went on to become important professors and teachers in the United States and elsewhere left Germany as students, recent graduates, journalists, librarians, and archivists, thus their influence in Germany was limited or impossible to determine.

If there was a brain drain in German musicology, it was more qualitative than quantitative. Although a qualitative decline is subtle and difficult to assess, we have already seen indications by reviewing Einstein's story, particularly Breitkopf & Härtel's need to carry on what was technically an illegal working relationship with Einstein in order to complete the new edition of Köchel and German scholars' continued respect for his work and reliance on his expertise, as in the case of Blume. More noticeable and widespread effects of the qualitative brain drain were felt in areas of systematic musicology. The emigration of two leading scholars, Sachs and Hornbostel, who also happened to be the only Jewish musicologists holding positions as professors in German universities, as well as most of their students and colleagues left a void that was difficult to fill. Hornbostel's departure left vacancies not only on the teaching staff but also in the renowned Phonogrammarchiv.[73] Upon his emigration, Fritz Bose, only twenty-eight, took over his courses, and Marius Schneider, age thirty, took over the directorship of the archive. In an appeal to the Education Ministry to be entrusted with the task of enlarging the music division of the institute to include a research center for comparative folk music research and musical race research, Bose listed among his qualifications his Aryan lineage, Nazi party and Studentenbund membership, and attempts to join the SA, as well as the distinction of being the only German student of Hornbostel and the only younger representative of the field besides Marius Schneider.[74]

A clear picture of the situation of Jewish academics before Hitler faded with time, especially since the Nazi period came to be viewed more and more as a surrealistic moment of insanity. Rationalizing the brutality of the Third Reich with the long tradition of German cultural achievement was an impossible task, and it was easier simply to assume that Hitler invented discrimination and forced it on German intellectuals against their will, rather than to allow that the seeds of hate had already been planted. Even as late as 1980, the major newspaper in Munich described Alfred Einstein's pre-1933 exclusion from academic life as more or less his own personal choice: "In those thirty years [1903–33] . . . this music researcher . . . never had an academic position, perhaps because he never tried to secure one, being in a profession in Germany in which the Jewish colleague was held at a respectful distance."[75]

But Einstein's own assessment of his career relays quite a different message, the message that emigration was the only way for the Jewish scholar to escape his isolated existence and to practice the profession for which he was trained and in which he excelled. Three years after leaving Germany, Einstein reflected on the effects anti-Semitism had on his career and saw how logically the entire episode had unfolded: "I have no academic track record. The same factors that have caused the dismissal and expulsion of Jewish scholars since 1933 were already preventing me in 1903 from doing my *Habilitation,* after receiving my doctorate."[76]

After seeing how productive he could be in the first few years of his first full-time academic position, acquired thirty-six years after his doctorate, one can imagine the bitterness over the many years he was kept from such productivity, but Einstein never deluded himself into thinking that such gains ever would have been possible in Germany. He enumerated his accomplishments while at Smith in a letter to Erwin Kroll in 1947 with the ironic remark: "Basically I cannot thank my Führer enough,"[77] and he elaborated on that sentiment in a *Time* magazine interview in 1950, upon his retirement from Smith: "When he found his German colleagues had become nonentities in brown uniforms, he decided he 'couldn't stand it any longer.' . . . Now Einstein looks on his years as a music critic as a 'nightmare' when he had time to be 'only a bricklayer in musicology.' By chasing him out of his rut and back to work as a master mason in music scholarship, Adolf Hitler, he says, became 'my greatest benefactor.'"[78]

NOTES

1. Curt Efram Steinzor, comp., *American Musicologists, c. 1890–1945: A Bio-Bibliographical Sourcebook to the Formative Period,* ed. Donald L. Hixon (New York, Westport, Conn.: Greenwood Press, 1989).

2. Converts to Christianity still had a definite advantage over practicing Jews, and objective sciences were more accessible to Jews than areas such as literature, classics, and other ideology-rooted disciplines. See Peter Pulzer, *Jews and the German State: The Political History of a Minority, 1848–1933* (Oxford: Basil Blackwell, 1992), 109–11.

3. Ibid., 271–72.

4. George Mosse, *The Crisis of German Ideology: Intellectual Origins of the Third Reich* (New York: Grosset & Dunlap, 1964), 271.

5. Contemporary statistics show that the percentage of Jewish *Ordinarien* (including baptized Jews) declined from 6.9 percent in 1909–10 to 5.6 percent in 1931–32, despite the fact that 14 of the total 114 in 1931–32 were at the newly established and notably liberal Frankfurt University (Pulzer, *Jews and the German State,* 276–78).

6. "Der Überfremdung der deutschen Hochschulen durch jüdische Lehrkräfte und Studierende ist ein Riegel vorzuschieben. Weitere Lehrer jüdischer Abstammung sind nicht mehr zu berufen. Für die Studierenden ist der Numerus clausus einzuführen" (quoted in Hans Peter Bleuel, *Deutschlands Bekenner: Professoren zwischen Kaiserreich und Diktatur* [Bern: Scherz, 1968], 189). This and all other translations of quotations are the author's.

7. Pulzer, *Jews and the German State,* 109.

8. "In einem 'Vaterlande' in dem die kleinsten Mediokritäten Ordinariate bekamen, wenn sie nur die vorschriftsmäßige Konfession hatten, konnte [Einstein] sich nicht einmal habilitieren. Mir persönlich ist wenigstens das zuteilgeworden, dank dem Drängen des unvergeßlichen Stumpf. Aber im übrigen habe ich nicht einmal an der Hochschule in vollen vierzehn Jahren eine ordentliche Lehrerstelle bekommen können" (Sachs to Moser [copy sent to Einstein], 9 Apr. 1949, folder 812, Alfred Einstein Memorabilia, Coll. No. 1, Music Library, University of California, Berkeley; hereafter cited as Einstein Papers).

9. Reich Education Ministry to Sachs, 6 Sept. 1933, and to Hornbostel, 24 Sept. 1933, file 1478 ("Professoren"), Universitätsarchiv, Humboldt-Universität zu Berlin.

10. Such generational differences prevailed in all fields. See Anthony Heilbut, *Exiled in Paradise: German Artists and Intellectuals in America, from the 1930s to the Present* (New York: Viking Press, 1983), 72–79.

11. For further discussion of others' experiences in emigration, see Potter, "Die Lage der jüdischen Musikwissenschaftler an den Universitäten der Weimarer Zeit," in *Musik in der Emigration, 1933–1945: Vorgeschichte, Vertreibung, Rückwirkung,* ed. Horst Weber (Stuttgart: J. B. Metzler, 1994), 56–68.

12. A letter addressed to the Munich musicologist Otto Ursprung refers to the obstacles Einstein faced "because Professor Sandberger turned down his intended *Habilitation,* in any event out of consideration of his being Jewish" (Decker to Ursprung, 2 June 1930, Otto Ursprung Papers [Ana 343], Manuscript Division, Bavarian State Library, Munich; hereafter cited as Ursprung Papers); and Sachs, in the same letter to Moser quoted above (see note 8), indicated that it was common knowledge that Sandberger treated Einstein "like a dog" because he was Jewish.

13. The lengthy and outwardly congenial correspondence between Einstein and Sandberger in the Einstein Papers ends with a letter from Sandberger dated 14 April 1938 (folder 817), but Einstein made no secret of his conviction of Sandberger's anti-Semitism in several letters to Theodor Kroyer (folder 568, Einstein Papers). In 1915 he refused to contribute to a Festschrift honoring Sandberger (9 Mar.) but agreed to contribute money to the venture out of an ironic sense of duty to "pay back" the man who had caused him so much pain out of anti-Semitic blindness: "It would even be fun if my own 'nobility' were to facilitate honoring a man who has, out of anti-Semitism, shoved insurmountable financial demands under my nose" (4 Mar. 1915). He also maintained that their relationship was always chilled by Sandberger's anti-Semitism: "Outwardly we got along just fine, but you know, he forgets nothing. And I am a Jew!" (17 Feb. 1925).

14. At the time of his emigration, he wrote: "It was [Sandberger] who, exactly fifteen years ago, informed me of my appointment as editor because he was aware of the injustice he had caused me" (Einstein to Kroyer [draft], 7 July 1933, folder 568, Einstein Papers). Three years later he reflected further: "However, I must say to his credit that he was the driving force [behind the decision] in 1918, when the 'Deutsche Musikgesellschaft' entrusted me with the editorship of its ZfMw—a post that was expressly explained as a compensation for [my] missed or obstructed academic activity" (Einstein to Notgemeinschaft der deutschen Wissenschaft [draft], 8 Sept. 1936, folder 1073, Einstein Papers).

15. "Ich weiss nicht, ob Sie über meine Lage ganz unterrichtet sind. Früher ein 'Privatgelehrter,' der seinen wissenschaftlichen Neigungen zwar eigentlich auch nicht hätte leben können, aber immerhin gelebt hat, bin ich heute, nach dem Verlust meines, unseres Vermögens durch die Inflation, ein Verlagsangestellter, d.h. meine Tätigkeit bei DMV gibt mir die durchaus nicht glänzende und breite Grundlage meiner wirtschaftlichen Existenz. Dass diese Tätigkeit nur halbtägig ist, verringert zwar jene Basis, aber ermöglicht mir wenigstens, dass ich die Verbindung mit meiner Wissenschaft nicht ganz habe aufgeben müssen. Diese Sklaverei dauert nun an die sechs Jahre. Die beste Zeit des Tages beschäftige ich mit Verlagsdingen, die mich innerlich nicht das Geringste angehen, die mich von den mir wesentlichen Aufgaben abziehen; es ist einfach unwürdig. Doch, ich will nicht klagen—ohne diese Sklaverei wäre ich eben samt meiner Familie schon längst verhungert, denn von dem Kritiker-Gehalt einer sozialdemokratischen Zeitung und den jährlichen 600 M Redaktionshonorar der ZfMw kann man nicht leben.

"Sie wissen, dass in München nichts für mich zu wollen ist, es ist mir jüngst wieder authentisch bestätigt worden: kein Angehöriger der bayerischen Volkspartei, ein innerlich unabhängiger Mensch, vor dem sich jeder *durchschaut* fühlt, und ein Jude! Es ist Hopfen und Malz verloren. Ich muss heraus aus diesen Verhältnissen, ich muss fort von München. Und nun zeigt sich ein Weg: Moser verlässt Heidelberg—wohin er geht, steht noch nicht fest, aber er verlässt es. Sagen Sie mir, ob Sie eine Bewerbung von mir für aussichtsvoll halten, und geben Sie mir als Kenner der Verhältnisse Winke, welche Schritte ich bei Fakultät und Ministerium tun soll. Am liebsten wäre mir, die 'Aufmerksamkeit würde auf mich gelenkt.' . . . Eine Art von Schicksalswink ist es, dass ich mütterlicherseits aus Heidelberg stamme—ich würde in eine Art von Heimat zurückkehren" (Einstein to Kroyer, 12 May 1927, folder 568, Einstein Papers).

16. Einstein to Kroyer, 23 May 1927, folder 568, Einstein Papers.

17. "... da er ja allerseits in der 'Zunft' sich durch stattliche Publikationen hohen Ansehen[s] erfreut. .... Aber Sie wissen natürlich ebenso wie ich, daß zwei große Schwierigkeiten bestehen: einmal, daß er nicht habilitiert ist, und dann sein Judentum—nicht wegen der politischen Richtung der Fakultät, die im Gegenteil überwiegend sehr liberal ist, sondern viel eher, weil bereits ein so starker Anteil von Juden vorhanden ist, daß das Ministerium wohl Bedenken haben würde, diese noch zu vermehren" (Moser to Kroyer, 28 May 1927, Kroyeriana, Manuscript Division, Bavarian State Library, Munich).

18. "Es wird für mich zu einer immer dringenderen Notwendigkeit, meine wissenschaftliche Seele zu retten, wieder *ganz* in mein Fach hinein zu kommen, nicht die besten Stunden des Tages an eine ganz unfruchtbare und mir innerlich fremde Tätigtkeit wenden zu müssen. Mit Bitterkeit denke ich an manchen, der das kann und der,—verzeihen Sie mir meine Anmassung—an Fähigkeit und Ernst tief unter mir steht" (Einstein to Adler, 3 June 1927, Guido Adler Papers, MS.769, Hargrett Rare Book and Manuscript Library, University of Georgia Libraries; hereafter cited as Adler Papers).

19. Ms. Eva Einstein (daughter of Alfred), interview with the author, El Cerrito, Calif., 27 Nov. 1994. One may ask why Einstein never tried to do his *Habilitation* in another city, and the only explanation he ever gave was that he was bound to Munich "out of family and economic considerations" and therefore was dependent solely on Sandberger's approval of his *Habilitation* in order to pursue his academic career (Einstein to Notgemeinschaft der deutschen Wissenschaft, 8 Nov. 1936, folder 1073, Einstein Papers).

20. "Aber ich glaube Boden zu fassen u. fühle mich jeden Tag wohler, jeden Tag glücklicher, München entronnen zu sein. Es war höchste Zeit, u. es war gerade noch Zeit. Sandberger schrieb mir eine Karte, in der er meinen Weggang bedauerte— aber er hat meiner Sklaverei im Drei M. Verlag viele Jahre zugesehen, ohne einen Finger für mich zu rühren. Jetzt erlebe ich jeden Vormittag, an dem ich für mich arbeiten kann, als ein wahres Geschenk des Himmels; da ich keinen Redaktionsdienst zu leisten brauche, kann ich endlich, endlich wieder zu wissenschaftlicher Arbeit zurückkehren" (Einstein to Adler, 16 Oct. 1927, Adler Papers).

21. "Sie sollten mich doch eigentlich gut genug kennen, um zu wissen, daß mir Antisemitismus im landläufigen Sinne fernliegt. Ich habe Ihnen aber auch nie einen Hehl daraus gemacht, wo ich die Gefahren und die Grenzen des Judentums innerhalb der deutschen Kultur erblicke. ... Bei der vorgesehenen Publikation handelt es sich nicht um Grundfragen des Judentums, sondern lediglich um eine Angelegenheit des Taktes. Das vorgesehene Werk ist, wenn es verkäuflich sein soll, nicht für die Musikhochschulen berechnet, sondern auch noch für weitere Musikschulen und die Kirchenmusikabteilungen innerhalb der verschiedenen Schulen bestimmt. Ich muß darauf bestehen, daß hierbei nach der konfessionellen Seite gewisse Rücksichten geübt werden; Empfindlichkeiten müssen geschont werden, wenn wir nicht große Teile der Auflage zur Makulatur verdammen wollen. J. S. Bach ist nun einmal besondere Angelegenheit für den gläubigen Protestanten und Sie sind nun einmal Jude; ebensowenig wie ich richtig finde, wenn Sie gerade diese Abteilung bearbeiten würden, könnte ich es gut heissen, selbst als Protestant irgendwelche besonderen Kernfragen der katholischen Kirchenmusik zu bearbeiten. ... Und endlich würden

Sie glauben, daß es in jüdischen Kreisen begrüßt werden würde, wenn ein Nicht-jude an einer besonders exponierten Stelle als Mitarbeiter für eine Darstellung we-sentlicher Teile des jüdischen Gottesdienstes herangezogen würde? Hier dürfte doch wohl unter allen Umständen nur ein Jude am Platz sein" (Waltershausen to Einstein, 2 May 1929, folder 997, Einstein Papers).

22. Einstein to Waltershausen, 23 Apr. [1929], folder 997, Einstein Papers.

23. See Jacob Katz, *From Prejudice to Destruction: Anti-Semitism, 1700–1933* (Cambridge, Mass.: Harvard University Press, 1980), chaps. 6, 15, 21, and 25.

24. Eva Einstein recalled in our discussion that her mother threw Heuss out of the house for making Nazi statements.

25. "Nur einmal ist es mir in meinem Leben nochmals begegnet, mich in Deutschland als 'Ausländer' bezeichnet zu sehen, das geschah wieder von Eurer Seite aus, die dabei ebenfalls den Anspruch machte, deutsches Wesen besser als ich zu vertreten: das war Hr. Aber.

"In gleichem Atemzuge wurde mit mir auch der andere 'Adolf,' Adolf Hitler näm-lich, der vier Jahre lang [und] [hunder]te von Malen sein Leben für die deutsche Sache hinzugeben bereit war, oder, schlichter ausgedrückt, als braver deutscher Sol-dat vier Jahren lang auf deutscher Seite kämpfte, als 'Ausländer' und, eigentlich noch schwerwiegender, als undeutscher Mann—so etwas wie 'erdrosselt' . . . ich gestehe dir's offen, so krass und unverhüllt ist mir persönlich jüdischer Geist noch nicht entgegengetreten. Du warst bis dahin für mich das sicherste *persönliche* Bollwerk gegen alle antisemitische Beeinflussungen. Es ist gefallen und ich muß mich nun mehr an meiner allgemeinen Anschauungen, die durch persönliche Erfahrung na-türlich nicht erschüttert werden können, halten" (Heuss to Einstein, 17 Apr. 1932, folder 454, Einstein Papers).

26. Otto Erich Deutsch was still given publishing opportunities because he was, according to Stefan Zweig, "taken for an Aryan" (Zweig to Einstein, 20 Dec. 1937, folder 1071, Einstein Papers).

27. "Wie der Klatsch wissen will, macht Breitkopf und Härtel, der Verleger der Zeitschrift für Musikwissenschaft, Einstein neuerdings das Leben schwer, indem er heftig Kritik übt an seiner redaktionellen Politik. . . . Nun kommt auch die allge-meine nationalistische Welle hinzu, die Deutschland gerade überflutet. Auswirkun-gen davon sind überall deutlich zu spüren. Nimmt Einstein Ihren Aufsatz und stellt solche von Deutschen zurück, so ist er möglicherweise als Jude einem gefährlichen Trommelfeuer ausgesetzt. . . . Übt nun der Verband [Deutsche Musikgesellschaft] gleichzeitig mit dem Verleger Kritik, so ist Einsteins Lage nicht gerade rosig. Und wir haben gerade an der Spitze der deutschen Musikwissenschaft ein paar sehr 'na-tional' empfindende Köpfe, von deren guter oder böser Meinung E[instein] keines-falls unabhängig ist" (Edwin von der Null to Bartók, transcribed in *Documenta Bar-tókiana* 3 [1968]: 161–62 [copy in folder 131, Einstein Papers]).

28. "Satzung der Deutschen Gesellschaft für Musikwissenschaft (früher 'Deutsche Musikgesellschaft')" (Ursprung Papers).

29. "Dem Herrn Reichsminister für Volksaufklärung und Propaganda senden die in Leipzig zur Neuorganisation der 'Deutschen Gesellschaft für Musikwissen-schaft' versammelten Vertreter der Musikwissenschaft von 18 deutschen Universi-täten und Hochschulen Treugelöbnis und ehrerbietigen Gruß. Sie bekunden den freudigen Willen, weiterhin mit dem Einsatz ihrer ganzen Kraft am Neuaufbau der

deutschen Kultur mitzuarbeiten, und sind sich der hohen Verantwortung bewußt, die ihnen zu ihrem Teil an der Verwaltung und Mehrung der unvergänglichen musikalischen Kulturgüter unseres Volkes auferlegt ist" (Schering to Goebbels, 26 Nov. 1933, Bundesarchiv Koblenz R55/1141 184). Herder (Propaganda Ministry) wrote back to the DGMW on 30 November 1933 giving the minister's approval (R55/1141 185).

30. Ludwig Schiedermair conjectured thus, and also greeted the change in editors, hoping that the "unpalatable boredom" and "colorlessness" of the journal of the last years would come to an end: "From the announcement of Mr. Einstein's resignation from the editorship of the journal effective at the end of the fiscal year, I assume that a restructuring is also taking place here [in the DMG]. Hopefully it will come to pass that the unqualified will retreat the background, and the often unpalatable boredom and colorlessness of the journal over these last years will come to an end" (Schiedermair to Sandberger, 2 July 1933, Adolf Sandberger Papers [Ana 431], Manuscript Division, Bavarian State Library, Munich).

31. Apart from the political circumstances, Einstein had been caught in the middle of a bitter conflict between Kroyer and Schering since the fall of 1932, which centered on an article by Kroyer on the question of a cappella performance that took issue with Schering. Kroyer's apparently tactless language compelled Einstein to urge him to tone down his attacks (Einstein to Kroyer, 16 Oct. 1932, folder 568, Einstein Papers), and the conflict escalated to the point where Schering threatened, among other things, to resign his post in the DMG if the article appeared. Einstein, caught in the cross-fire, knew very well that publishing the article would mean the end of his career as editor of the *Zeitschrift*, especially in light of a shaky relationship with Breitkopf & Härtel (Einstein to Kroyer, 21 Jan. 1933, folder 568, Einstein Papers) and the need to approach the state for financial support. Einstein tried desperately to mediate the conflict, but rivalries between Kroyer and Schering were too deep, and this only added to the heightened tension already caused by the uncertain status of the DMG in the new state.

32. DMG to Einstein, 24 June 1933, folder 1038, Einstein Papers.

33. "Was Sie gefürchtet haben und was ich in meiner Naivität für unmöglich gehalten habe, ist gekommen: man verlangt Ihre Abberufung als Schriftleiter der Zeitschrift. Der Vorstand hat sich vor einigen Tagen mit der Frage beschäftigen müssen und ist zu dem Ergebnis gelangt, daß es unmöglich ist, gegen die Zeitströmungen anzurennen, zumal das Unternehmen vom Staat Subvention verlangen muß" (Wolf to Einstein, 25 June 1933, folder 1038, Einstein Papers). In the same letter, Wolf announced that he was resigning from his seat on the executive board. One other member of the DMG, Annelise Landau, also withdrew from the society out of solidarity with Einstein (Landau to Breitkopf & Härtel, 28 Aug. 1938, folder 581, Einstein Papers).

34. "Ich bin nicht mehr Schriftleiter der ZfM. Am letzten Montag habe ich meine offizielle Verabschiedung erhalten. Glauben Sie nicht, daß die DMG etwa von oben herunter 'gleichgeschaltet' worden wäre. Ich habe das durch Furtwängler, der ja sich und den Herren Hinkel u. Consorten täglich abgeben muß, noch besonders feststellen lassen. Sondern meine Absägung ist das Werk von Herrn v. Hase [Breitkopf & Härtel], der mit der—ja mir allzu plausiblen—Begründung, die DMG müsse an die neue Regierung mit der Bitte der Unterstützung herangehen, die 'Untrag-

barkeit' eines nichtarischen Schriftleiters unwiderrufich dargetan hat" (Einstein to Kroyer [draft], 7 July 1933, folder 568, Einstein Papers).

35. Einstein to Heuss, 17 July 1933, folder 454; to Kroyer (draft), 7 July 1933, folder 568; and to Erwin Kroll, 13 Dec. 1933, folder 567: Einstein Papers.

36. "Wirklich untergebracht worden sind eine Anzahl von Gelehrten, und zwar dadurch, dass eine Reihe englischer Fachgenossen auf einen Teil ihres Gehaltes verzichteten. Es sind meist Physiker, Chemiker, Psychologen gewesen; für Musikwissenschaftler ist Ähnliches kaum zu erwarten" (Einstein to Kroll, 13 Dec. 1933, folder 567, Einstein Papers).

37. Einstein to Kroll, 27 Dec. 1947, folder 567, Einstein Papers.

38. Folder 573, Einstein Papers.

39. Scholes to British Consul in Zurich, 15 Nov. 1938, folder 919, Einstein Papers.

40. Recounted by Eva Einstein in a letter to Nicolas Slonimsky, 1 Oct. 1979, folder 852, Einstein Papers. Albert's letter undoubtedly contributed to the misconception that he and Alfred were cousins, as some reference works claim. According to Einstein's daughter, they knew each other as schoolmates in Munich and as neighbors in Berlin, especially since they lived near each other and often received each other's mail.

41. Josten to Einstein, 10 Apr. 1939, folder 508; W. A. Nielsen (President of Smith College) to Einstein, 16 Feb. 1940, folder 672: Einstein Papers. Eva Einstein further explained to me that the family left England because of a lack of prospects (an offer came through to teach at Cambridge at the last minute, but they had already decided to leave for the United States). Ms. Einstein further stressed the family's great indebtedness to Werner Josten for his efforts to arrange the position at Smith.

42. Einstein to Kroll, 21 Dec. 1947, folder 567, Einstein Papers.

43. Ibid.

44. Interview with Eva Einstein.

45. Foreword to *Chronologisch-Thematisches Verzeichnis sämtlicher Tonwerke Wolfgang Amadé Mozart,* 6th ed., ed. Franz Geigling, Alexander Weinmann, and Gerd Sievers (Wiesbaden: Breitkopf & Härtel, 1964), lv; and Breitkopf & Härtel to Hans David, 4 May 1954, folder 251, Einstein Papers.

46. Raabe to Einstein, 1 Apr. 1930, folder 757, Einstein Papers.

47. Bärenreiter to Einstein, 7 and 9 Sept. 1936, folder 122; Max Hinrichson (Peters) to Einstein, 21 Apr. and 8 May 1937, folder 464: Einstein Papers.

48. Blume to Einstein, 22 Sept. and 18 Oct. 1934, folder 169, Einstein Papers. See also Blume's introductions to the Eulenberg edition (1934) of Mozart's Piano Concerto in C Major, K. 467, iii and vii; and to the Eulenberg edition (1935) of the Piano Concerto in D Major, K. 537, iii and ix.

49. Einstein to Schott (draft), 7 Nov. 1938, and Schott to Einstein, 8 Dec. 1938, folder 829, Einstein Papers.

50. Einstein to Slonimsky, 24 Mar. 1947, folder 851, Einstein Papers.

51. Einstein to Slonimsky, 11 Mar. 1951, folder 851, Einstein Papers.

52. Blume asked Oliver Strunk to write an entry on Einstein, and Einstein's widow reports that her husband was opposed to the idea and to being mentioned in the work at all. Strunk to Einstein, 23 Oct. 1951, folder 885; Hertha Einstein (wife of Alfred) to Slonimsky, 25 May 1952, folder 851: Einstein Papers.

53. Einstein to Kroll, 16 May 1948, folder 567, Einstein Papers.

54. Einstein wrote to Adler shortly after his arrival: "We have been set up here for two months and consider ourselves quite fortunate . . . it all has a friendly and informal air. My harem is delighted to be living in a comfortable house once again and to be able to keep house with ample resources." (Einstein to Adler, 13 Oct. 1939, Adler Papers). Eva Einstein indicated in our discussion that her father's impression of the United States changed dramatically for the better after his arrival.

55. "Aus diesem Deutschland der Bestialität kann niemals wieder ein Deutschland der Humanität werden; wer sich mit ihm identifiziert, hat das Recht verloren, die Namen Mozart, Beethoven, Goethe, Schiller auch nur in den Mund zu nehmen. An das Deutschland dieser Namen muß ich mich in Zukunft halten, das kann mir niemand rauben" (Einstein to Heuss, 17 July 1933, folder 454, Einstein Papers).

56. "Ich gestehe, dass ich hier unter den bescheidensten Verhältnissen sehr glücklich bin; mein Deutschtum, meine Liebe zu allem was wirklich deutsch ist, im Gegensatz zu den verschauspielerten Deutschtum eines Staates der moralisch geistig kulturell tief unter dem Negerstaat Liberia steht, kann mir ja niemand rauben" (Einstein to Kroll, 13 Dec. 1933, folder 567, Einstein Papers).

57. Gerstenberg to Einstein, 21 Feb. 1949, folder 367; Einstein to Slonimsky, 30 Mar. 1949, folder 851: Einstein Papers.

58. Heilbut, *Exiled in Paradise*, 325–30. Heilbut outlines the positions of a few prominent émigrés, including Albert Einstein, whose attitude bears many similarities with that of Alfred.

59. Draft of letter, 13 June 1938, folder 89, Einstein Papers.

60. Einstein to Mark Brunswick, 7 Dec. 1948, folder 197; Einstein to Kroll, 16 Aug. 1948, folder 567: Einstein Papers.

61. Einstein to Eric Blom, 25 Aug. and 10 Oct. 1948, folder 167, Einstein Papers.

62. Draft of letter to Internationale Stiftung Mozarteum Salzburg, 16 Dec. 1949, folder 13, Einstein Papers.

63. Draft of letter to Kestenberg, July 1936, folder 521, Einstein Papers.

64. Liuzzi to Einstein, 20 July 1938, folder 611, Einstein Papers.

65. "Wir verlassen Italien—die 'difesa della razza' wird zwar von ihrem Urheber als Original-Leistung gerühmt, kommt uns aber äußerst vertraut vor" (Einstein to Lotte Medicus, 21 Aug. 1938, folder 635, Einstein Papers).

66. Einstein (writing in English) to Geoffrey Sharp, 17 June 1945, folder 842, Einstein Papers.

67. Einstein to Kroll, 16 May 1948, folder 567, Einstein Papers.

68. Einstein to Slonimsky, 25 Mar. 1949, folder 851, Einstein Papers.

69. Einstein to Eric Blom, 10 Oct. 1948, folder 167; and to Slonimsky, 6 July 1949, folder 851: Einstein Papers.

70. Einstein to Kroll (on Haas and Engel), 16 Aug. 1948, folder 567; Einstein to Slonimsky (on Müller-Blattau), 15 Dec. 1947, folder 851: Einstein Papers.

71. Disciplines that were similarly receptive included psychoanalysis, as opposed to fields such as philosophy. See Lewis A. Coser, *Refugee Scholars in America: Their Impact and Their Experiences* (New Haven: Yale University Press, 1984).

72. Of Steinzor's thirty-five leading scholars, eleven of the nonrefugees received some or all of their training in Germany.

73. Colleagues who emigrated included musicologist/librarian Robert Lachmann and psychologists Wolfgang Köhler and Max Wertheimer; students and younger colleagues included Mieczylaw Kolinski, Walter Kaufmann, Hans Hickmann, Manfred Bukofzer (all students of Sachs and Hornbostel), Klaus Wachsmann, Ernst Emsheimer, and Edith Gerson-Kiwi. Albrecht Schneider, "Musikwissenschaft in der Emigration," in *Musik im Exil: Folgen des Nazismus für die internationale Musikkultur,* ed. Hanns-Werner Heister, Claudia Maurer Zenck, and Peter Petersen (Frankfurt: Fischer, 1993), 192–97; idem, "Germany and Austria," in *Ethnomusicology: Historical and Regional Studies,* ed. Helen Meyers (New York: W. W. Norton, 1993), 85.

74. Bose to Reich Education Ministry, 31 Mar. 1934, Zentrales Staatsarchiv Potsdam, REM Nr. 1475, Bl. 480; Bose, "Lebenslauf," 25 Nov. 1941, Universitätsarchiv, Humboldt-Universität zu Berlin, Bose file.

75. "Der Musikforscher . . . hat in den dreißig Jahren . . . keinerlei Universitätsamt innegehabt, vielleicht auch nicht angestrebt innerhalb einer Zunft, die in Deutschland dem jüdischen Kollegen eher mit achtungsvoller Distanziertheit begegnete" (Albrecht Roeseler, "Gelehrter und Essayist," *Süddeutsche Zeitung,* 30 Dec. 1980 [copy in folder 17, Einstein Papers]).

76. "Ich habe keine akademische Laufbahn hinter mir. Die gleichen Gründe, die seit 1933 zur Entl[assung] u[nd] Austreibung jüdischer Wissensch[aftler] geführt haben, haben schon nach 1903, nach meiner Doctorierung, mich verhindert, mich zu habilitieren" (Einstein to Notgemeinschaft der deutschen Wissenschaft [draft], 8 Sept. 1936, folder 1073, Einstein Papers).

77. Einstein to Kroll, 21 Dec. 1947, folder 567, Einstein Papers.

78. "A Star of Knowledge," *Time,* 24 Apr. 1950.

Immigrant Musicians and the American Chamber Music Scene, 1930–1950

Walter Levin

The influence of emigration on American chamber music between 1930 and 1950 was in various ways both extensive and problematic: extensive in that performing musicians, ensembles, teachers, and composers fleeing fascist Europe irrevocably reconfigured the American musical landscape in terms of performance quality and style, in terms of repertoire, in terms of audience types and sizes, and in terms of institutional structures; problematic in that very few of the ensembles that came to the United States during the 1930s survived intact. Those that did, adapted both repertoire and performance practice to already dominant aesthetic norms in the New World; others, who turned to theoretical work and pedagogy, encountered significant resistance. However, in that curious fashion somehow so typical of the United States, even in emigration the most avant-garde traditions of European chamber music left their mark in the form of institutional innovations such as ensemble residencies, chamber music festivals, lecture-recital series, fellowships, and commissions that have both shaped many of the younger international ensembles and been directly responsible for much of the chamber repertoire of the twentieth century.

Before trying to assess the influence that refugees from Europe have had on the development of chamber music in this country between 1930 and 1950, we will have to take a look at the state of chamber music here prior to this period. This would include early performing groups: the economics of their financial support, their management, the concert-giving organizations that engaged them, and, as far as can be ascertained, certain stylistic characterizations and instrumental idiosyncrasies. I will concentrate here on string quartets, which have overwhelmingly dominated the American chamber music scene.

Professional chamber music performance in America developed rather recently. Early organizations, more or less permanent, were formed in Boston and New York around 1850. Among the most important were the Harvard Musical Association, which initiated an annual series of chamber music concerts in 1844 that continued for five years, and the Mendelssohn Quintette Club of Boston (consisting of five string players, two of whom doubled on flute and clarinet), which was active from 1849 to 1895. The Mendelssohn Club went on nationwide tours and eventually traveled as far away as Hawaii, Australia, and New Zealand. Probably the most outstanding of the early groups, however, was the Mason/Thomas Quintet, founded by Boston-born pianist William Mason in 1855. Mason had studied with Moscheles in Leipzig and with Liszt in Weimar, where he met Brahms. Upon his return to the United States he settled in New York and, together with the twenty-year old Theodore Thomas, leader of an established string quartet, organized the "Mason/Thomas Soirées" of chamber music, which continued until 1868.

The string quartet component of this group, the Thomas Quartet, was the first truly professional string quartet in America. The ensemble's first program in November 1855 included Schubert's *Death and the Maiden* Quartet and Brahms's First Piano Trio, op. 8, which had been published just a year before. In between these two formidable works was a typical variety program that included "Lied an den Abendstern" from *Tannhäuser,* Chopin's "Fantaisie-Impromptu," Variations for Cello and Piano by Mendelssohn, and a song by Otto Nicolai. Such eclecticism was typical at the time, both in Europe and in America. As late as the 1930s and early 1940s, concert organizers in smaller American towns still considered an all-quartet program too demanding for their audience, and often included a soloist for variety, having Efrem Zimbalist play a violin solo, for instance, or Rose Bampton sing some lieder in between quartets. Most members of these early organizations were born and trained in Germany and Austro-Hungary. Thus professional chamber music in the United States was, from its start in the mid–nineteenth century, predominantly the domain of immigrants.

The musicians of the Mendelssohn and Mason/Thomas groups were only part-time chamber music players, however. For economic reasons they also had to play in orchestras. In fact, up to about 1950, income from chamber music playing could only in the rarest instances fully support the members of an ensemble. To this day, most chamber music groups have to rely on some sort of outside financial and institutional support to survive.

The development of professional chamber music performance in America was made possible first and foremost by the financial support of wealthy, enthusiastic private sponsors, the counterpart of such earlier aristocratic patrons as Counts Lichnowsky and Razumovsky in Vienna and Galitzin in St. Petersburg, who commissioned new works from contemporary composers and supported Ignaz Schuppanzigh's quartet, the first full-time string quartet in Europe. In America, federal support has been minimal at best; rather, chamber music has depended on benefactors, such as Gertrude Clarke Whitall, Edward de Coppet, and, more recently, Rosalie Leventritt and Alice Tully.

One sponsor, however, towers above all others: Elizabeth Sprague Coolidge. The development of chamber music in this country after World War I was advanced to an overwhelming degree by the enlightened initiative and extraordinary generosity of Mrs. Coolidge. Born in Chicago in 1864, Mrs. Coolidge exercised a significant influence during the entire period under consideration here. Her sponsorship eventually embraced all aspects of chamber music performance: the commissioning of new works; the organization of festivals for their performance; the creation of a foundation at the Library of Congress in Washington to provide concerts there and in schools and universities around the country; the allocation of funds for building a chamber music auditorium at the Library; helping universities to engage groups permanently as ensembles-in-residence; and last but not least, the active support of virtually every important chamber music group, American or foreign, at special festivals and concert series which she sponsored throughout this country and abroad. A major portion of the twentieth-century quartet repertoire was composed as a result of her commissions. These works include Bartók's Fifth Quartet, Schoenberg's Third and Fourth Quartets, Webern's op. 28, Prokofiev's First Quartet, two quartets by Malipiero, Copland's Piano Quartet, Honegger's Third Quartet, and Piston's Fourth Quartet. Mrs. Coolidge died in Cambridge, Massachusetts, in 1953. Such sponsorship was the model for many other benefactors who founded private chamber music societies in cities across the country, such as the Wurlitzer family of Cincinnati. In addition to universities and colleges, it is these private societies which to this day have remained the backbone of professional chamber music in the United States.

Early interest in chamber music in cities across the country was stimulated by local ensembles formed by members of the resident symphony orchestra. The most successful and famous of these early groups was the Kneisel String Quartet of Boston, which toured nationally and internationally. Its career from 1885 to 1917 exemplifies the transition from orchestral dependence to independent professional ensemble and marks the earliest association between a chamber music ensemble and a professional school of music. The quartet was formed by Romanian-born Franz Kneisel when he came to Boston in 1885 as concertmaster of the recently established Boston Orchestra. While there were other quartets active before and during the career of the Kneisel Quartet, this group seems to have had the greatest influence on the development and chamber music activity in the United States in the period between 1885 and 1917. In 1903 the group members resigned from the Boston Orchestra in order to devote themselves exclusively to quartet playing, the first American quartet to do so without outside financial sponsorship. For a quarter of a century they performed regular concert series at Harvard, Yale, and Princeton, in New York City and in Philadelphia, later expanding their activities to Chicago, the West, and eventually to the entire United States. In 1905 Kneisel was approached by Frank Damrosch, head of the newly organized Institute of Musical Art in New York (later a component of the Juilliard School) to head the string department together with other members of the quartet as faculty. The Kneisel Quartet thus became the first professional resident string quartet at a school of music in the United States, establishing a tradition of chamber music coaching based on the idea of "in residence" ensembles that has steadily spread over the past ninety years to music schools and universities throughout the country. Today virtually every major American ensemble is associated with an institution of higher education, an association that usually includes, in varying mixes, the elements of teaching, coaching, concert series, lecture-recitals, concerts for young people in the community and in public schools, and of course, time for touring.

Parallel to the Kneisel Quartet, a younger group began playing regularly in New York in 1904: the legendary Flonzaley Quartet. The well-nigh utopian circumstances of this quartet's inception have probably never been duplicated. The idea of forming a permanent string quartet devoted exclusively to the study and performance of the quartet literature without outside obligations and free from any financial concerns arose out of private chamber music sessions with the pianist-wife of the Swiss-American banker Edward J. de Coppet. He became the Flonzaley's sponsor.

The Flonzaley members' background in the Franco-Belgian school of violin playing made famous by Ysaye, together with the possibility of unlimited rehearsal time, resulted in a quality of quartet playing hitherto unheard of in this country. The Flonzaley Quartet was decidedly of the twentieth century, a modern group by any standard, featuring constant vibrato, expressive portamenti rather than slides of convenience, moving tempi with sparing rhetorical gestures, equality of the four voices, clarity of the contrapuntal fabric, and no undue dominance of the first violin. The quartet was not even named after the first violinist, as had been the custom of most quartets prior to World War II. Its repertoire included many twentieth-century works. The group gave the American premiere of Schoenberg's First Quartet, and Stravinsky's Concertino is dedicated to them. The Flonzaley Quartet stopped playing in 1929. In twenty-five years, they played over 3,000 concerts, 500 of those in Europe, 2,500 in America in more than four hundred towns. By this time, and not least due to their efforts, chamber music in America had reached a level of ensemble virtuosity and professionalism comparable with contemporary European standards.

The stock market crash of 1929 and the resulting depression created enormous difficulties for musicians and concert organizers during the 1930s. It was the worst possible time for a new wave of immigrants to arrive in the United States. For musicians, a precondition for obtaining an immigration visa was either an appointment to an institution of higher learning, a contract with a major symphony orchestra, or a guarantee of financial support from a U.S. citizen (the famous "affidavit"). Many highly qualified potential refugees failed to meet these stringent conditions and were denied access. Those that did succeed faced considerable hardships in the depression years.

Musical performance in the United States had long been dominated by foreign musicians: soloists and chamber music groups, singers and conductors had been coming from Europe regularly for engagements and nationwide tours. The arrival of European groups fleeing Nazi persecution in the mid-1930s and wanting to settle in the United States was therefore hardly noticed by concert audiences, who knew most of these artists from previous visits. Of the string quartets that fled the Nazis, the Busch, Kolisch, Pro Arte, and Budapest all had been heard on tour in this country before. The Léner Quartet had already emigrated to the United States in 1929.

Of those groups that did manage to immigrate to the United States after 1933, only one, the Budapest Quartet, survived the depression and World War II as a successful chamber music organization.[1] Even so, this was possible only thanks to the help of a powerful backer, Mrs. Gertrude Clark Whitall, who provided the funds for the appointment of the group to the newly created position of quartet-in-residence at the Library of Congress. There they performed an annual series of concerts on the set of four Stradivari instruments that Mrs. Whitall had previously given to the library. The quartet retained this position from 1940 until 1962 and acquired the status of a quasi–national institution, enjoying enormous media exposure, regular nationwide radio broadcasts, and eventually the first ever live quartet telecasts. The arrangement with the Library of Congress gave the quartet financial security with ample time for nationwide and international touring and for study. For a whole generation, the name Budapest Quartet became synonymous with professional chamber music in the United States; indeed, their notoriety made them the subject of cartoons, advertising, and even jokes. For instance: "What is one Russian? One Russian is an anarchist, two Russians are a chess game, three Russians are a revolution, and four Russians are the Budapest Quartet."

The mixture of professional smoothness and personal mystique, plus the charismatic second violinist, Alexander Schneider, made the Budapest Quartet eminently marketable, a fact confirmed by their exclusive recording contract with Columbia Records. In 1962, sales of their records amounted to well over $2 million, leading Columbia proudly to hail the Budapest as "incontestably the world's best-selling quartet." They were masters of public relations. The coup of playing Mozart's Clarinet Quintet with jazz clarinetist Benny Goodman gained them notoriety among millions of jazz fans around the country. In August 1951, at the Ravinia summer festival in Chicago, they drew an audience of more than fifteen thousand people. Their YMHA concerts in New York outsold those of their competitors by a margin of better than five to one, at prices twice as high as those for other groups. The activities of this group in fact made chamber music economically viable for the post–World War II generation of American-trained chamber music players. Single-handedly, the Budapest Quartet made chamber music a quasi-popular mass entertainment.

From a latter-day vantage point, the Budapest was a rather conservative group. In their early days in Europe, first in Budapest and later in Berlin, they had played a fair amount of new music. But once settled in America, this adventurousness was tempered by the tastes of changed personnel, the preferences of American audiences, and the influence of managers and sponsors who cautioned against the inclusion of contemporary music. Part of the success of the Budapest Quartet certainly lay in the members' willingness to adapt to such requirements. Although they did play works by quite a few contemporary American composers, mainly neoclassical in style, their repertoire became predominantly classical and romantic, with a strong emphasis on Beethoven. They recorded the complete cycle of Beethoven quartets three times (!) and, eventually, as a result of their success, became cast as the model of classical and romantic interpretation. Some Bartók, Hindemith, and Prokofiev, even the early Schoenberg quartets and *Verklärte Nacht,* would occasionally appear in their programs, but they avoided the twelve-tone works of Schoenberg and never played any Webern or Berg, let alone any works by the postwar American or European avant-garde.

The Budapest Quartet was by far the most successful group in the period 1930–50, and thus was enormously influential in shaping audience expectations and tastes, in addition to serving as role models for a younger generation of American quartet players. However, the subtle influence of others, though initially less perceptible, proved ultimately more long-lasting.

The Budapest Quartet had come to the United States in 1938. Arriving just a year later, the Kolisch Quartet did not survive immigration. While they finally decided to stay in America just before the outbreak of the War in 1939, it was by then too late to establish a financially viable career based exclusively on the North American continent. The quartet, moreover, was famous for championing new music. It had given the U.S. premiere of Bartók's Fifth and Sixth Quartets and played all the works of Schoenberg, Berg, and Webern, including first performances of two works commissioned by Mrs. Coolidge: Schoenberg's Fourth Quartet (premiered in Los Angeles in January 1937 as part of the group's famous cycle, sponsored by Mrs. Coolidge, coupling the four Schoenberg quartets with four late Beethoven quartets); and Webern's op. 28 (in the fall of 1938 at South Mountain, Massachusetts).

But the very qualities that make the Kolisch Quartet's achievements of continuing relevance even today stood in the way of popular success in the United States of the 1930s. The group's programs were uncompromisingly serious. Not only was there no potpourri mixing in of fiddlers or solo singers, but the quartet persisted in playing "unpopular" programs that included demanding *new* pieces as well as big, difficult older ones. Their debut performance in 1935 at the Library of Congress, while on a U.S. tour, was typical: Beethoven's op. 130, in the original version with the "Große Fuge" finale; Berg's *Lyric Suite;* and the premiere of Bartók's Fifth Quartet.

Kolisch's ideas on musical reproduction owed much to the performance criteria developed by his teacher Schoenberg and practiced in the Verein für musikalische Privataufführungen. In essence, these established the primacy of the composition over the performer. As Hermann Danuser observed: "Among the most important motives of Schoenberg's theory of performance must rank the development of a performance practice that would protect not only his own works but also those of the *past* from the arbitrariness of the interpreter. The same holds true for the performance theories of other members of the Viennese School, particularly Rudolf Kolisch, Erwin Stein, René Leibowitz, Theodor Adorno, and Hans Swarowsky."[2] The Kolisch Quartet's interpretations of the standard repertoire were radically different from the norm represented by the Budapest Quartet. They played with less rubato, tighter tempi, practically no portamenti, utmost dynamic contrast, a fierce fidelity to the score coupled with a style of rhetorical expressivity that Kolisch referred to as "the Viennese espressivo," and, most characteristic of all, a historically founded disdain for the limitations and restraint imposed by the aesthetic of the "beautiful tone."[3]

The transparent clarity of their readings went largely unnoticed. The fact that this quartet was the first to play much of the repertoire, including many contemporary pieces, from memory was not appreciated by audiences in the provinces used to soloists playing recitals from memory as a matter of course and unfamiliar with the standard practice of chamber music groups to play from music. As a matter of principle, every piece the Kolisch Quartet learned was rehearsed from full score by everyone instead of the customary one-line parts. It seemed obvious to the members that intelligent decisions could be made only if *every* player knew *every* voice in the score, not just his own. This is a lesson yet to be absorbed by younger quartet players even today.

The quartet disbanded in April 1939 when, as violist Eugene Lehner later explained, they realized that you could not live from concerts on one continent alone. Things had become financially difficult already in 1933, when Germany was lost to the quartet, though tours to America had compensated by providing an alternative forum. Evidently the Kolisch Quartet never considered a residency at an American university as a solution; after they had disbanded, however, Mrs. Coolidge claimed she could have obtained one for them with a single telephone call. Cellist Benar Heifetz joined Toscanini's NBC Orchestra, second violinist Felix Khuner went to San Francisco, and Lehner joined the Boston Symphony.

A short digression on quartet economics may illustrate the problem. The financial aspects of string quartet touring are historically bleak. Even today, fees are relatively low, usually considerably less than a soloist gets. Expenses, however, are fourfold: quartet members pay all of their own travel and lodging expenses, and managers deduct 20 percent of the gross fee. A group is doing well if at the end of a tour every member receives 10 percent of the fee. In the period under discussion, $500 fees were just about the top, and even the Budapest Quartet often played for $400 or less. Assuming a $400 fee, then, it would take one hundred concerts for a player to earn $4,000. But most ensembles booked no more than about twenty to thirty concerts a season. Without some sort of permanent income, such as a residency at the Library of Congress or a university provided, a quartet could hardly survive.

For a while Kolisch struggled to salvage the quartet, but with America's entry into the war he realized it was impossible, so he was forced to freelance in the New York area. In a letter to Schoenberg dated 23 July 1942 he wrote: "I made some new efforts to gain pupils and maybe an orchestra position. I am thinking of odd jobs in radio stations, shows, etc."[4] In December 1942 Kolisch actually accepted a job playing in the orchestra of a Broadway musical called *Rosalinda*.

The forced interruption of Kolisch's quartet activities did, however, have one positive result: it marked the emergence of Kolisch as a lecturer, theoretician, and teacher. "Musical Performance—The Realization of Musical Meaning" was the title of a course he gave at the New School for Social Research in New York. It was a subject that was to remain one of Kolisch's preoccupations for the rest of his life.

A second focus of interest for Kolisch was Beethoven. "Elements of Performance in Beethoven's Music" was the subject of seminars held at Black

Mountain College in 1944 and later that year at the University of Wisconsin in Madison, where Kolisch replaced the first violinist of the resident Pro Arte Quartet and started to teach. Although Kolisch acquired a devoted following as a teacher, a wider dissemination of his ideas has been hampered by the fact that many of the texts of these seminars (and also those given between 1967 and 1978 at the New England Conservatory in Boston) remain unpublished among Kolisch's papers at the Houghton Library of Harvard University. A projected book of Beethoven analyses for Schirmer, and an edition of Beethoven quartet parts in full score, never progressed beyond the planning stage.

Beethoven had also been the subject of a lecture which Kolisch gave at the 1942 annual meeting of the American Musicological Society in New York. This, his most extensive theoretical study, was published in 1943 in the April and June issues of the *Musical Quarterly* under the title "Tempo and Character in Beethoven's Music." After fifty years, a thoroughly revised version of the lecture appeared for the first time in German (the language in which Kolisch had originally written the lecture), and an English translation of this updated version was published in the *Musical Quarterly*.[5]

In a carefully reasoned analysis Kolisch attempts to establish the relationship between specific tempi in Beethoven's instrumental oeuvre and characteristic motivic types and rhythmic configurations. He examines Beethoven's metronomic indications as well as his relationship to the inventor of the metronome (or rather, its perfecter), Johann Nepomuk Maelzel, and goes on to extrapolate tempi for movements lacking metronome markings by comparing them to movements of a similar tempo category and character configuration to which metronome markings were assigned by Beethoven, a provocative and complex procedure. The lecture must have touched a raw nerve of the assembled notables, who included Artur Schnabel, Otto Klemperer, Oliver Strunk, Ralph Kirkpatrick, Felix Greissle, William Schuman, Edward Steuermann, and Alexander Schneider.[6] Kolisch's argument seemed to threaten that jealously guarded sacred domain of individual expression: the personal choice of tempo. The reaction was mixed, as could be expected.[7] Kolisch could hardly have expected, however, the almost total disregard of the substance of this seminal research on the part of performers who for over half a century have consigned this ground-breaking study to oblivion. Very few of them seem to have taken the trouble to study this paper, and from the evidence of Beethoven performances worldwide it seems that even fewer performers tried to implement these findings, with the notable exception of some younger American-trained quartets, or conductors such as René Leibowitz, Michael Gielen, and, more recently, Roger Norrington, Nikolaus Harnoncourt, and John Eliot Gardiner.

As this example perhaps indicates, there seems to be a persistent resistance to things theoretical among performers everywhere. This applies equally to older texts containing important information for the performer as it does to essays like Kolisch's and to more recent studies. Instrumentalists are rarely interested in reading Quantz, C. P. E. Bach, or Leopold Mozart. The separation of "Heart and Brain in Music" has not really changed much since Schoenberg wrote this article in 1946 with its central tenet that "it is not generally agreed that poets, artists, musicians, actors and singers should admit the influence of a brain upon their emotions."[8] In the end, any influence Kolisch's lectures and courses may have had was limited to a relatively small circle of students, many of whom were musicologists and theoreticians rather than performers.[9] Kolisch was never invited to teach at any of the major centers of instrumental training such as Juilliard or Curtis.

Ironically, however, it is by way of the Juilliard School that some of the thinking and practice of the Kolisch Quartet was transmitted to the generation that came after World War II. In 1946 the school, under the forward-looking leadership of its new director, William Schuman, engaged a young American string quartet to become ensemble-in-residence: the Juilliard Quartet. Its artistic mentor in the early days was Eugene Lehner, violist of the Kolisch Quartet from 1927 until it disbanded in 1939.[10] Lehner had enormous influence on the initial orientation of the Juilliard Quartet, not least on their choice of repertoire. This was the first American-born quartet to play the six Bartók quartets and the entire body of quartet compositions by Schoenberg, Berg, and Webern and to consistently champion new works. The Juilliard Quartet ushered in a period of lively experimentation that revolutionized the American chamber music scene. The group's 1946 Town Hall debut included Webern's Five Movements, op. 5, and Beethoven's op. 130 in the original version with the "Große Fuge," which only the Kolisch Quartet had played in America previously. The Juilliard's daring programs and exciting intensity swept away the middle-of-the-road conventionality that had become the norm of much of the American chamber music scene by 1950. Even Kolisch's Beethoven lecture finally bore fruit, provoking new interest in Beethoven's metronome marks. The result was a radical change in performance practice by some of the younger quartets.

It is interesting to compare Beethoven performances in the United States in the late 1950s and 1960s with those of contemporary European quartets, such as the Amadeus, Italiano, and Vegh. As a group, the Europeans continued to favor slower tempi—sometimes up to 30 percent slower—than those indicated by Beethoven. The American chamber groups, which by then included the New Music, Juilliard, and LaSalle Quartets, played more tightly controlled, often considerably faster tempi, and sharper delineations of other parameters such as dynamic contrasts, accents, and agogic scanning. A comparison of the scherzo in Beethoven's op. 59, no. 2 is particularly revealing.

The difference, I believe, can be traced directly to Kolisch's work on interpretation, which has thus had a subtle but profound influence on the orientation of chamber music performance in the United States in the second half of the century.[11]

⌒

Another great musician initially prevented by the adverse circumstances of immigration from fully developing his enormous potential influence as a performer and a teacher was Adolf Busch. Quite independent of Kolisch, Busch seems to have arrived at some surprisingly similar results concerning tempo and style already in the early 1930s.

The Busch Quartet's recordings of Beethoven's op. 95 and op. 59, no. 3, made in 1932 and 1933 respectively, clearly suggest that Busch, possibly through his close association with Toscanini, was also aware of the Beethoven metronome marks. All of op. 95 flies in the face of a performance tradition that persists even today despite concrete evidence of a different vision on the part of the composer. Less rhetorically inflected than the performances of practically any other group then and since, the playing of the Busch Quartet reveals great linear clarity and a persistent renunciation of subjectivity in favor of classical vigor and discipline.

Of all the musicians who emigrated to the United States in the 1930s, Adolf Busch had the reputation, experience, and versatility that would seem to have offered every prospect for successful integration. He was famous as a soloist; his quartet was among the best in Europe, as were his duo and trio with Rudolf Serkin; and he toured with and led the Busch Chamber Orchestra, making records for "His Master's Voice" with all of these ensembles. He was a successful composer and an experienced teacher. At age twenty-seven he had been appointed professor of violin at the Hochschule für Musik in Berlin.

Busch had made an auspicious American debut in 1931 as soloist with the New York Philharmonic under Arturo Toscanini, playing the Bach A Minor Violin Concerto and the Beethoven. In 1933 followed the American debut of his quartet and the duo with Serkin at the Library of Congress, sponsored by Mrs. Coolidge, a friend, admirer, and powerful supporter of Busch in the United States.

Coming to America on tour was one thing; making a living here as an immigrant, however, proved very problematic, even for someone as famous as Adolf Busch. Trying to persuade his quartet colleagues, then still in Europe, to join him permanently in the United States, he analyzed the prospects very realistically. In a letter to his brother Hermann, the quartet's cellist, dated 22 January 1940, he wrote:

The situation here is such that in order to be able to get work, you first have to LIVE here. Playing quartets in this country you cannot earn enough to cover the cost of repeated Atlantic crossings. We have to reduce our concert fees and if possible play for very little more than the other quartets. Levin, the manager at NBC, told me last week that with an average fee of $500, he would hope to obtain twenty engagements. We are now trying—directly and through friends—to find employment for you, even something modest, at a college, university, or conservatory, and hope to succeed and expect that this would give you the basis for a modest existence here. The income from quartet concerts and other possible engagements would provide for a little better life. We and our friends are trying everything, but the difficulty is that no additional artists are being permitted into the country because it is felt that all of them are here already. In fact, big-name conductors, soloists, and lots of quartets are running around here with nothing to do and practically no work. But those capable people who have been living here for a longer time are eventually able to find work in this vast country.[12]

A month later, in a letter from New York to his brother Fritz, the conductor, Busch wrote:

For the time being there isn't much one can do with the quartet. Well-paid concerts are unobtainable. There are dozens of quartets here playing for very little, and between two complete works they program transcriptions such as the Gavotte by Gosseck and selections from famous string quartets: Andante Cantabile by Haydn and Andante Cantabile by Tchaikovsky. That should not be necessary, but if you are unwilling to do so and unwilling to play for less than $500 you get no engagements at all.[13]

As it turned out, the quartet never did obtain a position as quartet-in-residence. Second violinist Gösta Andreasson eventually accepted a teaching position at the Carnegie Institute of Technology in Pittsburgh, which forced him to leave the quartet.

It may be futile to speculate on the reasons why certain ensembles succeeded while others, equally qualified, failed. In a conversation I had in Basel in April 1994, Dr. Hedwig Busch, widow of Adolf Busch, recalled an incident that may shed some light. Discussing the problems of concert engagements for the Busch Quartet in the United States, a New York manager said to Busch: "You are not the right type for this country." Who, one is tempted to ask, *was* the "right type"? The most successful instrumentalists in America at this time were Russian immigrants: Horowitz, Rachmaninoff, Heifetz, Piatigorsky, Elman, Milstein. So strong was the mystique that, to make a successful performing career, some native-born Americans assumed Russian names. Thus pianist Mary Hickenlooper from Texas became Olga Samaroff. Could this have been another factor in the singular success of the four Russians of the Budapest Quartet at the expense of virtually all others?

What one could be tempted to read as a generous openness of Americans to émigré musicians may have been, at least in part, a romanticized cliché image of the Eastern European artist, with his genius, inspiration, and passion, a myth resulting in aesthetic politics often dubious at best. It is disturbing to think that considerations of ethnic and national background by those in control of music management may have played a role in determining the success or failure of an artist.

Busch, the successor of Joachim and Marteau at the Berlin Hochschule für Musik and known in America as the teacher of the young Yehudi Menuhin, who had sought him out in Basel in 1929, was never asked to teach at an American music school until, finally, he was invited to become instructor of chamber music at the Curtis Institute in Philadelphia for the 1952–53 season. Alas, he died in June 1952.

Just one year earlier, however, Busch, together with Rudolf Serkin, the Moyse family, and his brother Hermann, had founded the Marlboro School of Music. In the close to fifty years of its existence this summer school has been a haven for serious study and performance in the humanistic chamber music tradition of Adolf Busch. Here, together with some of the greatest musicians of our time, two generations of performers from all over the world have been able to study and play—away from commercial pressures—a wide repertoire of ensemble music, much of it rarely if ever performed elsewhere: pieces like the Reger Sextet, for instance; where can that ever be heard? Busch himself taught there only the first summer. But in the decades since, under the gentle firmness of Rudolf Serkin's direction, the Marlboro Music School, Busch's artistic legacy, has made a profound difference in the minds and attitudes of countless young musicians. Through its unique combination of uncompromising professionalism and utopian spirituality, the influence of Adolf Busch can still be felt.

Audience interest in chamber music during the 1930s and 1940s was greatly stimulated by the media. The weekly nationwide live broadcasts of the NBC Symphony Orchestra under Arturo Toscanini between 1937 and 1954, which included a series of live telecasts between 1948 and 1952, for example, did much to popularize not only symphonic music, but chamber music as well. Toscanini often included pieces from the chamber music literature in his programs, such as the Minuet and Finale of Beethoven's quartet op. 59, no. 3; the two middle movements of Beethoven's quartet op. 135 (in reverse order); Beethoven's Septet; Mendelssohn's Octet and the Adagio from his String Quintet, op. 87; and movements from quartets by Haydn and Boccherini. Toscanini was proud of the many string quartet players in his orchestra, including the violinists Felix Galimir and Daniel Guilet (formerly of the French Calvet Quartet), Josef Gingold and Oscar Shumsky; violists William Primrose and Milton Katims (for a decade the fifth member of the Budapest Quartet whenever two-viola quintets were on the program); and Benar Heifetz, cellist of the Kolisch Quartet. Toscanini championed their cause with the NBC management, and the result was a series of nationwide Sunday morning broadcasts of quartets from the NBC Symphony.

Outstanding among these groups was the Primrose Quartet. Between 1940 and 1942, when it disbanded, this group made recordings for RCA that included works by Haydn, Smetana, and Brahms. These performances offer a fascinating glimpse of a style of quartet playing directly related to that of Toscanini. The third Brahms Quartet is particularly astonishing: moving tempi, rhythmically controlled and terse, nevertheless allow freedom of declamation and a singing intensity of expression; hearing the crisp articulation and contrasting dynamics combined with razor-sharp ensemble and individual virtuosity, one gets the shocking impression of listening to the first performance of a new work. It must have seemed too extreme for the officials of RCA: they never released the recording![14]

So far this essay has dealt with those refugees actively involved in the performance and teaching of chamber music. There is, however, another large group of refugees that had a major influence on the growth of chamber music in the period under consideration: immigrant music lovers. It is worth taking a brief look at the effect of their activities.

The enormous expansion of professional chamber music performance in the United States, its decentralization across the country after the end of the war, was advanced decisively by countless Central European music lovers who, dispersed by the vagaries of immigration, had settled in American communities large and small. Bringing along their enthusiasm and appetite for the musical activities they had grown up with, they soon became involved in local organizations with the result that chamber music societies and music clubs sprouted up in great numbers after World War II. The prototype for many of these had been founded in New York City as early as 1936: the famous New Friends of Music.[15] A nonprofit enterprise dedicated to presenting "the best in the literature of chamber-music and Lieder," it sponsored sixteen concerts annually, with emphasis on eighteenth- and nineteenth-century repertoire ranging from solo sonatas to works for chamber orchestra. The New Friends of Music audience consisted in large part of Central European refugees, whence its nickname, "Old Friends of Schnabel."

When our quartet, the LaSalle, began touring from its new base as quartet-in-residence at Colorado College in Colorado Springs in the early 1950s, we were surprised time and again when our local concert hosts turned out to be immigrants from Berlin, Munich, Vienna, Prague, and any number of cities across Europe. In Albuquerque, New Mexico, for instance, we were the guests of Kurt Frederick, conductor of the Albuquerque Civic Symphony. To our amazement, Mr. Frederick proved to be an expert in the music of the Second Viennese School and in fact had given, with his semiprofessional forces there in Albuquerque, the world premiere of Schoenberg's *A Survivor from Warsaw* in 1948.[16] Kurt Frederick was a refugee musician from Austria. Moreover, I discovered only recently that between 1938 and 1942 Mr. Frederick was the violist of the Kolisch Quartet!

A letter that Frederick wrote to Rudolf Kolisch in 1971 poignantly summarizes the contribution this refugee chamber music player turned conductor has made to the musical life of a city in the Southwest, thousands of miles from New York or Boston:

> I am retiring at the end of this school year, although I was asked to continue my teaching activities at the University beyond the normal retiring age; but I feel that teaching in Albuquerque for thirty years is enough . . . I have worked during the past 30 years very hard. My main efforts went into building up a university orchestra and performing some good music in Albuquerque. Our orchestra introduced to Albuquerque and the Southwest compositions by Schoenberg, Berg, Webern, Bartók, Stravinsky, Schuller, Erb, Penderecki and many others. But I conducted also the first Albuquerque performances of Beethoven symphonies, not to speak of Bruckner and Mahler.[17]

When in 1953 the LaSalle Quartet moved to Cincinnati as quartet-in-residence at the College of Music, we were warned by the college administrator not to program much contemporary music. Cincinnati audiences, he said, would just stay away. We discussed this problem with our friend Dr. Ferdinand Donath from Vienna, a student of Sigmund Freud's and a member of Schoenberg's Verein für musikalische Privataufführungen, who had emigrated to Cincinnati after the Anschluß. Upon his suggestion we decided, in order to overcome the audience reluctance, to offer a free introductory lecture-recital on the contemporary work of our next program. It proved a huge success. As a result, Dr. Donath and his friends formed a group modeled on the Schoenberg Verein that met regularly to listen to similar introductory lecture-recitals of ours featuring contemporary works. Eventually the members decided to expand their activities by commissioning American and European composers to write new quartets for our meetings. The list of works that resulted from this initiative includes quartets by Hans Erich Apostel, Mauricio Kagel, Luigi Nono, Michael Gielen, Earle Brown, Henri Pousseur, György Ligeti, and many others. Furthermore, it was decided to establish a fellowship making it possible to invite young professional quartets to come to Cincinnati for a year of concentrated study with the LaSalle members at the University of Cincinnati. Some fine quartets emerged from this program, among them the Prazak from Prague, the Alban Berg from

Vienna, and the young Vogler Quartet from Berlin. Thus, the commitment and enthusiasm of one Viennese refugee in Cincinnati, Ohio, resulted in a significant contribution to the world of chamber music.

Is it possible to draw any conclusions from this conflicting evidence? The situation in the 1930s was certainly far from encouraging. For those arriving late in that tumultuous decade, there was little chance of establishing a presence until the end of the war. Recession and war made survival the first priority, and chamber music was necessarily relegated to a back burner. People had other worries. The educational institutions were slow to seize the opportunity of engaging talented and experienced immigrant musicians for their faculties.

With the end of the war, however, a vigorous growth in interest began. Chamber music societies emerged around the country, new ensembles were formed, music schools engaged ensembles-in-residence and started professional chamber music study programs. In 1946 the Juilliard administration even responded to the desire of the LaSalle Quartet to concentrate exclusively on quartet study by introducing a new major in string quartet performance, the first school anywhere to do so. In the large summer programs such as Tanglewood, Aspen, and particularly Marlboro, many European emigrant musicians at last found an appropriate opportunity to teach, as well as to play for and with a new generation of students. Participants in these programs were from this country and, increasingly, from abroad, since it had become clear at last that a disastrous void had been created in Europe by the driving into exile of most of its great performers and teachers. Of those who emigrated to the United States in the 1930s, some succeeded in building brilliant careers, though many others suffered considerable hardship—but at least they survived. It is with their help that America has since become a major center of instrumental and chamber music study for musicians from around the world.

NOTES

1. For details of the Budapest Quartet's career, see Nat Brandt's *Con Brio: Four Russians Called the Budapest String Quartet* (Oxford: Oxford University Press, 1993).

2. Hermann Danuser, "Zu Schönberg's Vortragslehre," in *Zweiter Internationaler Kongreß der Arnold Schönberg Gesellschaft* (Vienna: Elisabeth Lafite, 1984), 253–59.

3. In an article entitled "On the Crisis of String Players" published in the *Darmstädter Beiträge zur neuen Musik* in 1958 (85–90), Kolisch writes: "The language of the Viennese classics, particularly that of Beethoven, already demands a wealth of dynamic and expressive categories for which technical correlates would have to be

systematically developed. On this point traditional pedagogy has completely failed. The priests of this religion have placed but a single ideal upon their altar: that of the beautiful tone. This is an extramusical category insofar as no work of art music was ever written for 'beautiful tone'" (my translation).

4. In December 1942 Kolisch writes: "You may already have heard rumors about my whereabouts. Nonetheless you should have an authentic report. The ice has been cracked: I have broken into the amusement industry. That happened as follows: one night Korngold, who is preparing a Fledermaus production here in New York, called me in desperation complaining that his orchestra is miserable. He begged me to help. Nothing could have been more welcome and so I am now assistant concertmaster of the Rosalinda orchestra (the concertmaster had been engaged already) and have played some 30 performances since" ("Aus dem Briefwechsel Rudolf Kolisch/Arnold Schönberg," *Musik-Konzepte* 76–77 [July 1992]: 107; my translation).

5. See Rudolf Kolisch, "Tempo und Charakter in Beethovens Musik," *Musik-Konzepte* 76–77 (July 1992), translated as "Tempo and Character in Beethoven's Music," *Musical Quarterly* 77 (spring 1993): 90–131 and (summer 1993): 268–342. Thanks are due to Leon Botstein, editor of the new *Musical Quarterly*, for making this article available again.

6. See "Anhang II, Dokumente: Aus dem Protokoll des Meeting der American Musicological Society, Greater New York Chapter," *Musik-Konzepte* 76–77 (July 1992): 106.

7. Kolisch to Schoenberg [ca. fall 1943], reprinted in *Musik-Konzepte* 76–77 (July 1992): 108.

8. Arnold Schoenberg, "Heart and Brain in Music," in *Style and Idea: Selected Writings of Arnold Schoenberg*, ed. Leonard Stein (Berkeley: University of California Press, 1984): 53–76.

9. Kolisch was a close friend of Theodor Adorno. The two had planned to write a joint study of a "Theory of Musical Reproduction," but it was never completed. Adorno's musical writings were virtually unknown among performing musicians of the 1960s and 1970s in the United States and, I daresay, still are. *The Philosophy of New Music*, published in German in 1949, took twenty-four years to appear in an English translation. The work of most direct relevance to the performer, Adorno's *Der getreue Korrepetitor* (The faithful music coach), which was published in German in 1963, has yet to appear in English.

10. For details on the Kolisch Quartet's career in the United States and the Juilliard Quartet's beginning, see the interview with Eugene Lehner in "Les musiciens du quatuor, IV, dernier mouvement: Reprise—la musique de chambre aux USA, la renaissance en Europe: 1938–1987," film by Georges Zeisel and Catherine Zins (coproduction INA/LA SEPT/CST/MTV, Paris, 1991). For additional details on Kolisch in this period, see the article by Claudia Maurer Zenck, "Was sonst kann ein Mensch denn machen als Quartett zu spielen—Rudolf Kolisch und seine Quartette 1921–1924," *Österreichische Musikzeitschrift* (1998): no. 11, pp. 8–57.

11. The only publication dealing with Kolisch's ideas on interpretation currently available, in German only, is "Rudolf Kolisch: Zur Theorie der Aufführung," *Musik-Konzepte* 29–30 (Jan. 1983).

12. Adolf Busch, *Briefe–Bilder–Erinnerungen* (Walpole, N.H.: Arts and Letters Press, 1991), 397; my translation.

13. See ibid., 400; my translation.

14. The RCA recordings of the Primrose Quartet, including Brahms op. 67, were issued on CD in 1992 by Biddulph Recordings of England (LAB-052-53).

15. For the personal memories of Ira Hirschmann, founder of the New Friends of Music, see Hirschmann, *Obligato: Untold Tales from a Life with Music* (New York: Fromm International, 1994), esp. chapter 2: "Creation of the New Friends of Music."

16. See Ernst Krenek, "An Exceptional Musician: Kurt Frederick," *New Mexico Quarterly* 21 (spring 1951): 26–35.

17. Unpublished letter, Kolisch Papers, Houghton Library at Harvard University, Cambridge, Mass.

APPENDIX

Musicologists Who Emigrated from Germany, Austria, and Central Europe, ca. 1930–1945

NOTE

The scholars on this list were principally musicologists, or made contributions to musicology and theory, and received at least some of their musicological training before emigrating. The list has been compiled by Lawrence Gushee and Bruno Nettl, with help from Alexander Ringer, Herbert Kellman, Albrecht Schneider, Philip Bohlman, Donald Krummel, and others. We are grateful to Bruno Nettl (University of Illinois) for making it available and for suggesting that it be published in this book. Although this list cannot claim to be comprehensive, we hope that it may serve as a useful basis for further research.

Those listed emigrated to various places, not just the United States, as indicated below. Although no bio- or bibliographical information is provided here—suffice to say that the vast majority of individuals are no longer alive—the roster speaks for itself. That is, it represents an "honor roll" of those whose collective contributions to musical scholarship were significant, influential, and of lasting value. Since no such list has ever been published, it seemed appropriate to include it in this volume devoted to the musical migration which, after all, had a strong impact on musicology in particular.

RB & CW

ABER, ADOLPH (UK 1936)
ADORNO, THEODOR (USA 1934)
ALBERSHEIM, GERHARD (USA 1940)
APEL, WILLI (USA 1936)
ARMA, AAUL (FRANCE 1933)
AVENARY, HANOCH (PALESTINE 1936)

341

BARTÓK, BÉLA (USA 1940)
BEKKER, PAUL (USA 1934)
BERGER, JEAN (FRANCE 1931, USA 1939)
BERGMANN, WALTER (UK 1938)
BLAUKOPF, CURT (PALESTINE 1938)
BODKY, ERWIN (HOLLAND 1933, USA 1939)
BOTSTIBER, HUGO (UK 1938)
BRAUNSTEIN, JOSEF (USA 1938?)
BROD, MAX (PALESTINE 1939)
BUKOFZER, MANFRED (SWITZERLAND 1933, UK 1938, USA 1939)
CAHN-SPEYER, RUDOLF (ITALY 1933)
CARNER, MOSCO (UK 1938)
CONNOR, HERBERT (DENMARK 1935, SWEDEN 1937)
DAVID, HANS T. (USA 1938)
DEUTSCH, OTTO ERICH (UK 1938)
DORIAN, FREDERICK (USA 1936)
EINSTEIN, ALFRED (UK 1933, ITALY 1935, USA 1938)
EMSHEIMER, ERNST (USSR 1932, SWEDEN 1937)
ENGEL, ERICH (ARGENTIAN 1933)
ENGLÄNDER, RICHARD (SWEDEN 1939)
EPPSTEIN, HANS (SWEDEN 1936)
FERAND, ERNST (USA 1938)
GÄL, HANS (UK 1938)
GEIRINGER, KARL (UK 1938, USA 1940)
GERSON-KIWI, EDITH (ITALY 1933, PALESTINE 1935)
GOMBOSI, OTTO (USA 1939)
GRADENWITZ, PETER (PALESTINE 1936)
GRAF, MAX (USA 1938)
GUTTMANN, ALFRED (NORWAY 1939)
HAAS, KARL (UK 1939)
HALPERN, IDA (CANADA 1938)
HARICH-SCHNEIDER, ETA (JAPAN 1939?)
HELFRITZ, HANS (CHILE 1939)
HERNRIED, ROBERT (USA 1933)
HERTZMANN, ERICH (USA 1938)
HERZ, GERHARD (USA 1936)
HICKMANN, HANS (EGYPT 1933)
HIRSCH, PAUL (UK 1936)
HIRSCH, ARTUR (UK 1936)
HOFFMANN, SHLOMO (PALESTINE ?)
HOLDE, ARTUR (USA 1937)
HOLZMANN, RODOLFO (FRANCE 1933, PERU 1938)
HONIGSHEIM, PAUL (FRANCE 1933, USA 1938)
HORNBOSTEL, E. M. VON (USA, THEN UK 1934)

HOWARD, WALTHER (SWITZERLAND 1936? HOLLAND 1937)
ISTEL, EDGAR (UK 1936, USA 1938)
JACOBI, ERWIN R. (PALESTINE 1934, USA 1947)
JONAS, OSWALD (USA 1938)
KATZ, ERICH (UK 1939, USA 1943)
KAUFMANN, WALTER (INDIA 1934, UK 1946, CANADA 1947, USA 1957)
KAYSER, HANS (SWITZERLAND 1933)
KESTENBERG, LEO (CZECHOSLOVAKIA 1933, PALESTINE 1938)
KELLER, HANS (UK 1938)
KNEPLER, GEORG (UK 1934)
KOELLREUTTER, HANS-JOACHIM (BRAZIL 1937)
KOLINSKI, MIECZYSLAW (CSR 1933, BELGIUM 1938, USA 1951)
KRENEK, ERNST (USA 1938)
KUTTNER, FRITZ (CHINA 1939, USA 1947)
LACHMANN, ROBERT (PALESTINE 1938)
LANDAU, ANNELIESE (UK 1939, USA 1940)
LANDSHOFF, LUDWIG (FRANCE 1933, USA 1939)
LEICHTENTRITT, HUGO (USA 1933)
LENTSCHNER, SOPHIE (PALESTINE CA. 1935, USA CA. 1946)
LEVARIE, SIGMUND (USA 1938)
LEVY, ERNST (USA 1941)
LIUZZI, FERNANDO (BELGIUM 1939, THEN USA, ITALY 1940)
LIVINGSTONE, ERNEST (VENEZUELA 1939, USA 1946)
LOEWENBERG, ALFRED (UK 1934)
LOWINSKY, EDWARD E. (HOLLAND 1933, USA 1939)
MANDELL, ERIC (USA 1940)
MANN, ALFRED (ITALY 1937, THEN USA)
MAYER-REINACH, ALBERT (SWEDEN 1938)
MAYER-SERRA, OTTO (SPAIN 1933)
MEYER, ERNST HERMANN (UK 1933)
MEYER-BAER, KATHI (USA 1939)
MISCH, LUDWIG (USA 1947)
MOLDENHAUER, HANS (USA 1938)
MÜLLER-HARTMANN, ROBERT (UK 1937)
NADEL, SIEGFRIED (UK 1932, AUSTRALIA CA. 1953)
NATHAN, HANS (USA 1936?)
NETTL, PAUL (USA 1939)
NEUMANN, FREDERICK (USA 1939)
PAHLEN, KURT (ARGENTINA 1939)
PAUMGARTNER, BERNHARD (SWITZERLAND AND ITALY 1938)
PISK, PAUL A. (USA 1939)
PLAMENAC, DRAGAN (USA 1939)
PRAETORIUS, ERNST (TURKEY 1935)
RAWSKI, CONRAD (USA 1938)

REBLING, EBERHARD (HOLLAND 1936)
REDLICH, HANS F. (UK 1939)
REICH, WILLI (SWITZERLAND 1938)
REICHENBACH, HERMANN (USSR 1933, USA 1938)
RÉTI, RUDOLF (USA 1938)
RIEDEL, JOHANNES (ECUADOR CA. 1938, USA CA. 1950)
RINGER, ALEXANDER (HOLLAND 1939, USA 1947)
ROSENBERG, HERBERT (DENMARK 1935, SWEDEN 1943)
ROSENTHAL, ALBI (UK 1938?)
ROSENWALD, HANS (USA 1936)
ROTH, ERNST (UK 1938)
ROTHMÜLLER, ARON MARKO (SWITZERLAND 1935)
SACHS, CURT (FRANCE 1934, USA 1937)
SALZER, FELIX (USA 1938)
SCHNAPPER, EDITH (UK 1938)
SCHÖNBERG, JAKOB (PALESTINE 1935?)
SCHRADE, LEO (USA 1937)
SCHWARZ, BORIS (USA 1936)
SENDREY, ALFRED (FRANCE 1932, USA 1940)
SILBERMANN, ALFONS (HOLLAND 1933, AUSTRALIA 1938)
SIMON, JAMES (SWITZERLAND 1934, THEN HOLLAND)
SINGER, KURT (HOLLAND 1939)
SONDHEIMER, ROBERT (SWITZERLAND 1934, UK 1939)
SPECTOR, JOHANNA (USA 1947)
STEFAN, PAUL (SWITZERLAND 1938, PORTUGAL 1940, USA 1941)
STEIN, RICHARD HEINRICH (CANARY ISLANDS, 1933)
STERNFELD, FREDERICK (USA 1938)
STROBEL, HEINRICH (FRANCE 1939)
STUTSCHEWSKI, JOACHIM (PALESTINE 1938)
TISCHLER, HANS (USA 1938)
UNGER, ERNST MAX (SWITZERLAND 1933)
VINAWER, CHEMJO (PALESTINE 1933, USA 1938)
VOGL-GARRETT, EDITH (USA 1938)
WACHSMANN, KLAUS P. (SWITZERLAND 1936, THEN UK; USA 1963)
WALTER, ARNOLD (SPAIN 1933, CANADA 1937)
WEISSMANN, JOHN (UK 1937)
WELLESZ, EGON (UK 1938)
WERNER, ERIC (USA 1938)
WERNER, HEINZ (USA 1933)
WINTERNITZ, EMMANUEL (ITALY, USA 1938)
WOLFF, WERNER (USA 1932?)
ZUCKERKANDL, VICTOR (USA)

INDEX

abductees: defined, 55; musicological research with, 56–57
Aber, Adolf, 305
Abert, Claudia, 272n6
Abravanel, Maurice, 107, 142–43nn67,68, 147n87
acculturation, 9–11, 172–93; defined, 172; and identity, 157, 172, 179–86. *See also* adaptation; Americanization; assimilation
adaptation: adaptive/resistant dichotomy, 78–79, 82; desperate, 279; and identity, 157; to Nazi Germany, 102; necessary amount for survival, 172; Neumann, 27–28; *New York Times* on, 113; outward forms, 186n3; Stravinsky, 181; Weill, 160. *See also* acculturation; Americanization; assimilation
Adler, Guido, 59, 63, 157, 237n7, 303–4
Adler, Peter Herman, 105, 133n37
Adorno, Theodor W.: "Ad vocem Hindemith: Eine Dokumentation," 261, 262; character typologies in preconceptions of, 271; *Composing for the Films*, 230, 240–41n40; *Einleitung in die Musiksoziologie*, 262; European identity, 19n35; excess as positive moment, 85; and film scores, 229–30; "Fragen an die intellektuelle Emigration," 261, 276–77n56; *Der getreue Korrepetitor* (The faithful music coach), 338n9; on Hindemith, 261–62, 271, 272n3; *Impromptus*, 261, 262; on

intellectuals in exile, 7–8, 10–11, 85, 225, 229–30, 237n4, 238n10, 261–62, 276–77n56; Kolisch and, 338n9; *Minima Moralia*, 156; on "mutilation of self" caused by assimilation, 199–200; "nonidentical" theory, 156, 164; performance theory, 328; philosophy of music, 261–62, 272nn6; *Philosophy of New Music*, 156, 272n6, 338n9; on Rachmaninoff, 229–30, 240n35; role in postwar West Germany, 272n6; "Scientific Experiences of a European Scholar in America," 10–11; *Versuch über Wagner*, 230; on Wagner, 230, 240n39; on Weill, 220n66, 230, 261, 262, 272n7, 273n10, 277n56; "Zur gesellschaftlichen Lage der Musik," 262
Africans: abductees in slave trade, 56–57. *See also* "black" America
"aggressive defense": vs. "Americanization," 11–12. *See also* superiority feelings
Alban Berg Quartet, 336–37
Albers, Anni, 281
Albers, Josef, 281, 282
Albuquerque, New Mexico, 336
alienation, 17n14; of "black" America, 85; immigrants', 85, 266, 277–78n58; of Jews everywhere (Wagner), 80, 81. *See also* displacement; estrangement; exile; isolation
Allen, Warren, 49
American Federation of Musicians, 249

Papernow, Elizabeth: "People's March," 200; "Unto the New Day," 200

paradise: connotations of, xi; Schoenberg on new country as, 7, 79

paradox, of artist's position, 69–70

Paramount Pictures, 227, 239n24, 240n37

Paris: Boulanger, 174; Milhaud, 135–36n44; musical migration from, 133–35; musical migration to, 98–99, 106, 107, 142n66; Weill, 258, 266

parody: Stravinsky, 181; and Wolpe's Whitman song, 200

performance theory, 328

Perrin, Maurice, 189n56

personal identity, 155, 164–67, 172

Pétain, Marshal, 106, 135n41

Peters, publisher, 308–9

Petersen, Peter, *Musik im Exil,* 5, 12, 16n11, 17n12, 277–78n58

Petri, Egon, 111, 149n99

Petrillo, James, 249

Peyre, Henri, 27, 28

Peyser, Herbert, 93, 97–102

Pfitzner, Hans, 99, 102, 142n66, 311

Philadelphia: Curtis Institute of Music, 106, 141n58, 334; Music Teacher's National Association annual meeting, 43; Schoenberg's Violin Concerto at Academy of Music, 37–38; symposium of European scholars (1950s), 27–28; Wolpe teaching in, 50

Philadelphia Inquirer, 38

Philadelphia Orchestra, 37–38

Philadelphia Record, 38

philanthropy, American, 9–10

philosophy: full meaning of theory in, 87; of identity, 155–56, 164; of music, 70–71, 79–88, 261–62, 272nn2,6; and organic unity, 237n7; of reconciliation, 156

Phonogrammarchiv, 312–13

"Photophone" technique, 249, 260n9

Piatigorsky, Gregor, 97, 333

Pinson, H. S., 115

Pisk, Paul, 112, 139n52

Piston, Walter, 45, 174; Fourth Quartet, 324

poetic imagery, in Whitman's "Beat! Beat! Drums!," 203

poetry: "Black Mountain poets," 282; "Egotistical Sublime," 289; as "fringes," 87; Hartmann, 197; Hughes, 206–7; Ser-

vice, 196. *See also* Olson, Charles; Pound, Ezra; Whitman, Walt

Poland: immigrants and folk heritage of, 55; Nazi invasion (1939), 103, 111, 134n41

polarization: and artistic integrity, 186; home/estrangement duality, 70, 86, 292–93, 302. *See also* binary oppositions; dichotomies; duality

political identity, 155

politics: and American perspective on Schoenberg, 34–35; artists above (Kreisler), 96; exile, 5, 12, 67, 69, 71, 101, 129n25; in German universities, 299; McCarthyism, 294; musical emigration viewed separately from, 12, 13; and music (Lehmann), 136n45; Nazi policy controlling cultural life, 96–98, 128n23, 244, 306; Schoenberg retreat from, 76; twelve-tone system related to, 77; Weill mobilization, 201; Whitman, 195, 196–97. *See also* fascists; leftists; nationalism

Post College, Wolpe, 293

postmodernism: Black Mountain College and, 294; and European reception to Weill's and Hindemith's American works, 211; and Korngold, 236

Potter, Pamela M., 298–321

Pound, Ezra, 282, 289, 291; on Whitman, 194; *Women of Trachis* translation, 284

Pousseur, Henri, 336

practice, and theory, 28, 266, 267–68

pragmatism: Schoenberg, 184, 185, 192n79; U.S., 176, 180, 185, 224; Weill, 268

Prague: Nazi invasion, 59, 133n37; Nettl, 58, 59, 60, 61; Prazak Quartet, 336; Szell, 104

Prazak Quartet, 336

Preetorius, Emil, 127n17

press. *See* journalism; media

Preuss, Hugo, 23–24

Primrose, William, 334–35

Primrose Quartet, 335

Princeton: Institute for Advanced Study, 19n30, 28; Rathaus, 50; Schoenberg, 34; Westminster Choir College, 59

Princeton Radio Project, Newark, New Jersey, 10

Pro Arte Quartet, 38, 326, 330

Prokofiev, Sergei: Budapest String Quartet, 327; First Quartet, 324

Protestants, German, 304, 305

Designer:	Nicole Hayward
Compositor:	Prestige Typography
Music setter:	Rolf Wulfsberg Music Engraving Service
Text:	Baskerville
Display:	10/12 Baskerville
Printer and Binder:	Thomson-Shore